WATSON'S PLAY at BRIDGE

*the text of this book is printed
on 100% recycled paper*

WATSON'S Classic Book on the PLAY of the HAND at BRIDGE

by LOUIS H. WATSON

New Edition
Enlarged and Modernized
by SAM FRY, JR.

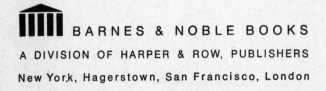

BARNES & NOBLE BOOKS

A DIVISION OF HARPER & ROW, PUBLISHERS

New York, Hagerstown, San Francisco, London

INTRODUCTION

I had the great good fortune to be the good friend and frequent tournament partner of Louis Watson. But despite the kind mention of me in Louis' original introduction, I had very little to do with the original publication of this book; a few chats, some rereadings, some hands furnished and that's about all.

As a matter of fact, callow youth that I was at the time and flushed with my first bridge trophies, I had never even deigned to read the larger portion of Part I. That has turned out happily now, for what might have been an editorial chore for the past few weeks became a delight and a pleasure. I was amazed by the lucidity of Louis' presentation, his insight and his thoroughness and above all his up-to-dateness, vintage 1958.

The changes that I had to make were few and far between. Virtually nothing Louis said about the play of the hand in 1934 is untrue today; Louis said much more and said it much better than anything done on the subject since. A few modernizations of phrase or terminology, a tiny clarification or two, some corrections of typographical errors—that's just about all I did in editing Part I. One warning to the average and advanced player. You'll get a kick and perhaps even learn a good deal when you read Part I. But don't be upset, as I soon learned not to, whenever Louis seems to stop a bit too short in the early part of the book, in analyzing a particular hand or situation. He's deliberately not clouding the issues, at this point, for the benefit of the less advanced. He'll get to it later.

In Part II, I had to change the bidding on some of the hands because of now obsolete conventions, or because of changed valuations for certain types of bids. But this was not too often. Please remember that any hand, in 1934 or 1958, can be bid correctly in several different ways, depending on the partnership system used and other factors.

Also in Part II, I replaced part of Chapter X and added Chapters XII and XIII for reasons which will become obvious. I hope they're up to the standard of the rest of the book.

Now may I quote from Louis' original Introduction:

"This book is an earnest endeavor to codify the successful present-day principles of the play of the cards. Insofar as it is possible, the author has attempted to correlate the established technique of the masters of the past with the modern methods of the champions of today. Only proven ideas of playing strategy that have withstood the test of fire are included in this work. The reader may rest assured that the various plays described here are the winning methods now used by the world's foremost masters of Contract Bridge.

"To assist bidders in fulfilling their contracts as well as to show the Defending Side how bidders may often be defeated in their efforts, is the purpose of this book. Practically all variations of play, both in attack and in defense, are explained and illustrated in the two major sections of this work, entitled 'Fundamentals of Play' and 'Advanced Play and Expert Technique.'

"Every playing possibility which may occur cannot, of course, be included here. To do that would require no one knows just how many different example hands, but it would probably run to a million or so out of the several billion possible combinations of cards in four hands which may be dealt. That is to say, the reader will find himself faced with hands which call for different applications of the principles he finds explained in this book, and which call for different combinations of those principles. To put it simply, one deal may offer a choice between a finesse and a drop; another may offer a choice between a finesse and a squeeze. Some hands are simple; others are complex. Many hands would be played in six different ways by six different expert players — and, in a manner of speaking, they would all be right! That is part of the reason for the fascination of the game. If it were possible to codify the play into forty-eight simple rules which would tell the whole story, devotees of Contract Bridge would forsake the game in droves.

"The effort here is to present the *fundamentals of play* (in Part I) and to follow them up (in Part II) with an elucidation of *advanced play and expert technique* that enable master players to get the most out of their cards. The strategy of play dominates every page. Only fish grab at worms without looking to see whether they are wound on hooks. Good bridge players never grab — they look carefully, consider every possibility, and take what seems to be the best course. If the ensuing pages enable you to choose the best course in 80 per cent of the hands you play, they will have accomplished far more than the author ever dared hope when he wrote this book. For of all the complex subjects that have ever plagued the mind of man, who is after all a rule-making as well as a rule-breaking animal, the play of the hand at Contract Bridge is the least susceptible of hard-and-fast regulation according to fixed formulas.

"Before any authority on Contract Bridge gets very far with his readers, he should be fair to them and say that in this intellectual game of wits and wisdom, if he has said Never, he means, of course, Almost Never, or if he has said Always, he means, if you please, Almost Always.

"The reader of this book will notice that Part I contains practically no mention of bidding. This is because the types of play explained do not depend to any large extent on the auction which has preceded the final contract, and because it would be useless to clutter up the text with a futile narration of the bidding where the play is not affected.

"In Part II the bidding is usually given and explained before the play so that the reader can learn to form certain deductions regarding the location of outstanding cards from his knowledge of what each specific bid means. In order to permit the reader to apply the same principles to the hands in Part I (although this is not really necessary) he is invited to bid all the hands according to his own favorite system. In almost all cases he will find that the final contract reached is the same as the one given in the text."

In closing may I say simply that I am indebted to both Louis Watson and also his many fans of the world of bridge for the opportunity of editing this book.

New York City   Sam Fry, Jr.
January, 1958

CONTENTS

PART II

Advanced Play and Expert Technique

PART I

FUNDAMENTALS OF PLAY

Introduction to Part I

You will find in Part I a detailed analysis of the fundamental aspects of the play of the hand at Contract Bridge. Here you have solid ground-work to proceed with the advanced play which will be explained in Part II. Every play used by an expert—every advanced play of whatever kind—depends upon the fundamental plays covered in the first part of this book. No beginner or even average player can hope to make successful use of advanced technique until he has mastered the elementals. Postpone your study of Part II, then, until you are confident that all the subjects covered in Part I hold no mysteries for you.

In any event, the table of Contents can be your guide as to the chapters of Part I you feel you can dispense with and as to the particular place where you feel your study can properly begin. *

---

* Louis Watson was an exceedingly modest as well as talented young man. It is our considered opinion that there is much meat for even the advanced player as early as Chapter VII of Part I (and each subsequent chapter gets meatier).—S. F. Jr.

CHAPTER I

THE POWER OF HONORS

BEFORE you can learn anything about the play of the hand at Contract Bridge, you must first understand that each card has a value and a meaning. Of course, you know that the Ace is the highest card in a suit, and that the King beats the Queen, and that a Queen is always better than a Jack, and so on. But it is entirely possible that you have never learned the full power of these cards, for they will do far more, if properly handled, than merely win a trick over any lower card.

First of all, then, you must study the relationship of the various cards in the pack to each other; and you must particularly study the relationship of the honor cards (the five highest cards in each suit, namely, the Ace, King, Queen, Jack, and Ten). Do not be contemptuous of this seemingly elementary knowledge, for only if your *basic* knowledge is sound can your later refinements be worth striving for. The player who *thinks he knows*, because he has participated in a few hundred rubbers, and who wants to plunge immediately into squeeze plays and coups, will never be a good Contract player. His parboiled knowledge has not allowed for the general principles of play which must be the higher law of every hand. Someone who masters the general principles, but cannot for the life of him tell you what a Double Grand Coup is, will win more points than the specialist in the Grand Coup—for those miraculous plays come very seldom in a Bridge player's lifetime.

The various "honor-trick" and "quick-trick" valuations, as well as the different "point" counts used in valuing honors, are not arbitrarily determined by the experts who recommend them as a basis for bidding. Every such valuation is theoretically based upon the relationship of those honors and honor combinations *in the play of the hand*. The fact that an Ace is given the value of "1 honor-trick" means that the Ace is almost certain to win a trick *in the play*. The King is usually valued at "$1/2$ trick" because it will on the average, win a trick about half the time—that is, a guarded King, without the Ace, will win 1 trick about 50 times out of 100 (on the average), and be captured by the Ace or by ruffing the other 50

3

times out of 100.* It is thus clear that all bidding valuation, to be of any use, must be based on what is expected to happen in the play. If you understand the relationship of honors—and also of lower cards—in the play, your bidding should then become more imaginative and more accurate. In fact, the ultimate object of anyone undertaking to learn more about the play of the hand at Contract Bridge should be to improve upon the mathematical averages ascribed to honors and other cards for bidding purposes. Your object should be, not to take a trick with a guarded King half the time, but *sixty percent of the time!*

THE MEANING OF RANK

Each card in the pack holds a special rank one position above the next highest card of the same suit. Thus any Ace outranks the King of the same suit by one position, the Queen by two positions, the Ten by four positions, and so on. The King outranks the Queen of the same suit by one position, but the same King outranks the Jack of the same suit by two positions. It would therefore seem that the Ace should take the first trick in a suit, the King the second in that suit, and so on. Everyone knows that this is not necessarily true, for the first trick in a suit—the first *round*, as we say—may be won by a low card like the seven-spot. Why does the Ace not always win the first round? Simply because there is no compulsion for a player to win a trick with his Ace (except when it is the only card he holds of the suit led)—he may find it better to keep his Ace until a later round, when it may actually be more valuable to him. The manner in which he decides to play his Ace (or King, or any other high card), sooner or later, is explained in this book. Just now the important thing to learn is that as each round of a suit is played, the rank of the *remaining cards* (those as yet unplayed) changes. It is obvious that if the Ace and King of a suit are played on the first round, the Queen thereupon becomes the highest card of the suit—the Queen is promoted to the position of first command, so to speak. The Queen now controls the next round of the suit; that is, the holder can win the next round with the Queen, if he so

---

* A strict mathematical average, of course, never develops in practice. The "1/2 trick" value, and other similar approximations, are generally too high for a poor player, and too low for an expert.

wishes. The foregoing principles may be stated as a general truth:
Whenever an honor is played to a trick, each lower card automatically goes up one position in rank.

This is illustrated by the following situation:

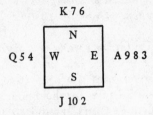

Suppose that yours is the South holding (J 10 2). Ordinarily you would not regard the Jack as being of much value. But suppose that East (the Opponent on your right) leads a low card (the three-spot), and you play the Ten, East plays the Queen, and North, your Partner, plays the King. Your Jack now suddenly becomes of much greater value, for it has been promoted to second position in the suit—only the outstanding Ace can beat it. In other words, you are now able to take the third round of the suit, when, before the first round had been played, you could not even expect to take the fourth round! Suppose that East led his Ace at the first opportunity, and your Partner led his King at the next opportunity, and the Queen was played from the West hand on the third round—your three cards would have fallen on the three leads, without winning a single trick. It is apparent, then, that the manner in which the cards of a suit are played may greatly affect the rank of the cards in the suit.

The principle of this axiom could be carried on indefinitely. For instance, if three honors are played to a trick, the card next below the lowest of the three played honors gains three positions in rank. Thus, in the preceding example, the Ten, Queen, and King having been played to the first round, East's nine-spot is promoted three positions, from the sixth rank to the third. Before any rounds of the suit were played, the rank of the cards was A K Q J 10 9; after the first round, as given, the rank became A J 9 8 7 6. Though the nine-spot is not an honor, it can become the third highest card of a suit after the first round has been played. Therefore, when we speak of "honors" we are usually referring to the commanding cards of a suit, and we may at times find that nines or eights are even such.

Now that you appreciate something about the rank and position of the cards in a suit, in relation to one another, you can realize the importance of *promoting* the rank of your lower cards as often as possible. *Whenever you win or attempt to win a trick, you should try to gain as many positions of rank as possible for your lower cards in the suit.*

There are two fairly obvious ways of carrying out this principle. One way is to lead high cards and pray that the intervening high cards held by the adversaries will drop (that is, that the holders will have to play them because they hold no other cards of the suit). Another way is to force an Opponent to lead a high card which can be captured by your own higher card. Thus, if you win an Opponent's King with your Ace, you bring your Queen up one position in rank—in fact, you promote it to the highest ranking card of the suit. Even if you hold the Jack (and not the Queen), by winning the adverse King with your Ace you promote your Jack's rank two places, when the play of the Ace without winning an adverse honor will promote your Jack only one place. The second way—forcing an Opponent to lead—is therefore the better way to accomplish your purpose: to promote the rank of your lower cards as fast as possible.

You must see that to lead an Ace is very like trying to stab an enemy in the dark—without even knowing where he stands! The chances are pretty good that you will miss your mark, and do no damage. For certainly if you lead an Ace your two Opponents are not going to drop an honor each just to oblige you. They will play the lowest cards they have, holding on to their King and Queen (against your original holding of Ace-Jack) which you have automatically promoted for them by your immediate lead of the Ace. However, if you let one of the Opponents lead the suit in which you hold Ace-Jack, and if the second Opponent is also obliged to play ahead of you (that is, you play the last card to the trick), either the King or the Queen must be played by the Opponents or you will win the trick with your Jack. On the King or Queen you will then play your Ace, leaving only one card outstanding that is higher than your Jack, when there were two before.

Therefore, *in trying to promote lower cards of a suit, remember that it is easier to capture adverse higher cards whenever you play after one or both Opponents.* The following situation illustrates this:

964

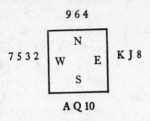

7532   W   E   K J 8

A Q 10

Suppose that you are sitting South with A Q 10, and it is your turn to lead. If you lead the Ace, your right-hand Opponent will play low. If you follow with the Queen, your right-hand Opponent will win with his King and take your Ten with his Jack. If you follow the Ace with your Ten, your right-hand Opponent will win with his Jack and take your Queen with his King. You can readily see the disadvantages of this mode of procedure. But let your right-hand Opponent do the leading and see what happens. If he leads his eight-spot, you will win with your Ten; if he leads his Jack, you will win with your Queen; if he leads his King, you will win with your Ace. No matter what card of the suit the Opponent leads, you will be able to win the trick.

The following situation is slightly more complex:

8753

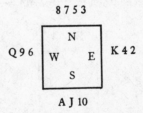

Q 96   W   E   K 42

A J 10

If you are sitting in the South position with A J 10, and you lead the Ace before any other cards of the suit have been played, East and West will hold on to their King and Queen, with which they will win your Jack and Ten on the second and third rounds of the suit. Even if you improve slightly upon the immediate lead of the Ace, and lead your Jack first, your left-hand Opponent will play low and your right-hand Opponent will win the trick with his King. By this procedure you have accomplished nothing whatever toward promoting the rank of your Ten. You have merely sacrificed one of your honors to an honor adversely held. Now try letting your left-hand Opponent do the leading and see what happens. Your right-hand Opponent will have to play his King to prevent you from winning the first round with your Jack or Ten. You take the King with your Ace, and lo! one card—and only one—is left outstanding against your Jack and Ten. You may drive out the Queen whenever you wish by leading one of your two equals, Jack or Ten (either one, since they are in sequence and therefore are equal in value in your hand), leaving your third card in command of the suit.

The Developing Power of Honors

We have already hinted that honors may not only promote lower honors to higher rank, but, when the honors have been played, still lower cards attain the rank of honors. You must get in the habit of thinking not only of the five or six highest cards, but try to picture each suit as containing thirteen cards. The very fact that the number of cards in each suit is *uneven* is significant, since an even number of cards (four) must be played on each round of the suit. Thus if three rounds are played when every player follows suit, only twelve cards are played, leaving the thirteenth card still outstanding. For example, suppose the heart suit is distributed in the four hands as follows:

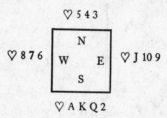

The player in the South position is fortunate, indeed, in his heart holding. With such a holding, and the distribution 4-3-3-3 around the table, you may lay down the Ace, King, and Queen in succession, and your Opponents must follow suit, leaving you, after these three rounds have been played, with the deuce as the only unplayed heart. You may now lead the deuce and take a trick with it (assuming that there are no trumps to ruff it). What has actually happened is that the Ace, King, and Queen of hearts have *developed the deuce* and promoted it from the thirteenth ranking card—lowest in the suit—to the first ranking card for the fourth round!

Consider now the following situation, which is less simple:

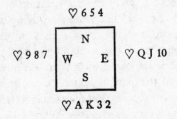

Again the distribution among the four players is 4-3-3-3, and you, sitting South, have the four cards headed by Ace-King. You may lead the Ace followed by the King, and then lead your trey (three-spot) to the third round. East must, of course, win the third round, but thereupon your lowly deuce is again developed, and has become the highest card of the suit for the fourth round! The only difference between this example and the preceding one is that in this example you lose 1 trick in the process of developing the deuce into a trick winner. A card thus developed into a trick winner is also said to be *established*.

The developing power of honors comes about, quite obviously, because the rules of the game require that a player "follow suit" by playing a card of the suit led whenever he has one. In fact, if a player does not follow suit when able to do so, he is guilty of a revoke, and may be severely penalized according to the laws of Contract Bridge. It should also be clear that this developing power of honors ceases to exist if the combined hands of yourself and Partner do not contain more cards of the suit than the Opponents hold in their combined hands. If you hold the controlling top honors, of course, your suit is already established. Suppose that the distribution of the diamond suit, for example, is as follows:

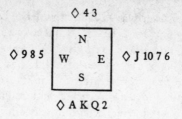

your holding is the same as in the distribution of the heart suit pre-viously discussed. You can lead the Ace, King, and Queen, but you will never develop your deuce into a trick winner. The reason is that your Opponents hold seven diamonds against your six. Since the most the Opponents can play on three rounds is six diamonds, their seventh card of that suit is bound to become established.

In the process of developing lower cards into trick winners—that is to say, establishing lower cards—the honor strength does not need to be all in one hand, as in the examples thus far given. Consider the following distribution of the club suit:

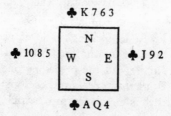

Here the thirteenth club can be established by the simple expedient of leading the Ace and Queen from the South hand, and going over to the North hand by leading the four-spot to the King. These three rounds draw the six clubs held adversely, leaving the three-spot established in the North hand.

In all the preceding examples, the ratio of length held by each side has been seven cards of the suit held by one partnership and the other six cards of the suit held by the other partnership. It naturally follows that if the suit is divided eight cards on one side and five cards on the other, the possibilities of developing low cards into trick winners are increased, for the Opponents hold only five cards with which to oppose the establishment of the suit. Generally speaking, when you hold only seven cards of a suit in your own and Dummy's hand, four in one and three in the other, you can only *hope* that the other six cards of the suit will be divided evenly between the Opponents. But if you hold five cards in one hand and three in the other (your own hand and Dummy's), you can *confidently expect* that the other five cards will be divided three and two. While it is not unusual for six outstanding cards to be divided four and two in the Opponents' hands, it is less common for five outstanding cards to be divided four and one.

Carrying the principle further, you should be able to see at once that with nine cards in your own and Dummy's hands, and only four in the Opponents' hands, the chances of developing low cards are still greater. In fact, there is a point at which the honors cease to be necessary as developing cards. When the principle is carried to its ultimate conclusion, we find a situation like the following distribution of the spade suit:

♠ 9 7 5 2

♠ A K   ♠ Q J

♠ 10 8 6 4 3

If you are South, as Declarer, your two hands lack the four top honors in spades, yet because you have nine spades against four held by the Opponents, you can develop spade tricks without the aid of spade honors. With the four outstanding honors divided two and two, as shown, you need only lead spades twice to establish 3 spade tricks—actually winning 1 spade trick more than the Opponents, who hold four honors between them! This distribution is not common, but it is a good illustration of the principle of developing low cards by eliminating the higher cards.

You have learned the power of honors in promoting lower cards to a higher rank in their suit. You have seen that sometimes even a card lower than an honor—even the deuce—may rise to the rank of an honor when all the higher cards have been "killed off." When a card reaches the top rank in the remaining cards of its suit, that card is said to *command* the suit. A good Bridge player often finds it desirable to keep control of a suit by retaining the commanding card in it, or by promoting a lower card to the position of the commanding card. This matter of control, indeed, is of vast importance in the play of the hand at Contract Bridge.

CONTROL

To have control of a suit means to hold the highest unplayed card in that suit. If you do not have the highest or commanding card, but if you do have the second or third highest, with some protection below it, you still have some measure of control—what may be called *secondary* control as distinguished from the *primary* control assured by holding the highest card. For example, if the highest outstanding spade is the Jack, and you hold the Ten and nine of spades, the Ten gives you secondary control of the spade suit (the holder of the Jack has primary control), because the nine protects the Ten. If you hold the Ten and eight, or the Ten and seven, the eight or the seven is merely indifferent protection, for if you have to play a spade before the holder of the Jack, your Ten may be forced since the eight or seven will not drive out the Jack if the nine-spot is with it. Any lower card than the seven held with the Ten against the Jack can only be regarded as doubtful protection.

For the time being, you need consider only primary control of a suit. If you realize the value of this, you will have taken an important step toward mastery of the play of the hand. Once primary control of a suit is relinquished, the Opponents will lose no time in proceeding to capture tricks with their lesser honors and lower cards. To prevent the Opponents from doing just this, you must keep primary control as long as possible, in order to have freedom and time to increase the rank of your lower cards in other suits. In fact, you should *never surrender control of a suit without an excellent reason for so doing.*

SUMMARY

The points thus far brought out are the promotional and developing power of honors, in raising the rank of lower cards, and the principle of controlling a suit to keep the Opponents from surging in with their released strength in that suit. There are very few playing situations in Contract which are not in some way affected by these fundamental principles, especially the promotional and developing power of honors.

Because of the fact that each card holds a rank one position above the next highest of the same suit, whenever an honor is played to a trick each lower card automatically goes up one position in rank—in relation to the cards of that suit which are as yet unplayed. In this connection, the following rules should be remembered:

Whenever you win or attempt to win a trick, try to gain as many positions of rank as possible for your lower cards in the suit.

In trying to promote lower cards, remember that it is easier to capture adverse higher cards whenever you play after one or both Opponents.

Never surrender control of a suit without a good reason for so doing.

CHAPTER II

THE POSITIONAL VALUE OF HONORS

In our discussion of honors thus far, we have assumed that the lead must be made by South (you) or an Opponent. We have not mentioned that the North or Dummy hand may also lead—in fact, must lead when it is that hand's turn to lead. In short, the Declarer playing a hand at Contract Bridge must pay particular attention to this matter of which hand has the lead—himself or Dummy—and so plan his play that the lead will always be in the hand where it is to his best advantage to have it at any particular moment. This appears even with such a simple thing as the holding of a King with only small cards below it in the same suit. Though this holding is valued at $^1/_2$ trick in most bidding systems, because it stands a fifty-fifty chance of winning a trick in the play, it can actually win a trick only if the King is played in a certain way, and that way depends on how the suit is led.

You can see at once that with several honors in a row, or in *sequence*, as we say—such as K Q J of a suit in one hand, and a few small cards of the same suit in the Dummy—it makes no difference which hand leads the suit or which of the honors is played first. Any one of the three high cards, since all are held by the same side, will drive out the Ace, leaving the other two in command of the suit. That is, a holding of K Q J in the same suit will certainly take 2 tricks (barring the possiblity of being ruffed). The same is true if the three honors are divided between the two partnership hands, as in the following heart distribution:

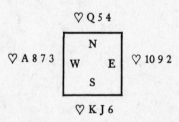

This combination is bound to produce 2 heart tricks for North-South no matter which hand leads—always provided the player is not silly enough to play his Queen and the King or Jack to the same trick.

But when the cards held are not equal in playing value—that is, when they are not in sequence—the matter of the *direction* of the lead becomes of vital importance. For example, suppose your heart holding is as follows:

♡ 4 3

♡ K 2

You are South, with the King of hearts guarded by the deuce, and Dummy has the four and trey. Suppose you lead the King (no hearts having been played). The player holding the Ace of hearts will certainly win the trick, and whatever heart he leads will then capture your other two small hearts, one in each hand. Thus played, the heart King is not worth ½ trick, for it can never win. How, then, does it become a winner? It has a fifty-fifty chance of winning if you lead from the hand containing the four and trey, *toward* the guarded King. If your right-hand Opponent (East) holds the Ace, with some other hearts, he can play the Ace or not, as he chooses. If he plays his Ace, you play your deuce, and your King is promoted to a sure winner for the second round of hearts. If your right-hand Opponent does not play his Ace, you play your King, which wins the first round. Whenever your right-hand Opponent holds the Ace, then, this method of playing your guarded King will win a trick. But, you ask, what if the left-hand Opponent holds the Ace? Then you can do nothing, for he will win the King no matter whether you lead it directly or play it by leading up to it from the other hand. Please note that it is the possibility of the left-hand Opponent's holding the Ace that makes the guarded King worth only ½ trick in bidding valuations—otherwise the guarded King would be worth a full trick, wouldn't it? The fact that there are two Opponents, and that only one of them can hold the Ace, gives the guarded King its fifty-fifty chance of winning—hence the $1/2$ trick valuation, which means 1 trick half the time and 0 trick the other half. In playing the hand as in anything else you do, never forget the truism that *a fifty-fifty chance is better than no chance at all!* To lead the King in the preceding heart holding is futile; to lead up to the King may win.

The same principle is applicable when two or even three honors are held in sequence. Assume the following club distribution:

♣ K Q 2

♣ 7 6 4

The holding of the King and Queen of clubs, together with a small club in the same hand, is regarded as worth about $1^1/2$ tricks for bidding purposes—to the prospective Declarer or Dummy. That is, if a Declarer plays this combination of cards, he will make either 1 club trick or 2 club tricks, depending on how he plays the clubs, and on his luck. The way to be sure of making only 1 trick is to lead the King from the North hand, letting the trick be won by the Ace, and the Queen is then good for the next round. Can the Opponents be prevented from winning all the club tricks but one? If you are going to try to stop them, you must lead from your weak hand toward the strong hand—that is, lead the four-spot up to the King-Queen holding. If West plays low, you then play the King or the Queen (they are equal in value) from the North hand, and if East does not have the Ace, you win the trick. You can repeat this process by *returning* to the South hand (by leading a card of some other suit, which we will assume you hold, that can be won in the South hand, giving that hand the lead again) and leading the six-spot. If West still plays low, you play your other high card, and win the second round—2 club tricks. That is, if West holds the Ace of clubs, this method of playing your club holding will always win 2 tricks, for if West plays the Ace on the first or second round, you merely play your deuce from the

Dummy (North*). If East holds the Ace, of course, you will make only 1 trick—but remember the truism about some chance being better than none!

The principle of leading from the weak hand toward the stronger, to avoid unnecessarily throwing a high card under an adverse Ace or other winner, applies with equal effect if one hand holds K Q J 3 and the other hand three small cards of the same suit. The hand with the three small, by leading three times toward the stronger hand, can win 3 tricks in this suit if the left-hand Opponent holds the Ace—even if that Ace has three small cards with it! Indeed, it is a good general rule, whenever you play an honor combination that is not in continuous sequence, to *lead from the weak hand toward the stronger*.

How to Play Tenaces—The Finesse

Up to this point we have discussed only the play of honors that are in sequence. Yet, in actual play, most of the honor combinations you hold will be broken up so that sometimes the honors are one position apart (with one intervening card missing), and sometimes more widely separated (with more than one intervening card missing).

A broken sequence of honors—that is, a combination of honors *not* in continuous sequence—is known as a *tenace*.** In the days of Whist, the best and third best cards of the suit formed the "major tenace," and the second and fourth best cards the "minor tenace." For all practical purposes in Contract Bridge, however, any combination of two or more high cards not in sequence may be regarded as a tenace.

Any tenace holding, as already stated, should be played *up to* or

---

* Hereafter, for simplicity, the Declarer will always be the player sitting in the South position in the diagrams, and the Dummy will always be the player sitting in the North position. Hence, East and West will always be the Opponents, who are playing defensively against the Declarer (South), who manipulates both his own hand and the exposed hand of the Dummy. The North hand, face up on the table, is thus always open to the view of all players. Every player *sees* twenty-six cards—his own hand and the Dummy's—but only the Declarer *plays* twenty-six cards. In actual play, of course, the position of the Dummy depends entirely on the outcome of the auction (bidding).

** The word "tenace" has no relation to either "Ten" or "Ace," but is French in origin and is closely related to the word "tenacious," carrying the connotation of *holding*. As a matter of fact—though it is of small importance—the tenace was originally, in Whist, a holding, by the fourth hand to play, of a combination of high cards, such as the major or minor tenace, which gave him the winning position over an adversary with the missing honors. Later the word was applied to such a broken honor combination held by any player. The word is pronounced with the accent on the first syllable, and the *a* long as in *Ace*.

toward rather than away from.   The so-called major tenace, or Ace-Queen holding, clearly shows the advantage of this, as follows:

$\Diamond$ A Q

$\Diamond$ 3 2

All bidding valuations give the Ace-Queen the value of $1^{1}/_{2}$ tricks. Yet if you lead the Ace and follow it with the Queen, you have practically no chance of making 2 tricks—your only chance, indeed, depends on the King being a singleton in an Opponent's hand.   The best chance, then, is to lead the deuce toward the Ace-Queen, so that, if West plays the King, you can win with the Ace from Dummy, or if West plays low, you can play the Queen from Dummy, hoping that East does not have the King.   Whenever West holds the King, then, with the diamond holding shown, the Ace-Queen is worth 2 tricks, but it is worth only 1 trick if East has the King.

You may ask why, if West holds the King, he does not play it?   He holds it up for the simple reason that it would do him no good to play it, since he cannot thereby affect the winning power of Dummy's holding of Ace-Queen.   Indeed, West has a very slight chance of gaining something by holding up his King, for if you cannot afford to take the fifty-fifty chance that East does not hold the King, you will be obliged to play the Ace from Dummy.   This is a rare situation, however; it is mentioned here only to emphasize further the definite advantage of leading from your weak holding toward your stronger holding in playing tenaces.

This manner of playing tenaces has a name familiar to every card player.   It is called taking a *finesse*.*   Though a finesse is an ex-

---

* Writers on Bridge have used the word "finesse" very carelessly.   So that there may be no misunderstanding, the reader should note the correct usage observed in this book, as follows: *To finesse a card* is to play that card; thus, in the example just given, the Queen is finessed.   The outstanding King is the card finessed *against*, or the card the player hopes to capture by his finessing maneuver.   Thus, you finesse against a missing honor, but you finesse the card you yourself play, the card finessed being so played that it has a chance of winning against the missing higher card.

tremely elementary play, it is also a very important play. The greatest of experts use finesses. Some unthinking players regard a finesse as a gamble, and get the idea that they may lose something by taking a finesse. Unless there is some better play available, a finesse stands to win and *actually loses nothing*—for it may win a trick which would be lost if the honors were led in rotation or led directly into the Opponents' hands. Every finesse is so planned that only one of the two Opponents is given an opportunity to win the trick with his higher card (if he has it), as against a sure-to-lose method of play whereby either Opponent is given the chance to play that higher card and win the trick. Thus, in the example just given, by finessing the Queen you give only one Opponent, East, the chance to play the King if he has it. But if you lead the Queen, before or after the Ace, you give either Opponent a chance to play the King on it and win it. *A finesse is therefore a strategic play which is sure to win a trick if the higher missing honor is in a favorable position.*

The Ace-Queen tenace is the simplest combination to finesse, but it is by no means the most common. Consider, for example, the following spade distribution:

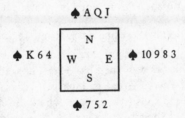

You know by now that the only way to launch an attack in this suit is to lead the deuce from your own hand, as Declarer. If West plays his King (you don't know he holds it, of course, but you hope he does), you will be able to take 3 tricks with Dummy's spades. But if West does not play his King, you finesse the Jack, which holds (wins the trick). You now have good reason to believe that West holds the King, but you must assume that it is still guarded. The only safe way is to return to your own hand and lead low again, this time finessing the Queen if West plays low. Only in this way can you be sure of winning 3 spade tricks if West holds the King.

Even suppose that the spade situation is as follows:

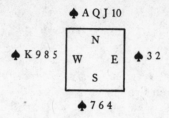

On the first round of spades, you lead low from your hand, as Declarer, finessing the Ten—assuming that West always plays low, since it will avail him nothing to play the King before he has to. You then return to your hand, and finesse the Jack on the next round. Eight spades have now been played, and you hold three of the five remaining. There is a pretty good chance that the King will drop on the next round, but why should you take this unnecessary risk? After all, West may hold the two remaining spades, and you will then lose your Queen. If you can still return to your own hand, by way of another suit, you should do so, leading your last low spade toward the Ace-Queen left in Dummy's hand. Only in this way can you be absolutely sure of winning 4 spade tricks, assuming that West has the King with three small cards guarding it.

The finesses thus far explained have been characterized by the play of a high card *third hand*—that is, next to the last card played to the trick. A finesse may also take place when the high card is played first (led), provided the situation is such that only the last Opponent to play to the trick really has an opportunity to win it, if he holds the card you are finessing against. The following two suit holdings illustrate this type of finesse:

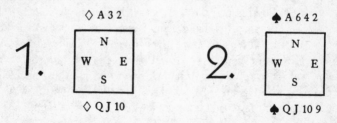

If you lead low from Dummy toward your hand (South), as Declarer, you give East and West equal opportunity to play the King and win the trick. Notice, however, that if, for example, in the first situation, you lead the Queen of diamonds toward the Ace in Dummy, only East ever has a chance to *win* the trick, for if West plays the King, you win with Dummy's Ace and your remaining Jack and Ten are good. The same is true of the second situation, if you lead the Queen of spades toward Dummy's Ace. In the diamond situation, if West holds the King you can make 3 diamond tricks by taking this type of finesse against the King. In the spade situation, you can make 4 spade tricks, even if West holds the King and three small cards with it, by leading three times toward Dummy's Ace, winning the fourth trick with the Ace if the King is not played earlier.

Following are four more situations, in which the Ace, Queen, Jack, and Ten of a suit are held in the two hands, more or less divided. But the principle of finessing against the King remains the same:

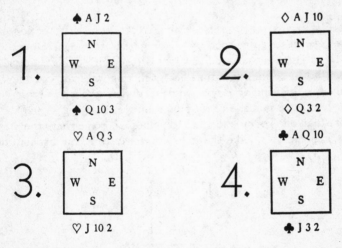

In the first two situations (Nos. 1 and 2) you should lead the Queen to finesse against the King, and in the other two (Nos. 3 and 4) you should lead the Jack. Notice that in all four the lead is toward the Ace; in other words, the lead is toward the hand which holds the commanding card of the suit, so that the card against which you are finessing *can be captured if it is held by the intervening Opponent.*

Any of these four suit holdings should develop 3 tricks for you, as Declarer, if the King is favorably located—that is, in West's hand.

In the finesses we have explained up to this point, the attempt has been to encircle or finesse against the King. This has been just an accident, though natural enough, considering that the King, next to the Ace, is the most impressive card to keep from taking a trick. It is equally possible and advantageous, of course, to finesse against out-standing Queens, Jacks, and even against lower cards on occasion. One great player once boasted of finessing against a five-spot, thus:

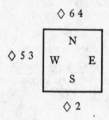

Obviously, if you lead the deuce and West plays the trey, you can finesse against the five-spot by playing the four from Dummy—assuming these are the last five cards of the suit. This example is just a curiosity, and is not given because it is at all likely to come up.

After all, finessing is easy enough to understand and accomplish when the finesse is made against only one outstanding higher card. If more than one honor is missing, the finesse is somewhat more complex. For example, take the following fairly common distribution:

$$\heartsuit A 3 2$$

```
      ┌─────────┐
      │    N    │
      │  W   E  │
      │    S    │
      └─────────┘
```

$$\heartsuit Q 6 5$$

The question very frequently arises, how should this combination of cards be played for the best results? At first thought, a beginner is likely to say that the Queen should be led from Declarer's hand to-ward the Ace in the Dummy, and that if West plays low, Dummy should play low. This is incorrect; in fact, it is a losing play. Just consider what the West player may hold and what he may do if you play in such a fashion. If the remaining hearts are as follows:

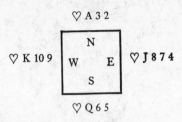

and you, as Declarer, lead the Queen, West will cover it with his King and you will win with the Ace in the Dummy. Now where do you stand with this suit? You have remaining exactly the six, five, trey, and deuce, none of which stands the slightest chance of taking a trick against the Opponents' remaining Jack, Ten, nine, eight, and seven! Yet the King is in the West hand, where you hoped it would be when you attempted to finesse by leading your Queen toward Dummy's Ace. All right—reverse the East and West holdings, thus:

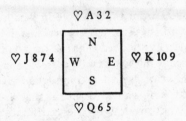

Now suppose you play the same way—leading the Queen toward Dummy's Ace. Obviously, West must play low and East wins with the King. The Opponents now hold a sequence from Jack to seven-spot, any one of which can drive out your Ace, leaving the remaining cards all trick winners. It is thus demonstrated that the lead of the Queen toward the Ace in the holding given is always a losing play, no matter which Opponent has the King.

Is it possible, then, to play the combination of Ace and two small in one hand, with Queen and two small in the other hand, to make 2 tricks? It is, and this is how it is done. The lead is made toward the guarded Queen, so that, if East has the King, he must play it, thereby establishing the Queen (for you then play low from the South hand), or, if East plays low, you play the Queen, which wins—except half the time, when West has the King. If you first play the Ace of hearts from Dummy, and follow with a low card to the Queen, this finesse will be seen to follow the principle of leading from the weak hand toward the stronger, thus:

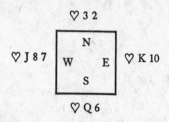

♡ 3 2

♡ J 8 7   N   ♡ K 10
          W   E
              S

♡ Q 6

It should be evident that the only way the Queen can win a trick is either for East to lead, or for East to be made to play before the South hand—as when a small heart is led from Dummy (North) toward the guarded Queen. Here the object is not to capture the King, but to prevent it from capturing your Queen!

How does this differ from the example in which it was proper to lead the Queen toward the Ace? Ah, when this was the correct way to finesse, you should have noticed that the Jack or Ten was also held. In other words, when a finesse may be correctly made by *leading* the card finessed, another card is also held in sequence with it, and hence equal to it in trick-taking value, so that if the card led is killed by being covered, no tricks are lost by the sacrifice, and control of the suit is still retained. A moment's thought will clarify this for you.

The following suit distribution is an extension of the principle that *you can profitably finesse a card by leading it only when you hold another card in sequence with it:*

◊ A 7 5

◊ K 10 6   N   ◊ 9 8 4 3
           W   E
               S

◊ Q J 2

Now you may lead the Queen, hoping that West has the King, for if the Queen is covered, and you win with Dummy's Ace, you still have the Jack left to control the suit.   By leading the Queen, you successfully finesse against West's King, for whether West plays the King or plays low, you must make 2 diamond tricks.   You cannot make 3 diamond tricks, because West's Ten will win the third round no matter what you do, assuming that the King is played on the Queen. You can readily prove this by trying the various plays yourself.   The best procedure, then, is for you to finesse your Queen, and take your Ace, abandoning the suit for attacking purposes, since 2 tricks are all you can get out of it.

The Ten, it appears, may be a very vital card.   Suppose we merely interchange the Ten and the seven-spot in the preceding example:

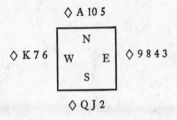

Now you may finesse twice against the King—first by leading the Queen toward the Ace, and, if it holds, following with the Jack, for you still hold the Ten if the Jack is covered and you are forced to win with Dummy's Ace.   Put another way, it is profitable to finesse by leading an honor in such a way that it may be covered only if the next lower card is held, which will thereby be promoted to command of the suit.

You should form the habit of regarding finessing as a method of *winning tricks*, and not as a method of eliminating the missing higher card.   Ask yourself: Can I win 2 tricks with this combination if the position of the outstanding higher card is favorable, or will this method of play gain a trick, or will it establish the cards held by the Opponents if I am forced to play my highest card to win the trick?

SUMMARY
You have learned in this chapter that the trick-taking power of honors depends on their position in relation to the other cards of the suit distributed around the table.

You have learned the elementary ways of finessing, or encircling a card adversely held so that that card cannot deprive you of a trick you might win by finessing. Two rules may be usefully memorized, as follows:

Whenever you play an honor combination that is not in continuous sequence, plan to lead from the weak hand toward the strong hand.

You can profitably finesse a card by leading it, only when you hold another card in sequence with it.

CHAPTER III

DOUBLE AND COMBINATION FINESSES

A RULE was laid down in the preceding chapter, to the effect that to win as many tricks as possible with honors not in sequence, you should lead from the weaker holding toward the stronger. This rule applies equally well to the more complicated finesses, when more than one card is finessed against. In the double finesse, for example, an endeavor is made to encircle two outstanding higher cards, as shown in the following:

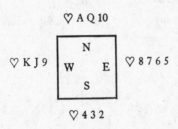

You first apply the principle of leading from the weaker toward the stronger hand. You must therefore, as Declarer, lead from your own hand (South), the deuce. If West now plays the nine, your first impulse may be to try to encircle only the King, and finesse Dummy's Queen. However, this would be an unfortunate choice, as it would eliminate any chance you might have of making 3 heart tricks. For if the Queen is played and holds, the King and Jack are still left outstanding, one of which must win a trick. How can you play for 3 tricks in this suit, then? Simply by finessing the Ten, which, in this instance, will hold the trick, and you have only to return to your own hand, lead the trey, and finesse the Queen on the second round. No matter how West plays, if you follow this procedure your left-hand Opponent's holding of ♡ K J 9 becomes worthless.

The logical objection to this line of play is that it really stands very little chance of success. The probabilities are that at least one of the missing honors (King or Jack) is located on your right. However, you must not forget the definition of a finesse. A finesse, you recall, is not a gamble—that is, you do not risk something to make something more. You risk nothing. You merely play to get something half the time which you would otherwise not get at all! So even if East, in the preceding heart situation, does hold one of the missing honors, he will only win a trick that the Opponents must win any-way—so nothing has been gained, but also nothing has been lost. In fact, if East has to win the Ten with the King, your Ace and Queen are both of them commanding cards in the suit. If East wins with the Jack, you can still re-enter your hand and take a second finesse against the King. Even if East has both King and Jack, you have lost nothing, for if they are guarded, they must win anyway.

So much for the simple and double finesse. The combination finesse, so called, is probably even more common, for it can take many different forms. Study the following diamond distribution:

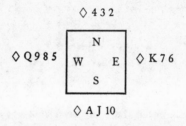

This is one of the examples used in the first chapter to illustrate the advantages of the lead being made by an Opponent rather than by the Declarer (South). It was shown that if West is obliged to lead diamonds, South must win 2 tricks in the suit. Unfortunately, however, it is not always possible to compel your Opponents to lead as you wish, so that you are frequently forced to launch the attack yourself. Suppose that you are faced with the diamond distribution given above. Can you be sure of 2 diamond tricks even if you have to lead the suit yourself? You can. You lead a low diamond (the deuce) from Dummy, on which East will play low. You then play your Ten (not the Ace), not with any expectation that the Ten will win, but in order to *establish a future finesse*. Here West wins the Ten with his Queen, but your Jack has now been promoted one position. With the first round out of the way, the situation is:

```
                          ◊ 4 3
                    ┌───────────┐
                    │     N     │
        ◊ 9 8 5     │  W     E  │     ◊ K 7
                    │     S     │
                    └───────────┘
                          ◊ A J
```

This is a simple finessing situation. You simply re-enter Dummy's hand and lead low through East. You have thus placed yourself in a position to take a simple finesse against East's King. You are sure of 2 tricks in the suit whenever the King and Queen are divided.

But there are two other possible combinations, as follows:

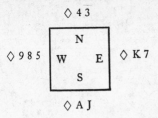

```
              ◊ 4 3 2                              ◊ 4 3 2
        ┌───────────┐                        ┌───────────┐
        │     N     │                        │     N     │
1. ◊965 │  W     E  │ ◊ K Q 8 7   2. ◊KQ87  │  W     E  │ ◊ 9 6 5
        │     S     │                        │     S     │
        └───────────┘                        └───────────┘
            ◊ A J 10                              ◊ A J 10
```

In the first situation, it is still essential for you to lead low from Dummy, and, if East plays low, your Ten will hold the trick. You still make 2 diamond tricks, for if East plays one of his honors, you win with your Ace and then either your Jack or Ten will drive out the other honor, leaving you an established trick. In the second situation, all your strategy will fail, since the Ten must lose to the Queen, and on the second round the Jack will lose to the King. However, our original argument is still sound, for nothing has been lost which would not have been lost anyway, and you have the satisfaction of having played the best way to *have a chance* of making 2 tricks.

FINESSING AGAINST LOWER HONORS THAN THE KING

So far we have given no specific examples of finessing against honors other than the King; yet it should be apparent that occasion for finessing against some lower honor must often occur. Suppose we consider a finesse against an outstanding Queen, as in the two situations given below. Though these two examples may seem at first glance to resemble each other very much, they are actually quite different.

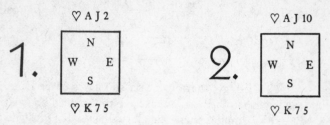

The vital difference in these two situations lies in the fact that in the second the Dummy has the Ten (an honor instead of a small card). Before proceeding to the explanation which follows, it would be a good idea for the reader to consider the aspects of these two situations very carefully.

In the first situation, the Declarer has only one chance of securing 3 tricks in suit. In the second situation, the Declarer has two chances of making 3 tricks—that is, he has open to him two possible methods of play. In No. 1, if you wish to finesse against the Queen of hearts, your only chance lies in leading low from your own hand (South), and playing the Jack from Dummy if West plays low. In other words, 3 heart tricks are possible in No. 1 only when West holds the Queen. Why can't you lead the Jack from Dummy and hope to capture the Queen if East holds it? Simply because, if you do this, East will cover your Jack with his Queen, and you will be forced to win the trick with the King, leaving you with A 7 5 2, a combination which can obviously win but 1 more heart trick. The situation is exactly analogous to the situation in the preceding chapter when the Declarer held the Queen and two small cards in one hand and the Ace and two small cards in the other hand. You will remember that leading the Queen could not possibly gain anything in that situation. For the same reason, leading the Jack cannot gain anything in No. 1 above.

The difference in No. 2 should be at once apparent. You can play low and finesse either the Ten or the Jack if West plays low also. However, if you think it more advisable, you can also finesse against the Queen by leading your Jack from Dummy, when, if East covers with his Queen, you can win the trick with your King, thus promoting your Ten to equal rank with your Ace, completely commanding the the heart suit. You thus see that we are retracing our steps—we are refusing to take a certain type of finesse (that in which an honor is led) unless we hold honors in sequence.

The natural question arises as to which play is the right one in the second situation just analyzed. The answer is that, lacking additional information, the chances are exactly even. It is a pure guess which Opponent holds the missing Queen. Later on, when we study card reading, we will find that it is often possible for a skillful player to locate cards from information disclosed during the bidding or revealed by discards of the Opponents during the play. Yet even the most skillful player must at times resort to mere guesswork in such a situation as No. 2, since the Opponents do not always give information as to the key cards they hold. For the present, you may believe that the position of the Queen depends wholly on a guess—with a fifty-fifty chance of any player guessing aright, and let it go at that.

The finesse against the Queen also occurs in the following situations, in which the cards of Nos. 1 and 2 are arranged somewhat differently:

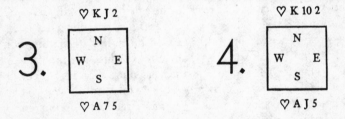

In No. 3 your only hope of success is to lead low from your own hand (South) and finesse the Jack from the Dummy. In No. 4 you have a clear choice; that is, if you think West holds the Queen, you should lead low from your own hand and finesse the Ten, but if you think East holds the Queen, you should lead low from Dummy and finesse the Jack.

There are even more intricate ways of encircling adverse Queens. Consider, for example, the following spade situation:

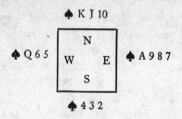

The same old principle applies: you must lead first from the weak hand (South).   Clearly West will play low, and you must finesse the Ten.   Just as when you held A J 10 in a previous example, you do not expect Dummy's Ten to hold the trick.   In other words, you are not making any wild attempt to finesse around the Ace.   The only card you are interested in circumventing is the Queen, and you are hoping that West holds it, for if he does, East will be forced to capture the Ten with the Ace if he wants to win the trick.   If East does win with the Ace, you plan to re-enter your own hand and lead low again in order to finesse the Jack.   In this fashion your negligible spade holding of K J 10 may succeed in winning 2 tricks against the Opponents' powerful combination of both Ace and Queen.

An objection to this play is bound to occur to everybody, and that is that the Ten will lose to the Queen whenever East holds it and West has the Ace, so that the first trick in the suit could actually have been won with the King.   The answer is that, if this is done, only 1 trick will be won in the suit anyway.   In fact, if the K J 10 combination is led in rotation, one of the three honors must win a trick, netting you 1 trick no matter where the Ace and Queen are located.   Your only hope of making *2 tricks* is to proceed as explained above.

The following situation is likely to arise frequently in our ensuing general discussion of hands:

$\Diamond$ K J 2

	N
W	E
	S

$\Diamond$ 4 3

Let us assume that you need to win only 1 trick in this suit.   To do this, you lead the trey or the four-spot toward the Dummy's King-Jack.   Now if West plays low, you may play the King, hoping that East does not have the Ace though he may have the Queen, or you may play the Jack, hoping that East does not have the Queen though he may have the Ace.   It merely is guesswork; the chances are even.

The combination of K J 10, to carry this principle further, may be variously divided, thus:

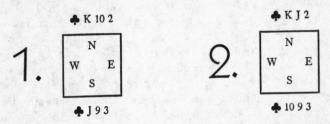

In both situations, the proper play is to lead the honor from the weak hand and play low from Dummy if West plays low.   However, note one very essential factor in both these situations which was lacking in preceding examples.   This factor is the presence of the nine-spot—an extremely important card here.   This brings us back to the principles governing the proper way to play Ace and two small cards in one hand and Queen and two small cards in the other.   To make this clearer, consider the combination when the nine-spot is missing:

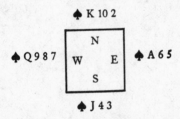

If Declarer (South) plays the Jack, and West follows with the Queen, North must play the King and East the Ace.   This is an extreme example of the promotional power of honors.   All four top honors have gone on one trick, and the Dummy's Ten has suddenly become the commanding card, gaining four positions.   Note that something else has happened.   West's nine, eight, and seven have also been promoted, so that West can be sure of winning the third round of the suit.

We may therefore come to the conclusion that a holding of K J 10 (divided between the two hands) without the nine-spot is not a particularly attractive finessing combination. In fact, the chances are that such a suit should not be attacked by the Declarer at all. It is true that, even without the nine, the suit is very valuable if West holds both Ace and Queen, but such a distribution is unlikely.

The same principle holds true for lower cards than K J 10. In fact, a holding of Q 10 9 should be treated in the same fashion. There is a kinship of pattern between K J 10 and Q 10 9 which a moment's thought should make as clear as daylight. If the Dummy holds Q 10 9 and you have three small cards in your hand, you lead—always remember!—*from the weak hand toward the stronger*. It would be excellent practice if you would go back to the finessing situations thus far given and substitute, in the examples, lower cards for those given. For the King substitute the Queen; for the Ten the nine-spot. Cards below honors may be finessed in exactly the same way as honors.

Some Miscellaneous Examples

The reader must surely comprehend the finessing principle by this time. However, it is sufficiently important to justify including here certain combinations which it may be well to recognize when they occur. Note, for example, the difference between the following two situations:

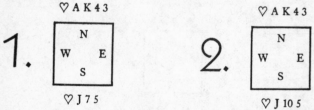

In No. 1, if you play the Jack first, you cannot hope to gain anything, for the simple reason that if the Queen is played the Opponents' Ten and nine-spot must be promoted into potential trick-takers. In No. 2, however, if the Jack is led and the Queen is played on it by West, you can win the trick with Dummy's Ace or King, and your own Ten will be promoted to a commanding position. In the first instance, the lead of the Jack needlessly wastes an honor; in the second, the lead of the Jack hopes to gain a trick.

While we are discussing these particular suit distributions, take note of the fact that they contain seven cards for the partnership and therefore have extremely good chances of developing a small card as a trick. In the first situation of the two just given, it is impossible to take all 4 tricks. In the second situation, however, it is entirely possible to take 4 tricks if the adverse cards are evenly divided and if West has the Queen, thus:

Leading the Jack on the first round nets the Declarer 4 heart tricks.

Another rather common finessing situation is the following:

This presents a slight variation known, for want of a better name, as a "postponed finesse." The finesse undergoes postponement simply because a sure winner is led before any finesse is considered. This play is made to secure the maximum degree of safety in the event that a certain peculiar distribution happens to exist, such as the following:

The normal way to finesse in this situation (the adverse distribution being, of course, unknown) would be to lead a low card from the weak hand, finessing the Jack. With the Opponents' cards distributed as shown, this play will lose a trick to the Queen held by East. To insure against this situation, it is a wise play for the Declarer first to win a trick with the Ace or the King, postponing his finesse of the Jack until the second round. The degree of safety is worth while.

Summary

You have learned in this chapter how to finesse against more than one outstanding higher card. You have also learned how to finesse against lower honors than the King. The manner in which you attempt to encircle an adversary's honor should now be an open book to you, and you should find it as simple a matter as the proverbial rolling off a log. The *names* of the finesses you have learned do not matter; they are merely convenient tags to use in discussing them in a textbook of this kind.

CHAPTER IV

WHEN NOT TO FINESSE

THE thoroughness with which we have gone into the subject of tenaces and finessing may give the reader the wrong impression that finesses are compulsory whenever a finessing position appears. Please be patient and do not take anything for granted; by the time you have finished this book you will be able to decide for yourself which may be the better play in any given situation.

A warning may very appropriately be inserted at this point to the effect that just because certain combinations of honors are held, and other honors are missing, you need not feel obliged to attempt to encircle the honors not held. In fact, *when a suit is divided in the two hands in such a way that a missing honor seems likely to drop on the lead of a higher honor, to finesse against the missing honor is usually not a good play.* Consider the following diamond situation:

◇ 6 5 4 3

◇ A Q J 10 9 8 7

You have seven diamonds, and Dummy has four. The Opponents, therefore, have only two diamonds, and the chances are good that each Opponent holds one. If so, you will capture both adverse diamonds by leading your Ace; the King then drops. Of course, one Opponent may hold both missing diamonds. In this event, the lead of your Ace will not capture the King. You may assert that to finesse would have been better; but a finesse will work only when East holds both missing diamonds.* The fact remains that experi-

---

* The missing diamonds may be divided in any one of the four following patterns:

W.	E.	W.	E.	W.	E.	W.	E.
◇ K	◇ 2	◇ 2	◇ K	◇ K 2	◇ —	◇ —	◇ K 2

Obviously, an attempted finesse made by a low lead from Dummy (North) will *apparently* succeed half the time. Actually, in the second situation, when East has the King alone, the attempted finesse develops at once into the drop, for East must play the King willy-nilly, whereupon South puts on the Ace. The King therefore drops half the time, whether the Ace is led or is played on a low lead from Dummy.

ence has shown that it is better in a situation like this, to play for the drop (by playing the Ace on the first round) than to finesse. To be sure, you thereby give up any chance of encircling the King if it does not drop. That is unfortunate, but it is not your fault. You have made the best play under the circumstances.

However, reconsider the preceding diamond situation with one less diamond in your hand and Dummy's. The Opponents then have three diamonds, thereby greatly reducing your chances of dropping the King. Your best play is then to finesse, by leading from Dummy's hand toward your Ace-Queen tenace, hoping East holds the King.

The same principle can be extended to Queens and Jacks, as, for example, in the following spade situation:

♠ A 10 9 8

♠ K J 7 6 5

You have nine spades in your two hands, including the two top honors. The Opponents have only four spades, one of which is the Queen. With your two top spades, you have two leads on which the Queen may drop. Whenever the adverse spades are evenly divided, you can drop the Queen, and to finesse may lose. Also, if the Queen is alone in one hand, it will drop on the first round. If an Opponent holds the Queen twice guarded (Queen and two small spades), the honor will not drop. However, unless you have obtained some information from the bidding or from some previous play which locates the Queen for you, to play for the drop is a better play, all things considered, than to finesse for the Queen.

As a matter of fact, when you hold two top honors in a suit, it is always better to lay down one of them on the first round, so that if the missing honor happens to be a singleton,* it will drop—even when a finesse is indicated as the best play on the second round.

* "Singleton" as a term for only one card of a suit dealt originally has been common for centuries in the language of card games. By a similar word-formation, "doubleton" for a two-card suit and, less common, "tripleton" for a three-card suit have come into use.

Consider now the following heart situation:

$\heartsuit$ K 10 9 8 7

```
        N
    W       E
        S
```

$\heartsuit$ J 6 5 4

Following the principle of finessing, you must lead from your own hand first, as it is the weaker hand. If West plays low, you must decide whether to attempt a finesse against the Queen, or to capture the Queen. The Opponents hold only two heart honors. If West holds $\heartsuit$ Q 3 and East $\heartsuit$ A 2, your best play is the seven-spot from Dummy. But if West holds $\heartsuit$ A 2 and East $\heartsuit$ Q 3, the King would be a better play because it would hold the trick and the Queen would fall automatically on West's Ace on the next round. The play is essentially a guess, though information disclosed during the bidding or previous play may often eliminate the guess.

Note that here you had nine cards in the suit in the combined hands so that if you guess (correctly) to play the King on the first round there is a good chance that the Ace and Queen will fall together on the second round. But if your combined holding consists of eight or fewer cards, the Queen, not the Ace, should be finessed against on the first round as clearly the best chance of losing only one trick in the suit.

SUMMARY

In this short but important chapter you have been warned that occasions arise when a finesse is not advisable; that is, when some other method of play against a missing honor offers better chances of success. In fact, when a suit is divided in the two hands in such a way that a missing honor seems likely to drop on the lead of a higher honor, to finesse against the missing honor is usually not a good play.

Whenever your partnership hands contain nine or more cards of a suit, it is worth considering whether to play for the drop is not more likely to succeed than to play for the finesse. With nine cards against the Queen, or with eleven cards against the King, it is best to play for the drop.

CHAPTER V

ENTRIES

T ENACE positions have been discussed thus far as though they were a separate department of play. The necessity of leading from the weak hand toward the strong hand has been emphasized repeatedly; it has been pointed out that it may be necessary to lead in this way two or three times. To do just this—to lead from the hand desired—certain cards in other suits also have to be considered.

Cards which enable a player to get at will into the hand from which he wishes to lead are appropriately called *entries*. An *entry* card is a winner which puts the hand containing it in the lead whenever the winner is cashed in. An *entry* is sometimes called a *re-entry* when it permits a player to return to the hand after he has already led from it and lost the lead for the time being.

When a good player utilizes an entry, he is entering the hand containing it in order to accomplish a particular purpose which he has in mind. No good player makes any play in a haphazard fashion. For this reason, you must get in the habit of paying careful attention to the distribution of entries in your partnership hands.

Entries are of various kinds; they may be high cards or low cards. Sure winners are, of course, sure entries. Other cards, which are only probable or possible winners, because of cards out against them, are doubtful entries. Even the doubtful entry may be of great importance in planning the play of a hand.

The following situation, for instance, illustrates the sure entry:

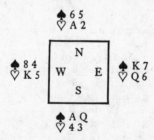

Here, as Declarer (South), you are faced, let us say, with the problem of how to take 3 more tricks when the lead is at the moment in your own hand. Obviously, if you lead your Ace of spades, you will not accomplish your purpose, for the King of spades will thereupon be established against you, and either the King or Queen of hearts must win. You remember that the Ace-Queen combination is one of those tenaces with which it is imperative for the lead to come from the other hand. What do you, therefore, do? You lead one of your small hearts and win the trick with Dummy's Ace. You are now in the Dummy with the lead—that is, you have entered the Dummy with the Ace of hearts, and you can lead a low spade toward your Ace-Queen, taking a simple finesse. The Ace of hearts was your sure entry for this play; if the Ace of hearts had been in your own hand at this point, the finesse would have been impossible.

Take the following slightly different situation:

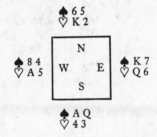

Suppose again that you are Declarer, and the lead is in your hand. How can you win 3 tricks more? The situation is the same as the preceding one, except that you have no sure entry to the Dummy's hand. Instead you have a doubtful entry (the King of hearts). At any rate, you must make the best of the situation. You therefore lead a heart from your own hand, playing the King from Dummy if West plays low, hoping that the King will hold the trick. In the situation given, the King does hold, and a doubtful entry has become a certain entry. If West plays the Ace, the King is then promoted to a sure entry on the next round.

Very often one entry is not enough, especially when it is desirable to lead from the same hand two or three times. Since, in finessing, you always lead from the weaker hand, it behooves you to develop as many entries as possible in the weaker hand, so that you will have them available when you need them. Study the following situation, in which, since the weak hand (in spades) is the Declarer's hand, the lead must come from South toward North:

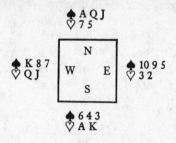

The lead is in the Dummy. Since, assuming that West holds the King of spades, you must lead from your own hand twice in order to capture it, your first play at this point must be to get back into your own hand. You do this by leading a low heart and winning it in your hand with the King (or Ace). If you now lead your Ace of hearts, you sacrifice what is otherwise a situation in which you can take all the remaining tricks, for you destroy the second sure entry into your hand. Instead, you lead a low spade toward Dummy's spade tenace. If West plays low, you finesse the Jack from Dummy. Now you return to your hand, using the heart Ace as your second entry, and lead another low spade toward Dummy's Ace-Queen. West is helpless; if he plays low, you finesse your Queen, and your Ace of spades wins the last round; if he plays the King, you win with your Ace and the Queen wins the last round.

To follow this principle a little further, study the following:

If West holds the spade King, you should see clearly that, as Declarer, you can win all the rest of the tricks by taking the spade finesse.

Even if West holds the King thrice-guarded (King and three small), you can still win, provided you are able to lead from your hand three times. Your three top honors in hearts give you the three entries you need. Any player, in the given situation, who leads those three hearts one after the other, is bound to lose a trick to West's thrice-guarded King. The proper procedure is to lead a heart from Dummy (assuming the lead is in Dummy's hand at this point), winning in your own hand. Then you should lead a spade toward Dummy's tenace, finessing the Ten if West plays low. You then re-enter your hand by leading a heart from Dummy; next you lead a small spade, finessing the Jack if West again plays low. You can return to your hand a third time with your third heart, taking the spade finesse a third time by playing the Queen from Dummy if West still plays low. Notice that if on the second round of spades East follows suit, you know that West's King is now unguarded and will fall on your Ace. The third finesse is therefore unnecessary when East follows suit. If East does not follow suit on the second round, you know that the third spade finesse is required.

Tenace positions very often occur in both hands. Your problem then reduces to trying to get the maximum number of tricks out of whatever combinations you hold. Assuming that the missing honors are favorably placed for finessing purposes, you will find the following situation a good illustration of this point:

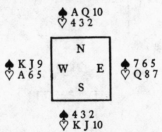

If the lead is your own hand, as Declarer (South), you must lead spades first; if the lead is in the Dummy's hand, you must lead hearts first. Otherwise the lead at this point does not affect the trick-taking power of the tenaces held. Assume, for the sake of illustration, that the lead is in your own hand. You lead a low spade, finessing the Ten if West plays the nine-spot. The Ten holding, you find yourself in the Dummy, whereupon you lead a heart, finessing the Ten in your hand if East plays low. You thus force West to play his Ace if he wishes to win the trick, and you have secured enough information about the adverse honors to know that you are going to win the balance of the tricks. Having won with the Ace of hearts, West must lead a heart or a spade. If he elects to lead a spade, you need not worry about entries, for you merely play the Queen from Dummy (or the Ace if West leads the King). If he chooses a heart, your entry problem is also solved, for your King-Jack is in perfect tenace position over East's Queen. In fact, if West leads a heart and East plays the Queen, you can take both your King and Jack of hearts before leading the low spade to finesse the Queen.*

This subject is sufficiently complex to be discussed at indefinite length. But only three more examples, all simple, will be given here to clinch the points that have been made. They are the following, all occurring at the eighth trick. In all three the Declarer (South) must be very careful to utilize all his entries properly, for, if he fails to do so, he is extremely liable to find himself in the wrong hand and be forced to lead from his own tenaces—with fatal consequences.

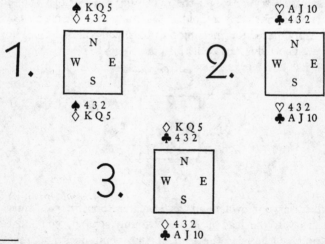

* The combination of cards given in this example would hardly occur in actual play, for it is perplexing to try to figure out how the other twenty-eight cards could have been played to the first 7 tricks in order to arrive at such a situation as this. However, the distribution, invented though it is, serves as a good illustration of the use of entries.

The Vital Meaning of Tenaces

Suppose we briefly re-examine the meaning of a "tenace position." Assume that you hold the Ace and Queen of a suit in your hand. From what hand should the lead be made in order for you to have the maximum likelihood of taking 2 tricks with the Ace and Queen? The answer is that the lead should be made *from the hand on your left.* In other words, if your left-hand Opponent leads that suit, you will be the last to play to the trick, and you will therefore be in a position to win the trick with whatever card is required. In fact, whenever the lead comes from the hand on your left, your expectation of winning 2 tricks with your Ace-Queen tenace becomes a 100% certainty.

What is the next most advantageous lead? The answer is that there are two equally advantageous directions from which the lead may come, provided it cannot come from the left-hand Opponent. You may lead the suit yourself, from the Dummy's hand up to your Ace-Queen. Also, if your right-hand Opponent leads the suit, it comes up to your Ace-Queen with equal advantage. In both situations, your Queen may be finessed; it wins whenever your right-hand Opponent has the King, and loses when your left-hand Opponent has it.

The third possible direction of the lead, from your own hand, is the worst, as you know. To lead from your own tenace is disastrous, except in the few rare instances when the missing honor is a singleton and you lead the Ace. In other words, if you must lead from your Ace-Queen holding yourself, you stand practically no chance of winning 2 tricks in that suit.

The situation may be boiled down to the following general truths bearing on the proper play of a suit in which you hold the Ace-Queen tenace in your own hand as Declarer:

If you lead from your own hand, you accomplish nothing.

If you lead from Dummy's hand, or if your right-hand Opponent leads the suit, you are in a position to take a simple finesse.

If your left-hand Opponent is forced to lead the suit, you are presented with an "automatic" finesse—in other words, your Ace-Queen is placed in a definitely winning position over BOTH Opponents.

To control the lead so far as your hand and the Dummy's are concerned, you must pay strict attention to your available entries and utilize them to your best advantage. As to the problem of securing a lead from either Opponent, especially when it will be to your advantage, that will be solved as soon as you learn some of the further strategy of play, explained in later chapters.

Every combination of cards in which one or more honors is missing is but a variation of the Ace-Queen tenace. The direction of the lead has exactly the same effect upon it. Whenever the lead is from the Opponent on the *left* of the tenace, the tenace has the best chance to win. A lead from the *opposite hand* is equal in value to a lead from the Opponent on the *right* of the tenace. To lead from the *tenace itself* is the least likely to prove at all profitable. Every situation that ever arises in the play of the cards, even if it seems different, is governed by this fundamental principle. No matter what different aspect any combination of cards may appear to take, it is only wearing a cloak—you need but apply this principle in some form, and the problem is solved. This will become clearer and clearer as you progress from elementary to advanced play.

Summary

The essential lesson of this chapter has been the importance of entries. Only by being able to lead from the proper hand at a strategic moment can you hope to reap the full harvest of your winners and probable winners. On entries depends your freedom of choice in handling your cards. Watch all entry cards—and cherish them. Develop further entries, and plan to have entries available as you proceed. You will learn many ways of doing this as you take up the ensuing chapters.

And remember that the best lead for any suit of yours which is not solid must come from the left of your tenace, and that the next best is from the opposite hand, or from the right of your tenace, but that to lead from the tenace itself is the least advantageous.

CHAPTER VI

GENERAL PRINCIPLES

Now that you are somewhat acquainted with the proper methods of handling various two- and three-card combinations of honors, you are about ready to take up the study of the play of a complete deal of fifty-two cards—of which you and your Partner hold half and the Opponents hold the other half.

Let us digress just a moment to contemplate the *meaning* of a hand. Ask yourself this question, What is the fundamental principle underlying the game of Contract Bridge? In short, just what is the *idea* of the game? The idea, or the object, of the game is to obtain a larger number of points (in the score) than your Opponents. To do this, you must always plan to take as many tricks as possible. This holds true in any playing position, whether you are the Declarer or are playing defensively against the Declarer. Of course, before you can plan to take any tricks, the auction must take place in which one or more bids are made for the contract. The bidding is nothing more nor less than an estimate of the number of tricks which a partnership believes it can win. When a player secures the contract, he undertakes to win the number of tricks named in his contract in addition to the book (first 6 tricks for his side). If a player becomes the Declarer with a contract of one no-trump, he undertakes to win 1 trick more than his book, or 7 tricks in all—at least. If his contract is three no-trump, he must win 9 tricks to make his contract. If his contract calls for a Grand Slam (any contract of seven-odd), he must win all 13 tricks. If he fails to make his contract, owing to the fact that his Opponents have won more tricks than he should have let them win, the Declarer is penalized for being set, and the Opponents score the points for that deal.

How are tricks won? There are two kinds of play, namely,

no-trump play and *trump* play.   Of these two kinds, no-trump play
is the easier to understand.   At no-trump all four suits have equal
value in the play, and the highest card of the suit led always wins the
trick to which it is played.

The Ace is obviously the most conspicuous high card, for it is the
highest card in each suit, and cannot therefore be defeated (captured)
by any other card in the same suit.   Next in order come the other
honors: Kings, Queens, Jacks, and Tens.   You have already seen
that if a suit is solid with top honors, those top honors must win in
that suit.   If any honors are missing, the suit must usually be developed in some way to secure its maximum trick-taking power.

These facts are all very simple.   Any novice cannot fail to realize
that certain cards of high rank are bound to take tricks.   However,
contracts cannot be made by means of such high cards alone.   As
you have already learned, honors have other functions to perform
besides winning tricks right off the bat, so to speak.   They must
stand by to assist in the development of lower cards as trick winners.
The tricks won directly by honors may be named, for convenience,
high-card tricks.   The tricks which are won with lower cards, developed by honors, are usually what are known as *long-suit tricks*.
They are so called because they depend on suit length for their exist-
ence.   You will recall that in the following spade distribution, for
example, South must win 4 tricks:

♠ 5 4 3

♠ J 8 7   N W E S   ♠ 10 9 6

♠ A K Q 2

Of these, 3 are high-card tricks, won with the three top honors, and
the fourth is a long-suit trick, won with the deuce, which remains
after the top honors have captured all the outstanding lower cards.
But with the following spade distribution, of course, the deuce cannot
be developed into a long-suit trick:

♠ 4 3

N
W E
S

♠ 9 6 5   ♠ J 10 8 7

♠ A K Q 2

Thus it appears that long-suit tricks belong to the Opponents when they hold the greater length. Note that in the example just given East and West hold seven spades as against the six held by North and South.

There is an apparent exception to the rule that the greater length means the development of long-suit tricks, as in the following situation:

♠ 4 3

N
W E
S

♠ A K Q 10

Here North and South hold only six spades, and the Opponents have seven. However, South may occasionally develop his Ten into a trick winner. This is possible whenever the Opponents' Jack drops on one of the first three rounds of the suit. This will happen whenever the Jack is accompanied by two small cards or fewer, but it cannot happen when West holds the Jack with three small cards.*

High-card tricks and long-suit tricks are all that you will have to consider in no-trump play. Another kind of trick is possible in trump play, but you need not worry about that till you come to it. High-card and long-suit tricks are present in each of the four suits. If they are not in your hand and not in your partner's hand, they will be found in the hand of one of the Opponents. The primary objective in play, then, is for you to establish as many tricks as you can, for yourself and your partner, before your Opponents can establish theirs. The high-card tricks are usually handled without difficulty. The

---

* Another method of play, of course, is to finesse on the second round against four spades to the Jack in the East hand.

real problem is to bring in your long-suit tricks before your Opponents can bring in theirs.

The play thus develops into a sort of race between the two opposing partnerships. While you are trying to establish certain high cards by driving out the higher cards held by the Opponents and while you are also trying to develop lower cards because of your superior suit length, the Opponents are trying to do exactly the same thing with *their* high cards and *their* suit lengths. If you win the race, you will probably succeed in making your contract, but if you lose the race, you will probably be set 1 or more tricks.

No matter what happens, there are only 13 tricks which may be won in each deal. Nothing could be more absolute—there are 13, no more and no less. Unless the deal is voided in some way under the laws of the game, 13 tricks must be scored, divided between your side and the opposing side. It is entirely possible that the *potential* trick winners in the different hands around the table may total more than 13. Suppose, for instance, that your hand contains 12 *sure* trick winners, and that one of the Opponents has 8 *sure* winners. That makes 20 tricks in all. What happens to the 7 tricks in excess of the 13 to which the ultimate play is limited? Just this:

If you are the Declarer (South) at a no-trump contract, you have what you naturally regard as 4 sure heart tricks, 4 sure diamond tricks, and 4 sure club tricks—12 in all. You are willing to concede 1 spade trick to the Opponents. As a matter of fact, however, you can take only 5 tricks in the example given, for the very good reason that West has what he regards as 8 sure spade tricks—and he is right, *for he has the lead*. Since you are the Declarer, it is West's privilege and right to make the first lead. He leads his Ace of spades, and follows it with the seven spades in sequence. You are helpless, for you cannot capture any of West's spades. What is worse, you must discard—throw away—seven of your sure winners on West's good spades (your singleton spade goes on West's first spade trick). You must take the last 5 tricks, but what a sorry result from your beautiful hand, all because your Opponent *got there first* and cashed in 7 of his winners before you could cash in any of yours. Thus only 13 tricks were won, though both of you apparently had enough to total 20 tricks before the play started.

The hand just given is fantastic, both because such a distribution of cards is very freakish and very rare, and also because it is unlikely that the bidding would result in a no-trump contract for South. But the hand vividly illustrates the importance of the *time element* in the play. This element of time—the matter of getting there first with your winners—occurs in all hands. It is a factor in every known play, and may determine the success or failure of any contract. Many a Bridge player has clung tenaciously to an Ace (a sure winner) only to find the thirteenth trick approaching without his having cashed it in, and owing to the *time element* the Ace is not a winner!

Keep a sharp eye on the watch for the *time element* and notice what a vital part it plays in every example deal which is given in this book. The *potential* winners in any hand develop into *tricks* in the play only when they are utilized *before other winners crowd them out*.

THE CONTRACT IS THE THING

Another fundamental principle must be emphatically stated and duly impressed upon every player's mind, as follows: always let the first object of your play as Declarer be *to make your contract*, ignoring the possibility of extra tricks whenever to play for them places your contract in jeopardy. *

If your contract is one-odd, calling for 7 tricks, your primary objective must be to win 7 tricks. Do not yield to the fascination of a possible *eighth* trick, if by so doing you run any risk whatever of falling short of that essential, all-important 7 you have undertaken to win.

A simple arithmetical calculation will show how important the contract objective is. Suppose you have contracted for a game, not vulnerable. The value of the game is about 450 points to your side, considered as an average, for you not only secure the trick score (from

---

* This admonition and the paragraphs that immediately follow apply to rubber (or money) bridge. At match-point duplicate play it may very occasionally be wise to jeopardize one's contract in a quest for overtricks.—S. F. Jr.

100 to 120 points), but you also gain an advantage, since, having won a game, you have that much better chance to win a *second* game before your Opponents can win two games.   If you win that second game before your Opponents win two games, you score the handsome rubber premium.   If you have contracted for a game *when vulnerable*, already having won one game, the value of that second game is worth just about 600 points to your side.   The most that you can expect to gain by extra tricks is from 20 to 40 points, as a rule.   Does it seem to you to be a good gamble to risk from 450 to 600 points to make an extra 20 to 40 points?   Of course not.

First of all, then, learn to count.   Form the habit of counting the number of tricks you are sure of making.   If that falls short of your contract, count the number of tricks you have *some expectation* of making, and then plan your play to make those tricks if possible *regardless of any other consideration*.   At no-trump, your high-card tricks are certain, your long-suit tricks uncertain.   As the play of the hand progresses, some of the uncertain tricks may become actual tricks.   As soon as you have won enough tricks to take care of your contract, then (and not before) you can consider possible extra tricks.

Summary

You should appreciate the important fact that Contract Bridge is a contest in which each side (two players in partnership) endeavors to score as many points as possible.   Points may be scored in two ways, primarily; these two ways are scoring points for Games, Slams, and Rubbers (that is, for tricks won over the book), and scoring points in penalties against the opposing side (by winning enough tricks defensively so that the opposing Declarer cannot make his contract).

A session of Contract Bridge is won, then, first of all, by getting into a contract suited to the partnership hands, and, secondly, *by winning tricks in the play*.   From the time the Dummy goes down to the fall of the cards on the last trick, the object of both sides is simply *to win every possible trick*—except that the first object of the Declarer must be to make his contract, ignoring the possibility of extra tricks whenever to play for them may forfeit the contract.

You learned that at no-trump there are two kinds of tricks, namely, high-card tricks and long-suit tricks.   Until they are actually cashed in during the play, all tricks are merely potential winners.   The potential winners in any hand develop into tricks in the play only when they are utilized before other winners crowd them out.

In other words, there is a *time element* in the play, which depends on the fact that only 13 tricks are possible, no matter how many potential tricks may seem to be available.   Thus, if you have a chance to take all 13 tricks, by virtue of the fact that you have the first opportunity to do so, you should seize that chance, thereby forcing your Opponents to waste potential winners by discarding them on your good tricks.

CHAPTER VII

ESTABLISHING A SUIT AT NO-TRUMP

THE preceding pages have taught you how to treat various card combinations in a suit in order to obtain the greatest possible number of tricks from each combination. The next step is for you to learn how to discriminate—how to choose between the different suit holdings which exist in your hand. You must learn how and why one suit is selected for development rather than another.

We shall continue to assume that every hand is played at a no-trump contract, mainly because most principles we shall take up are common to both no-trump and suit play. The special aspects peculiar to suit play will be taken up later. By the time the principles of no-trump play are mastered, the peculiarities of suit play will be very easy to comprehend.

The characteristic feature of no-trump play is that all suits are of equal rank in trick-taking power, so that, as a consequence, high cards lord it over the others. However, even high cards become helpless when one side is winning tricks by leading out a series of established winners in low cards. The high cards will probably win tricks eventually, but they should frequently be made to play a wholly secondary role for the time being.

We have already emphasized that the chief object of the Declarer at a no-trump contract is to win as many tricks as he can. Now it is true of his hand that the high cards he holds will generally take care of themselves, and are almost certain to take tricks some time. The low cards, however, are not sure winners. They require development and establishment, and to develop and establish low cards is impossible without some definite *plan of play*. Anyone can win with Aces and Kings, but it takes a fair amount of skill and strategic foresight to win with sevens and eights. When you stop to think that there are only twenty honors (high cards) in the whole deal, as against thirty-two cards ranking nine or lower, you suddenly see how important the manipulation of low cards becomes. In fact, no one can ever play Contract Bridge successfully without learning how to make the most of low cards.

Though high cards must be led or played at some stage of the game, in order to cash in the tricks they represent, they should always be led or played with some purpose in the player's mind. Many beginners (and, no matter how much they play, many persons never pass beyond the beginner stage) think they must take all their tricks as quickly as possible. They suffer under the delusion that if they do not cash in their high cards immediately, they will lose them. What is the result of this foolhardy mode of play? The result is that after the Declarer has taken all his high-card tricks, the Opponents swoop down like hungry birds of prey and snap up the remaining tricks with the lowly sevens and eights which the Declarer so generously established for them.

Contrary to the beginner's notion, it is not necessarily disastrous to lose the lead by letting an Opponent take a trick. In fact, it is often advisable. Remember that the most advantageous position for you, if you are holding certain tenaces, is for your left-hand Opponent to lead. However, you should never give up the lead to an Opponent unless you know why you are doing it, and have a good reason for so doing. If you concede a trick to one of the Opponents' honors, you should be planning to take tricks later with some lower cards which cannot be utilized until they are established. Any sacrifice of tricks must be made to secure the promotion of lower cards to positions of importance.

The following deal is a simple example:

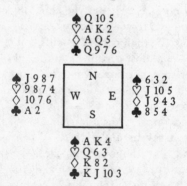

Let us say that you are playing a contract of six no-trump, which, in view of the cards you and your partner (South and North) hold, is not unduly ambitious. Suppose that the opening lead is a spade which you win with the Ace in your own hand. The fact that you should win this first trick is an obvious result of your spade holding, which cannot help taking the first three rounds. Normally, however, as soon as the opening lead is made, you should stop for a few moments *to study the hand and mentally explore its possibilities*. This momentary hesitation is always important. It should determine where you want the lead placed at the second trick, whether you wish to develop a suit, whether you may have to finesse, and a number of other things which you will learn anon. Even at this stage of your knowledge, you can make some plan of play. It may not be the right plan. When you know more, you may find better plans. But the habit of stopping to look ahead is the important thing.

In the hand just given, you win the first trick. You pause then to see what is ahead of you, bearing in mind that you must win 11 more tricks. You see at once that you can be sure of 2 more spade tricks, 3 heart tricks, and 3 diamond tricks, making a total of 9 tricks. After these tricks are taken, the only outstanding high card will be the Ace of clubs. Your King or Queen of clubs will drive out the Ace, leaving you the remainder of the club tricks. In other words, it looks very much as though the Opponents will win just 1 trick—with their club Ace.

Suppose, then, that you proceed with cashing in the tricks in the order in which you have mentally noted them. You take 3 spade tricks, 3 heart tricks, and 3 diamond tricks. If you are watching each trick like a hawk (as you should, no matter how simple the play may seem to be), you will notice that every player follows suit on the three rounds of spades, three rounds of hearts, and three rounds of diamonds. That leaves one card outstanding in each of these suits. As you can see in the example, since the hands are all exposed, West is left with the Jack of spades, the nine of hearts, and the Ace and deuce of clubs. You know that a diamond is also outstanding (the Jack), and you can see in the diagram that this is held by East. Now suppose that you lead your club King to force out the Ace. West wins the trick and what happens? Do you think he will lead back clubs to you so that you can cash in those last 3 club tricks? Not by a long shot—if West is a player who knows how to count. He will know that he has 2 other tricks: the Jack of spades and the nine of hearts. By leading these two cards (which you have established for him), he will set your Small Slam contract by 2 tricks. In other words, by recklessly taking your high-card tricks in spades, hearts, and diamonds without a moment's thought for the future, you have established 2 long-suit tricks for the Opponents. (You have actually established 3 long-suit tricks, but East cannot cash his in because he has no entry.) The situation would be even worse for you if West held the Ace of clubs singleton, and had one more diamond, for he would then hold the fourth diamond also, to cash in against you if you play as first planned.

It is easy enough to see where the mistake was made. In your partnership hands you had originally only six spades, six hearts, and six diamonds. In other words, even if the adverse cards of these suits are divided as evenly as possible between the Opponents, four in one hand and three in the other, the immediate play of the three rounds by you will automatically establish at least one card in each suit for the Opponents.

Therefore, to cash in your high-card tricks immediately is lacking in purpose, for it accomplishes nothing for your side. It helps the Opponents, not you. It cannot possibly help you, no matter how the Opponents' cards are distributed. Nor can the postponement of cashing in these tricks cause you to lose any of them.

What, then, should your plan of play be? You should endeavor to establish your clubs at once. In the example given, this is very easy. You simply lead the King of clubs, sacrificing it to West's Ace at the second trick. (If West holds up his Ace, you win the trick, and lead another club to your Queen.) As soon as West takes his Ace of clubs, at the second or third trick, he must lead a card which you will be able to win and the rest of the tricks are yours.*

The principles involved in the example hand just given are the

---

* When the remaining tricks unquestionably belong to the Declarer (or to any other player), that player may lay down his cards and claim the rest of the tricks, indicating any particular mode of play if such is necessary for him to secure the tricks he claims. This procedure of claiming obvious tricks is commonly followed by all good players in order to save time which would be consumed in actually playing the hand out without any benefit (in pleasure and experience) to either side. That is, no good player considers it "fun" to lead out and haul in tricks that belong to him as surely as the nose on his face. The beginner should be warned, however, not to claim the rest of the tricks in this fashion unless he is *sure* they belong to him no matter how the Opponents may play. The correct procedure for claiming tricks and for penalizing a player who falsely claims the rest is covered in the Laws of Contract Bridge, October 1, 1948.

fundamental principles of all no-trump play. You should, as a rule, never attempt to establish a suit in which the Opponents hold more cards than you do, and you should not play your high cards until it is absolutely necessary. This latter admonition is a modification of the earlier principle of not giving up *control* of any suit without an excellent reason for so doing. The Opponents may also be establishing their suits at the same time.

It is extremely important to watch every card that is played to every trick. You should form the habit of counting the cards in each suit as they are played or discarded. Your mental calculation might go something as follows:

"Let's see now. Spades have gone around twice. I still hold two spades, and the Dummy has one. Since everybody followed suit on the two rounds, that makes eight plus three—eleven spades have been accounted for. Therefore there are two outstanding. One Opponent may have both of them, or each Opponent may have one."

A mental calculation similar to this should be gone through for each suit during the play of every deal. You should always know how many cards of each suit, and, if possible, their denominations, remain unplayed at any point in the game.

Establishing a Suit Before Eliminating Entries

The following deal is slightly more complex. It illustrates the importance of establishing a suit before taking out entries which may be required to cash in the established low cards later in the play:

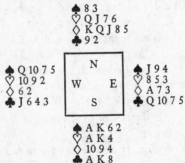

```
                    ♠ 8 3
                    ♡ Q J 7 6
                    ◇ K Q J 8 5
                    ♣ 9 2
        ♠ Q 10 7 5      N       ♠ J 9 4
        ♡ 10 9 2                ♡ 8 5 3
        ◇ 6 2       W       E   ◇ A 7 3
        ♣ J 6 4 3      S       ♣ Q 10 7 5
                    ♠ A K 6 2
                    ♡ A K 4
                    ◇ 10 9 4
                    ♣ A K 8
```

Suppose you are the Declarer (South) playing a contract of six no-trump. West's opening lead is the five of spades, on which, since there is nothing to be gained from playing the eight-spot, you play the trey from Dummy. East plays the Jack (not the four, since he wishes to drive out as high a card as possible from your hand). Naturally, you win the trick with the King. You do not need to hesitate about taking this first trick with your King, for you still have the Ace to keep control of the spade suit.

At this point you should start planning your play. Your first object will be to try and develop the suit containing the greatest number of potential tricks. You can already see 1 more trick in spades, and no more than 2 tricks in clubs. Your hearts are very strong: you have the greatest possible high-card strength, consisting of the four top honors, and you also have seven cards of the suit, leaving only six divided between the Opponents. In fact, you have 4 sure heart tricks.

Having won the first trick with the King of spades, you might then proceed to cash in those 4 heart tricks, which, with another spade trick, and 2 club tricks, will make 8 tricks. But what of the other 4 tricks you need? If for no other reason than that you have not yet planned how to make your whole contract, to cash in your sure heart tricks at once is certainly imprudent. Indeed, it would be insane, as events will prove. You have the four top honors in hearts and control of every other suit eventually; there is, therefore, no reason for being precipitate in hearts. You can cash in those heart tricks whenever it suits you to do so.

Look now at that diamond suit. You have eight diamonds—five in the Dummy's hand and three in your own. Your sequence is complete from the King down to the eight-spot. That is, the only outstanding card which can beat you in diamonds is the Ace. Don't you think, then, that it might not be a bad idea to get rid of that diamond Ace first of all? As soon as that Ace is eliminated, you can draw a breath of relief, for nothing will be left to interfere with your cashing in your remaining tricks. The only possibility of calamity in this particular hand lies in that outstanding diamond Ace, which is a menace as long as it is unplayed.

The proper playing plan, therefore, is to lead the Ten of diamonds to the second trick, playing the five from Dummy. (Or the four could be led from your hand, and the eight played from Dummy.) Your object is to force the Opponents to play their Ace if they wish to win this diamond trick.   If East at once takes the Ten with his Ace, you can count your sure tricks as follows: 1 spade trick already won, 1 spade trick to come, 4 heart tricks, 4 diamond tricks (now sure), and 2 club tricks, making a total of 12.   Thus you will make your contract of six no-trump.

However, suppose that East does not play his Ace on your lead of the Ten of diamonds.   What then?   Ah, something happens which is the particular lesson you are to learn from this hand.   Your Ten of diamonds wins the second trick.   Thereupon you lead the nine, which is allowed to win the trick.   Now you lead the four, playing the Jack from Dummy (the eight and five having already been played).   East, now having only the Ace, is forced to play it and win the third round of diamonds.   All very well, you say, for now, no matter what East leads, you can win the next trick and proceed to make your contract.   Yes, it is indeed all very well since you have developed your diamonds at once.   But pause for a moment and consider what would have happened if you had cashed in your 4 heart tricks before establishing your diamonds.   You would then be faced with the following situation:

♠ 8
♡ —
♢ K Q
♣ 9 2

```
        N
    W       E
        S
```

♠ A 6
♡ —
♢ —
♣ A K 8

Four rounds of hearts exhausted the hearts from Dummy, and on the fourth round you discarded a spade from your hand.   Three rounds of diamonds exhausted all the diamonds in your hand.   You have taken 1 spade trick, 4 heart tricks, and 2 diamond tricks.   But now you cannot get over to the Dummy to cash in those 2 good diamonds.   East would not lead a diamond even if he had one, and you have no diamonds left which you can lead yourself.   In other words, your King and Queen of diamonds are rendered useless. How did this happen? It happened because you took your heart tricks too soon, eliminating entries from the Dummy. By playing according to the other plan, developing diamonds before playing hearts, the situation develops as follows:

♠ 8
♡ Q J 7 6
◇ K Q
♣ 9 2

N
W   E
S

♠ A 6 2
♡ A K 4
◇ —
♣ A K 8

Now, no matter what East leads, you win the trick. After two rounds of hearts which you win with your Ace and King, the four of hearts led to Dummy will enable you to enter Dummy's hand to cash in your remaining heart tricks and also those 2 good diamonds. Your hearts are, therefore, useful to you as *entries*. Remember what you learned about the importance of entries. Not only does the immediate play of the hearts accomplish nothing to your advantage in this hand, but it also costs you 2 tricks and your contract. The problem of establishing suits is always closely linked with keeping adequate entries available in both hands.

Choosing Between Two Establishable Suits

Quite often a no-trump hand will contain more than one suit which should be established without delay. The natural thing is to try and establish them both, but sometimes there is not time enough for you to do this. You must therefore decide which suit is to be established first. The answer is to try to establish the *longer* suit first in most instances. For example, suppose you have to choose between spades and hearts, ignoring all other factors, thus:

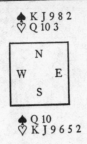

♠ K J 9 8 2
♡ Q 10 3

♠ Q 10
♡ K J 9 6 5 2

In both suits you have a solid sequence with only the Ace missing. However, you have nine hearts and only seven spades. By driving out the Ace of hearts first, you establish 5 tricks, whereas, by driving out the Ace of spades first, you establish only 4 tricks. Clearly you should proceed first with what yields the larger profit, namely, establishing the 5 heart tricks.

If the hand contains two suits of equal length both of which are establishable, prefer the suit which offers the greatest number of tricks. Consider, for example, the following deal:

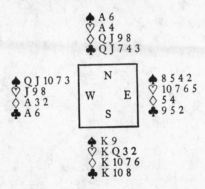

♠ A 6
♡ A 4
♢ Q J 9 8
♣ Q J 7 4 3

♠ Q J 10 7 3
♡ J 9 8
♢ A 3 2
♣ A 6

♠ 8 5 4 2
♡ 10 7 6 5
♢ 5 4
♣ 9 5 2

♠ K 9
♡ K Q 3 2
♢ K 10 7 6
♣ K 10 8

The contract is three no-trump; you are Declarer (South). West opens the spade suit (with the Queen), and, since the question of which hand wins the trick is not of immediate importance, you win in your own hand with the King. Now is the time to stop and plan your play. You have 2 certain spade tricks and 3 certain heart tricks (4 tricks in hearts are out of the question since the Opponents hold seven hearts to your six). These 5 tricks are the only ones on which you can absolutely rely. However, your diamond and club sequences contain potential tricks if you can drive out the opposing Aces. Which of these two suits do you try to develop first? If you drive out the diamond Ace, you will be able to take 3 diamond tricks, but if you drive out the club Ace, you will be able to take 4 club tricks. This difference exists in spite of the fact that you have an equal number of diamonds and clubs; the explanation lies in the distribution of the cards. Your diamonds are evenly divided, but your clubs are longer in Dummy's hand than in your own. The most advantageous suit to develop first is therefore clubs. You immediately play your club King, and continue the suit until, eventually, West is forced to win with his Ace, giving you 4 sure club tricks. Your contract is now assured.

You are curious to see what would happen if you develop diamonds first? All right; let's delve a little deeper into this hand. Suppose that, after winning the first trick with the spade King, you decide to play diamonds. West wins the first round of diamonds with his Ace and returns a spade. You can now take 2 spade tricks, 3 heart tricks, and 3 diamond tricks, making a total of 8 tricks. What are you going to do next? Develop clubs, you say. Very well; you do so, and West wins the first round with his Ace of clubs and cashes in his 3 established spade tricks against you, defeating your contract. Thus you see that, by developing the least profitable suit first, you did not secure enough tricks to make your contract before West could drive out your controlling spades and get in the lead to cash in his spade tricks. Therefore, when you hold two establishable suits, *always try to establish first that suit which promises the greater number of tricks by being established.*

SUMMARY

You have learned in this chapter the primary steps you must undertake to make sure of deriving the greatest possible profit from your low cards in long, establishable suits. The lessons embodied are pithily summarized in the following precepts:

When you are Declarer, as soon as the opening lead is made, stop to study the hand and formulate some fairly definite plan of play.

Never attempt to establish a suit in which the Opponents hold more cards than you do.

Do not play your high cards in suits of which you hold fewer cards than the Opponents, until absolutely necessary.

Count the cards of each suit as they are played or discarded so that you will always know how many remain unplayed at any point in the game.

When you hold two establishable suits, always try to establish first that suit which promises the greater number of tricks by being established.

CHAPTER VIII

ESTABLISHING A SUIT AT NO-TRUMP (CONTINUED)

ALTHOUGH you may not have noticed it at that time, the examples of suit establishment given in the preceding chapter were confined to those suits in which the Declarer held but one losing card (the Ace). Naturally, it is often necessary to try to establish suits against which the Opponents hold more than one winning card. As a matter of fact, most suits which the Declarer ever tries to establish contain more than 1 losing trick, or at least 1 sure loser and 1 possible loser. However, this should not discourage anyone from trying to set up* his low cards in such suits. Admittedly his task is more difficult than in the hands you have already studied, but this is overcome by somewhat greater skill. If the Opponents are bound to win 2 tricks in a suit, do not let this upset you.

The following hand is a good example for study:

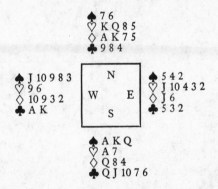

Again you are Declarer (South), with a contract of three no-trump. West's opening lead is the spade Jack, which you naturally win in your own hand with any one of your three top honors (say, the Queen). Now comes your pause to consider your plan of play. You first look for the suit which promises the most tricks if established. In spades you are sure of 3 tricks, and in hearts you are sure of 3 tricks. You cannot hope to take more than 3 heart tricks be-

---

* *Set up* is a familiar synonym for *establish*.

cause you have only six hearts against the seven held by the Opponents, so that it is quite likely that one Opponent will have a winning heart set up after you have taken the first three rounds. You have 3 certain diamond tricks, and you may find a 4th diamond trick if the adverse diamonds are evenly divided. In clubs you have 3 sure tricks if the Opponents can be forced to play their Ace and King.

You know by this time that your solid high cards will win at any time. There is no reason for you to cash in your 3 spade tricks, 3 heart tricks, and 3 diamond tricks right away. Your first objective must be to attack the suit in which you have to drive out opposing higher cards. It is true that your potential winners in diamonds number 4, which is 1 more than you can ever expect to win in clubs. However, you are sure of 3 of those diamond tricks no matter what happens. The 3 club tricks are merely possibilities until the Ace and King are played. Therefore, after considering everything, you are going to try to develop 3 club tricks first, instead of the 1 long-suit trick in diamonds. Though at first glance it seems that the diamond suit is more profitable, actually the club suit is the best bet. By trying clubs first, you may gain 3 tricks, and you *can* lose 1 diamond.

To the second trick, then, you lead a club—any club, since you hold a solid sequence from the Queen down to the six-spot. Say, you lead the Queen. West wins this trick with his King and returns a spade. This does not worry you, for you win the trick and still retain control. Now you lead another club which must drive out West's Ace. Your 3 club tricks are now assured, and—you do not need that 4th diamond trick. You can discard the fourth diamond on one of those 3 club tricks. It is not necessary for you to take any chance that the adverse diamonds are not evenly divided.

Indeed, if you had tried to develop a 4th diamond trick before going after those 3 club tricks, you would have found out, in this particular hand, that West held four diamonds originally and East only two. In other words, West would be presented with an established diamond trick which he would cash in the moment you led a club. By developing clubs first you made 11 tricks. By developing diamonds first you can make only 10 tricks. To be sure, the difference is only 30 points, an extra trick, but inasmuch as your contract is never jeopardized, you may as well play for it.

In choosing between establishing a suit in which you hold the top cards but wish to promote some lower card, and establishing a suit in which the Opponents hold the top cards but you have the long cards, the latter is generally the best hope. A 4th long-suit trick depending on twelve cards falling on the first three rounds of a suit—depending, that is, on a 4-3-3-3 distribution of the suit—is a possibility which can be tried any time.

The Time Element in Establishing a Suit

In the example hand just discussed, West returned a spade at his first opportunity to do so. He was attempting to establish his long spades by driving out your Ace, King and Queen. Meanwhile you were attempting to establish your long clubs by driving out West's Ace and King. You won the race, as Declarer, because your battle was against only two controlling clubs while West's battle was against your *three* controlling spades—the *time element* again.

This matter of time may be reduced to units. Every lead is a time unit, for the lead gives a player the chance to lead the suit he wishes to establish. The right to lead may be called an *offensive* unit (attacking unit). Every high card held is also a factor, for it represents one more obstacle which the adversary must overcome in trying to establish the suit. A controlling high card may be called a *defensive* time unit. West was one offensive unit ahead of the Declarer, in the example just given, for he had the first or opening lead. But against this the Declarer held one additional defensive unit—the third controlling spade.

To illustrate this point, a slightly different deal suffices:

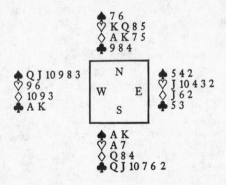

South is still playing a contract of three no-trump. West opens the spade Queen which Declarer has to win with the King (or Ace). If Declarer leads a club, West wins with his King. Now West leads his second spade, driving out Declarer's Ace. Declarer's only two defensive units in spades (Ace-King) are now gone, but West still has one of his two defensive units in clubs. Now if West obtains the lead, Declarer's contract will be defeated, for West will immediately cash in his good spades, of which Declarer knows that he holds at least three.*

What should Declarer do? He must abandon all hope of establishing the club suit, because it would be fatal for him to relinquish the lead at this juncture. The only course open to him, with any hope of making his contract (three no-trump), is to turn his attention to some other suit. Now the diamonds come into their own, for there is the possibility of a 4th diamond trick. What was not worth considering as long as there was a chance to make 3 club tricks now becomes Declarer's only hope.

Just what is the trick situation? Counting, we learn that Declarer has 2 spade tricks, 3 diamond tricks and 3 heart tricks—a total of 8. If Declarer is lucky enough to find the outstanding six diamonds divided 3-3 he can still make his contract of 9 tricks. The proper lead here is therefore the diamond Queen, followed by a small diamond which is won by Dummy's King. Now the Ace is led and, as can be seen from the diagram, both Opponents have to follow suit, leaving Dummy's fourth diamond set up for the needed 9th trick.

Now that Declarer's contract is assured (he makes sure of it by taking his 3 heart tricks and that 4th diamond trick before he does anything else), he can experiment with the clubs. However, it is hopeless, for the moment he leads a club West claims the rest of the tricks with his club Ace and remaining good spades.

The two hands just given—in the first you establish 3 club tricks and in the second Declarer establishes instead a 4th diamond trick—will repay careful study. They illustrate two very important prin-

---

* Actually West will cash in 4 spade tricks if he gets the lead at this point. Declarer knows that the Opponents must have at least 3 spade tricks because there are five spades outstanding, of which the best possible distribution for Declarer is 3-2. The fact that the five spades are distributed 4-1 in this hand means only that the Declarer is worse off than he might be.

ciples of play, as follows: (1) *when you are not crowded for time, do not be afraid to lose the lead by letting an Opponent win tricks which are his anyway;* and (2) *when an Opponent, on obtaining the lead, may be able to cash in enough established tricks to defeat your contract, try to keep the lead while doing the best you can with whatever winners you have left.*

ESTABLISHING A SUIT BY FINESSING

Suit establishment does not always take place by the lead of cards of equal value in order to drive out opposing high cards. The missing high card or cards can often be eliminated by finessing. Such a finesse must be taken boldly when it gives some chance of making an otherwise impossible contract, for some chance is better than none, as you recall. Even though, if the finesse fails, an Opponent may be given the opportunity to cash in several established low cards, this is no reason for you to get panicky and decide to take your high-card tricks in other suits at once. Your best procedure is always to take the chance of losing by a finesse rather than to accept the certainty of losing by foolishly abandoning your only hope of winning!

Take, for example, the following deal:

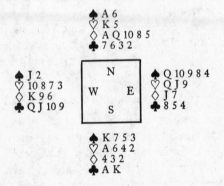

You are playing a contract of four no-trump, against which West opens the club Queen. In your examination of the possibilities, you find no promise in the spade, heart and club suits beyond the 2 certain tricks in each guaranteed by the two top honors. But that makes only 6 tricks, to which you may add the sure trick represented by the diamond Ace. More than the Ace must be developed in diamonds in order to make your contract. In spite of the fact that two diamond honors are out against you, you must do what you can. You may lose a trick to each of them, or to neither. But you must take the chance of losing in order to have any hope of winning.

You proceed against the adverse King and Jack of diamonds, not by leading your high cards, but by finessing as you learned in preceding chapters. The finesse here offers a better chance of gain than the direct lead of honors. Therefore you lead a low diamond from your own hand toward Dummy's Ace-Queen tenace. When West plays the six, you play Dummy's Ten, finessing it against both the King and Jack (a double finesse, you recall). Of course, as you can see by the diagram, East wins with the Jack. This is momentarily discouraging, and the gloom increases when East (as was to be expected) returns a club (his partner's suit). This trick you can win, but it takes out your last defensive unit in clubs. However, you still have a chance. Just because East held the Jack is no reason to suppose that he holds the diamond King also. If West has the King, you can still make your contract. Therefore you lead another low diamond and, when West plays the nine, you boldly finesse Dummy's Queen. The trick is yours! East follows suit, and your count tells you that eight diamonds have been played. Since your hand and Dummy's contain four more, you know that West's King must drop on your Ace and all your remaining diamonds will be established, giving you 2 spade tricks, 2 heart tricks, 4 diamond tricks and 2 club tricks—a total of 10 tricks.

A Second Look at the Double Finesse

Let us digress a moment to look at that diamond finesse again. You may say that the finesse of the Ten was futile because it fell prey to East's Jack. Suppose you finessed the Queen instead of the Jack. You would win the first round of diamonds, drop East's Jack with your Ace on the second round and concede 1 trick to West's King. The result is the same as before—you have lost 1 diamond trick. The finesse of the Ten loses 1 trick to the Jack; the finesse of the Queen ultimately loses 1 trick to the King. What difference does it make? The finesse of the Ten is better, for by finessing the Ten first you have a chance of making all 5 diamond tricks. You also have a chance of forcing the King immediately which leaves only the

Jack out against you. To finesse the Queen first gains nothing and costs you all hope of making 5 diamond tricks.

The number of diamonds you hold makes a difference, though. When you have eight diamonds against the Opponents' five, to finesse the Ten first is the best play. But if you are lucky enough to hold nine diamonds against the Opponents' four, you must bear in mind that there is an excellent chance that those four adverse diamonds will be evenly divided, two in West's hand and two in East's. In this situation, the better play is to finesse the Queen first (hoping West has the King), following it with the Ace (hoping to drop the last two diamonds).

Reserving an Entry for a Second Finesse

Never lose sight of the necessity for reserving an entry against a possible emergency, especially when the establishment of a suit may depend on it. Blind leads of high cards can never be justified. You should lead out high cards only when you have a purpose, or when all the remaining tricks are clearly yours.

The following deal shows how true this is:

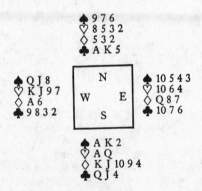

Study the foregoing hand as though you were South, playing as Declarer to make a contract of three no-trump. The opening lead is a lucky break for you—a small heart up to your Ace-Queen tenace, giving you an automatic finesse. That makes you sure of 2 heart tricks. But there seem to be only 6 more sure tricks, namely, 1 more heart trick, 2 spade tricks, and 3 club tricks. It is apparent that your only hope of more tricks lies in the diamond suit. Also, to make these diamond tricks, you must lead from the Dummy. Since the first trick, which you won with the heart Queen, places the lead in your hand, you must enter the Dummy. To do this you lead a low club to Dummy's Ace-King, winning with the King. Notice that you cannot follow this up by taking your Ace of clubs at once, for you need that Ace as a second entry. You therefore lead a low diamond, and, when East plays low, you finesse the nine-spot. As you should remember in connection with finessing, you are not hoping that the nine will win. You are hoping that East holds the Queen and West the Ace, and that the nine will drive out the Ace. If West wins the nine with his Ace, your King is established, and something more—you now know that East holds the Queen, and your King-Jack is in perfect tenace position over him.

Having won with his diamond Ace, if West returns a heart, you must win the trick with the Ace in your hand, and lead another club to Dummy's Ace in order to re-enter that hand for the second diamond lead. This time you finesse the Ten if East plays low. You know that West does not have the Queen, for if he had it, he would have played it on your nine before. The Ten holds, and your count of diamonds tells you that the Queen must drop on the next round under your King. You may claim 6 more tricks at this point, since they will easily be won with your remaining high cards.

Summary

You have added to your knowledge of the technique of establishing suits that it is better to seek to gain long-suit tricks by driving out high cards held by the Opponents, or by capturing such high cards by a finessing maneuver, than to hope for the development of long-suit tricks by dropping outstanding cards on the successive leads of your own high honors. This is true, of course, only when you have a choice. When there is no choice, you must make the best of whatever you have to work with.

In successfully handling the time element, you have found that offensive and defensive units are invaluable. Whichever player has the advantage in these units will win the race for suit establishment, provided he makes the most of his holdings.

When you are not crowded for time, you do not need to be afraid to lose the lead by letting an Opponent win tricks which are his anyway, sooner or later. But when an Opponent, on obtaining the lead, may be able to cash in enough established tricks to defeat your contract, try to keep the lead while doing the best you can with whatever winners you have left.

CHAPTER IX

THE STRATEGY OF CONTROL AND THE HOLD-UP

HAVING gone through a necessary amount of groundwork in suit establishment, you are now ready to return to a subject which was but touched upon in the first chapter, namely, the *control* of a suit.

In the handling of no-trump hands, which permits of considerable flexibility, you have learned that it is important to establish a suit netting you a profitable number of tricks before leading out your good cards without any purpose in view. So far, however, you have not been confronted with a hand in which you have been unable to retain control of the adverse suit which might be established against you. To make the preliminary explanation simpler, you were deliberately given example hands in which a suit was attacked by the Opponents, but in which you were also provided with adequate defensive units to circumvent the attack.

Unfortunately, in playing Contract Bridge you will have to handle whatever cards fate deals out to you, and you can by no means expect to have double control cards in every suit in the majority of hands you will get. Very frequently you will find yourself with but one defensive time unit in one of your suits, and you will be annoyed when your Opponents are usually discerning enough to choose that suit for their immediate attack!

Naturally, if you have but one defensive unit against them, the Opponents will ultimately establish their suit in spite of everything you can do, especially if they keep on leading it. You can minimize the danger to some extent by keeping the Opponents from getting the lead. If you cannot keep both Opponents out of the lead, you can try to confine the lead to one Opponent and hope that he is the one who does not hold the established cards in the suit you fear.

It may usually be taken for granted that the player who opens a suit (that is, the player who first leads that suit) is the one who holds the greater length in it. Later you will have to remember that this rule is not invariable, but just now let us assume that it is always true. Your object will then be to hold on to your controlling card in that suit until there is a fairly good chance that the Opponent who is not leading the suit will be exhausted of it. Then, if you have to give up

the lead, you will try to let that Opponent have it who quite probably
has no cards left of his partner's suit to lead to him.   This sort of
play is called, in Bridge language, the *hold-up*, because you refuse
to play ("hold up") the controlling card until you have to play it.

The following deal illustrates the successful use of the hold-up:

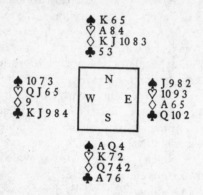

You are the Declarer (South), faced with the problem of making 9
tricks at no-trump. West opens a low club to start the attack in a
suit which may net him some long-suit tricks. East plays the
Queen, hoping to force your Ace. The weakest point in your armor
is being attacked: your club Ace is your only stopper (controlling
card) in that suit, but you have two or more controlling cards in each
of the other suits. You cannot afford to release the Ace of clubs immediately, for you do not have enough high cards to make your contract in the teeth of an established club suit against you. The
moment you lose the lead, when your club Ace is gone, the Opponents will cash in you have no idea how many club tricks (at the
worst, as many as 6). Meanwhile you earnestly desire to set up some
diamond tricks on your own behalf, and you can do this by forcing
out the adverse Ace. But you cannot take your club Ace and then
let an adversary take his diamond Ace, for he will surely come right
back with a club. If the clubs are divided 4-2 (there are six outstanding), the Opponents will then make 4 club tricks and 1 diamond
trick—enough to set your contract.

Though it is true that if the adverse clubs were originally split 4-4,
the loss of 3 club tricks and 1 diamond trick will not defeat your con-

tract, you have no right to expect such a favorable break in the club suit. The fact that West has opened the suit suggests that he has fair length in it, probably five cards. Indeed, if West has five clubs, and his partner the other three, there is a way you can nip the plans of your Opponent in the bud. You have only to refuse to win the first two rounds of clubs, *holding up* your Ace until the third round. By doing this, you wait until East is exhausted of clubs before you release control, so that, if East also has the diamond Ace, he will not be able to lead a club to his partner when he gets the lead with that sure winner. In fact, if East has no clubs at that time, he will have to lead a suit in which you have the controlling cards.

The play proceeds. You play your six of clubs on East's Queen. East returns a club, on which you play the seven-spot. Whichever Opponent wins, the suit is continued. Now East has to play his last club, and you have to play your Ace. On this third round, incidentally, you discard a heart from Dummy's hand. You have to make some discard, since Dummy has no more clubs, and you must retain as many diamonds as possible. Since you can take at the most only 2 heart tricks the discard of a heart is indicated.

Your next step, since it is now your lead, is to lead a low diamond while murmuring a prayer to the gods of chance. You are practically certain that West holds the two outstanding clubs. If he also holds the diamond Ace, all is lost. When West plays low on the diamond lead, you have reason to hope. You play the King from Dummy, and you sigh with a measure of relief when East wins with the Ace. Even if East has another club, his partner has one also, so that the loss of a club trick cannot defeat your contract. As it happens, East has no more clubs, and must lead a spade, a heart, or a diamond. Whichever of these suits East chooses, you can claim the balance of the tricks.

The hold-up is one of the simplest bits of strategy in the play of any hand, but it is also one of the most important plays in any good player's repertoire. There is a strangely prevailing opinion among average players that the use of the hold-up is confined to Aces. Actually the play can be used with cards as low as the Jack.

One more example of the hold-up is not out of place here. Follow it through carefully so that you will surely be able to recognize the play whenever it comes up in your own experience at the card table:

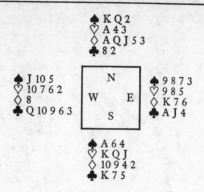

The principle is the same as in the preceding hand. West opens a small club against your no-trump contract. East plays the Ace and returns the Jack. The King is your only defensive time unit against the establishment of the club suit. You must therefore hold on to it as long as possible. Hence you play a low club on the second round, holding up the King. Really, you have less reason to be afraid on this hand than on the preceding one, for you are worried about the location of only one card, the diamond King. If West holds it, you can finesse against it successfully. If East holds it, the chances are better than even that East held originally three clubs at the most. If this is so, the hold-up will prevent any established clubs from winning. When East leads his last club, you win with the King, and you follow this up by taking the diamond finesse. The finesse consists of leading your Ten through West, letting it ride up to East when West does not cover. East wins with his King, but he is exhausted of clubs. Whatever East leads you can win and claim the balance of the tricks.

When the Situation Does Not Call for the Hold-up

The *hold-up* is not the proper play when you hold more than 1 potential trick in that suit. In the two examples just given, the hold-up was effective because you held only one possible stopper in the suit attacked by the Opponents. Sometimes the suit opened against you is one in which you hold the Ace accompanied by certain lower cards which can be developed if you do not employ the hold-up, but which will be valueless if you hold up the Ace. This fact is due to the promotional value of honors. The hold-up should be employed only when you have no chance at all of promoting a lower card in the same suit. Whenever there is a chance of making a trick with a lower card, it is better strategy to cash in the controlling card immediately in order to have that chance of making a second trick in the suit.

The following hand contains a situation in which the hold-up should *not* be employed:

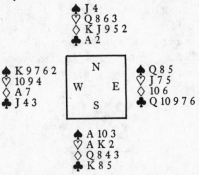

♠ J 4
♡ Q 8 6 3
♢ K J 9 5 2
♣ A 2

♠ K 9 7 6 2   ♠ Q 8 5
♡ 10 9 4   ♡ J 7 5
♢ A 7   ♢ 10 6
♣ J 4 3   ♣ Q 10 9 7 6

♠ A 10 3
♡ A K 2
♢ Q 8 4 3
♣ K 8 5

West opens the six of spades against your (South's) three no-trump contract. You might play the Jack from Dummy, hoping to force East to play an honor. You may consider that if East has the Queen and plays it on the Jack, you can win with your Ace and thereby have a chance of making a trick on the third round with your Ten. However, since you play after East, what is to be gained by playing the Jack? If East does not play his Queen, your Ten will win the trick, since you play after East. The proper play is the four-spot from Dummy, and, when East plays the Queen, the immediate play of the Ace from your hand. To hold up will, as it happens, cost you a trick. By retaining the Jack in the Dummy and the Ten plus a small card in your own hand, you hold two cards which can be beaten only by the King. This means that one of your two cards must win a trick. You ultimately establish your diamonds in this hand and come out at the end of the play with 11 tricks piled up for your side.

The play of the hand just given provides the novice with a chance to do two things wrong. The first, the wrong play of the Jack in-

stead of the four-spot from Dummy, has already been discussed.
To play the Jack is senseless.   The second is the mistaken use of the
hold-up by letting East's Queen hold the first round of the suit.
Notice what would have happened if South did this.   East's Queen
would hold the trick.   In the lead, East would return the eight of
spades.   Committed to the hold-up, South must let this card ride
through also, letting West win with his King.   The third lead of
spades will now drive out the Ace, and West will regain the lead
with his Ace of diamonds, whereupon he can take his 2 established
spade tricks and defeat South's contract by 1 trick.

This principle of not holding up when the Ace is accompanied by
lower cards which may be promoted to trick winners is applicable
even to cards as low as Tens and nines.   Consider, for example, the
following deal:

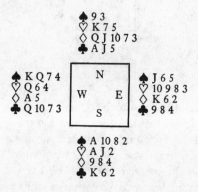

West leads the four of spades against your three no-trump contract.
You play the three from Dummy (*not* the nine, which would avail
you nothing since you hold the eight in your own hand).   East
plays the Jack, and you must play—what?   The Ace, of course;
no other card will work out so well.   By capturing the Jack you promote your Ten, nine, and eight to a higher rank in the suit.   Since
you hold two of these cards guarded in one hand, you can successfully
withstand the further bombardment in the suit which will occur
when the Opponents play their King and Queen.   You should be
able to perceive immediately that this situation does not call for the
hold-up.   If you hold one less spade in your own hand, well and
good—hold up your Ace then, because your Ten, nine, and eight will

all fall together on the adverse King and Queen. Without an original holding of four spades you would not have a potential second spade stopper.

Having won the first round of spades, then, with your Ace, what do you do next? You probably see all sorts of finessing situations confronting you. You can finesse against the club Queen; if West holds this card, you will make 3 club tricks. You can also finesse against the heart Queen; if East holds this card, you will make 3 heart tricks. What can be gained by taking these finesses immediately? They will be available somewhat later, if you find it advisable to take them. Your main object should be, instead, to try to establish *certain* winners before you do any fooling around with *possible* winners. After all, good though a finesse may be in the proper time and place, it cannot compare with the certainty of developing tricks by establishing a suit along lines of play which are almost sure to succeed.

Look, for instance, at your diamond holding. If you concede 2 tricks to the Opponents for their Ace and King, you establish 3 tricks in the suit. You must also lose the King and Queen of spades, and that will make 4 tricks for the Opponents. However, you are certain of winning the fourth round of spades, so that if the spades are divided adversely 4-3 you can lose no more than 2 spade tricks. Has the finessing possibility any advantage over developing diamonds? None. Indeed, even if both finesses succeed, they will not assure you of your contract, and it will still be necessary to attack the diamond suit. The best procedure is clearly to make the diamond attack without delay.

You will find it enlightening to follow this hand play by play.

Trick 1. West leads ♠ 4, North plays ♠ 3, East plays ♠ J, and South wins with ♠ A.

Trick 2. South leads ◇ 9, West plays ◇ 5, North plays ◇ 3, and East wins with ◇ K.

Trick 3. East leads ♠ 6, South plays ♠ 2, West wins with ♠ Q, and North plays ♠ 9.

Trick 4. West leads ♠ K, North discards ♡ 5, East plays ♠ 5, and South plays ♠ 8. West's lead holds the trick.

You are now perfectly content with the developments, for you know that there is only one spade outstanding, and your Ten will beat it. It makes no difference what West decides to lead.

Trick 5. West leads ♠ 7, North discards ♣ 5, East discards ♣ 4, and South wins with ♠ 10.

Trick 6. South leads ◇ 8, West wins with ◇ A, North plays ◇ 7, and East plays ◇ 2. The situation at this point is as follows:

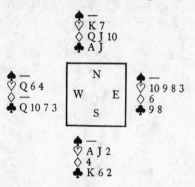

With 7 tricks still to be made, you are certain of winning 2 club tricks, 3 diamond tricks, and 2 heart tricks—your contract.

Suppose that, instead of playing as just recommended, you decide the spade suit is dangerous and that you must take the club and heart finesses at once. You have only a one-way finesse, for you cannot lead the Jack blindly without having the Ten to back it up (see complete hand on page 76). You might lead the King of clubs from your own hand and follow it with a low club, finessing the Jack on the second round if West plays low. It so happens that this will hold the trick and you can turn your attention to hearts. By following the same procedure here, the Jack will lose to West's Queen. This would be enough to set your contract 1 trick, for East and West still hold the King and Queen of spades and the Ace and King of diamonds against you, making 5 tricks won by your Opponents.

Suppose you refuse to win the Jack of spades on the first trick with your Ace. Notice how the play develops trick by trick:

Trick 1. West leads ♠ 4, North plays ♠ 3, East wins with ♠ J, and South plays ♠ 2.

Trick 2. East leads ♠ 6, South plays ♠ 8, West wins with ♠ Q, and North plays ♠ 9.

Trick 3. West leads ◇ 5, North plays ◇ 3, East wins with ◇ K, and South plays ◇ 4.

Trick 4. East leads ♠ 5, South wins with ♠ A, West plays ♠ 7, and North discards ♡ 5.

Trick 5. South leads ◇ 9, West wins with ◇ A, North plays ◇ 7, and East plays ◇ 2.

Trick 6. West leads ♠ K, North discards ♣ 5, East discards ♣ 4, and South plays ♠ 10. West's King holds the trick.

At the sixth trick, East and West have taken 3 spade tricks and 2 diamond tricks, enough to defeat South's contract by 1 trick. In other words, your refusal, as South, to promote your lower honors immediately has resulted in the loss of your contract.

Should Dummy Play High or Low Second Hand?

The question came up, earlier in this chapter, whether Dummy should play a high or a low card on the opening lead coming from Declarer's left. The statement was made that it was inadvisable to play a high card when there was no good reason for doing so. This statement requires elucidation. Notice the following distributions of spades for Declarer (South) and Dummy (North):

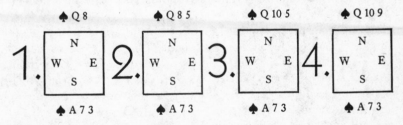

The contract is still no-trump, and spades are opened against you by West on the first lead. Say, the four of spades is the actual opening lead. Slightly different treatment is required in each distribution.

Consider No. 1, with Queen-eight in Dummy. If you play the eight, East will probably play the nine, Ten, or Jack, forcing you to win the trick with your Ace, thus permitting the outstanding King to capture Dummy's Queen some time later. You must always weigh the possibility of making as many tricks in any suit as you can. Your only chance of making 2 spade tricks in No. 1 is to play the Queen immediately, hoping that the King lies with West. If East covers the Queen with the King (which he may, of course, have), you must refuse to win that trick, and also refuse to win the second round of spades. In other words, if the Queen does not hold the first trick, you proceed to hold up your Ace. *

The situation in No. 2 requires other tactics. Now you should not play the Queen.* The better procedure is to play low from Dummy, and, if East plays the nine, Ten, or Jack, win the trick with the Ace in your own hand. Thereafter you should try to put East in the lead rather than West, in order to keep West from leading through Dummy's guarded Queen. If West does happen to gain the lead and return a spade, you must play your Queen and hope for the best. If East ever leads a spade, Dummy's guarded Queen becomes a sure trick in that suit.

What is the essential difference between No. 1 and No. 2? In the first situation, if the Queen is not played on the first trick, it gets left alone there in the Dummy and is of no value. That is, you may as well play it at once, and gain whatever advantage you can from it. In the second situation, if you play a low card you still leave the Queen guarded, and consequently the Queen may win later.

Look now at No. 3. Dummy's holding is a little bit stronger. Your best play from Dummy is the Ten, in the hope that it will force the King from East's hand.* You can then win with your Ace, leaving the Queen to control the second round of the suit. If East covers the Ten with the Jack, you are in the same situation as you were in No. 2. You win with your Ace and try to let East lead (not West).

Now take No. 4. Here 2 spade tricks are practically certain, but there is a chance for you to win 3 tricks. In fact, you will probably make 3 tricks, by playing properly, if the suit is distributed thus:

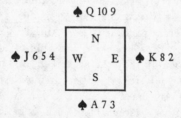

You play the nine from Dummy and, if East plays his King, you win with your Ace. The Queen-Ten in Dummy now forms a perfect tenace over West. All you have to do is lead spades through

* In all of these instances there are exceptions, depending on special factors which may exist in a particular hand. These are covered in the advanced sections.—S. F. Jr.

West, or let West lead the suit. The best play, therefore, is the nine from Dummy, in the hope that East has the King. It loses nothing, and stands to gain a trick, as you see.

You should have been able to follow the logic of the four situations just discussed. In your playing experience you will often be faced with exactly such simple decisions as these. If you fear you may forget the logical analysis, memorize the situations and the proper card to play in each. The profit you will make on the tricks accruing from your correct play will more than repay you for your efforts.

Indeed, this is probably as good a spot as any to insert three other common situations, in which the King and Queen of a suit are held by Declarer and Dummy when the suit is opened against no-trump. These three situations are as follows:

In No. 1, if a low diamond is opened by West, it should be apparent that to play the Queen will do no good whatever, for if East has the Ace and wins the trick, you are reduced forthwith to but one defensive time unit in the suit (your King). If West holds the Ace, the Queen will win the trick, but you have seriously endangered your King. Whenever East obtains the lead, he need but return a diamond through your guarded King up to West's Ace, and where's your King? You will find it best always to play low from Dummy in this situation, on the off-chance that East will play the Ace anyway (if he has it), giving you 2 sure tricks after that. If East plays some other card, such as the nine, the Ten, or the Jack, you win in your own hand with the King. If West holds the Ace, you need but lead low toward Dummy's guarded Queen to be sure of another diamond trick.

In No. 2, however, all is changed. To play Dummy's eight can by no stretch of the imagination hope to induce East to play the Ace if he has it, for he will much prefer to keep the Ace for the second round and surely capture that lone Queen left in the Dummy.

(East knows, you see, that an Ace which captures an honor has done heavier duty than an Ace which merely wins a trick.)   On Dummy's eight, East will play some card which will force you to play the King if you wish to win the trick, and Dummy's Queen is as good as dead. Your only hope of gain is to play Dummy's Queen boldly on the first trick (on West's low lead).   To be sure, if East captures the trick with the Ace, you have accomplished nothing, but you have also lost nothing which you would not otherwise have lost.   What is more pertinent, if East does *not* have the Ace, the Queen will hold the trick, leaving you with secondary control of the suit (your guarded King). From this point, you will find it to your advantage to keep East out of the lead, if possible, by throwing the lead into West's hand whenever you have to lose it.   You pursue these tactics, of course, to protect your King from a fatal lead by East up to West's Ace.

Situation No. 3 is almost exactly the same as No. 3 in the first group (page 79).   On West's low diamond lead, you must play the Ten and hope that West (not East) has the Jack.   The Ten must then force the Ace, or else hold the trick.   If East covers the Ten with the Jack, you win the trick with the King, but you can still hope that West has the Ace so that you can lead through it and make a trick with Dummy's guarded Queen.

Keeping a Weather Eye Open for Suit Control

The high-card situations just discussed are vitally important in suit control.   The effort, you should perceive, was always to keep some measure of control in the suit West attacked in his opening lead.   The following deal illustrates how these tactics—always keeping a weather eye open for suit control—are carried out:

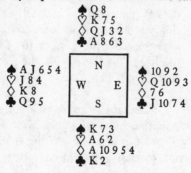

Your contract, as South (Declarer), is three no-trump. West's normal opening lead is a low spade. By now you should not need to hesitate about which card to play from Dummy. You know that your best play is the Queen, so you go up with it promptly. You are happy to notice that the Queen wins. Looking a bit ahead, you see that only the diamond suit offers any possibility of development. Your lead is therefore the Queen of diamonds to the second trick, on which you play low from your hand. You can take this sort of finesse, you recall, because you hold the next lower card (Jack). The diamond Queen loses to West's King, but this does not help West much. If he cashes in his spade Ace, he knows that your King will be set up for a sure trick. He will probably decide to lead some other suit in the hope of putting his partner in the lead to return a spade through your guarded King. However, as you can see from the diagram, West's hope is a forlorn one; East cannot get in the lead.

You must make your contract with 1 spade trick (already taken), 2 heart tricks, 4 diamond tricks, and 2 club tricks. If West should lead the spade Ace after all, you make an extra trick (spade King).

What a difference if you had played low from the Dummy on that first trick! East would have covered with the nine, forcing you to win with your King. Your next step would have been to enter Dummy's hand with the heart King in order to take the diamond finesse. The finesse, of course, would have failed, and West, having gained the lead, would have played his spade Ace, capturing Dummy's now unguarded Queen. West's 3 additional spade tricks would have defeated your contract by 1 trick.

A Hold-up in a Suit With Two Stoppers

Don't think you are through with hold-ups, for you've just begun. In a later chapter you will be given further examples of hold-ups with unusual card combinations. Before going on to some other basic and more essential principles of no-trump play, however, you should give some study to the following deal, which illustrates a hold-up with two defensive time units (stoppers) in the suit which is led against the Declarer, who is playing a three no-trump contract:

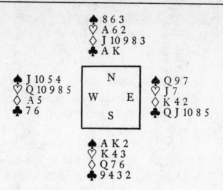

♠ 8 6 3
♡ A 6 2
◇ J 10 9 8 3
♣ A K

♠ J 10 5 4
♡ Q 10 9 8 5
◇ A 5
♣ 7 6

♠ Q 9 7
♡ J 7
◇ K 4 2
♣ Q J 10 8 5

♠ A K 2
♡ K 4 3
◇ Q 7 6
♣ 9 4 3 2

The first few tricks in this hand require careful attention.

Trick 1. West leads ♡ 10, North plays ♡ 2, East wins with ♡ J, and South plays ♡ 3. You, as South (Declarer), purposely refuse to win the first round of hearts because you can see at once that you are a time unit behind your Opponents. You must establish your diamonds if possible, and you must do it while under fire from your Opponents in their efforts to establish hearts for themselves. Since you have only two defensive units in hearts, and they have two defensive units in diamonds, apparently they must win the battle because they already have the advantage of having made the first lead. Your only hope is that one of the Opponents will be exhausted of hearts as a result of your hold-up.

Trick 2. East leads ♡ 7 (returning his partner's suit), South wins with ♡ K, West plays ♡ 5, and North plays ♡ 6.

Trick 3. South leads ◇ 6, West plays ◇ 5, North plays ◇ 8, and East wins with ◇ K.

Trick 4. East leads ♣ 8, South plays ♣ 2, West plays ♣ 6, and North wins with ♣ K. What you hoped would happen, has happened! By holding up for one round of hearts, you eliminated all hearts from East's hand so that, in the lead at this trick, he has had to lead some other suit.

Trick 5. North leads ◇ 3, East plays ◇ 2, South plays ◇ Q, and West wins with ◇ A.

At this point, West can establish his hearts by driving out Dummy's Ace, but it is too late. Your strategy of holding up to exhaust East of hearts has offset the advantage the Opponents had in their one defensive unit. If you win the first round of hearts, East will obtain the lead soon enough to return a heart, enabling West to establish the suit in time to benefit when he gains the lead on the second round of diamonds. In fact, if you fail to hold up in hearts,* even with two stoppers, you must be set 2 tricks.

Though it is too early to bring up the subject of defensive play, it may be mentioned here (to forestall any criticism by some alert reader) that East could defeat your contract on this hand by good play in spite of your hold-up in hearts. He needs only to switch from hearts to clubs at the second trick. In other words, he abandons trying to establish his partner's suit and seeks to set up a suit of his own. The full explanation of this defensive strategy will come in a later chapter.

The subject of the hold-up play has not been exhausted in this chapter. A further discussion of this important play may be found in Chapter IX of Part II.

SUMMARY

Surely the great mystery of "card sense" now begins to clear up a little. You can even feel some confidence in your ability, for by now you should be well on the way toward realizing the value of controlling cards. You have learned when the hold-up may be to your advantage, and when it may not. Always it is the lure of tricks that goads you on to whatever you do. If to hold up looks profitable, you hold up; if not to hold up may mean gaining a trick, you refuse to hold up.

---

* Someone is sure to ask why he cannot win the first round of hearts with, say, his Ace, and hold up the King on the second round. Won't East be exhausted of hearts just the same? Oh, yes; East will be exhausted of hearts eventually, no matter what else happens, but will it do *you* any good? If you win the first round, and hold up your second stopper on the second round, West will simply overtake his partner's heart lead and return the suit. Then where are you? Play the hand with actual cards if you still do not see the point.

CHAPTER X

UNBLOCKING

Passing now to the phase of play known as *unblocking*, you are really taking up an extended phase of an old subject, namely, entries. The underlying principle of an unblocking play is so to arrange a hand that it will contain sufficient entries for you to cash in whatever established cards that hand contains. What we call unblocking is nothing more nor less than the best means of accomplishing this result.

Three simple types of unblocking situations are shown below:

◊ K Q J 10 2   ◊ A Q J 10 2   ◊ A K J 10 2

	N	
W		E
	S	

◊ A 8   ◊ K 8   ◊ Q 8

Disregarding the rest of the hand* entirely, assume that you find it necessary to cash in the tricks you have in diamonds in each of these situations. Notice that in each one, if you lead the eight-spot from your own hand (South) and win with a card in Dummy, you must lead to the second round from Dummy, and, if you lead a card which you win with the lone high card remaining in your hand, you have *blocked yourself* in diamonds. In other words, having won the second round in your hand, the lead is now there and you have no more small diamonds to lead to Dummy's set up cards. If you have no entries in any other suit, the diamonds in Dummy are then worthless to you. What is worse, the blocking has been your own fault. All you have to do to unblock yourself in all three situations is to *lead the honor first* from your own hand, following it with the eight-spot on the second round.

---

* The fact that the word *hand* is used in two ways in Bridge terminology is often confusing to the beginner. Usually, a player's *hand* consists of the thirteen cards dealt him originally, and continues to be called the *hand* at any point during the play as long as any cards remain unplayed by that player. In this sense, there are four hands around the table. The word is also used in a larger sense to mean a complete deal of four hands. To avoid confusion, the word *deal* or the term *complete deal* is frequently employed in this work to mean all four hands. Otherwise the context shows clearly which sense is meant.

It is an excellent idea to get in the habit of unblocking; that is, always to play each solid suit so that the lead remains in the *long* hand when the hand containing the fewer cards is exhausted of the suit. Precisely stated, the rule is that, *whenever a solid or nearly solid suit is split between the partnership hands, you should lead the suit in such a way that on the trick which exhausts the shorter hand the lead will remain in the long hand.*

Unblocking by Leading a Singleton Honor

It is frequently necessary to unblock a suit when one of the two hands contains a singleton honor. Such a card must usually be led as quickly as possible to get rid of it, as in the following hand:

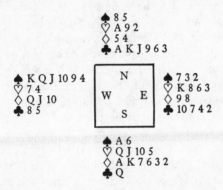

You are playing a contract of three no-trump* and West opens the King of spades against you. You hold but one controlling card in this suit; in fact, you have only four spades altogether. The hold-up is not likely to do you much good, but, since it can do no harm, you allow West to win the first round. He immediately returns spades, which you must win with your Ace. By now you should have looked ahead a little, but there is one play which requires no further thought. You must lead that singleton club Queen at once and let it ride through, holding the trick. You need not overtake it in Dummy, since Dummy's heart Ace is a perfectly good entry for the clubs.

* Lest the reader become suspicious, let it be said here that not all hands are played at three no-trump. It so happens that, in illustrating no-trump play (which logically precedes suit play), a deal showing a legitimate contract of three no-trump is the most natural situation for bringing out the effectiveness of various principles.

You may now stop and consider to your heart's content, for you have avoided any possibility of blocking yourself in clubs later on. Your long diamond suit of eight cards looks dazzling, but you cannot try to develop it because the Opponents hold five diamonds between them—and every one of those five diamonds is higher than every one of yours except the Ace and King. Obviously, the greatest number of adversely held diamonds that will fall on your Ace-King leads is four; in other words, to lead two rounds of diamonds is sure to present the Opponents with a diamond trick. You cannot afford to let them have this, for they will still hold five good spades between them, at least three of which (and probably four) they will be able to make. Any notion of developing diamonds is therefore squelched at once.

The next best bet—in fact, the best bet—is the club suit. To make good on your clubs you must enter Dummy's hand. The Ace of hearts will accomplish this all right, but, speaking of hearts, what about that sequence of Queen-Jack-Ten? And the nine in Dummy? A heart finesse seems simple—and alluring. If it works, we can add 3 or 4 heart tricks to all those club tricks and make about 12 tricks!

One thing you should have learned by this time, however, is that in Contract Bridge it never pays to be too greedy. The player who gorges himself every time he sits down to the Bridge table, always hoping that he will gulp down all the tricks before his Opponents even get started, finds that the occasions when he is interrupted—and starved (defeated)—more than offset the times when he succeeds.

Though it is true that the finesse in hearts may succeed, there is an equal chance that it will fail. If it fails, the Opponents will cash in their good spades at once, and will probably defeat your contract. In other words, you are betting a practically sure game (three no-trump) against the possibility of making at most 110 extra points. You have already taken 1 spade trick and 1 club trick; you can surely take 2 diamond tricks, 1 heart trick, and almost surely 5 club tricks. Your count of clubs should show you that the Opponents have left only four clubs between them. You control three more rounds of that suit (Ace-King-Jack). Your three leads will drop all the adverse clubs unless all four of them are in one hand, which is the worst of all possible distributions. A 4-0 division of the adverse clubs is extremely unlikely, however; the chances are about *twenty to one against it*. Mathematically stated, your chance of making your con-

tract by being content with 1 heart trick and at once leading the clubs
is about 95% certain, while the heart finesse is only 50% certain.   The
percentage is all in favor of spurning the heart finesse as too risky and
taking the almost sure game that immediately cashing in clubs offers.

As you can see from the diagram, the contract is made this way
without difficulty.   As soon as both Opponents follow suit on the
Ace of clubs your fears are over.   But if you had taken the heart
finesse, East would have won the trick and returned a spade—giving
his partner 4 more spade tricks, and you would have been set 2 tricks.

Unblocking by Overtaking an Honor

Another way of unblocking a suit is sometimes advisable, consisting
of overtaking a perfectly good card in the opposite hand.   The following deal brings out this mode of play:

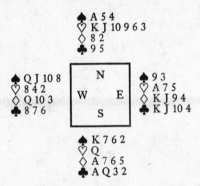

West's opening lead against your three no-trump contract is the spade
Queen.   Your first decision must be in which hand you should retain an
entry in spades, since you have one in each.   You see that the Dummy
is the hand which contains the greater length of the only establishable
suit (hearts), and therefore win the trick with the King in your hand,
leaving the spade Ace in Dummy for an entry.   (Note that no hold-up
in spades in necessary, for you hold more spades than your Opponents
though you cannot expect to win more than 2 tricks in the suit.)

What do you do at the second trick?   Quite clearly something
must be done toward establishing the heart suit.   You run smack up
against the annoyance of the singleton Queen in your own hand.
That Queen is annoying for the simple reason that if you lead it and

the Opponents refuse to win with their Ace, you will have to use your only entry into the Dummy (spade Ace) in order to lead hearts again. The Opponents then take their Ace, and what happens to the rest of the hearts? They are as useless to you as all the gold in Davy Jones's locker.

Do you see the way out of your difficulty? You lead the Queen and *overtake* it by playing Dummy's King on it. If the Opponents refuse to win the trick, you're then in the Dummy to lead the Jack. If the Opponents still hold up the Ace, you follow by leading the Ten, and even the nine-spot. It makes no difference to you now when the Opponents take their Ace, for you hold over their heads that enormous bludgeon in the shape of the spade Ace, which will enable you to get back into the Dummy to belabor your Opponents with the balance of your hearts as soon as the Ace comes out of hiding.

Proceeding thus, you find that East wins the third round of hearts—with the Ace. He returns a spade, let us say (his partner's suit). You win with Dummy's Ace, and are ready for those other three hearts. But wait a minute! Did you notice something as you counted those spades? (Surely you have formed the habit of counting every suit as it is played.) Eight spades have been played, and you still hold three, which leaves the Opponents, at the most, only 2 spade tricks. Consequently you no longer have much cause for anxiety about the spades. Therefore you lead your good hearts, chalking up 7 tricks for your side as you face the following situation at the 9th trick:

You have discarded your two small spades and three little diamonds on the last five rounds of hearts led from Dummy's hand. Your contract is safe, for you have 2 more tricks in those Aces looming in your own hand. However, there is that club finesse, which looks tempting. If East has the club King, why not enjoy grabbing that extra trick? Probably you think you should not jeopardize your contract by taking that finesse when all you have to do is cash in the two Aces to be home. Of course, you should not jeopardize your contract at any time in exchange for a sure thing. But look at this situation again. You recall that just a few tricks ago we decided that the Opponents had left 2 spade tricks *at the most*. Your count of spades proved this. They have won already only the Ace of hearts, so that, even if the club finesse fails (falling to West's King, if he has that card), the greatest number of tricks the Opponents can take is 4 (1 heart trick, 2 spade tricks, 1 club trick), for you still retain control of the two unplayed suits (diamonds and clubs).

Here, then, you should by all means take the club finesse, for it does *not* place your contract in jeopardy. You take no chances. You merely play to make an extra trick if the location of the club King is favorable, and you *lose nothing* if it is not. As it happens, East has the club King, so you risk nothing and gain a trick by finessing. If there had been even the remotest possibility that West could take 3 spade tricks, it would have been insane to take the club finesse.

When Failure to Unblock Immediately Means Defeat

Very often an unblocking play must be made on the very first trick. In such situations, if the unblocking is not done on the first trick the contract may be defeated right then and there. In the following deal, for instance, the Declarer may quite easily find himself set:

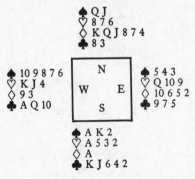

Against your three no-trump contract, West's opening lead is the spade Ten.   You play the Queen (or Jack) from Dummy, and East plays low.   The crisis is already upon you: which spade do you play from your own hand?   If you play the deuce, which seems natural, you will later on find yourself with some perfectly beautiful diamonds in the Dummy without being able to do a thing about cashing them in. Notice that the Dummy contains no tricks outside the diamond suit, and you can't overtake a diamond trick in Dummy, for the Ace, the highest card, is alone in your hand.

You can make sure of an entry for those diamonds by a very simple expedient.   Do not thoughtlessly play the deuce on that first spade trick.   Overtake Dummy's Queen (or Jack) with your Ace (or King), *keeping the deuce*.   Then lead the Ace of diamonds out of your own hand in order to unblock the suit.   After doing this you find that you can enter the Dummy by leading the deuce of spades to Dummy's remaining honor, which enables you to cash in all of the diamonds.

It should be obvious that failure to unblock the spades on the very first trick, to retain an entry in the Dummy, means losing eventually at least 3 club tricks and 2 heart tricks.

Unblocking by Discarding

Quite often a lowly Ten, nine, or even eight may be in exactly the right position to choke an otherwise vital suit to death.   The Declarer must always be on the alert to remember that a certain card may block a suit or he may suddenly find himself marooned helplessly in the wrong hand.   On the following type of deal, for instance, many players go wrong out of sheer carelessness:

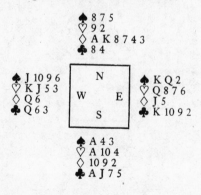

West's opening lead is the Jack of spades. Your contract, as South, is three no-trump. East covers the Jack with his Queen (the correct play, as you will learn later), and you refuse to win the trick. This may seem rather pointless, since you not only are limited to one stopper in spades but you have only one stopper in hearts as well. However, you let the first round of spades go by. East naturally continues by leading his King, and this time you decide to take your Ace, realizing that a switch to hearts will prove even worse than a continuation of spades.

It takes but little examination of the hands to see that the success of your contract depends on the diamonds. No other tricks can be developed, and that's all there is to it. Indeed, to make 9 tricks you cannot afford to concede even 1 diamond trick to the Opponents. You must find the adverse four diamonds evenly divided or you are lost. The only way to play the suit, if you are to make your contract at all, is to lead a diamond from your hand at once, win with Dummy's Ace, and come back snappily with the King. If all four adverse diamonds drop, you are all right, for you will make 6 diamond tricks and three side Aces. If the diamonds do not fall, your contract is hopeless. And if the diamonds do not break 2-2, there is absolutely no other way of making your contract. Having no choice, you must try the diamonds on this basis.

You find, on playing your Ace and King of diamonds, that the adverse diamonds do fall. If you have been careless, however, you now find that, on top of your joy at seeing everybody follow suit to the first two rounds of diamonds, swift gloom descends as you notice the denomination of the diamond left in your hand. You have carelessly, from force of habit, played the lowest diamonds from your hand on Dummy's Ace and King. Your Ten now hopelessly blocks the suit and the Dummy has no outside entry.

It is essential in this hand to unblock the diamonds by leading the *Ten* (not the deuce) up to Dummy's Ace-King, and by playing the *nine* (not the deuce) on the second round. Playing this way, at the third round of diamonds you find the deuce in your hand which falls harmlessly under Dummy's eight-spot, leaving the road entirely clear for leading out the rest of the suit from Dummy's hand.

This unblocking play really is simple, isn't it? To fail to make it is inexcusable. Yet to make it requires both thought and care. The foresight is well repaid, though, for it means the making of a game contract which will otherwise be irretrievably set 3 tricks. Even an eight-spot or a nine-spot can cause an unwary player's downfall if he is not careful.

UNBLOCKING TO DISCOVER HIDDEN ENTRIES

Sometimes certain low cards in the Dummy, which ordinarily would not be regarded as trick winners, may become entries—and perhaps direly needed entries—by the simple process of unblocking.

In this connection, let us return for just a moment to the subject of suit distribution. Normal distribution is *even* distribution, or as near even distribution (with an odd number) as possible. If five cards are outstanding, the normal expectation is that they will be divided between the partners 3-2 (three in one hand, two in the other); likewise, if seven cards are outstanding, the likelihood is that they will be divided 4-3. Bearing this fact in mind, you will frequently find that it enables you to establish additional entries in a hand which has a scarcity of winning cards.

Such entries, which are established during the play of a hand, are termed "hidden" entries because they do not appear until the play of higher cards has uncovered them. Another reason for the name is the fact that the entries are usually harmless looking small cards, which seem absolutely useless for communication purposes. The establishment of these entries depends entirely on applying the principle of unblocking. Look, for instance, at the two suit distributions given below:

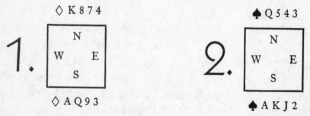

Suppose that you find it absolutely essential to discover two additional entries in Dummy's hand. In the first situation, if you lead the trey from your hand and go up with Dummy's King, the three cards remaining in your own hand will be higher than any of those in the Dummy's hand. Hence, any chance of establishing an additional entry *in the Dummy* in this suit will be eliminated. However, try playing your Ace first, following on the next round with your Queen. If both Opponents follow suit each time, a count of diamonds shows you that eight cards have been played, and you still hold four. This means that the Opponents can hold but one more diamond. You can therefore lead the nine and overtake it with Dummy's King, retaining the trey in your hand. This lowly three-spot will enable you to enter the Dummy in diamonds by leading your low card to Dummy's high eight. That eight-spot was a hidden entry which you uncovered by your manner of playing the diamond suit.

The second situation illustrates the same principle. The technique is exactly the same as that applied in the first situation, if you wish to find two extra entries in the Dummy. You lead your Ace and King so that, if both Opponents follow suit on both rounds of spades, you will succeed in your purpose. You lead the Jack to the third round, overtaking it with Dummy's Queen. All the spades have now been played except the two you have left. You can lead the deuce from your hand, when you are ready, and enter the Dummy, for Dummy's trey will overtake your deuce!

In the second situation just analyzed, if it were important for you to enter your own hand three times, and the Dummy were otherwise well supplied with entries, this unblocking play in spades would be unnecessary. The Ace, King, and Jack in your hand serve very easily as entries, and the complication of the overtaking play in Dummy would not take place.

The whole point here is that unblocking in this fashion is for the purpose of establishing entries *if those entries are needed*. The suits just considered may be played whichever way is most desirable. You need only estimate how many entries you require in each hand and play accordingly.

SUMMARY

You have learned how to clear the road in a suit so that all the available tricks in it may be secured. That is, you have learned to unblock, so that you will not suddenly find yourself cornered. The player who blocks himself in one hand or the other through failure to look ahead, is akin to the fellow who paints himself into a corner, or to the chap who sits on the outer edge of a limb to saw it from the main trunk. In this connection, *whenever a solid or nearly solid suit is split between the partnership hands, you should lead the suit in such a way that on the trick which exhausts the shorter hand the lead will remain in the long hand.*

Finally, you learned that application of the unblocking play may not always have for its object the cashing in of tricks in the suit in which the unblocking occurs. Unblocking may also be used to develop additional entries in one hand or the other.

CHAPTER XI

DUCKING

T HE mode of playing a suit known as *ducking* closely resembles the hold-up, but it differs in the object of the procedure. The hold-up is intended to prevent the Opponents from establishing their suit until it is too late for them to cash in the remaining cards. Ducking is intended to preserve entries for the Declarer so that he may cash in *his* good cards. Sometimes to duck is an essential play; sometimes the player ducks purely for reasons of greater safety.

The following heart situation illustrates ducking in its most elementary form:

♡ A K 8 7 5

```
      N
  W       E
      S
```

♡ 4 3

You have seven hearts, and you are in a situation where you must establish hearts in order to fulfill your contract. Suppose that the Dummy (North) contains no entries outside this suit. It looks as though 2 heart tricks are all you can expect, but, on analyzing the situation, you discover that the Opponents have only six hearts between them, which may break 3-3. If the adverse hearts break thus evenly, you can drop four of them on the lead of your Ace and King, concede the third round to the Opponents, and have 2 established hearts left in the Dummy. However, if it is the *third round* that you concede to your Opponents, you cannot use those 2 good hearts left in Dummy, for you have no entries.

You have only one chance of making more than 2 heart tricks with this suit holding. You must lead a small heart and *play low from Dummy*, no matter what West plays. Or, if an Opponent leads hearts, you must play low from both hands on the first round, thereby "ducking" the trick by holding up your Ace and King. This is called ducking rather than holding up because here you, as the Declarer, are trying to establish your suit—not trying to keep the Opponents from establishing theirs. You thus concede the *first round* to the Opponent, so that, if the adverse cards are evenly divided, your winners will drop them on the second and subsequent rounds, leaving you with the lead in the hand which contains the established cards if the ducking play succeeds.

By leading the Ace and King immediately, you stand no chance of making more than 2 heart tricks. By giving up the first trick, even though one tempo or time unit is sacrificed, you have some chance of establishing the suit and of being able to cash in all the good cards in it.

The following hand shows the ducking principle carried to an extreme:

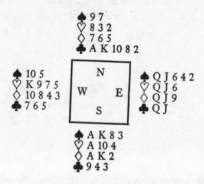

Suppose that West opens the five of hearts against your three no-trump contract. You play low from Dummy, and East plays the Jack. You naturally hold up in this suit, playing the four-spot from your hand, as you have no lower cards which you can hope to establish. East returns the Queen of hearts, and again you play low. You are forced to win the third round of hearts with the Ace, but you have watched the cards played and noted with inward satisfaction that only one heart is left outstanding. Taking stock at this point, you note that you have lost 2 tricks, and can afford to lose at the most 2 more (9 tricks are necessary to fulfill your contract). You have only 6 sure tricks left in your hands, now that the heart Ace has been cashed in. Obviously, then, you must look for 2 tricks among your lower cards. The club suit is the only one long enough to be worth trying to establish. You therefore, at the fourth trick, lead a low club toward Dummy's hand, playing the Ace, on which East drops the Jack, making it look very much as though East had only a doubleton to start with (Queen-Jack), at the most. If this is true, the Queen will drop on the King, giving you 5 club tricks, 2 spade tricks, 2 diamond tricks, and 1 heart trick—a total of 10 tricks.

So far your reasoning is all right, except that you have not considered the possibility that East's Jack might have been a singleton. In this case, by leading the King you give up every chance of ever establishing enough clubs to make your contract, for the Dummy contains no outside entry and there is no chance of discovering any hidden entry in that slag heap of small spades, clubs, and diamonds. You are now faced with an important choice: is it better to hope that East had a doubleton in clubs originally, and play for 10 tricks on that basis, or to consider that East had a singleton originally, and play West for the Queen? For, if East's Jack was a singleton, you can return to your own hand and lead the nine of clubs, passing it if West plays low. This way you can also make 10 tricks if West turns out to have the Queen, but make only 9 tricks if East has this card in his hand.

Again the guiding principle of Contract play comes to the fore. *Always make sure of your contract* whenever that is possible. It is much safer in the foregoing hand to assume that East's Jack may have been a singleton and plan to concede him his Queen if he turns out to have held it, for in this way you are *absolutely sure* of making 2 spade tricks, 1 heart trick, 2 diamond tricks, and 4 club tricks—just three no-trump. Furthermore, you are not worried about any other suit as you hold control of all of them.

You therefore, at the fifth trick, return to your own hand (in spades or diamonds) and lead the nine of clubs, playing low from Dummy when West plays low. East wins with his Queen, it so happens—but do not kick yourself for not taking a chance! Your contract is certain, for no matter what East leads you can cash in your remaining tricks. Had you gambled and led out both Ace and King immediately, and had East's Jack actually been a singleton, you would have been hoping to make 30 extra points by your gambling play but, in failing, you would have sacrificed 100 points for the game plus the value of that game toward winning the rubber. The ducking play is the only correct one, considering the odds.

In the following deal we have an extreme application of the ducking principle. This hand actually occurred in a game among experts:

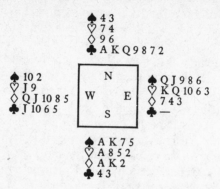

The opening lead by West was the diamond Queen against South's contract of three no-trump. South won with his Ace, and, holding nine clubs in the partnership hands, he now led a low club and won it with Dummy's Ace. West had played the five-spot, and East showed a void in clubs by discarding another suit. Already South is irrevocably committed to being defeated by 1 trick, no matter what he does from this point on! Yet he could have made this contract by remembering what surety the simplest of ducking plays would offer. Holding the controlling cards in the other three suits, all he had to do was to lead a small club from his hand and *play low from the Dummy*, as, say, the seven-spot on West's five. By thus ducking the first round of clubs he would be taking out full insurance against the possibility that East would be void, and, even if East were void, South's contract would be as sure as sunrise. In spite of the fact that the 4-0 break in clubs would occur only about once in a hundred times with this distribution, the ducking play is the *only sure way* to make this contract. In Bridge, only the sure way is always the only correct way. As a matter of fact, in this hand, Dummy's seven of clubs will hold the first round, winning West's five-spot—but South would make the play, not to win the trick, but *to safeguard 4 club tricks* if East is void, for West's thrice-guarded Jack will then stop the club suit, and South has no outside entries in the Dummy.

DUCKING TWICE TO ESTABLISH A SUIT

Frequently it is necessary to duck twice in order to establish a suit. Such a play may seem rather hopeless to the beginner unless he gives proper weight to the probabilities of suit distribution. It is also well to bear in mind that in Bridge there is no such thing as a hopeless hand. The old admonition to keep a stiff upper lip even when things look dark is never truer than in Bridge. No matter how discouraging the prospects of a hand look at first glance, there is always some chance of developing sufficient tricks. In no-trump play, particularly, you must remember that the *worst* distribution should not be expected (except when you are in a position to make a play that will insure you against the worst distribution, as in the previous hand.)

Consider, for example, the following deal:

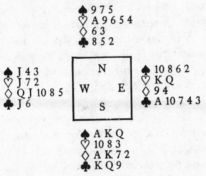

♠ 9 7 5
♡ A 9 6 5 4
◇ 6 3
♣ 8 5 2

♠ J 4 3
♡ J 7 2
◇ Q J 10 8 5
♣ J 6

♠ 10 8 6 2
♡ K Q
◇ 9 4
♣ A 10 7 4 3

♠ A K Q
♡ 10 8 3
◇ A K 7 2
♣ K Q 9

Having to make a contract of three no-trump, you find yourself confronted with the opening lead of the diamond Queen. The situation in this deal does look rather gloomy. You hold a few top tricks (exactly 7), but no suit looks easily establishable. However, this is not the time to act like a coward by cashing in all the available tricks without more ado. You may as well inject a little hope into a hopeless situation! There is a right way to play, even here, which may yet pull you out of the morass.

You win the first trick with your diamond King, realizing that to hold up can be of little avail, particularly in view of the fact that the club suit is also dangerous. Your only long suit is hearts, so you attack in this suit without delay. But observe that you cannot take the Ace of hearts out of the Dummy at once, as to do so will eliminate your only entry into that hand. There is no finessing possibility at all, so you must content yourself with leading the trey from your hand, and, assuming that West plays the deuce, you play the four from Dummy, conceding the trick to East, who wins it with the Queen. East returns the nine of diamonds, and you play low on this trick, figuring that it will do no harm to make sure that your right-hand Opponent is stripped of diamonds before you lose control of the suit. West overtakes the trick with the Ten, and returns the Jack of diamonds. You win this trick with your Ace, as there is no purpose in holding up further, since East discards a club.

Now the time has come for your desperation play—even if it is a forlorn hope, it is hope. You lead the eight of hearts and, when West plays the seven, you again duck the trick by playing low from the Dummy. This is a double ducking play, and is the only way you can ever hope to make 9 tricks on this deal. As it turns out, East is forced to win the trick with his King, and has to lead back either a spade or a club. Whichever East does, you are assured of your game, for you have, against the odds, developed 3 good heart tricks in the Dummy, in which the Ace still remains as an entry. You have already taken 2 diamond tricks and hold also 3 spade tricks and 1 club trick.

True, if West held the Ace of clubs, you would be set 2 tricks in spite of your "double duck" in hearts, for that card would serve as an entry for West to cash in 2 good diamond tricks. However, you remember that you held up on the second round of diamonds in the hope that East would be stripped of the suit and not be able to lead a diamond, assuming that he has the club Ace and will ultimately gain the lead. Everything worked out as you hoped.

Right here is a good place to state that you do not *know*, of course, that the cards are distributed as you *hope* they are. Not even an expert knows that, on a deal such as that just discussed. You merely analyze the situation and discover that, *IF* the cards are distributed so-and-so against you, you have a chance of making your contract by playing on that assumption—but you cannot make your contract if you play any other way (no matter how the cards are really distributed).

At the point where East wins the second round of hearts with his King after your second duck, the situation is as follows:

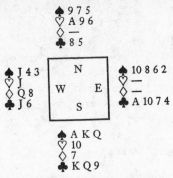

Let us assume that East returns a spade, which you win with the Ace. You now lead your Ten of hearts and win with Dummy's Ace, which places you in that hand to lead the nine and six, both of which are now good. East discards clubs on these three rounds of hearts. You discard the nine of clubs and seven of diamonds on the last two rounds, from your own hand. Now you must not lead out your King and Queen of spades, for, if you do this, you will immediately establish the long spade in East's hand, and he will win the last 2 tricks with the Ten of spades and the Ace of clubs. You must first, therefore, play clubs to drive out the Ace. No matter what East returns, you can then win the last 3 tricks.

This example presents three very interesting points.

The most important point is the development of the heart suit. Five hearts were outstanding, and the Dummy had no outside entry. If you played the Ace on the first round of hearts, the hand would then have been hopeless indeed, for you could not have secured any long-suit tricks in hearts at all. By ducking twice, keeping the Ace until the third round, you still had a small card in your own hand to lead to the Dummy at the proper time. Thus, instead of but 1 heart trick, you made 3!

The second interesting point is the hold-up in diamonds on the second round of that suit. If East had held three diamonds and West only four, you would have lost your contract by taking the second round of diamonds with the Ace. This would have given the Opponents a total of 2 diamond tricks, 2 heart tricks, and 1 club trick, defeating you by 1 trick. The fact that the hold-up was unnecessary on this particular hand does not affect the correctness of the play.

You have the best chance of making the hand by holding up on the second round of diamonds. In the long run, it is the odds that count, not the particular hand.

The third interesting point concerns the location of the club Ace. If West had held this card, you would have lost 2 more tricks than you did. But there was no reason to proceed on the assumption that West held it, since to do so would do you no good whatever. You hoped that East held it, which was your only chance of making the contract.

How to Decide Whether to Duck

Consider the following diagrams of heart distribution:

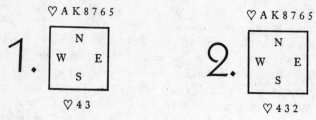

The first shows a partnership holding of *eight* cards headed by Ace-King; the second, a partnership holding of *nine* cards headed by Ace-King. Naturally, the second combination is considerably better than the first. The first is a simple illustration of the necessity to duck a round of hearts in order to preserve an entry: you merely concede the first round of the suit to your Opponents, hoping that the distributon of the five adverse hearts is 3-2 (if they are otherwise distributed, there is nothing you can do about it—to duck is still your best play).

The second situation is somewhat different. With only four hearts outstanding against you, you can lead the Ace and King and drop all four if they are divided 2-2. But it is altogether possible—and even likely—that the four adverse hearts are distributed 3-1. What, then, should you do? The answer is that you cannot tell without seeing the rest of the outstanding cards. If the Dummy contains a re-entry outside the heart suit, the proper play is to lead the Ace and King pronto, and, if these two leads fail to capture all the adverse hearts, you should lead another heart right away. But if the Dummy does not contain a re-entry, you cannot afford to take the chance of finding the adverse hearts divided 2-2, particularly if you hold a certain degree of control over the other three suits. In other words, if you can see your way clear to making your contract even though you concede 1 heart trick to the Opponents, you should lose that trick faster than you can say Jack Robinson—so that you can be *sure* of 5 heart tricks eventually, and not *hope* for 6 heart tricks and perhaps take only 2! You do this, of course, by leading a low heart from your hand, and ducking in the Dummy no matter what West plays.

If, in the end, it turns out that your ducking play in the second instance has actually lost you a trick on this particular deal, the number of points you have sacrificed is not great enough to offset the safety value of the ducking play. Again, if the situation is so desperate that you cannot afford to give up 1 heart trick at once, thereby losing the lead, you cannot afford, naturally, to play safe. The man who is dying of starvation cannot afford to pay for life insurance! But whenever you are certain that the loss of a few tricks at once, to insure a measure of safety, will not in any event cost you your contract, you *must* "play safe."

DUCKING BY REFUSING A FINESSE

One rather unusual type of ducking play involves the deliberate refusal of a finesse. Before studying this play, recollect what you learned about the promotional value of honors, and store away in your mind the fact that honors may be thus promoted defensively (by the Declarer's Opponents) as well as by the Declarer. Then look at this deal:

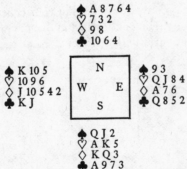

Let us say that West's opening lead against your three no-trump contract is the four of diamonds.   East wins with his Ace and returns the seven-spot, which you win with the Queen.   Your spades offer what is apparently your only chance for development of long-suit tricks, and since you hold the Jack too, you are perfectly safe in laying down the Queen.   West covers with the King.   Your first impulse is now to win with Dummy's Ace, thus capturing West's King by a finessing maneuver.   However, just stop and think a moment.

The Opponents held five spades, including the Ten and nine, besides the King which West has just played.   That all these cards will fall together is very unlikely.   Just suppose you do win with Dummy's Ace, and take the second round of the suit with your Jack. West's play of the King on the Queen has promoted the Ten or the nine as a winning card for the Opponents, since it is impossible for five cards to fall on two rounds.   But notice what has happened to you.   You have completely shut yourself out of Dummy's hand.

You can avoid shutting yourself out of Dummy's hand by a ducking play.   Since you may have to lose a spade trick,* why not lose it at once?   By letting West's King hold the trick, you refuse the finesse and, if the suit is divided 3-2, you are sure of 4 spade tricks eventually.

West wins the trick, then, and returns (for lack of anything better) another diamond.   You win with the King and play the spade Jack. Both Opponents follow suit, which means that there is now but one spade remaining in their hands.   You lead your last spade, winning with Dummy's Ace, which places you in position to run off the last 2 tricks in that suit.   You thus have 4 spade tricks and 2 diamond tricks, needing only 3 more tricks to make your contract, which are assured by your Ace and King of hearts and Ace of clubs.

Following is a slight variation of the same situation:

♠ A 8 7 6 4

♠ Q J 10

---

* The play of Dummy's Ace can win against a 3-2 distribution of the adverse spades only when West has K 5 3 and East 10 9—a remote possibility.

These cards are the same as in the foregoing example, except that the deuce has become the Ten. Does this alter the problem? When you lead the spade Queen, which West covers with the King, should you now win with Dummy's Ace where you previously ducked? You have the Ten yourself, so you need not fear its establishment in the Opponents' hands. Therefore you think, perhaps, that you can well afford to go up with the Ace. As a matter of fact, if the rest of Dummy's hand is the same as in the foregoing example, you must still let West's King win. You must duck the trick in order to unblock the suit, for, if you win with Dummy's Ace, your own Jack and Ten are high, preventing you from getting into the Dummy for those last two small spades. In this particular situation, the ducking play—in order to unblock—is just as essential with a practically solid suit as it was before with a suit that was not solid.

DUCKING IN DESPERATION

The following suit distribution illustrates a ducking play which will work only about once in a half-dozen tries. Yet it may be the only possible play in hands where desperate measures are the only ones available:

◇ A Q 8 6 3

◇ 4 2

Assume that with this distribution, you must make 4 diamond tricks, or you are lost. You must play, then, as follows: (1) lead the deuce and, no matter what West plays, play low from the Dummy, deliberately losing the trick—thus four diamonds are gone, Dummy still has four, and you hold one, making a total of nine accounted for; (2) praying that the four remaining diamonds are divided adversely, 2-2, and that West has the King, you lead your four-spot as soon as you regain the lead, and finesse the Queen—if the Queen holds, part of your prayer has been granted; (3) you then lead the Ace and, if both Opponents follow suit again, you have won your required 4 diamond tricks.   The success of this ducking play is only a slender hope, but there occur situations in which such desperate plays are the only choice.

Another interesting ducking situation is the following:

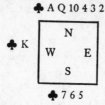

♣ A Q 10 4 3 2

♣ K

♣ 7 6 5

Assume that the distribution of your other suits is such that you cannot enter the Dummy outside the club suit.   Your problem is to retain a low club in your own hand after the suit has been established. If you do not succeed in doing this, you will find yourself unable to take advantage of that pretty length in the Dummy.   Hence, when you lead the five from your hand, and West plays the King, your best hope is to let the King hold the trick.   The fact that West plays the King seems to indicate that he held a singleton originally, which means that East has three clubs to the Jack.   If this is so, and you play your Ace-Queen on the first two rounds, you will have to lose the third round of clubs.   Without an outside entry to the Dummy, your remaining clubs are useless.

This suit distribution may be played in a still better way.   Assuming that your own hand contains the necessary re-entries, you can capture the King with Dummy's Ace and return to your hand by means of some outside entry card.   You then lead another low club, and, if West fails to follow suit, you give up the trick to East's Jack on the second round, leaving you with one low club in your hand which you can use to get into the Dummy later.   Of course, this accomplishes the same result as the first suggested way of playing, as you still concede 1 club trick to the Opponents, but it is a better method of play because it allows for the rather remote possibility that West held the King-Jack doubleton originally.   Of course, if getting back into your hand after winning the first round of clubs with Dummy's Ace seems at all problematical, or if it cannot be done without removing an important controlling card, the first method of play must be followed.

A Matter of Judgment

Situations which call for a ducking play are not at all hard to recognize, but sometimes the player's perspicacity is clouded by greed. If a player sees that he *may* be able to establish a suit without losing a single trick in it—provided the adverse cards "break right"—he is often very loath to concede a trick for the sake of retaining an entry card.

The following suit distribution shows a common error:

♡ K 9 8 7 6 4

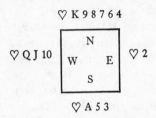

♡ Q J 10   ♡ 2

♡ A 5 3

Suppose you (South) must establish this suit, and the Dummy contains no outside entries. You naturally lead your Ace, on which West drops the Ten and East plays the deuce. You now play the five, on which West plays the Jack. At this point only the Queen is outstanding. You note that, if East has the Queen, you can take all 6 tricks in hearts by going up with your King on this round. However, if West should hold the Queen (as he does in the example given), this card will win the third round and take away your only means of running off the remainder of the suit. This is the time to make a sacrifice for the good of the entire hand—a principle quite as worth while in Bridge as in other forms of human activity. You must make sure of winning 5 heart tricks, rather than hoping to win 6 at the risk of losing all but 2. Even if the Queen shows up in East's hand after you have let West's Jack hold the second round, you must not be disappointed, for you have made the best play.

Summary

Whenever giving up a trick that does not lose your contract guarantees that you will win the balance of the suit, to lose that trick is more profitable, in the long run, than to take any chance of blocking the suit for the sake of making a possible extra trick if the distribution is favorable. The ducking play either gives you your only chance of getting the most out of a suit, or it gives you security against the worst possible distribution of the adverse cards. It is not a good play, of course, if losing the trick by ducking means the certain defeat of your contract.

CHAPTER XII

TRUMP MANAGEMENT AT SUIT PLAY

THE time has come to consider not only no-trump play, but play at a suit contract. The distinguishing characteristic of suit play is that one of the four suits (that named in the final bid, which becomes the contract) has greater trick-taking power than any of the other three suits. This is the *trump* suit. Thus, if the final bid is three diamonds, the trump suit for that hand is *diamonds;* if the final bid is any number of no-trump, there is *no* trump suit for that hand. Any card of the trump suit wins a trick to which it is played provided no higher trump is played to that trick. Whereas, at no-trump, *the highest card of the suit led* wins the trick, at suit play the highest card of the suit led wins *except* when one or more trumps are played, when the highest trump wins. The trump suit therefore becomes of extreme importance in suit play. At no-trump all the suits are of equal value; you would just as soon have a long club suit as a long spade suit. At a suit contract, length in the trump suit is of first and overwhelming importance. This elementary preamble is stated here so that the player will remember that trump plays are based on the commanding power of the trump suit.

Except when the trump suit is led, a player may play a trump only when he cannot follow suit. This fact, which every Bridge player knows, brings to the front another distinguishing feature of suit play. As soon as the Declarer, playing a suit contract, is void in a suit and also possesses trumps, he controls the void suit with his trumps. A trump may therefore be a controlling card, in addition to the high cards which were the only controlling cards at no-trump.

Also, the reader must remember that *every principle of no-trump play is applicable to suit play as well.* The only change is the dominating position of the trump suit. And just as soon as all the trumps are played, which may quite often happen long before the full 13 tricks are won or lost, the remainder of even a trump hand must be played exactly as in no-trump. The factor of first importance in suit play, as distinguished from no-trump play, is the trump suit itself. That suit is so valuable that its proper management for the best interests of the whole hand is absolutely essential.

110

To be sure, whenever the contract is at a suit, it may be taken for granted that nine times out of ten the Declarer and Dummy will hold more trumps than the Opponents. All systems of bidding require that a suit cannot be bid unless it contains at least four cards, and require further that a player cannot support a suit bid by his partner unless he holds at least three cards in it. The partnership hands will, therefore, in reaching a suit contract, contain at least seven trumps, and probably more. These trumps may not include all the high cards of the suit. The Opponents may even win trump tricks, but this is no cause for alarm, as a rule.

When to Lead Trumps

The problem of when to lead trumps, and when *not* to lead trumps, is one of the most difficult for the beginner to solve correctly. More hands are wrecked by failure to lead trumps at the right time or by leading trumps at the wrong time than by any other form of poor play. And this error in judgment is nearly always inexcusable. The proper management of trump leads is really so simple that, once understood, it should never bother any player.

Trumps are controlling cards. The fact that if a player cannot follow suit he may play a trump and thereby win a trick headed even by the Ace or King of the suit led, is the clearest indication of the controlling strength of trumps. The deuce of trumps may quite often be far more valuable than the Ace of any other suit.

You will recall that, at no-trump, when a player holds only the Ace of a suit the Opponents are likely to win 5 or 6 tricks in that suit as soon as the Ace is driven out. At a suit contract this unhampered cashing in of established tricks in an adverse suit is impossible, for as soon as either the Declarer or the Dummy becomes exhausted of that suit he can step in and halt the run with a small trump. Hence the establishment of a suit by the Opponents, when the contract is at a suit, need not be a source of half the anxiety it may cause the Declarer playing a hand at no-trump.

That the most valuable trumps are high trumps is axiomatic. Low trumps may become "high" as soon as all higher ones have been played. If all the trumps from the Ace down to and including the seven-spot have been played, and the Declarer still has left in one hand the six, five, four, and three, he is just as certain of taking 4

tricks with these cards as he would be of taking 4 tricks with four
Aces at no-trump.   No matter how many high cards the Opponents
may hold in the other suits, nothing can prevent the Declarer from
taking 4 tricks with his remaining four high trumps.

However, if the higher trumps have not been played, the small
trumps may be captured by higher trumps held adversely. This
can be prevented by ridding the Opponents' hands of their trumps
at the earliest opportunity. This is called *drawing trumps*. As a
general principle, except in the instances when other factors must be
considered, the Opponents' trumps should be drawn at once. This
may be effectively stated as follows: *at a suit contract, the first suit
the Declarer should try to establish is almost always the trump suit.*
The low trumps are established, or made high trumps, in exactly
the same ways that a regular suit is established at no-trump. If
you hold the high trumps to start with, you must lead them until
the Opponents have no more. If you do not hold the high trumps
originally, but have the greater length, you must still lead trumps in
order to exhaust the Opponents so that your own lower trumps will
be in full control later.

The following deal is a simple example of drawing trumps:

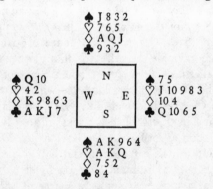

You are the Declarer (South), playing a contract of four spades.
West opens the club King, which you must let win the trick.   West
follows with the club Ace, which also wins, since you cannot prevent
it.   West thereupon leads a small club for the third round of the suit,
on which East plays the Queen.   You see now the difference between
no-trump and suit play; at no-trump East's Queen must win.   But

here spades are trumps.   Since you have no more clubs, you can play a small spade (the four-spot), thereby winning the trick by *ruffing*.* By virtue of the fact that you held only two clubs to start with, you have control of the third and later rounds of clubs by means of your trumps.

You are now in the lead, having trumped the third round of clubs. At this point, surveying your prospects, you know that you can lose no more club tricks, and assuredly you can lose no heart tricks, for your only three hearts are all high.   In diamonds you have a clear finesse against the King; if the finesse succeeds, you make 3 diamond tricks, and if it fails, you make 2 diamond tricks.   The diamonds must wait, however, until your spades are taken care of, for spades are trumps.

You have four spades left in your hand, and four in the Dummy, making nine accounted for (you have already played one).   The Opponents hold only four trumps between them, then.   If these are divided 2-2, they will fall on your Ace and King; if they are divided 3-1, you will still capture them all if the singleton is the Queen. In any event, this suit must be the point of your immediate attack. You lead your Ace at once and follow it with the King.   When both Opponents follow suit on both rounds, you know that your own trumps are fully established. Instead of cashing in your remaining spades by leading them, as you would at no-trump, you retain them as control cards in the event that they may be necessary.   They protect you, as you have seen, from the Opponents' established clubs.

You are now free to turn your attention to the diamond suit, by leading low from your hand.   You finesse the Jack, which holds. Returning to your own hand with the heart Ace, you take a diamond finesse again, this time playing the Queen, which also holds.   You can now lose no more tricks—all the rest are yours.

Look back a moment and see what would have happened had you not led trumps instantly you got the lead.   Suppose you fooled around with the other suits first, letting trumps wait a bit.   You

---

* "Ruffing" and "trumping" are synonymous terms.   "Ruff" was the name of an old game of cards preceding and closely resembling Whist.   The name came to be applied to the act of trumping because this mode of winning a trick was the outstanding characteristic of the play.   At Whist all hands were played with some suit as trump; the no-trump contract came into use with Bridge.

play as before, ruffing the third round of clubs, and then you lead a small diamond to finesse the Jack. Returning to your own hand with the heart Ace, you lead another low diamond and finesse the Queen, successfully. Another heart puts you back in your hand. Still ignoring trumps, you lead a diamond to Dummy's Ace, and West follows suit. But East surprises you (though why you should be surprised, after eight diamonds had been played on the two previous rounds, is something of a mystery), for East trumps with the five of spades, effectively killing your diamond Ace. East then returns a heart, which his partner (West) trumps. Thus, by your failure to lead trumps, you permit the Opponents to win 2 tricks with low trumps you should have eliminated from their hands early in the play.

The first thing a player should learn is to lead trumps as soon as possible. The second thing he should learn about trump management is that, on about half the hands he will play at a suit contract, leading trumps should be postponed—when the reason for doing so is clear in the player's mind. Generally speaking, unless some good reason exists for not leading them, trumps should always be led as soon as possible by the Declarer. Even though drawing the adverse trumps may not seem particularly advantageous, nevertheless a good purpose is served in establishing definite control cards.

If all of the Opponents' trumps but one have been eliminated, and this last lone trump is a small card, it is still advisable, usually, to get rid of it as quickly as possible—even if you have to use two of your own trumps (one from your hand and one from Dummy) to do so. As a rule, nothing can be gained by waiting. If you wait, the Opponent may find an opportunity to use his small trump to some advantage. But if the one outstanding trump is *higher* than any of yours, there is no good reason for you to waste two of your trumps in disposing of it.

For example, suppose the trump situation is as follows:

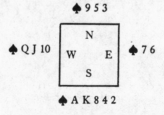

♠ 9 5 3

♠ Q J 10   N W E S   ♠ 7 6

♠ A K 8 4 2

Spades are trumps; you lead your Ace and King, dropping all the adverse trumps but the Queen in West's hand. This Queen is the highest outstanding trump, and must win a trick no matter what happens. In order to eliminate that Queen you must waste one of the trumps left in your hand and also the last trump in Dummy's hand. Yet you do not eliminate a possible adverse trick; you merely sacrifice two of your trumps unnecessarily to an outstanding trump which can never be worth *more* or *less* than 1 trick. Under these circumstances, it is much better to lead other suits and allow West, if he will, to use his Queen to ruff a trick.

The situation takes on still another color when there are two outstanding trumps, both high. Here there is always a chance that they will be divided between the Opponents and will therefore fall together. If they fall on the same trick, they win only 1 trick, but if they are allowed to remain unmolested, one Opponent may very often find a chance to make a trick with his trump separately from his Partner's. The following two situations illustrate this point:

	♡ 9 5				♡ 5	
1. ♡ Q 10 7	N W E S	♡ J 6 3	**2.** ♡ Q 10 7	N W E S	♡ J 9 6
	♡ A K 8 4 2			♡ A K 8 4 3 2	

In both situations you, as Declarer (South), hold seven trumps. Assuming that the rest of the hand does not throw a different complexion on the situation, your only troubles are centered in the trump suit. Your proper play in both instances is to lead out the Ace and King, followed by a small card on the third round. If the adverse trumps are divided 3-3, as in both examples above, this play assures you of losing but 1 trump trick. Even if the adverse trumps are not divided 3-3, nothing is lost by this mode of play, for the tricks that must be lost will have to be lost ultimately anyway.

When Not to Lead Trumps Immediately

A very common occurrence which necessitates postponement of the trump lead is a finessing situation which must be taken advantage of while entries are still available. The following deal drives home this point:

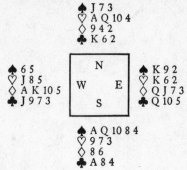

You are the Declarer playing a contract of four spades. West's opening lead is the King of diamonds, followed by the Ace, and, on the third round, the five of diamonds. When this third diamond trick comes up to your hand, you have no more of the suit led and therefore trump with the four of spades. Looking at the hand as a whole, you see that you have a perfect finessing position in trumps (spades), but you cannot finesse if you lead trumps immediately, for you are in the wrong hand. You therefore do not lead trumps at the fourth trick, but cast about for some means of entering Dummy's hand.

You have two certain entries to the Dummy: the heart Ace and club King. You have two more entries that are possible: the heart Queen and the heart Ten. The heart Queen offers a distinct probability as an entry card, but the Ten cannot be considered with any seriousness, for both the King and Jack must be in West's hand if the Ten is to become an actual entry. Which entry shall you utilize at this point? The heart suit offers a finesse, too—in fact, a double finesse (against King and Jack). However, by taking the heart finesse now, you run a risk of losing the lead and being obliged to postpone leading trumps until still later. The club King looks like the logical entry card to use at this juncture.

But (every good player, remember, goes through a mental process similar to this on every hand he plays), giving second thought to the use of the club King, you note that as soon as it is gone you will have left only one controlling card in that suit. Then if the spade finesse loses and the Opponents lead another club pronto, you will be forced to win with your Ace, while still holding a club that is sure to lose. If you put off relinquishing your control of the club suit, however, you may be able, eventually, to discard that losing club on the extra heart in Dummy's hand (you hold seven hearts against the Opponents' six).

After considering every angle, then, you decide to take the heart finesse at once. You therefore lead a low heart from your hand and finesse the Ten from Dummy. East wins with the King and returns a club. You can win this in either hand, but you decide to let the trick run around to Dummy's King, as you feel that leading trumps has been put off long enough. You must choose which of Dummy's trumps to lead. Not a low one, certainly, because, if you win in your own hand with either the Ten or the Queen, you will be obliged to do some squirming to find your way into the Dummy again. You must try to keep the lead in the Dummy in order to facilitate a second trump lead through East, who may not play the King on the first round. Therefore you lead the Jack, on which East plays low, you play low from your hand, and West also plays low. The Jack holds the trick, keeping the lead in the Dummy, from where you now lead a low trump, winning with the Ten in your hand. Your count tells you that the King is now the only trump outstanding, so you drop it by leading your Ace.

The rest of this hand is pie. The King of hearts is gone, leaving Dummy's Ace-Queen high. You lead these two rounds of hearts, dropping all the outstanding cards of this suit, throwing off your losing club on Dummy's four of hearts. You thus make the 10 tricks called for by your contract of four spades.

This hand contained three sharp points of interest. The first was the postponement of leading trumps in order to get into the opposite hand to finesse the suit. The second was the preference given to the heart suit for purposes of entry into the Dummy, so as not to relinquish control of a side suit (clubs). The third was the unblocking play in trumps (by finessing the Jack from Dummy first) in order to allow as many leads as possible from the proper hand. These three points or plays occur time and time again, and you will therefore be repaid for remembering their principles.

Summary

The principal lesson taught by this chapter has been to lead trumps as quickly as possible unless some excellent reason exists for doing otherwise. All sorts of dire fates have been predicted for the Bridge player who puts off leading trumps—for no good reason—until the adverse trumps come romping boisterously in to break up his peace of mind at just the wrong moments. The rule to lead trumps—or to think about leading trumps until it is crystal clear that the lead should be postponed—is far and away the most important of all in suit play. It is the good Bridge player's automatic impulse for self-preservation. He thinks first, in playing a suit contract, of the moment when he should lead trumps; always in the back of his mind, until every adverse trump has been played, is the prodding insistence of the thought: "Now shall I lead trumps? If not, why not?"

In fact, *at a suit contract, the first suit the Declarer should try to establish is almost always the trump suit.* As a corollary to the drawing of the Opponents' trumps in the process of establishing your own trumps, *whenever but one trump is left outstanding, almost always capture it if it is lower than your highest trump (even if it costs two of your trumps), but let it alone if it is higher than any of your remaining trumps.*

There are times when you should not lead trumps at the very first chance, though it is still true that you should lead them as soon as the time is ripe. Just bear in the front of your mind the constant checking thought: put off leading trumps, even for 1 trick, only when you have a good and sufficient reason for doing so—that is, *only when you gain some advantage* to compensate for the risk you run by letting the Opponents hold onto their trumps for any longer than you can help.

CHAPTER XIII

RUFFING POWER

THE principal difference between no-trump and suit play lies in the ruffing power of trumps at a suit contract. It is for this reason, of course, that all bidding systems give definite trick values to short or void suits in the hand supporting Partner's bid. A player who considers raising his Partner's suit bid does so with far more confidence when his hand contains even a doubleton, and more so still with a singleton or a void. The reason is that the Declarer, if he plays the hand at a suit contract, can eliminate the short suit from the Dummy and use Dummy's trumps for ruffing cards which would otherwise be certain losers. Thus the proper understanding of ruffing power becomes of extreme importance.

It is as clear as daylight that to make full use of Dummy's small trumps the Declarer must keep them in Dummy's hand. In other words, if the Dummy contains a limited number of trumps, the Declarer cannot afford to remove them immediately, even for the important purpose of drawing the Opponents' trumps. When the Dummy goes down on the table, and you see a singleton or a doubleton among your assets as Declarer, you must check at once that suit in your own hand in order to discover whether the shortness of the suit in the Dummy will be of any use to you. If you hold more cards in that suit than the Dummy, and some of these are clearly losers, you see at once that Dummy's shortness has a vital value.

A very simple illustration will serve to clarify this:

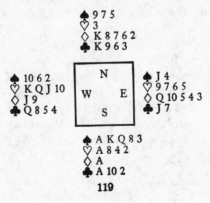

♠ 9 7 5
♡ 3
♢ K 8 7 6 2
♣ K 9 6 3

♠ 10 6 2   ♠ J 4
♡ K Q J 10   ♡ 9 7 6 5
♢ J 9   ♢ Q 10 5 4 3
♣ Q 8 5 4   ♣ J 7

♠ A K Q 8 3
♡ A 8 4 2
♢ A
♣ A 10 2

Suppose that you are Declarer and have to make a contract of seven spades.* That is to say, you cannot lose a single trick. The opening lead by West is the heart King, which you win with your Ace. You see at a glance that you lack enough high cards to guarantee the success of the contract. However, you have other tricks available—those which may develop from ruffing, for spades are trumps. You hold three absolutely worthless hearts—but the Dummy has no hearts at all! What is more, the Dummy also has three trumps—just enough to ruff your losing hearts. Unless you are over-ruffed (that is, unless an Opponent plays a higher trump on one of these ruffing-tricks of yours), you can utilize every one of Dummy's trumps, provided you do not eliminate any of them in trying to draw the Opponents' trumps.

At the second trick, therefore, you lead a low heart and ruff it in the Dummy. At the third trick, you lead a low diamond back to your Ace, following with another small heart which you ruff in Dummy. Re-entering your own hand with the club Ace, you lead your third low heart and ruff with Dummy's last trump. Every time you made one of these ruffing plays, you may well have held your breath lest one of the Opponents be exhausted of hearts and play a higher trump. However, this mode of playing this hand is the only chance of making the contract, and the risk must be taken. With the last of the heart losers out of the way, you begin to perk up hopefully.

The moment has come to draw trumps, for Dummy has none left to be sacrificed in this attack. You lead a low diamond from Dummy and trump in your own hand with the three of spades. (Note that the club King remains in Dummy as a re-entry for using the diamond King later.) You now lead your Ace-King-Queen of spades in rapid succession, felling all the Opponents' trumps. This leaves you with one trump in your hand and two small clubs. One of the clubs is led to Dummy's King. Then the diamond King is led from Dummy, on which you discard your remaining small club.

This hand is very simple because of the fortuitous opening lead made by West. You were able to realize the value of your short suit (hearts) without delay. Very often, however, you will find it necessary to go to work and establish the value of your short suit

---

* This contract would probably not be reached by normal bidding, but for the purpose of illustration let us assume that you (South) have to play to make 13 tricks.

by your own efforts. In the example deal just given, one lead of trumps by an Opponent would have upset the apple cart as far as the success of your contract was concerned. The enemy would then have been able to keep your ruffing activities down to two hearts. To be sure, the Opponents had only one opportunity to lead (the opening lead), but a trump lead then would have been a catastrophe.

STRUGGLING TO REALIZE ON A SHORT SUIT

This deal illustrates short-suit difficulties:

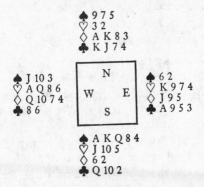

```
              ♠ 9 7 5
              ♡ 3 2
              ◇ A K 8 3
              ♣ K J 7 4
                  ┌─────────┐
  ♠ J 10 3        │    N    │        ♠ 6 2
  ♡ A Q 8 6       │         │        ♡ K 9 7 4
  ◇ Q 10 7 4      │ W     E │        ◇ J 9 5
  ♣ 8 6           │    S    │        ♣ A 9 5 3
                  └─────────┘
              ♠ A K Q 8 4
              ♡ J 10 5
              ◇ 6 2
              ♣ Q 10 2
```

The opening lead by West is the four of diamonds against your four spade contract. You win this first trick with Dummy's King. The hand does not look very promising, but you note with a quickening pulse Dummy's heart doubleton, because you have three hearts, all of no value, in your own hand. If you can wipe out Dummy's heart holding while the exposed hand still keeps a trump, you can gain a trick by ruffing your own last heart in the Dummy. This seems the best mark to shoot at just now, so you lead a low heart.

West probably wins the second trick with his heart Queen. Sensing your wish to ruff in the Dummy, West comes back with the Jack of trumps. You win with your Queen and promptly lead another heart. West wins with his Ace and retaliates with another trump! You win with your King, of course, and now you proceed to trump your last heart in the Dummy. Fortunately for you, your left-hand Opponent was one time unit behind you. In other words, he did not have time to remove all the trumps from the Dummy before you could lead the third round of hearts for the needed ruffing-trick.

Studying your prospects again at this point, you see that you can now lead trumps to advantage. To do this, you must enter your hand—by leading the diamond Ace and following with a low diamond which you ruff in your hand. Your last high trump drops the adverse spade remaining, and you have only the club Ace to lose.

Notice that your contract would have been defeated had the opening lead been a spade. However, the fact that the Opponent who first leads does not always choose the card to his best advantage is always to be considered. Incidentally, South's contract of four spades could have been defeated by another mode of defense. (See Chapter XXIV.)

RUFFING AFTER FIRST LEADING TRUMPS

The lead of trumps by the Declarer need not always be postponed in order to realize fully any available ruffing power. Sometimes the Dummy is so long in trumps that the short suit need not be attacked first. Trumps can be drawn first of all without losing any ruffing power, which may be utilized later.

This situation arises, usually, when the Dummy holds four trumps. Generally speaking, when the Dummy contains only three trumps, the drawing of trumps must be deferred until the Declarer has taken whatever he needs in ruffing-tricks. With four trumps in the Dummy, the Declarer may usually lead one round of trumps with complete safety. You must, of course, always notice how many losers you must dispose of in your hand, and how many trumps the Dummy has available for ruffing purposes.

The following deal is an illustration of ruffing after leading trumps:

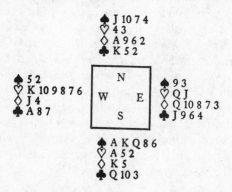

West's opening lead is a heart against your four spade contract. You win with your Ace. There is no escaping the fact that you must lose 1 heart trick some time, and that you must also ruff a heart in the Dummy. This does not require immediate attention, however. You require that only one trump be left in the Dummy, for your ruffing purposes, and consequently it will be well, first of all, to draw the adverse trumps.

At the second trick, then, you lead the spade Ace, following with the King. Both Opponents follow suit, showing that their trumps have been successfully drawn. (Even if the adverse four trumps had been divided 3-1, you could still safely lead a third round before reverting to ruffing that third heart.) At the fourth trick, you lead the heart you must lose, which is probably won by East, who returns a diamond. You win with your diamond King, and lead your last heart to ruff in the Dummy. Cashing in your diamond Ace, you lead a low diamond from Dummy to ruff in your own hand. The balance of your cards now look like this:

```
        ♠ J
        ♡ —
        ◇ 9
        ♣ K 5 2
      ┌─────────┐
      │    N    │
      │ W     E │
      │    S    │
      └─────────┘
        ♠ Q 8
        ♡ —
        ◇ —
        ♣ Q 10 3
```

You have lost but 1 trick thus far; you can therefore afford to lose 2 more. Indeed, 2 tricks are the most you can possibly lose, for your two remaining trumps are good, and you must certainly win 1 club trick. However, what if you can win 2 of those club tricks? You know that the high cards out against you are the Ace and Jack. The Ace must win, but you may be able to encircle the Jack by a finessing maneuver. You may as well take this finesse, for if it loses, you have lost no more than you must lose by any other method of play. You therefore lead the club trey from your hand; when

West plays low, you play Dummy's King, which holds the trick. The fact that East does not win with the Ace may be taken as a pretty good sign that he did not have it; in other words, West very likely has the Ace. Now you lead the club deuce from Dummy; when East plays low, you play—not the Queen, but the Ten! Since West holds the Ace, the play of the Queen can gain nothing as it will leave the Jack as the outstanding high club. But the play of the Ten, if East has the Jack, will force West's Ace, leaving your Queen high. What have you done? You have simply finessed against a Jack.

DIVERTING TO A NEW TYPE OF FINESSE

The last part of the preceding illustrative play involved a type of finesse which has not yet been discussed. The situation comes up repeatedly. We may, as a diversion from the subject of ruffing power, look at this new finesse more closely for a moment. Consider the following diamond situations:

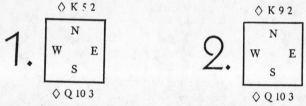

The first situation is quite the same as the one in the preceding example deal. The proper way to play this combination is to lead the three and go up with the King if West plays low, finessing the Ten on the way back if the King holds the trick. Would it be just the same if you lead low from the Dummy and finesse the Ten on the first round? Not quite. This play would be almost as good, but it would lose one time unit. In the first place, it might result in failing to establish a sure trick immediately, because, if the Jack wins the first round, the Ace is left outstanding. Furthermore, it does not take into account the possibility of finding West with either the lone Jack or the Ace-Jack doubleton. If West should have either of those combinations, the lead of the trey from your hand exposes the weakness and ends all your worries about losing 2 diamond tricks.

Still looking at the first situation, do you think it would be the same to lead low from Dummy and play the Queen on the first round? No, for if West wins with the Ace, you will no longer have any finessing position because the lead of the Ten on the third round will mean its certain covering by the Jack. This is the same as leading a lone Queen up to a lone Ace—if the Queen is covered, the finesse disappears. The situation remains unchanged if your Queen holds the trick on the first round, and you continue the suit—the Opponents must win 2 tricks. *To finesse when holding three honors—two in one hand and one in the other—first lead up to the single honor, keeping intact the tenace position with the double honors.*

Now glance back at the second situation. The cards are the same as in the first, except that the nine-spot is now held in place of the five. This nine-spot gives you a choice of plays. If you decide that West has the Ace and East the Jack, you must lead from your own hand toward the King, finessing the Ten on the way back. If you decide, however, that East holds the Ace and West the Jack, you must lead low from the Dummy (North), go up with the Queen on the first round, and finesse the *nine-spot* on the way back. The fact that you hold four cards which are higher than all but two (Ace and Jack) of the Opponents' enables you to play the combination either way, because your fourth card gives you control of the last round if the Ace wins the first round and the Jack the second, or vice versa. This was not true in the first situation.

UNBLOCKING THE TRUMP SUIT

Return now to ruffing power.

Just to prove that no-trump plays are applicable to suit contracts, look at the following partnership hands to be played at a five diamond contract:

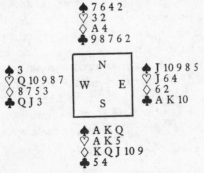

The opening lead is a spade, which you win with your Queen. You perceive at once that the hearts offer ruffing possibilities. Therefore you lay down your heart Ace and King, following with a low heart which you ruff in the Dummy. *But which of Dummy's trumps do you ruff with?* You must remember the principle of unblocking which you learned in connection with no-trump play. To unblock the trump suit you must ruff with Dummy's diamond Ace (not with the four-spot). You are using a card of equal value with your own nine-spot, for you hold an unbroken diamond sequence from the Ace down to the nine-spot. Having trumped with the Ace you can now lead the four-spot and draw all of the outstanding trumps. You then cash in your good spade tricks and simply concede two club tricks at the end.

The ruffing with Dummy's Ace is far from a pointless play. Had you ruffed with the four-spot and then led the Ace to start drawing trumps, you would have found that the trump suit was blocked. You would have been forced to try to return to your own hand by leading spades, and West would have trumped the second round of this suit and your contract would have been defeated by 1 trick. By unblocking the trump suit, which you did by ruffing with your Ace, you eliminated any chance of this happening.

Ruffing Power Is Confined to the Dummy

In all the example deals in this chapter, you may have noticed that ruffing power appeared only in the Dummy's hand, never in the Declarer's hand. Though it may seem incredible, there is practically no such thing as a ruffing-trick to be found in the long trump hand, which is almost always the Declarer's hand.*

The reason for this may be quickly explained. If the hand containing the greater number of trumps wishes to take tricks with them, he needs only to establish the trump suit. If he holds five trumps to the Ace-King, and his Partner holds four small ones, two rounds of the suit will probably catch all the adverse trumps, and the three trumps he has left in his own hand will all be high. If now he leads some card from the Dummy and plays a trump on it from his hand, he is not making a ruffing-trick—he is, as a matter of fact, not gaining

---

* In those rare cases where the Dummy contains the greater length in trumps, the play is simply reversed.

a trick at all. He could easily have accomplished the same result by *leading* the trump from his hand and discarding the card (which he led) from the Dummy. The high trumps in his own hand are good no matter how he plays them. Put this way, the lead of trumps for no reason at all, you see, gains nothing. Properly speaking, a *ruffing-trick* is a trump trick which cannot be made by leading trumps; it is always an extra trick, never an automatic trick.

This fact—that ruffing power is generally confined to the Dummy—is of importance because it crops up frequently in defensive play. It is a common failing among average players to take tricks quickly, as Declarers, with tricks in their own hands. Most of the time they do not realize that they are reducing their strength and weakening their position. The Declarer who takes out his own trumps immediately, under the delusion that he is making ruffing-tricks, is merely taking a few tricks early in the play with cards which he should be reserving as controls against later attacks.

SUMMARY

The general subject of this chapter has been the utilization of ruffing power in the Dummy. Whenever necessary, the lead of trumps should be postponed until full and separate use has been made of Dummy's trumps in gaining ruffing-tricks. This is true whether the Opponents lead your short suit or whether you find it necessary to lead it yourself in order to get at the precious nucleus of ruffing profits. You should lead trumps before ruffing, of course, if the Dummy is long enough in trumps to withstand one or more trump leads without being drained of ruffing power.

You learned about a new type of finesse, which came up incidentally—the finesse against Ace-Jack. To finesse when holding three honors (two in one hand and one in the other) you should first lead up to the single honor, keeping intact the tenace position with the double honors. This rule does not necessarily apply, however, when the three honors are supported by the next card in sequence below.

Finally, you learned that you may sometimes find it necessary to unblock the trump suit by ruffing with a high trump instead of a low one.

CHAPTER XIV

PLAYS POSTPONING THE TRUMP LEAD

I N the preceding chapter very brief mention was made of the fact that there are many hands which make the postponement of the trump lead more advantageous than the immediate drawing of the adverse trumps. There are, as a matter of fact, a fairly large number of trump plays in which the postponement of the trump lead is a prominent factor.

The most common situation which calls for the postponement of drawing trumps is the hand which contains losers that at all costs must be discarded before the Opponents regain the lead. Sometimes the Declarer can draw trumps anyway, but when the adverse trumps include a high one which cannot be surely captured, he must wait until he has taken the discards necessary to salvage those losers. This mode of play may risk the loss of a trick, but more often than not it actually shows a profit.

The following deal illustrates this play:

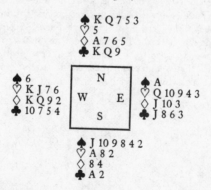

The contract is four spades (even perhaps six spades). West's opening lead is the diamond King, which you naturally win with your Ace.

Before playing another card, you must probe the possibilities of the hand as they now present themselves. You spot at once the trump trick you must lose (spade Ace), and you note with a sparkling eye Dummy's singleton in a suit of which you hold the Ace. Surely there are no heart losers in this hand. You can ruff your worthless hearts with Dummy's trumps. What is more, you need not postpone the trump lead on this account, for Dummy has plenty of ruffing power to take care of the hearts later. However, you cannot stop here. You must also look at diamonds and clubs.

You have 3 sure club tricks. But your hand contains a losing diamond, and there will certainly be no possibility of ruffing it. If you lead trumps at once, the Opponents will take their trump Ace, and return a diamond. In this way they will take 2 tricks, for you can do nothing to prevent them from winning that second round of diamonds—unless you can discard one. You have the three top clubs. You cannot follow suit from your hand on the third round of clubs, but, if neither Opponent has less than three clubs, you can throw off your losing diamond on that third round. Even if one Opponent has only two clubs, and ruffs the third round, it will do no harm to try this way of playing the hand, for you will still have discarded your losing diamond and will lose no more than 2 tricks in the entire deal no matter what happens.

Therefore you lead your club Ace, and follow with another club to Dummy's King-Queen. When Dummy's King wins, you lead the Queen, discarding the last diamond from your hand. Both East and West follow suit, and your diamond loser has ceased to threaten you. The rest is simple: you merely lead trumps, letting the Opponents have their Ace, and noting that no more trump leads are necessary, for both adverse trumps fall on the first trick. You ruff your two small hearts with two of Dummy's trumps, and now the rest of your hand contains nothing but good trumps. Thus you make six-odd, an impossibility if you had first tried to remove the Opponents' trumps.

To prove to you beyond any possibility of doubt that the loss of the third round of clubs, in the deal just given, if the Opponents ruff, does not really lose anything for your side, consider the following deal, in which just such a play does fail:

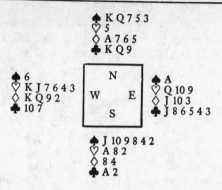

With the same opening lead as before (diamond King), you win with your Ace and lead three rounds of clubs. (Declarer's and Dummy's hands are just like those in the preceding example.) On the third round of clubs, you discard your diamond in exactly the same way as you did before, but this time, being exhausted of clubs, West ruffs with the six of spades. What tricks must you lose after this? Only 1 more—the spade Ace. You would still lose only 2 tricks even if you did lead trumps at once, and lost that diamond instead of the ruffed third round of clubs. Notice that in the preceding example your method of playing enabled you to make six-odd; in this example, you lose no more than you must lose by any other method of play. In other words, you risked nothing, and half the time you gained a trick!

The type of play just described is not good policy, of course, when the adverse trumps can be drawn without losing the lead. If you had held the Ace instead of the Jack of spades it would have been the height of folly for you to have led clubs first. You should then simply lead spades until the adverse trumps are exhausted, using your clubs for any necessary discards later. *Only when the Opponents are sure of obtaining the lead on the first round of trumps, and are then sure of making a trick they could not take later, must you avail yourself of this trump postponement play.*

POSTPONING THE TRUMP LEAD FOR A SPECIFIC DISCARD

You cannot simply make up your mind that you need to discard a loser, and then discard any small card at all. Very often it makes a

vast difference if you discard, say, a diamond instead of a club—
when you have a choice.

Consider, for example, the following deal:

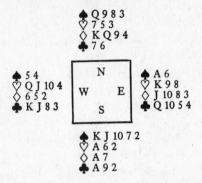

♠ Q 9 8 3
♡ 7 5 3
♢ K Q 9 4
♣ 7 6

♠ 5 4   ♠ A 6
♡ Q J 10 4   ♡ K 9 8
♢ 6 5 2   ♢ J 10 8 3
♣ K J 8 3   ♣ Q 10 5 4

♠ K J 10 7 2
♡ A 6 2
♢ A 7
♣ A 9 2

West's opening lead is the heart Queen against your four spade contract. You win with your Ace, and, glancing hurriedly at the trump
situation, you see that you have the Ace to lose. Looking at your
hearts, you see that each hand has 2 losers. Turning to your diamonds, you perceive 3 positive tricks and one round of diamonds from
Dummy available for a discard from your own hand. You have 1
losing trick in clubs, but the third round can be ruffed in Dummy.

The question is, should you lead trumps at the second trick? If
you do, the Opponents will obtain the lead and will probably cash in
2 heart tricks promptly. But this does not take away your discard
on the diamond suit, for you still have a losing club you would like
to get rid of. Why not lead trumps, then, and, after the Opponents
have taken 3 tricks, use the third round of diamonds to discard a
club?

This reasoning is wholly fallacious. What earthly good would a
club discard be? You would have left two clubs in each hand, and
only one round controlled (by the Ace). That is, you would still
have to lose the second round of clubs in spite of your club discard.
You would no longer have to ruff the *third* round in the Dummy, but
how does that help?

The discard of a club is purposeless. But the *immediate* discard of a
heart is imperative. The heart is a sure loser, while the club (the
one you contemplated discarding) is not a loser at all. Conclusion:

you cannot lead trumps at once, but you must take three rounds of diamonds in order to get rid of a heart. The play, then, proceeds as follows:

Trick 1.   West leads ♡ Q, North plays ♡ 3, East plays ♡ 8, and South wins with ♡ A.

Trick 2.   South leads ◇ A, West plays ◇ 2, North plays ◇ 4, and East plays ◇ 3.   South's lead wins.

Trick 3.   South leads ◇ 7, West plays ◇ 5, North plays ◇ Q, and East plays ◇ 8.   North wins the trick.

Trick 4.   North leads ◇ K, East plays ◇ 10, South discards ♡ 2, and West plays ◇ 6.   Success crowns your play—the diamonds broke 4-3.   The nine-spot left in Dummy is, of course, not high, for one Opponent still has the Jack.

Trick 5.   North leads ♠ 3, East plays ♠ A, South plays ♠ 2, and West plays ♠ 4.   East's Ace of trumps wins.

Trick 6.   East leads ◇ J, South ruffs with ♠ 7, West discards ♣ 3, North plays ◇ 9.   South's ruff wins.   The purpose of East's lead, since he saw the odd diamond left in Dummy's hand, was the hope that West could over-ruff whatever spade South played to the trick. However, since the Declarer held a solid sequence from the King down to the seven-spot, the seven was as good as the King for ruffing.

Trick 7.   South leads ♠ K, West plays ♠ 5, North plays ♠ 8, and East plays ♠ 6.

Trick 8.   South leads ♣ A, West plays ♣ 8, North plays ♣ 6, and East plays ♣ 4.

Trick 9.   South leads ♣ 2, West plays ♣ J, North plays ♣ 7, and East plays ♣ 5.   This is the trick that South must lose in clubs no matter what course he pursues.   He therefore leads it to dispose of it.

The rest of the tricks are easily accounted for.   South's last club is ruffed in the Dummy.

This hand illustrates once again the absolute necessity of making a careful plan before proceeding with the play of any hand, no matter how simple it looks at first glance.   Blindly leading trumps would have lost the contract.   South cannot think, with a little reasoning behind his thought, that he can take his discard just any old time.   By observing the crying need for a *specific* discard, he reached the right conclusion as to the proper play.

Another Way of Taking Discards Before Leading Trumps

In the preceding deal, discards were secured by leading out high cards in the suit which was to offer the discarding opportunity. Sometimes, however, the suit on which 1 or more losing tricks are to be discarded must first be established. A high card must be driven out of the Opponents' hands. The situation can usually be properly appraised by considering the time element of leads and realizing what may happen if you thoughtlessly present the lead to an Opponent.

In the following deal it will take but one lead of trumps by South to send his four spade contract down the river.

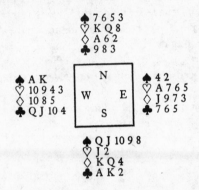

```
                    ♠ 7 6 5 3
                    ♡ K Q 8
                    ◇ A 6 2
                    ♣ 9 8 3
                 ┌──────────────┐
   ♠ A K         │      N       │      ♠ 4 2
   ♡ 10 9 4 3    │              │      ♡ A 7 6 5
   ◇ 10 8 5      │  W       E   │      ◇ J 9 7 3
   ♣ Q J 10 4    │              │      ♣ 7 6 5
                 │      S       │
                 └──────────────┘
                    ♠ Q J 10 9 8
                    ♡ J 2
                    ◇ K Q 4
                    ♣ A K 2
```

You win West's opening lead of the club Queen with your own King. What is to be your next play? You can, of course, lead your top trump with the idea of drawing trumps and losing 2 tricks immediately (spade Ace-King), but the Opponents will then continue the club suit to drive out your other stopper. They will thus chalk up against you 2 trump tricks, 1 club trick (the third round, for which the second trick in trumps provides them an entry), and 1 heart trick (Ace)—defeating your contract by 1 trick.

There is only one way you can save yourself. You must establish a trick somewhere on which you can quickly throw off that losing third club. The only suit that seems likely (to be useful for discarding, a suit must be shorter in one hand than in the other) is hearts. The fact that you have only five hearts is encouraging, for your shortness reduces the risk of an adverse ruff on the third round. At the second trick, then, you must lead the Jack of hearts and continue the suit if the Opponents do not take their Ace promptly. Whether the heart Ace is cashed in immediately or not makes no difference. The point is that you want to utilize the long (third) heart in Dummy's hand for getting rid of a club from your own hand. You can then draw trumps with perfect equanimity, knowing that the Opponents can win no more than 3 tricks altogether.

Note that the heart suit is the one to lead—not the diamond. You have 3 sure diamond tricks, but with the equal diamond length in both hands you develop no discarding opportunity and, furthermore, you run great risk of an adverse ruff on the third round. As already stated, a suit is useless for discarding purposes unless its length is greater in one hand than in the other. The greater length need not be in the Dummy—it can be in either hand. Discards can be made from Dummy on long cards in Declarer's hand, for the purpose of developing 1 or more ruffing-tricks, just as efficaciously as discards have been made (in preceding examples) from Declarer's hand on Dummy's long cards.

Glance just a moment at the following partnership holding (South being Declarer at a spade contract):

♠ K J 10 9
♡ A 2
♢ 7 6 5
♣ K 10 8 4

```
      N
   W     E
      S
```

♠ Q 8 7 6 5
♡ K Q 4
♢ A 6 2
♣ A 3

If the opening lead is a diamond, South must take his Ace at once. This leaves two losing diamonds in each hand, making a discard imperative before trumps are drawn (if possible). The Dummy has the Ace and one heart; Declarer has three hearts to the King-Queen. Clearly, then, the play is for South to take three rounds of hearts before leading trumps, discarding one of Dummy's diamonds on the third round. Trumps can then be drawn, and the Opponents will have to be satisfied with only 1 diamond trick—for South subsequently ruffs the other diamond loser in the Dummy.

SUMMARY

The general principles set forth in this chapter may be concisely stated—to refresh and intensify the memory—as follows:

Whenever the Declarer must discard 1 or more losers before the Opponents have a chance to lead the losing suit, he should postpone leading trumps—if by leading trumps he will permit the Opponents to regain the lead.

The necessity of postponing the trump lead in order to first discard a loser arises from the fact that to lead trumps will give the Opponents an opportunity to lead the suit containing Delcarer's loser.

Drawing trumps must also be postponed when, to afford a discard, a side suit must be established. Here the process of establishing the side suit necessarily gives the Opponents one or more leads, and to give them the additional lead assured by an adverse controlling card in the trump suit will prove fatal. By first establishing the side suit, particularly when the suit containing the loser has two stoppers, Declarer is able to find the necessary discard before drawing trumps, always provided, of course, he does not run into any distributional snag—which, in any event, he cannot help.

CHAPTER XV

NO-TRUMP PLAYS AT SUIT CONTRACTS

AT no-trump, the play of a hand consists almost entirely of making tricks with high cards and with the low cards which may be established in long suits—that is to say, high-card tricks and long-suit tricks. At a suit contract, on the other hand, the play consists chiefly of making high-card tricks and *short*-suit tricks (the latter are also called ruffing-tricks). The *long*-suit trick is occasionally present in suit play, but it is usually of minor importance.

With one type of hand, played at a suit, the long-suit trick does become of just about as much importance as the short-suit trick. This type of hand, because of the nature of the play, is really much more like a no-trump hand than a trump hand; in fact, it would be a no-trump hand if it were not for the fact that one of the four suits is the declared trump. This kind of hand is characterized, generally, by some fairly long side suit in the hand with the fewest entries.

This hybrid—the "no-trump-suit" hand—calls for a trump postponement play. The following deal is a good example:

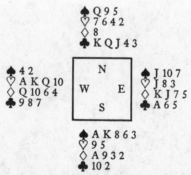

```
                    ♠ Q 9 5
                    ♡ 7 6 4 2
                    ♢ 8
                    ♣ K Q J 4 3
    ♠ 4 2              N            ♠ J 10 7
    ♡ A K Q 10                      ♡ J 8 3
    ♢ Q 10 6 4      W     E         ♢ K J 7 5
    ♣ 9 8 7            S            ♣ A 6 5
                    ♠ A K 8 6 3
                    ♡ 9 5
                    ♢ A 9 3 2
                    ♣ 10 2
```

The opening lead is the heart King against your four spade contract, which holds, and is followed by the Queen and then the Ace. You (as Declarer) ruff the third round of hearts with your trey of spades. The time has come to estimate your chances of making 10 tricks.

The adverse trumps offer no obstacle, for they can probably be drawn in three leads. Further, unless one Opponent has four spades

136

to the Jack, there is no adverse commanding trump. However, Dummy's singleton diamond focuses your attention on the fact that ruffing power is available there—Dummy's three trumps look like just the answer to the three losing diamonds in your own hand.

Now look just a bit further. Suppose you lead the diamond Ace, exhausting the Dummy of the suit, and follow with a small diamond which you ruff with Dummy's spade five. The only way you can re-enter your hand is to lead Dummy's last heart (three rounds of hearts have already been played, you know) and ruff it in your own hand. Now you lead the third round of diamonds, again ruffing in the Dummy. What then? You cannot get back to your hand. You would be forced to attack the club suit by leading the King—but the Opponents hold up their Ace on the first round, and where are you? You lead another club—and East wins with the club Ace. East then leads another diamond, which you would be forced to ruff with Dummy's spade Queen. Now, no matter what you do, East must win a trick with his spade Jack.

What is likely to be the best way to make your contract? Of course, you can first draw trumps and then establish the club suit, but East will certainly not be so accommodating as to play his Ace on the first round of clubs—and if he wins the second round, you will be shut out of the Dummy with a vengeance, for your only possible entry, the spade Queen, has vanished.

The only way to manage this hand is to play it exactly as though the contract were no-trump. You must, to avoid blocking yourself, establish the club suit before touching spades. Thus you retain the spade Queen in the Dummy as a re-entry for the set-up clubs.

Your cards now lie as follows:

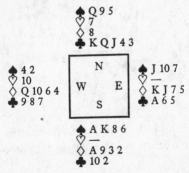

We are at the fourth trick, you remember. Three rounds of hearts were played, the first two won by West, and the third you ruffed. At the fourth trick, then, you lead the Ten of clubs from your own hand, playing low from Dummy. If East refuses to win the trick, you simply lead the club deuce and play the Jack from Dummy. This time East must go up with the Ace if he does not wish to have it ruffed on the third round. Suppose that East returns a diamond. You win with your Ace and immediately lead trumps. You must lead the Ace-King from your hand first, following on the third round with the six-spot to Dummy's Queen, which succeeds in removing all the trumps from the Opponents' hands and leaves you with the lead in the Dummy, where you want to be in order to cash in those last three good clubs. On those three club leads you discard the three small losing diamonds from your own hand.

Note that ruffing even one diamond in the Dummy would have proved disastrous. When the time came to draw trumps, you could then have taken only two rounds—if you wished to use the Queen as a re-entry for the clubs. This would mean that East would trump the fourth round of clubs, forcing you to wind up with one losing diamond, shattering all hopes of making your contract.

AGAIN ESTABLISHING A SIDE SUIT BEFORE LEADING TRUMPS

The following deal is another example of the establishment of a side suit before leading trumps:

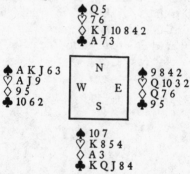

Your contract this time is four clubs, and the opening lead is the spade King. Nothing can prevent West from winning the first two rounds of spades, which he does.   At the third trick, West shifts to a club (deuce), on which you play low from Dummy, but East's play of the nine forces you to win with the Jack in your hand.   Now what? That long diamond suit needs establishing, but the Ace of clubs in the Dummy offers the only re-entry.   To draw trumps first will destroy that entry into the Dummy.   The first thing to do, then, is to attack diamonds.   You must run the risk of the second round being ruffed.

You therefore lead your diamond Ace, following with the trey and winning with Dummy's King.   Now you lead the Jack, on which East plays the Queen.   A count shows you that West now has no more diamonds, and he will surely over-ruff any low trump you play. Therefore you must not ruff low—you must ruff with a trump honor and hope that the adverse five clubs are divided 3-2.   You ruff with the club Queen and follow with the lead of the King.   At this point both Opponents follow suit, leaving but one trump outstanding. The low club to Dummy's Ace drops this last trump, and you are now in position to lead your three good diamonds, on which you discard three small hearts from your own hand.   This unguards your heart King, but you can concede this trick to the Opponents.

If you think you can make 10 tricks in this hand by leading out all the trumps, try it until you convince yourself that you are wrong.

Setting Up a Side Suit by Preserving Ruffing Power

In the following deal the lead of trumps is postponed in order to establish a side suit first, but the postponement is necessary here, not to preserve an entry, but to avoid giving up Dummy's potential ruffing-tricks, which are essential to the success of the hand.

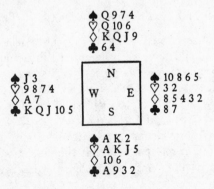

Your contract is four hearts, of which you have only seven against the Opponents' six, and, although scarcity of trumps may become one of your minor troubles, this need not worry you unduly since you are lucky enough to have controlling cards in all the side suits. However, West, like a worthy Opponent, makes things difficult by choosing for his opening lead the club King, thereby removing your only control card in clubs (your Ace).

Pondering your situation, you decide that you cannot afford to draw trumps at this stage. If you attempt to draw all of the trumps, you will eventually be forced to let West regain the lead with his diamond Ace, and then he will simply rake in 4 club tricks while you look on in agonized helplessness. You know from West's King lead that he has some club tricks, even if you are not sure he has as many as 4. Note that by drawing trumps, which requires four trump leads, you exhaust both your own hand and Dummy of hearts, so that you have no ruffing power available to stop that run of clubs by West.

You can escape this fate by first driving out West's diamond Ace— before you do anything else. If you do this, West will be forced to continue clubs at a time when you still have a trump in the Dummy to ruff the third round of clubs. Thus the Opponents are held down to 2 tricks—the club Queen and the diamond Ace. Note, by the way, that you never made actual use of Dummy's ruffing power. You merely preserved it long enough for it to be a threat over any attempt by West to run off his established club suit. Note in addition that the third round of clubs (if led by West) must be ruffed with the Ten of hearts in Dummy, for fear that East will over-ruff any lower card.

Establishing a Side Suit After Drawing Trumps

Some very good reason must always be present to delay the drawing of trumps. This should have been hammered into your permanent stock of playing principles by this time. To give it due weight, suppose we emphasize it once more: you should *postpone drawing trumps only when you have a clearly defined reason for so doing, and only when that reason is something to your advantage.*

The temptation to tackle an attractive side suit may be very strong, and yet it is entirely possible that the invitation to establish the side suit can be declined until trumps have been drawn. In fact in the majority of instances, the establishment of the side suit can wait until the drawing of all the adverse trumps has destroyed all threats of possible ruffs by the Opponents.

The following deal shows how trumps may be—in fact, should be—drawn before establishing a side suit, and it also teaches a new way in which a side suit can be set up (by ruffing):

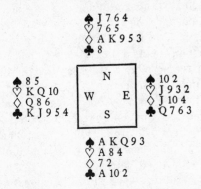

```
              ♠ J 7 6 4
              ♡ 7 6 5
              ◇ A K 9 5 3
              ♣ 8
                  ┌─────────┐
 ♠ 8 5            │    N    │        ♠ 10 2
 ♡ K Q 10         │ W     E │        ♡ J 9 3 2
 ◇ Q 8 6          │    S    │        ◇ J 10 4
 ♣ K J 9 5 4      └─────────┘        ♣ Q 7 6 3
              ♠ A K Q 9 3
              ♡ A 8 4
              ◇ 7 2
              ♣ A 10 2
```

Against your contract of four spades, West's opening lead is the heart King, which you win with your Ace. It does not take much time to learn that your contract is in no danger here. You have only 2 losing tricks (in hearts). Those two small clubs you can ruff in Dummy as soon as your Ace has eliminated Dummy's singleton.

Since your victory is certain, you may just as well look around for an extra trick or so. Those diamonds look intriguing, for you have seven against the Opponents' six. Of your seven, Dummy has five topped by Ace-King, so your own two small ones are well taken care of. Now what about those three small diamonds in the Dummy? Is there not some way of benefiting from your superior diamond length? There is. If the adverse diamonds are divided 3-3, or even 4-2, you can establish 1 or 2 long-suit tricks by ruffing Dummy's small diamonds in your own hand. You therefore plan to cash in Dummy's Ace and King of diamonds, and ruff the third round in your own hand. You thus take advantage of the fact that one of your suits happens to be the trump suit, but the principle involved here is basically a principle of no-trump play.

Should you develop diamonds immediately? No, for you hold all the high trumps, and the Dummy actually has four trumps, which means that the matter of entries is no source of worry. You can afford to lead at least two rounds of spades (trumps), and, if the adverse trumps do not all fall, you can refrain from leading the third round until you have ruffed your losing clubs.

At the second trick, therefore, you lead the spade Ace and follow it with the King. Fortunately, the missing trumps do fall, and you can go after the diamonds without a qualm. You lead a low diamond, winning with Dummy's King, and follow by cashing in Dummy's Ace. Now a low diamond from Dummy, ruffing in your own hand. You note that the Opponents always follow suit in diamonds, which means that they have no more. In other words, your two last diamonds in the Dummy are now high. All you have to do now is to lead the club Ace, followed by a low one which you ruff in the Dummy. Cashing in your two good diamonds, you throw off on them your two losing hearts. The next lead from Dummy is a small heart, which you ruff in your hand, and then trump your last club with Dummy's last spade. Thus you win all 13 tricks.

Some readers are doubtless agog with an earlier statement made to the effect that the Declarer's own hand practically never contains any ruffing power. At first thought, this example may seem to contradict this statement. When you ruffed the third round of diamonds in your hand you were not trying to make a ruffing-trick. You were trying to establish a long-suit trick in the Dummy. In other words, this was not a senseless waste of a trump which would have been a good trick in any event, but instead was the sacrifice of a good trump for the purpose of establishing some extra tricks.

The diamond distribution was very favorable for your purposes in this last deal. If the adverse diamonds had broken 4-2, you would have been obliged to trump two rounds of diamonds in your own hand. Instead of establishing 2 winners for discarding purposes, you would have been able to throw off only one heart, ultimately losing the other heart to the Opponents. Also, if the diamonds had been divided 5-1, you would have set up no diamond winners at all. There would then have been nothing you could do about it, but you would have lost nothing by trying. Your 2 losing heart tricks, which you saw at once when you first examined the hand, would then have been lost in spite of everything. However, at no time was your contract in any danger whatsoever.

Retaining Trump Entries Until a Side Suit Is Established by Ruffing

Suppose we now combine the two methods of play thus far discussed in this chapter. It is sometimes necessary to retain trumps in the Dummy for use as entries until a side suit has been established by ruffing.

The following deal offers a rather desperate situation illustrating this:

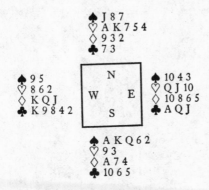

```
                    ♠ J 8 7
                    ♡ A K 7 5 4
                    ◇ 9 3 2
                    ♣ 7 3
    ♠ 9 5                              ♠ 10 4 3
    ♡ 8 6 2          N                 ♡ Q J 10
    ◇ K Q J      W       E             ◇ 10 8 6 5
    ♣ K 9 8 4 2      S                 ♣ A Q J
                    ♠ A K Q 6 2
                    ♡ 9 3
                    ◇ A 7 4
                    ♣ 10 6 5
```

Against your four spade contract, West's opening lead is the diamond King. Your first examination of your prospects is discouraging. Your one hope lies in how the adverse hearts may break. If the adverse hearts are divided 3-3, there is a chance of setting up a couple of long-suit tricks by ruffing the third round, but you are annoyed by the barrenness of the Dummy in the matter of entries. The only obvious entry is the Jack of spades, which will be killed by any premature drawing of three rounds of trumps. You might lay down the Ace and King of trumps, and then lead three rounds of hearts, but this will not obviate your difficulty if the hearts are unfortunately distributed. There is the further possibility of a ruffing-trick in clubs (third round).

At the second trick, then, you attack the heart suit, winning the first two rounds with Dummy's Ace-King. The third round, led from Dummy, you trump in your own hand. You are gratified to find the adverse hearts divided 3-3, as you had hoped. Now the value of those two good hearts in the Dummy depends entirely on the break in trumps. If they are not divided 3-2, you are lost. You lead out the Ace and King of spades, and follow with a low one to Dummy's Jack. When all the adverse trumps fall, your troubles are over. Your own hand contains 3 losing club tricks and 2 losing diamond tricks, but you can throw off two of these on Dummy's two established hearts. The other three you must lose, but you still make 10 tricks.

This example involved what was really a rather desperate play. The odds were decidedly against your fulfilling your contract, but you chose the only possible way to do it and were blessed by the gods of chance. In Contract Bridge, you see, it never pays to give up easily.

GAINING TRICKS BY REFUSING TO RUFF

In the following deal still another principle is exemplified:

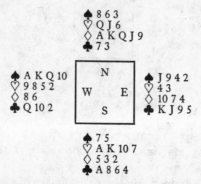

Your contract is four hearts, against which West opens the spade King, holding the trick. Your left-hand Opponent continues with the Queen, and then the Ace. On the third round you can ruff with a low heart, but before you do so, look over the situation. Never was the old proverb that you should look before you leap more true. An immediate ruff of spades can do you no good. The only suits offering any number of tricks are hearts and diamonds. You have only 1 other trick: the club Ace. You may discard some of your losing clubs on the long diamonds in the Dummy, but the number is limited. There are only two more diamonds in the Dummy than in your own hand, which means only two discards will be available.

If you ruff the spade trick (which you will lose if you do not ruff), you must ultimately lose a club trick instead. What if, instead of ruffing here, you throw off a club? Study the situation carefully.

If you trump, you will have only three trumps left in your hand and three in Dummy's hand. Before you can run off your diamonds, you will have to draw trumps. If the adverse trumps break 3-3, you will be all right, but if they should break 4-2, you will find yourself exhausted of trumps while the Opponents have one left. When you start leading your diamonds, the Opponents (actually West) will ruff the third round and lead clubs. If this happens, not even a miracle can keep you from losing 3 club tricks besides 1 more spade trick.

Now consider refusing to trump. Discard a low club on that spade Ace. West is left in the lead. If he leads another spade, he cannot force you to ruff in your own hand, for you can trump with Dummy's Jack of hearts and still retain your own four trumps untouched. West will probably lead a club, which you will win with your Ace, and then lead *four* rounds of hearts, removing all the adverse trumps. The rest of the tricks are then yours, for you have five good diamonds. Strange though it may seem, your refusal to ruff the third round of spades actually saves you 3 tricks.

Is Declarer or Dummy the Dominating Hand?

Most Declarers have a tendency to regard their own hand as the supreme one, and look upon the Dummy as merely supplementary or secondary. When they check over their losing tricks, they do so, almost invariably, from the viewpoint of their own hand. This is generally correct, but there are still many occasions when the Declarer's own hand must be looked upon as the secondary holding of the partnership. After all, it makes no difference which hand wins the bulk of the tricks so long as they are won by the partnership.

The following deal is a good illustration of this:

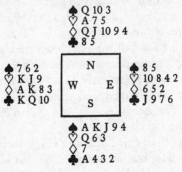

West opens the diamond King against your four spade contract. But as soon as West sees the diamond strength in the Dummy, he naturally shifts to something else for his second lead, realizing that Declarer can very likely ruff a second round of diamonds. Suppose he now leads a club (his best lead), which you win with your Ace. Looking at the possibilities entirely from the standpoint of your own hand, things look rather dark. You can give up a club trick immediately, and thus make available 2 ruffing-tricks in the Dummy. You can also hope that East has the heart King, so that you can finesse against it for 2 heart tricks. But if West should have the heart King, this mode of play will mean the loss of your contract by 1 trick.

There is another possibility. Perhaps you can lead some of Dummy's diamonds in order to trump in your own hand, and eventually establish a long-suit trick for discarding purposes. But if you do this, you will sacrifice your ruffing-tricks in clubs. What should you do? You can answer this question if you will pretend, for the moment, that your own hand is the Dummy, and the Dummy is Declarer.

Looking at the South hand as though it were the Dummy, you see that you can lead a low spade to North's Ten, and then lead out the diamond Queen, on which you discard from the South hand a small club! This gives up a trick which you do not have to lose, but it does more—it establishes 3 diamond tricks in the North hand on which you can get rid of three losing cards from the South hand. After West wins the trick with the diamond Ace, he will probably lead another club, thereby winning the third trick for his side. His best play is to lead still another club, which you ruff with the trey of spades, and lead the Queen—which you do not overtake in the South hand. This leaves one trump outstanding, and the success or failure of your contract depends on which Opponent holds it. You lead the diamond Jack, on which you discard the heart trey, and then lead the diamond Ten while murmuring a prayer. East, unable to follow suit and unable to trump, helplessly throws off a heart. You discard a heart from the South hand, and you have left only trumps and the heart Queen. The heart Ace in the North hand is good, of course, and so are the trumps.

If West had not led that third round of clubs, your problem would have been simpler. Suppose, for instance, he had led a heart. You must not bother with the finesse, but go up with Dummy's Ace, leading a low spade to your Ace, and then re-entering the North hand with the spade Queen. The three diamonds would then give you all the discards you need. Note how simply the play developed as soon as you looked upon the South hand (your own, as Declarer) as the secondary holding.

SUMMARY

Reduced to essentials, this chapter has told you how to watch for long-suit tricks which may be available at suit play. The likelihood of gaining a long-suit trick is sufficient justification for postponing the trump lead, provided you lose nothing by so doing. But you should *postpone drawing trumps only when you have a clearly defined reason for doing so*, and only when that reason is something to your advantage.

The talk about "no-trump play" as applied to suit contracts need not disturb you. As long as you understand each hand, and perceive the principle demonstrated, whether the principle rightfully belongs in the category of no-trump or suit play is not at all an important question. The hands are grouped together here because they are in many ways similar in kind, and because it is felt that the reader is sufficiently advanced to understand them.

The warning about not always looking upon the Dummy as the secondary hand, however, should be heeded. Again the terms used need not be remembered. You merely view your prospects from the standpoint of the combined hands. If it ever seems advisable to make Dummy the Declarer, you must do so.

CHAPTER XVI

MISCELLANEOUS TRUMP PLAYS

THE principal situations in which trumps should be drawn immediately, or in which the trump lead should be postponed in order to secure some other advantage, have already been covered. The principles thus far laid down will take care of practically all the elementary trump situations that will occur in the average evening's play. But there remain certain specific situations which must be handled in a particular way. These are the subject of this chapter.

On an earlier page a certain kind of trump play was referred to as the *cross-ruff*. It was not illustrated at the time, because it was first necessary to impress on the reader the difference between ruffing in the Dummy and ruffing in Declarer's hand. As a general rule, it is not worth while to trump with Declarer's own hand, but with a certain type of hand this becomes not only advisable but necessary. The hand calling for the cross-ruff, as this mode of play is named, occurs with relative rarity, but when it does occur it is essential that the player recognize it.

THE CROSS-RUFF

The cross-ruff consists of refusing to lead trumps so that the trump holding in each hand can be cashed in independently by ruffing first with the one hand and then with the other. The following deal is a good example:

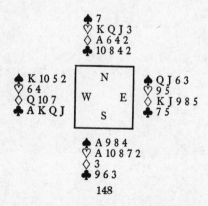

Your contract is four hearts. West opens the club King, continuing with the Queen, and then with the Jack, winning all 3 tricks. West now shifts to hearts, leading a trump, hoping by this lead to hamper your development of ruffing-tricks. You play a low heart from Dummy, letting this trick come around to your own hand, so that, if East plays the nine, you can win the trick with your Ten. The only high-card tricks you have, you now perceive (outside the trump suit), are the spade Ace and the diamond Ace. You also note that Dummy has only three trumps left to take care of the three losing spades in your own hand. Hence, not even one more round of trumps can be led.

The proper play at the fifth trick is for you to lead the spade Ace, and follow it with another spade which you ruff in Dummy. You now return the diamond Ace, and follow it with a low diamond which you ruff in your own hand. Next you lead a low spade, ruffing in Dummy, and then another diamond, which you ruff in your hand. You do this still once again, crossing from one hand to the other by means of ruffing—which explains why this play is called *cross-ruffing*. You have left at the thirteenth trick only the Ace of hearts, which drops the last two outstanding trumps. Thus you make the Ace of spades, the Ace and Ten of hearts, the Ace of diamonds, 3 ruffing-tricks in spades (with Dummy's King-Queen-Jack of trumps) and 3 ruffing-tricks in diamonds (with your own eight-seven-deuce). Note that after you ruff with your own deuce of hearts, all your trumps are higher than the two outstanding, which means that you are never in any danger of being over-ruffed.

Frequently, in playing the cross-ruff, it is necessary to trump with low cards and run the risk of losing to some higher trump held adversely. Many players, faced with this threat, are prone to trump with the highest trumps they hold, but this is not a good idea at all, for it succeeds only in postponing the inevitable. If you are going to play a hand by cross-ruffing, you must follow it through. If you refuse to take chances in the earlier stages, you will eventually reach a point where the only outstanding trumps will be higher than any you have left. You will then be in the predicament of having used up your high trumps unnecessarily, and your remaining low trumps will be over-ruffed. A suit which has gone around only once or twice may be safely ruffed, as a rule, with a low trump, but a suit which has gone

around three or four times stands no chance whatever of being controlled by low trumps against outstanding higher ones.

High-Card Tricks in the "Other" Suit

In hands which require cross-ruffing, two suits are being utilized for
ruffing purposes, and of course the trump suit is utilized also. The
"other" or fourth suit must not be ignored, for it may contain high-
card tricks. If the cross-ruff is begun early in the hand, the trumps
in Declarer's and Dummy's hands will rapidly be reduced, while the
Opponents (unable to over-ruff) still have some trumps left. Since
they do not over-ruff, the Opponents will have had some opportunity, as a rule, to make some discards, and they will probably discard that fourth suit in which you have high-card tricks. What will
happen then is that when you come to cash in those tricks in your
"other" suit, the Opponents will intrude with *their* developed ruffing-
tricks.

The way to avoid losing high-card tricks in the fourth suit, in a hand
which requires cross-ruffing, is to take them before the Opponents
have any chance to discard their losers in that suit. The following
deal, which is a rearrangement of the preceding example, shows what
is meant:

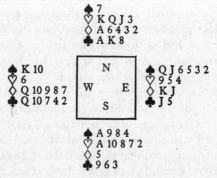

Against your contract of six hearts, this time West opens a diamond, which you win with Dummy's Ace. You find yourself considering a choice of plays. You can undertake to cross-ruff the
hand, or you can try to establish a long-suit trick in diamonds,
meanwhile drawing trumps. Surely the cross-ruff is preferable, for
you might easily fail to set up that long diamond, and, further, if it

should require three leads to draw trumps, you would have available no alternate play if the diamond trick did not materialize. In fact, the cross-ruff may actually develop more tricks as you can dispose of all your spades by this means.

Should the cross-ruff be started without delay? No, for to do so will give the Opponents a good chance to make discards—and they will probably throw off their clubs, since they can see your Ace-King commanding the suit in the Dummy. If this happens, you will probably find yourself at the end of the hand with your Ace and King of clubs struck down by adverse trumps.

Your first act, therefore, is to lead out your Ace and King of clubs before you do anything else. Both win, and you then lead one round of trumps, winning with Dummy's Jack. You can afford to do this, for you need only three trumps in the Dummy for ruffing spades. Proceeding with your cross-ruff, you trump spades in the Dummy and lead diamonds to ruff in your own hand. It now makes very little difference to you what cards the Opponents play on these tricks.

What a difference if you start the cross-ruff before leading clubs! East, with only two diamonds to start with, would discard a club on the third round of diamonds. This would automatically hold you to 1 club trick, as East could then ruff the second round. If by any chance you lead a fourth round of diamonds, East could discard his other club, holding you to no club tricks at all.

Like all other principles in Bridge, even this one can be carried to extremes. It is playing with dynamite to try to cash in as many as 3 tricks in a side suit before starting your cross-ruff. The third round of the side suit gives the Opponents the break they are always looking for, and they are likely to trump in and spoil the effectiveness of your cross-ruff by slapping a trump lead into the proceedings. It is consequently better, as a rule, to content yourself with two leads in a side suit—always provided, naturally, that the cross-ruff itself promises enough tricks to complete your contract. If the three rounds of a side suit offer the only likely way of making your contract, you have no choice but to be bold and try to make them.

Sacrificing a Principle to Efficiency

It has been stated that when the Opponents have left only one trump and that is high, it is costly to draw it if by doing so you must sacrifice two of yours—one from each hand.   It is better, you recall, to try to force the play of this outstanding high trump by leading a suit which will induce the Opponent to ruff with it.

An important exception to this rule occurs when the Declarer holds a strong side suit in a hand which lacks re-entries.   The principle must then be sacrificed for the greater efficiency of doing otherwise, and the high trump driven out.   The following deal shows this:

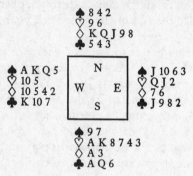

```
                    ♠ 8 4 2
                    ♡ 9 6
                    ◇ K Q J 9 8
                    ♣ 5 4 3
          ♠ A K Q 5    ┌─────┐   ♠ J 10 6 3
          ♡ 10 5       │  N  │   ♡ Q J 2
          ◇ 10 5 4 2   │W   E│   ◇ 7 6
          ♣ K 10 7     │  S  │   ♣ J 9 8 2
                       └─────┘
                    ♠ 9 7
                    ♡ A K 8 7 4 3
                    ◇ A 3
                    ♣ A Q 6
```

Your contract is four hearts.   West's opening lead is the spade King, which he follows with the Queen and then the Ace.   You trump the Ace in your own hand, thus reducing your trumps to five.   It is at once apparent that Dummy offers no ruffing power, but the diamond suit is unquestionably already established.   The best thing to do is to lead out the hearts (trumps), and then run off the diamonds, discarding clubs on the good diamonds when your hand has no more of the latter.   The club finesse need never be taken.

When you lay down the Ace and King of hearts, it pleases you to see both Opponents follow suit on both rounds.   This leaves but one trump outstanding—the Queen, which is high.   On this hand, if you follow the rule to let this Queen alone, on the assumption that it can never be worth more than 1 trick, you will never be able to make your contract.   Proceeding along these lines, you would lead the Ace and the trey of diamonds, and then a third round from the Dummy, which East would ruff.   You would discard a club from your hand on that same third round, but you would still hold a losing club which you could never dispose of.   The Dummy would be shut out of further play, with the two last diamonds as inaccessible as money in a closed bank.

Yet you can easily avoid this predicament. All you have to do is lead a third round of hearts, letting East win with his Queen. Then whatever East leads, you would still be able to take a trump trick, a club trick and 5 *uninterrupted* diamond tricks. By sacrificing one of your trumps to the high one held adversely (you would willingly sacrifice two, if necessary), you would secure a clear title to the rest of the hand.

This play would be unnecessary, of course, if the club Ace were in the Dummy instead of in your own hand. You would then simply lead all your diamonds until East ruffed, for you could use the club Ace to re-enter the Dummy. It would also not be necessary to draw that Queen if Dummy held one more trump originally, provided this trump would serve for an entry after East's diamond ruff.

ANOTHER EXCEPTION TO THE RULE

It was further stated, you remember, that when only two trumps are left outstanding, and both are high, an attempt should be made by the Declarer to drop both of them on one more trump lead—inducing them to fall together. This is not always the best play. Sometimes the danger involved is so great that it must be avoided, for if the Opponents are allowed to have the lead too many times, they may be able to run off their own established suit without interference. If you can still make your contract, you must permit the Opponents to take both of their trumps, not caring even whether they are divided or not. Again you must put *the making of your contract above all*.

The following deal brings out this exception to the rule:

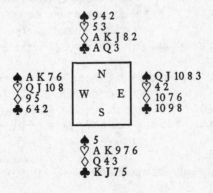

You are playing a contract of four hearts. West's opening lead is the spade King. He follows on the second trick with the spade Ace, which you trump in your own hand. You have left six trumps in your two hands, and the Opponents also have six. When you lead out the Ace and King, the Opponents follow both times. This means that you have two trumps left, and the Opponents also have two—but the pair held by the Opponents are both higher than yours.

Now if you lead a third heart, and the outstanding Queen and Jack are divided, you will drop them both and be left free to take the rest of the tricks, for you have all the top cards in diamonds and clubs and you will still have a heart to stem the run of the adverse spades. But suppose the Queen and Jack of trumps are not divided. If they are in one hand, the Opponent who holds them will certainly lead the second as soon as he wins with the first, eliminating trumps altogether. You then have no protection against spades, and you will have to throw away some of your good diamonds or clubs.

To lead another trump in the hope of dropping the last two high ones on the same trick is nothing but madness on this hand. You have already lost 1 trick, and you can afford to lose 2 more. All you have to do is to lead diamonds until at last West ruffs. This puts you one time unit ahead, for you have two trumps left to the Opponents' one. If West now leads a spade, forcing you to ruff, you continue with the rest of your diamonds and clubs until West ruffs again. As soon as this happens, the rest of the tricks are yours.

Successful as your play was on the example given, it might conceivably have lost a trick. If the hearts had been adversely divided 3-3 instead of 4-2, you could have made 11 tricks very easily instead of only 10. But why risk the success of your contract for a nebulous extra trick? The way you played, your contract was never in jeopardy. The loss of an extra trick is insignificant against the loss of a game contract.

Perhaps you say, "Well, what if the contract was five hearts?" Ah, this puts a different complexion on things. You have a chance of making your contract by trying to drop the Queen and Jack of trumps on the same trick. You also risk being set 4 tricks. It is entirely a question of how good a gambler you are. If the contract is not doubled, and your side is not vulnerable, the chance should be taken, for you can lose only 200 points at most. But if the contract is doubled and your side is vulnerable, the chance should not be taken, for you are running the risk of losing 1400 points—certainly not worth pitting against the five hearts bid and made, which you are gambling to make. It is much better to be discreet (doubled and vulnerable), and accept the set of 1 trick—which you can be sure will be no worse if you let the Opponents ruff with Queen and Jack separately— which is only 200 points. Doubled and not vulnerable, or not doubled and vulnerable, the gamble is at about even odds, and de- pends on the player's temperament. Choices of this kind frequently arise, and the best way to play is always determined by considering what you stand to lose if your procedure fails to work.

PLAYING A HOPELESS TRUMP CONTRACT

In all the example deals thus far analyzed, you have been presented automatically with fairly strong trump holdings. In actual play, you will not always be so lucky. The best players will now and then bid rashly and find themselves suddenly plunged into rather weird contracts, considering their holdings. Mr. Oswald Jacoby, one of the world's great Contract Bridge players, often boasts that he is the most expert player of hopeless contracts on earth. Anyone who has ever seen him play a hopeless hand will agree that he has considerable right to make such a boast. But the fact that he can make the boast is clearly an indication that even he must get into hopeless contracts occasionally, and if Mr. Jacoby can, you can—and will.

The following deal is certainly an example of a hopeless contract if there ever was one:

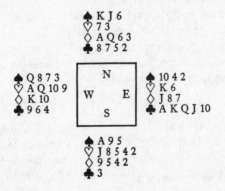

```
                ♠ K J 6
                ♡ 7 3
                ◇ A Q 6 3
                ♣ 8 7 5 2
                  ┌─────────┐
♠ Q 8 7 3         │    N    │    ♠ 10 4 2
♡ A Q 10 9        │         │    ♡ K 6
◇ K 10          W │         │ E  ◇ J 8 7
♣ 9 6 4           │    S    │    ♣ A K Q J 10
                  └─────────┘
                ♠ A 9 5
                ♡ J 8 5 4 2
                ◇ 9 5 4 2
                ♣ 3
```

Suppose you are South and that you must try to make a contract of three hearts; we need not discuss how you ever got into such a contract. West's opening lead is the nine of clubs, which East wins and continues the suit—but you ruff the second round with your deuce of hearts. It can take only a moment to tell you that your contract is indeed hopeless. All you can attempt to do is to hold your loss down to as few tricks as possible.

Only a madman would try to draw trumps here. If you start it, your Opponents will gladly lead them for you, and will then satisfy their appetite for slaughter by running off 3 more club tricks. Never were desperate measures more urgently required. It is barely possible that your Opponents will not discover the woeful weakness of your trump holding until it is too late to do much about it.

At the third trick, therefore, you lead a low spade and nonchalantly finesse the Jack. When, to your surprise (which you do not reveal), this holds, you come back to the spade Ace in your own hand. Another spade puts you in the Dummy with the King. These three rounds hold, and you have won 4 tricks. You now speculate as to whether one of those silly-looking small trumps in your hand might not take another trick. You therefore lead a club and ruff—and it holds. Luck is with you. Quickly you lead a diamond and finesse Dummy's Queen. Then you cash in your diamond Ace—and stop to get your breath. After all, out of this mess of rubbish you have managed to eke 7 tricks. It is difficult to see how you can make any more, but you must keep on playing. You lead a low diamond, throwing the lead to East—and the story is ended. You are down 2 tricks. Still, it looked much worse at first glance!

This hand teaches little, except that it is but another instance when trumps should not be drawn immediately. The reason for inserting it at this point is to lend contrast to the following deal, which shows a situation in which many players would hesitate to lead trumps because of the weakness of the suit.

LEADING TRUMPS WITH A WEAK SUIT

In the following deal (contract four hearts) trumps must be led even though the Declarer holds but seven trumps against the Opponents' six, and the six adverse trumps include the Ace, King, Queen, Ten, and nine-spot!

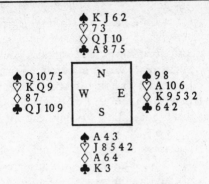

Again it is hard to see how North and South reach a contract of four hearts, but that is not pertinent here. In spite of the tremendous trump strength in top cards against you, if you are South you must lead trumps because this offers your only chance of making anywhere near 10 tricks. If you fail to lead trumps, the time will come when the Opponents will start ruthless ruffing. As soon as they find that they are both out of certain suits, they will start trumping everything in sight. This means that they will make their trumps separately rather than together, and consequently will pile up just that many more tricks against you.

West opens the club Queen, which you win with your King. You can see that your trump suit is as weak as water, and you would welcome something to brace you up. Your chief solace lies in the fact that your other suits contain several tenaces. If you play around with them a bit (you say to yourself), you may be able to wangle a few tricks before the Opponents can trump in. Your first thought, then, is to take a spade finesse by leading low toward the Jack in Dummy. But this would be a mistake!

There is one loophole by which you may escape from the Waterloo that is marked down in the cards for you. Look for a moment and try to spot this way out. It is a chance, and some chance is always better than none. If you see this means of escape you must attempt it at all costs.

Think, first, that the Opponents' six trumps may be divided 3-3. If they are, their imposing rank is of less consequence. Three generals are worth no more than one private if they stand in a line to be shot! What is equally consoling is the fact that every time an Opponent takes a trump trick he must lead something back which may produce a trick from one of your tenace positions. Certainly one trump lead can do no great harm, and suppose you try it and see.

Leading a low heart from your own hand,* you watch West play, let us say, the nine-spot, which holds the trick. He returns the club Jack, which you win with Dummy's Ace, establishing the suit for the Opponents. But this is not so bad, for eight clubs have been played, and Dummy still has two. Now you may as well try one more round of hearts. This time East plays the Ten and West wins with the Queen. Well, well! The outstanding trumps are now much less formidable—in fact, they are only two, Ace and King. If they are divided, and the Ace kills partner's King—but you will soon learn. A third round of clubs now comes upon you, which you ruff. Both Opponents follow, leaving only one club out. Having two trumps left, you bang down another one (even if the trump Ace-King are not divided, you can bear up under the loss of a trick to that one outstanding club), and—the trump top honors fall together.

East is in the lead, but it makes no difference what card he leads. Indeed, it does not matter which Opponent leads, or what he leads. If it is a club, you can ruff with your last trump. And West has the spade Queen, which means that your spade finesse will win, and East has the diamond King, which means that your diamond finesse also wins. Thus, by making the best of a bad situation, you tally your 10 tricks, four hearts—and the better to make it sound when you tell it to your friends, let us hope that the contract, this once, was doubled and redoubled!

SUMMARY

There is little to be said in the summary of this chapter. You should be sure, of course, that you understand cross-ruffing, and realize the necessity of cashing in a side suit before allowing the Opponents to get in some discards while you are occupied with your cross-ruff.

The other example hands, like many of those which follow, illustrate situations which tend to clarify what is, after all, a highly complex subject. No two Bridge hands are exactly alike, and these little analyses of what may seem to be minor bits of strategy will all prove of value in your playing experience.

---

* The compulsion to lead from the weaker holding toward the stronger need not embarrass you here, for neither hand is of sufficient strength to warrant more than a split second's consideration.

CHAPTER XVII

ELEMENTARY DEFENSE AGAINST NO-TRUMP

T HE preceding chapters have given the first essentials of play by the Declarer, both at no-trump and at a suit contract. Every situation could not be covered, for the very good reason that Declarer's play is governed, to a very large extent, by what the Opponents do. Therefore, before taking up the more complex aspects of the play of the hand, we must turn for a bit to the Defending Partnership, not only to teach the reader how to defend against an adverse Declarer, but also to teach him to understand, when Declarer, what his Opponents may be up to.

Most expert players agree that defensive play is the most difficult phase of Contract Bridge. Bidding can become pretty well standardized between any pair of players, and even two players who have no common bidding system can generally coördinate their ideas of bidding to such an extent that they will have some notion of what each is doing. The play of the Declarer is comparatively simple, for he always manipulates half the cards in the deck (twenty-six in all, his own hand and Dummy's), all of which he can see. Generally there is nothing to prevent the Declarer from making the maximum number of tricks his hands afford, except, of course, lack of knowledge, or possibly the complexity of a hand which offers more than one likely method of play.

The player on the Defending Side has no such advantage. He can see his own thirteen cards, and he can also see the Dummy's thirteen cards. But the only cards he can play as he chooses are his own thirteen, and he cannot see his Partner's hand at all. Even though the sight of the Dummy does help each defending player, it cannot ever be of as much help to the Defending Side as to the Declarer (the Attacking Side).

Of course, the auction, with its opportunity for each player to make a bid, provides some information as to partnership holdings. It is quite possible that the players who find themselves defending against an adverse contract have made one or more bids during the auction preceding the play. By bidding honestly a player can very often give his Partner clues to his holding which will prove of great value in the subsequent play. Even a pass (the absence of a bid) can imply the negative information that sufficient strength for a bid was not held. The distribution may also be indicated by the bids of a partnership. From the partnership bidding, and from the inferences which must also be drawn from the Opponents' bidding, certain ideas may be logically arrived at before the play starts. The inferences to be drawn from the bidding, of course, depend very largely upon what bidding system the players are using,* and how closely they stick to its principles, and how well they apply those principles. It is assumed that the reader is already using some bidding system. Discussion of this phase of the game is not within the scope of this book.

After the auction has ended, the player at the left of the Declarer makes the first or opening lead. He will naturally select a card which seems to him to be of some advantage to his side. From the opening lead, then, all the other players may draw certain inferences also, which tell something about the leader's hand. In fact, every subsequent lead during the play, and to a great extent every card played, tells its own story. If two rounds of spades have been played, and everyone has followed suit, the good player knows that eight spades have gone—two from each player's hand, and he has noted which two each player played. From this, and from other inferences he has drawn as to high-card holdings and distribution, he may have a fairly good notion where the other five spades (such as he does not hold himself and are not in the Dummy) are located.

Still more information can be conveyed by the fall of the cards. Certain conventions** of leads, and to some extent of plays, particularly discards, are now in fairly general use by all good players. Some of these have come down from the days of Whist, which was a card game in which all four hands were concealed, so that no player had any more idea of his Partner's hand than what he could deduce from the fall of the cards. Indeed, in Whist there was no bidding, so that

---

* It should be made known to all the players at a table what system of bidding each player is using. In tournament play, only recognized bidding systems and conventions may be used, unless the individual variation, if any, can be simply explained in a very few words before the game begins.

** A *convention*, whether of bidding, leading, or playing, is a generally understood agreement with respect to the *meaning* of the bid, lead, or play, respectively. The convention, to be ethical, must be a known one.

the play of each deal started entirely in the dark (except that the Dealer's last card was turned up, or exposed, to indicate the trump suit, and this one card became known to all the players). The value of signals* in the play can thus be well understood, and the best of these signals have been carried on into Contract Bridge, with a few new ones which have come about as a natural development of the modern game.

When a player has a choice of cards to play, therefore, he must bear in mind not only the advantage to himself, but what his Partner may infer from the card he chooses. No player can afford to play his cards in haphazard fashion. If you play carelessly, your Partner may deduce something about your hand which is not true. Of course, the Declarer may play as he wishes, for he manipulates the Dummy himself and is not therefore able to deceive his "Partner," but we are speaking now of defensive play. The information that can be conveyed by leads and discards is, after all, limited, so you must always make the most of whatever opportunity you have.

But, you may say, if we play in such a way that our Partner learns something about our hand, and if that signal is known and understood by the Declarer too, will it not "give away" our hand to the Declarer? True, but you must also remember that your partner may be in a better position to interpret your signal than is the Declarer, and also that even if the Declarer interprets the signal correctly, it may be of far more value to your Partner than to the Declarer. In fact, to the Declarer it may often be the handwriting on the wall, telling him that he is about to be defeated unless your Partner is as blind as a bat. If, when you become more expert, you are able to satisfy yourself that to signal your partner will give valuable information to the Declarer, you may then—and not until then—modify your play on a particular hand. But never forget that whenever you undertake to mislead the Declarer, you run the risk of misleading your partner also.

---

* By "signals" the use of well-understood playing conventions is meant. The signal is made entirely by the denomination of the card played, and not by any special manner of playing it or by any gesture of the player himself. Any signal other than the denomination of the card, or any private understanding whatever between partners, is unethical and is absolutely taboo among all Bridge players worthy of the name, who spurn the use of any language other than the language of bidding and the legitimate language of the cards. A good Bridge player who plays the game for the intellectual enjoyment he gets out of it would not think of marring his pleasure by using any unethical tools.

Opening Leads Against No-trump

First, let it be understood that for the time being, in setting forth the elementary principles of making the opening lead, we are going to assume that every lead is made "blind"—that is, we are going to ignore the bidding so far as our own partnership is concerned. You have entered upon the play of each hand without you or your partner having made any sort of bid (except a pass). In other words, you know nothing about your partner's hand beyond the fact that he never made a bid.

The object of the Defending Side, incidentally, is the same as the object of the Declarer—to win as many tricks as possible. If the tricks won are sufficient in number to defeat the Declarer's contract, so much the better, but even if the adverse contract is not defeated, every trick won by the Defending Side means that *that* trick at least cannot be scored by the Declarer as an extra trick. In other words, every trick won defensively represents a certain number of points, either saved from being scored by the Declarer, or scored by the Defending Side in penalties.

Now, the Defending Side has no time to lose in developing tricks, for the Declarer already has the advantage of manipulating twenty-six cards visible to him. The moment the Declarer gains full control of the hand, he will make his contract without more ado, and perhaps extra tricks as well. It behooves the Defending Side, then, to get busy right from the start, and there can be no better beginning than the opening lead.

The better to understand the situation, review for a moment how Declarer goes about making a no-trump contract. He first endeavors to establish a long suit—as soon as he gets the lead, of course. He will let the Defending Side win tricks, perhaps, but he will always be endeavoring to line up enough tricks to make his contract, and as soon as he does that, he will cash them in.

The Defending Side at no-trump, then, should do precisely the same thing—try to establish *their* long suit. The trouble is that the Defending Side cannot be sure what is their best suit. The longest suit of one defending player may be the shortest suit in his Partner's hand. When neither Partner has made a bid, the choice of the suit to develop depends entirely on the player's own hand until he hears from his Partner by means of the cards Partner plays on his leads.

You also remember from the principles of Declarer's play that certain tenace combinations, such as holdings headed by Ace-Queen, King-Jack, and the like, are worth more tricks when led up to than when led away from. This is just as true of a hand in a defending position. Therefore, it is often unwise to lead from such tenaces, and better to wait until the suit is led by Partner or by Declarer, if you are to make the most of such holdings.

Generally speaking, there are four types of leads against no-trump, namely, the honor-sequence length lead, the plain length lead, the short-suit sequence lead, and the desperation short-suit lead.

The Honor-Sequence Length Lead:

When holding four cards or more of a suit headed by three honors in sequence, or by two honors in sequence and the third card not more than one step lower, the top card (except when it is the Ace) should always be led.* Partner may then readily infer that you hold the next two lower cards in the suit, or the next lower card and the third not more than one rank lower. If you lead anything but the top card from such a sequence, Partner will be more or less in the dark about your holding in that suit. The top card, if consistently led, will give Partner definite information right away. For example, in the following suit holdings the underlined card should be led:

$$♠ \underline{K} Q J 3 2$$
$$♡ \underline{Q} J 10 3 2$$
$$◇ \underline{J} 10 9 3 2$$
$$♣ \underline{K} Q 10 3 2$$
$$♠ \underline{Q} J 9 3 2$$
$$♡ \underline{J} 10 8 3 2$$

Note that in every one of these holdings, the *top card* is led. The first three holdings show three honors in sequence, or three cards at the head of the suit in sequence. The second three show three cards almost in sequence—the top two in sequence, but the third one rank below. Remember this lead, for it is one of the best leads against no-trump: the highest card from a sequence of three cards, or the highest card from a sequence of two cards if the third card is not more than one step lower.

---

* In the present discussion, "lead" must always be taken to mean "opening lead," and any reference to leading is meant to apply to the first lead of the deal.

Do you see why these leads are the best choice against no-trump? First of all, the lead of the top of a sequence attacks the suit without delay, forcing out a higher card held by the Declarer if he wishes to win the trick, and thereby is effective in establishing the suit. The King from King-Queen-Jack is the only lead required to set up the suit immediately. From a suit headed by Queen-Jack-Ten, two leads are theoretically required, but Partner will now and then hold one of the missing honors. The lead of the Jack from Jack-Ten-nine is perhaps not quite so promising as the others, but it starts the definite establishment of tricks in a suit of five or more cards. Do not overlook the fact that your position as the first leader gives you automatically one time unit advantage over the Declarer.

To lead the King from a suit headed by King-Queen-Ten establishes that suit at once when Partner holds the Jack. Similarly, to lead the Queen from Queen-Jack-nine establishes the suit when Partner holds the King. By leading the Jack from a five-card suit headed by Jack-Ten-eight, you may start the ball rolling in plenty of time to get some long-suit tricks if Partner holds even King-nine or Queen-nine.

The following suit combinations also belong in this category, and are known as *intermediate* sequence leads. In each holding, the underlined card should be led—the top of an *inner* sequence:

$$\spadesuit \ A \ Q \ J \ 5 \ 4$$
$$\heartsuit \ A \ \underline{J} \ 10 \ 5 \ 4$$
$$\diamondsuit \ A \ \underline{10} \ 9 \ 5 \ 4$$
$$\clubsuit \ K \ \underline{J} \ 10 \ 5 \ 4$$
$$\spadesuit \ K \ \underline{10} \ 9 \ 5 \ 4$$
$$\heartsuit \ Q \ \underline{10} \ 9 \ 5 \ 4$$

Any other honor combination requires different treatment. A holding of A 9 8 3 2 or of Q J 8 3 2, for example, requires the lead of a low card rather than a high card, and comes under the classification of a length lead.

The Plain Length Lead:

Roughly speaking, the lead of a low card from a suit of four or more cards is the second most advantageous opening lead against no-trump. The reason is, again, that it is the second most likely lead to develop into establishing 1 or more tricks in the suit.   For example, if you hold ♣ Q J 8 3 2, and lead a low card, the suit is established at once if Partner plays the King, forcing Declarer's Ace.   Even with a combination of cards not quite so strong as that just given, you have a chance of finding the Declarer with no more than two stoppers in that suit, which means that the suit must be set up eventually.

All length leads, needless to say, are not made with any definite hope of profit.   Yet such a lead may be the *best* hope that the hand affords, even if it is from a suit as weak as ◇ 10 7 6 3.   And even that hope may occasionally materialize, as witness the following possible distribution of the suit:

◇ A 8 4

	N	
◇ 10 7 6 3	W E	◇ Q J 5
	S	

◇ K 9 2

Let us say you are West, leading against South's no-trump contract. It is clear that only two leads in diamonds are necessary to give your side 2 tricks.

In leading a low card from a long suit (four or more cards), the card selected should always be the *fourth best*, counting down from the top. This is of very great importance to your Partner, for, if you stick to this rule of leading the fourth best when you do not lead the top card of an honor sequence, you will enable him to apply what is called the Rule of Eleven (explained in the next chapter).   Even though the fourth best card is not the lowest card, you should lead it.   Any lead but the fourth best will upset Partner's count and may ruin his entire defense for the rest of the hand.   For example, from the following holdings lead the underlined card:

♠ Q J 8 3 2	◇ 10 7 6 3
♡ J 9 3 2	♣ Q 8 7 5 4 3 2

Leads From Ace-King Suits:

A suit headed by Ace-King presents one of the most difficult problems in defending against no-trump.   Some excellent players recommend the lead of the King first if the suit contains four or more cards; others recommend the lead of a low card even when such a suit contains six cards (provided the Queen and Jack are not also held). With Ace-King alone, or Ace-King and one small card, it is just as well, generally speaking, not to select the suit for the opening lead, for the simple reason that your shortness in the suit indicates that the Declarer may have length in it, and you will only aid him to set up his suit. Furthermore, these cards may prove to be valuable entries to your longer suit.

Consider the following Ace-King combinations:

1. ♠ A K Q 2   **2.** ♡ A K J 2   **3.** ◇ A K 10 9

With these combinations, whether of four cards or more, the King is generally the best opening lead. In No. 1 the advantage is obvious, for the Queen can be led to the second round, and control of the suit is retained. In No. 2, the King may be led so that if it subsequently develops that Partner can lead through Declarer's Queen, that advantage may be gained. In No. 3, the King is led to explore the suit, but the suit is to be discontinued if Declarer seems to hold the Queen, for then Partner's Jack can be led through and the Queen captured.

With practically all other combinations of four or more cards, of which the top two cards are the Ace and King, the best lead is usually a low card. The low card is sent out to reconnoiter, as it were, while you still have two sure stoppers in the suit. If Partner holds the Queen, the whole suit may be established at once.

In Ace-King suits the proper lead is never the top card of the sequence. This is the only exception to the rule that the top card of a sequence should be led. If you wonder how your Partner is going to tell from your King lead whether you hold the Queen or the Ace, since the King may be led from either sort of sequence, the answer is that your Partner probably cannot tell unless he holds the missing card himself. However, he should be satisfied with the information that you hold either the Ace or Queen, and he will know before long which one you have—or, if he cannot deduce it after a while, he is not the sort of player you will want for a Partner over any great length of time.

Continuation Honor Leads:

With honor combinations such as A K Q, K Q J, or Q J 10, the problem very often arises as to the proper procedure if your first card led holds the trick. For instance, which should you continue from A K Q after your King has won? As a rule, it pays to lead the card which gives Partner the maximum amount of information. In the A K Q instance, the Queen is the best continuation, because the lead of the Ace the second time fails to tell Partner anything about the location of the Queen, while the lead of the Queen informs Partner *definitely* (except under certain desperation circumstances) that the Ace is held.

The reason for the above is apparent when the same principle is applied to the lower honor combinations. With a holding of K Q J, for example, the King should be opened and the Jack continued. This card affirms the possession of the Queen. Similarly, from Q J 10, the opening of the Queen and continuance of the Ten shows the Jack.

Leading the Ace:

As a matter of sober fact, very few expert players ever lead the Ace of a suit as their opening lead against no-trump. This is so universal that it is almost safe to tell the beginner never to make an Ace his opening lead against any no-trump contract, for the Ace is a key card which the Declarer is always burning up to locate.

Occasionally, when revealing the location of the Ace cannot help the Declarer, the Ace may be the first lead. But such occasions are rare, for only some such holding as ♡ A K Q J 3 2 justifies leading the Ace to start with. With such a powerful six-card suit, you may as well lead the Ace and follow right down the line with the rest of the suit. Since you will take 6 tricks nine times out of ten, your lead makes little difference to anybody, but it is a fairly well-established convention to lead the Ace first with such a six-card suit, and also with ♠ A K Q 7 6 3 2 (a seven-card suit). The only advantage gained, incidentally, is a rather negligible one. In fact, it involves only a question of discarding. This will be discussed later.

Choosing Between Two Length Leads:

When you have a choice of opening leads, between two suits of some length, let us say, you should prefer the longer suit except when

the shorter suit offers an honor-sequence length lead. For example,
suppose you hold:

1.
♠ K J 8 6
♡ J 8 7 6 3
◇ Q 5
♣ 10 3

2.
♠ Q J 10 9
♡ Q 9 8 4 3
◇ Q 5
♣ 10 3

In No. 1, you have two long suits available—spades and hearts. The
six of hearts is a better opening lead than the six of spades, principally
because the heart suit is longer and may develop more tricks. But in
No. 2, the spade Queen is the better opening lead because it will develop tricks *more quickly* than a plain length lead in hearts (four-spot).
Sure developable tricks are better than doubtful developable tricks.

When the choice is between two honor-sequence length leads, the
decision is never difficult. When the suits are of the same length, the
stronger should be preferred; when the equally long suits are of the
same strength, the one should be chosen in which the fourth or fifth
card is the higher. When all cards in the two suits are exactly the
same, you might just as well toss a coin. There is little justification
for preferring a major suit to a minor.

When the choice is between two plain length leads, the decision is
more difficult. As a general thing, the *weaker* of two four-card suits
should be preferred, because this enables the stronger suit to be retained to furnish a possible entry, while the lead of the stronger suit
immediately would probably leave practically no hope of an entry at
all. For instance, if the choice is between ♠ A 10 3 2 and ♡ K 9 3 2,
the latter should be opened (the heart). If the choice is between
♡ K 10 6 4 and ◇ J 9 8 3, the latter should be opened (the diamond);
in fact, even if the choice is between ◇ Q 9 7 3 and ♠ 10 7 6 4, the
latter should still be opened in preference, for it will generally prove
more advantageous in the long run.

This principle of selection cannot be adhered to relentlessly. With
♣ Q 7 6 3 and ♡ 8 6 4 2, for example, the suit headed by the Queen
is the better one to open.

When the choice is between two five-card suits, the principle should
be reversed, and the stronger suit opened, because this offers more
chance of developing sufficient tricks to set the contract immediately.
As for two six-card suits there is no particular need to consider the

question, for with such a holding you are most likely to be the Declarer yourself!

Short-suit Sequence Leads:

The so-called short-suit sequence leads consist of the lead of the
top card of a sequence from a three-card or shorter suit.   This lead
has two objectives: (1) the hope that this particular suit will turn
out to be Partner's long suit and that he will be able to develop it
before the Declarer can establish his suit; and (2) the desire to avoid
leading from tenace combinations since to do so may give the Declarer tricks he would not otherwise make.   A typical hand calling
for such a lead is the following:

$$\spadesuit \ \text{K J 8 5}$$
$$\heartsuit \ \text{J 10 3}$$
$$\diamondsuit \ \text{Q 10 7 5}$$
$$\clubsuit \ \text{K J}$$

If the bidding has gone *one no-trump—two no-trump—three no-trump*
by the Opponents, any lead looks unattractive.   But, since you are
compelled to lead from this hand, the heart Jack is by far the best
choice.   It cannot really sacrifice a trick, and if partner should have
four hearts to the King-nine or Queen-nine (or better), the development of 2 heart tricks is in the offing.   Another lead may look better,
and on some distributions may be better, such as the five of diamonds,
but this runs a greater risk than the heart Jack as it may plunge right
into Declarer's holding of $\diamondsuit$ A K J.

The short-suit sequence lead can also be the top of such suit hold-
ings as $\heartsuit$ Q J 2, $\clubsuit$ 10 9 2 or even $\spadesuit$ Q J, $\diamondsuit$ J 10, or $\heartsuit$ 10 9.   A lead
from any King-Queen short suit is not recommended, for it is very
dangerous and loses a trick more often than not.   It is possible now
and then to open the King from three cards headed by Ace-King,
but it is almost always better to preserve this suit for entry purposes.
In fact, strictly speaking, a lead of this kind comes under the heading
of a desperation short-suit lead.

Short-suit Leads (Desperation):

The desperation short-suit lead is indicated when you have nothing
you care to develop, no entry cards, and very little hope of doing the

Declarer any damage. With such a barren hand, the top card of a doubleton or of a three-card worthless suit may blindly hit upon Partner's best suit now and then. For example, suppose you hold:

♠ 9 8 2
♡ 7 5 4
♢ 10 7 4 3
♣ J 8 6

It is obvious that a length lead in diamonds is hopeless, for even if your fourth diamond should become established, you will never get in the lead to use it. The best chance is to lead the nine of spades or the seven of hearts—and pray for luck. Most good players would select the nine of spades, feeling that a nine-spot is more likely to aid in developing Partner's suit than a seven-spot, and after all whether Partner's suit is spades or hearts is entirely a guess.

Do not confuse desperation short-suit leads with short-suit sequence leads. The latter are made *to avoid leading from tenaces;* the former are made *only when there is no hope.* For example, the following hand does not call for a short-suit lead:

♠ K 10 8 4
♡ 9 7
♢ Q 10 4 3
♣ K 6 2

Here the best lead is the diamond trey, with a gay hope of finding one or more diamond honors in Partner's hand. To lead the nine of hearts may get you into a spot where you will have to begin discarding very soon—before you have gained any inkling of what Partner may hold.

It is only fair to say that not all expert players agree with the preceding paragraphs. However, the author has found in his long tournament experience that short-suit opening leads very rarely pay any dividends when the leader holds one or two suits of his own which stand some chance of becoming established. It is true that the weaker you are in a suit, the stronger your Partner is likely to be. At the same time, Partner has to be very strong for a lead from such a suit as hearts, in the preceding example, to prove profitable. If the nine of hearts is to gain anything, your Partner must have ♡ K J 10 or ♡ Q J 10—a pretty long gamble. The diamond lead can easily gain an advantage if Partner holds as little as the Jack.

LEADING PARTNER'S SUIT

The preceding "blind" leads, made when Partner has made no bid, are listed approximately in the order of their value. This scale of values is based on average expectation; there is nothing mysterious about it at all. Any player will find that these leads work out in practice—over a large number of no-trump hands—just about as analyzed here.

We come now to the vastly different situation when Partner has made one or more bids. Assuming that the Opponents are playing the hand at three no-trump, if Partner has named a suit during the auction the Opening Leader's selection of a good lead becomes much more standardized.

When you hold four or more cards in the suit bid by Partner, you should lead the *fourth best* (counting down from the top). The importance of this will become apparent in the next chapter, when the Rule of Eleven is explained. Only one exception occurs to this rule, and that is when the suit is headed by some sort of sequence. In each of the following situations, the top card should be led.

    1. ◊ Q J 7 2   **2.** ◊ K Q 7 2   **3.** ◊ J 10 7 2

You will notice the disregard of the rule of holding a card only two steps below the lowest ranking honor. This is of no importance so long as your Partner has bid the suit. Combination honors or split honors require slightly different treatment.

When you hold only three cards of Partner's suit, and the top card is an honor higher than the Ten (such as the Ace, King, Queen, or Jack), *lead the lowest card.* * This may appear speculative, but you must consider that the Declarer, who sits on your right, may hold a potential double stopper in the suit which you can discount only by holding on to that honor in back of him. For example, consider the following heart distribution:

♡ 4 3

```
        N
♡ Q 8 6  W   E   ♡ A 10 9 7 5
        S
```

♡ K J 2

---

* This is the first time in 171 pages that modern practice differs at all from Watson's 1934 script. But it differs only in degree. It subscribes wholeheartedly to Watson's principle but goes a bit further. We therefore feel safe in postponing the description of the modern extensions to Chapter XII, Part II, one of those we have added.—S. F. Jr.

Declarer has what may become a double stopper in hearts. If you lead the Queen (as West), you automatically assure the Declarer of his double stopper, for he must then make 2 heart tricks no matter what happens. But if you open the six-spot, your Partner wins with the Ace and returns a low card. Since you play after the Declarer, his King-Jack is held to 1 trick.

With all holdings of three-cards headed by the Ten or lower,* and with all two-card holdings of Partner's suit, always lead *the highest card*. The reason for this is that it gives Partner a partial reading on the hand even though the lead itself may not be particularly constructive. If such a lead is the Ten or lower, Partner knows that you have three cards or fewer; if the lead is an honor, he knows that it must be from a sequence containing four cards or more, or that it indicates only a doubleton—and he can tell which very soon after he sees the Dummy and looks again at his own hand.

In choosing the proper card to lead from combinations containing two honors, the same general rules apply. The top of two touching honors should always be led, such as the King from K Q 3 or the Queen from Q J 3. With K 10 3, Q 10 3, etc., the question is very close. As a rule, however, the low card is preferable.

Choosing Between Your Own Suit and Partner's

You may occasionally hold a hand from which Partner's suit does not appear to be the best lead, particularly if Partner has bid his suit only once. The decision must depend on which suit seems likely to develop the most tricks *the most quickly*. You may take it as a safe rule that you should always lead Partner's suit when you hold four or more cards, or when you hold three cards headed by an honor, in that suit. With less than this, you should prefer to make an honor-sequence length lead of a King or a Queen in some other suit. The top card of three little ones of Partner's suit should be preferred to the lead of Jack from Jack-Ten in some other suit, and should also be preferred to almost any other length lead. If you have only a doubleton or singleton in partner's suit—well, a point is now reached when so many other factors, psychological and otherwise, enter into the situation that it is best, temporarily, to duck the subject.

In conclusion, for the time being, it can only be said that this dis-

---

* See footnote at bottom of previous page.

cussion of leads has been kept on a general footing, but as you learn more about defensive play the matter of opening leads will tend to become clearer, in one sense, and will become more complex, in another sense, for you will discover why even expert players are very frequently baffled when it comes to selecting the best possible opening lead. No one is clairvoyant, after all, and, if one were, the game of Contract Bridge would lose its element of variety which is its greatest charm.

SUMMARY

In summarizing opening leads against no-trump, it seems best to make a somewhat arbitrary list, in the order of preference, of the choices the leader is likely to be confronted with. The following tabulation of the more common type of leads should guide the beginner until he knows that some other lead is better under the particular circumstances.

When Partner has not bid—

1. The highest card from four or more cards headed by a sequence of three cards (except when the top card is the Ace). (K Q J 2)

2. Same as No. 1 if the sequence consists of two cards with the third not more than one step lower. (Q J 9 8)

3. The top card of an inner sequence of two or more cards, from a suit of five or more cards, when there is a skip between the sequence and the top card. (K J 10 3 2)

4. Fourth best from four or more cards not headed by an honor sequence.

5. The top of a two-card sequence (if an honor) from a three-card suit.

6. The top card of a worthless three-card suit or a doubleton.

When Partner has bid a suit—

1. From four or more cards, fourth best—unless an honor sequence of two or more cards heads the suit, when the top honor should be led.

2. From three cards, the lowest card if the top card is an honor higher than the Ten, but the highest card otherwise.

3. From two cards, the highest card always.

4. A singleton—more often than not a suit of your own is chosen.

CHAPTER XVIII

THIRD HAND DEFENSE AGAINST NO-TRUMP

T HE fact that opening leads against no-trump occupied the entire preceding chapter does not mean that the opening lead is the most important feature of defensive play; in fact, the chief purpose in devoting so much space to the subject was to emphasize the importance of certain conventional leads so that Partner will always know, within limits, what he has a right to expect of the leader's hand. Without this groundwork it would be impossible to continue the discussion of defensive play with anything like clarity.

We come now to the player known as Third Hand—the Partner of the Opening Leader. We are going to consider what takes place in his mind when he sees the opening lead and the Dummy's hand go down on the table. For the moment we will assume that the only information he can derive comes from his own hand, the cards in the Dummy, and inferences drawn from Partner's opening lead. The contents of his own hand and the Dummy are obvious. Deductions to be made from the opening lead require some study.

The most likely opening lead Third Hand will have to consider is a low card. Those fine honor combinations mentioned in the preceding chapter are but seldom held, and it is also true that Partner's hand will rarely be so impoverished that he will have to resort to a short-suit desperation lead. By far the greater part of the time his lead will be the fourth-best card from some long suit headed by one or two honors at the most.

Put yourself now in the position of the Third Hand. Looking upon your Partner's low-card lead as probably the fourth-best card from a suit of four cards or more, your first thought should be to help your Partner to establish that suit. You must deliberately sacrifice your own high cards in that suit, knowing that, as you do so, you are promoting your Partner's cards. In playing your high cards you seek to drive out whatever stoppers the Declarer may have in his own hand or in the Dummy. If you succeed, you will enable your Partner, at some later time, to cash in his established low cards in the suit and perhaps keep the Declarer from making his contract. This principle of playing your highest card on Partner's lead goes by a very old

name or slogan which you probably have heard, namely, "Third
Hand high."* This means that in playing to a trick as the third
player, you should always play your highest card of the suit led. The
rule is by no means absolute, however, as will be seen in a moment
when we discuss it more fully.

The Rule of Eleven

Assuming that Partner's low-card lead is the fourth best of his suit
you can apply what is known as the "Rule of Eleven," which has been
in use by card players since the days of Whist. The rule gets its
name from its arithmetical operation, which is simply this: if you
deduct from 11 the number of pips or spots on the card led, the remainder is the number of cards higher than the card led which are
held by yourself, Dummy, and Declarer together. That is, if Partner leads a five-spot, you deduct 5 from 11, and you know that only
6 cards higher than the five-spot are to be found outside the leader's
hand. The following diagram shows how the rule works:

♠ Q 10 4

Lead ♠ 6   N W E S   ♠ K 9 5

You are East, and your partner leads the spade six. You deduct
6 from 11, which tells you that five cards higher than the six are held
by North, South and East. Of these five higher cards, you yourself
(East) hold two, and Dummy (North) holds two more. That means
that you know the location of four of the five cards outstanding higher
than the card led (King, Queen, Ten, and nine). Where is the other
one? It has to be in the Declarer's hand. In other words, of all the
cards higher than the six which you cannot see, the Declarer holds
but one, and Partner holds the rest (you know, of course, that if
Partner's lead is fourth best, he must hold *three* cards higher than his
lead).

The value of this formula—the Rule of Eleven—now becomes ap-

* Originating from an old Whist maxim glibly set forth as "Second Hand low, Third
Hand high," but nowadays more often abused than properly respected. The subsequent analysis will throw much light on the efficacy of this principle of play, or, under
certain conditions, its disadvantages.

parent. With the particular distribution of spades in the diagram you know that the Ace, Jack, eight, and seven of spades are missing. If you had no way of telling where any of these might be, you would be up a tree to choose your play if Declarer plays the four from Dummy. But since you know that Declarer holds only one of these missing higher cards, you can play with much more confidence.

You thus see how the Rule of Eleven works. It is mathematically sound, provided Partner's lead is his fourth-best card, which you must usually assume unless or until you have reason to suppose otherwise. The mathematical reasoning underlying the rule is not important.*

Having found your first clue as to your Partner's holding in the suit he has led, you are ready to consider your play. It may safely be said that you should follow this rule 99 times out of 100: *Whenever Partner's opening lead against no-trump is obviously a plain length lead and your (Third Hand's) highest cards are not in sequence, you should play your highest if the Dummy has no more than three cards of which the highest is the Ten or lower.* It is understood that your "highest card" is better than the Ten, of course.

This may seem rather complicated, but it is really extremely simple. Suppose your Partner leads a card between the two-spot and the six-spot. If the Dummy goes down with a singleton, a doubleton, or a tripleton headed by no card above the Ten, you must play the Ace, King, Queen, or Jack, if you hold it and do not have the card directly below it—no matter what card is played from the Dummy. The following diagram is a simple illustration:

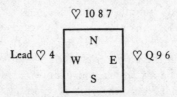

♡ 10 8 7

Lead ♡ 4   N W E S   ♡ Q 9 6

---

* Mr. R. F. Foster, a famous Whist and Bridge authority, claims to have first formulated the rule. Whether he did or not, the rule is so simple that, given the premise of the lead of fourth best, any arithmetician would be likely to derive the formula sooner or later. It is based on the fact that there are 13 cards in the suit of which, since he has led his fourth-best card, Partner holds three higher than his lead. Since three cards are accounted for, only 10 cards remain to be considered. Of these, only the card led and those ranking below it need be deducted to determine how many other cards there are higher than it. However, there is no one-spot (the

Partner leads the heart four, on which the seven is played from Dummy. You are East, and *you must play your Queen.*

What have you done? You first applied the Rule of Eleven. You subtracted 4 from 11, which left 7. You can see six cards in your own hand and the Dummy which are higher than the four-spot. You therefore know that the Declarer holds only one card higher than the four, which can be only the Ace, the King, the Jack or the five-spot. If Declarer has the Ace, you know your Partner holds King-Jack; if Declarer has the King, you know your Partner holds Ace-Jack; if Declarer has the Jack or the five-spot, you know your Partner holds Ace-King. In any one of these events, it is impossible for the Declarer to secure more than 1 trick in hearts if you play your Queen, and he can make 1 trick only if his higher card is the Ace or King—otherwise your play of the Queen will keep him from making any heart tricks at all. It is quite possible that your Partner is leading the fourth-best card from a suit headed by the Ace-King and he may have anywhere from four to six cards in the suit.

When Third Hand's "Highest" Is in Sequence With the Card Below It:

In the rule just given, it was specified that to play your highest card you must not have the card directly below it in rank. There was a reason for this. If you do have two or more high cards of Partner's led suit, and these are in sequence, you should not play the highest card, but the lowest card of the sequence. This is true for any number of cards in unbroken sequence at the top of the led suit. If you hold Ace-King, you play the King; if you hold King-Queen, you play the Queen; if you hold King-Queen-Jack, you play the Jack; if you hold K Q J 10, you play the Ten.

This rule holds true, as a matter of fact, throughout Third Hand's play, even after the first trick. It helps your Partner to read your hand during the later play. In playing Third Hand high, then, you

---

Ace being high), so 1 must be added to compensate for the non-existent lower card (or the same result may be accomplished by subtracting from 10 *one less* than the number of pips on the card led). Obviously, the number of pips on the card led accounts for its own rank and also the rank of all lower cards, so that to deduct its denomination from 11 gives the answer desired.

The rule may be explained another way. Deduct the denomination of the card led from 14, and you know how many cards in the suit are higher than it. Of these the leader holds three. Subtracting these, you have the same result as though you had deducted the denomination of the card led from 11 in the first place.

always select the *bottom* card of a sequence heading the led suit. Put another way, whenever you have cards of equal value so far as taking the trick is concerned, you *lead* the highest, but *play* the lowest. We will now explain this principle.

Why, in leading, should you choose the highest of a sequence, but in playing, the lowest? Perhaps the following diagram will make the reason clear:

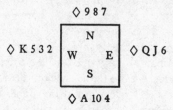

Your Partner, let us say, leads the diamond deuce against no-trump. The seven is played from Dummy. Sitting East, you blindly choose your highest card—the Queen. Now suppose Declarer wins with his Ace, and, later on in the hand, your Partner regains the lead. What does he know about the distribution of diamonds? Nothing whatever—beyond those he can see in his own hand and in the Dummy, plus the four that have been played. Anyone may have the Jack of diamonds; anyone may have the Ten. Partner's only high card is the King, now the commanding card of the suit. He will probably lead, therefore, some other suit.

Now suppose that, as East, you play the *Jack* (instead of the Queen) on the opening lead. Declarer wins with his Ace. Partner later regains the lead. Now what does he know about diamonds? He knows a great deal. He saw you play the Jack, and noticed that Declarer won with the *Ace*. Now if Declarer had held the Queen, wouldn't he have used it to win that trick, since the King was still outstanding? He certainly would have. Consequently since Declarer did not win with the Queen, your Partner knows that you have the Queen (obviously it is not in the Dummy). He can thus lead another low diamond with the knowledge that you will win the trick and return the suit, enabling him to take 2 more tricks with his King and five-spot.

This conventional play of the bottom card of a sequence is of the utmost importance. Never depart from it. Since your cards in sequence are of equal value, the card you play can make no difference to you, but it makes a vast difference to your Partner—so play the bottom one. This applies to any number of cards, no matter how many cards heading the suit are in sequence. If Partner leads low in a suit of which you hold K Q J 10 9, your proper play is the *nine-spot*, which, for trick-taking purposes, is every bit as good as the King. If you hold 9 8 7 3 2 in the suit Partner leads, and your play is to choose your highest card, you play the *seven-spot*, which ranks equally with the eight and nine.

When Not to Play "Third Hand High"

We now come to those instances in which you should not play, as Third Hand, the highest card you hold on Partner's lead. The first and most obvious instance occurs when the Dummy plays a card higher than any you hold. Then there is nothing to be gained by throwing a high card away, like flinging oneself under the wheels of the Juggernaut. The other situation involves what we may term "finessing around the Dummy," and occurs very often.

You have probably been told many times that you should *never finesse against your Partner*. If you understand this admonition, all well and good. But the chances are that you have been putting a false meaning into those words. Let us see.

Partner leads, and Dummy goes down with no card higher than the Ten in the suit led. The situation may be as follows:

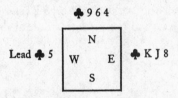

Partner having led the five-spot, it is foolish for East not to play his highest card—which is to say, his strongest forcing card, to drive out Declarer's Ace if he has it. It is senseless to play the Jack, figuring that Partner may hold the Queen. What if he does have the Queen? Your partnership holding of King-Queen-Jack represents three cards of equal trick-taking power, so it makes no difference which one is played on the first round of the suit. However, to play the Jack makes a great deal of difference if your Partner holds the Ace and *Declarer has the Queen.* By playing the Jack you present the Declarer with a trick he could not otherwise make.

In the situation just given, if East plays the Jack, he is really finessing against his Partner, for, in playing the Jack, he hopes that his Partner holds the Queen. Such a finessing attempt, as you have just seen, is no less than folly.

Now finessing against the Dummy is something entirely different. When you attempt this, you are really making a "sure-thing" sort of play. You are trying to win the trick as cheaply as possible, or, failing that, you hope to drive out one of the Declarer's high cards with as little expenditure of power as possible. The following diagram makes this clear:

♡ Q 7 3

```
             ┌───────┐
             │   N   │
Lead ♡ 4     │ W   E │   ♡ K J 10
             │   S   │
             └───────┘
```

Now if, on Partner's lead of the four, the trey is played from Dummy, you should see that to play the King is sheer lunacy. So far as this particular trick is concerned, the Queen is dead, for the hand holding it has played some other card. You therefore remember that you should play the bottom of your cards of equal value, and play the Ten, which will either win the trick or force Declarer's Ace.

The following three situations are less simple at first glance:

♡ Q 7 3   ♡ Q 7 3

```
              ┌───────┐                          ┌───────┐
              │   N   │                          │   N   │
1. Lead ♡ 4   │ W   E │  ♡ K 10 2    2. Lead ♡ 4 │ W   E │  ♡ K 9 2
              │   S   │                          │   S   │
              └───────┘                          └───────┘
```

♡ Q 7 3

```
                ┌───────┐
                │   N   │
3. Lead ♡ 4     │ W   E │  ♡ K 8 2
                │   S   │
                └───────┘
```

The first thing to do in each situation is to apply the Rule of Eleven. Subtracting 4 from 11, you get 7—which tells you that there are seven cards higher than the four outside your Partner's hand. In each situation, you find four of these cards in your own hand and in the Dummy. This means that the Declarer must hold *three* cards higher than the four-spot, which gives him fairly good control of the suit. Now should you, as East, play your highest card immediately or not?

In the first place, you know that your Partner holds *only four hearts*. How do you know this? Elementary—you can see the trey and deuce in your hand and Dummy, and Partner led the four; since his lead was his fourth best, he can hold no lower cards. You can confirm this deduction. Your application of the Rule of Eleven told you that Declarer has three cards higher than the four. Adding your three cards and Dummy's three, you have a total of nine hearts accounted for. That leaves only four for Partner.

Take the first example. If Declarer has the Ace, to play your King is suicidal, and gives the Declarer at least 2 tricks (for Dummy has the Queen), and 3 tricks if he has A J. If Partner has the Ace, Declarer probably holds J 9 8, which will give him 1 trick anyway. In what way, then, can you play to gain a trick?

In this situation, the best play is your second best card, assuming that a low card is played from the Dummy. The reason for this is demonstrated by the following diagram:

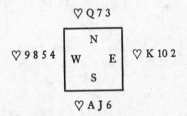

Partner has led the four-spot, and the trey has been played from Dummy. If you (East) play the Ten, the Declarer will win with the Jack but he cannot afford to continue the suit. If Declarer ever leads the Queen from Dummy, you simply play your King and Partner's nine will be promoted to command. This is equally true if your Ten is exchanged for Partner's nine or eight, as illustrated in Diagrams 2 and 3.

But let us suppose that Declarer does not hold the Ace, but the perfectly terrible combination of J 8 6, as in the following diagram:

♡ Q 7 3

♡ A 9 5 4

```
N
W   E
S
```

♡ K 10 2

♡ J 8 6

Now, with the same lead and the same play from Dummy, you can win the trick by playing the King, but then there will be absolutely no way of preventing the Declarer from winning at least the third round of the suit. By playing the Ten, you allow him to take his 1 trick immediately, but any time thereafter, as soon as you regain the lead, you have available 3 tricks in the suit.

To delve into this matter even further, there is a situation in which to play the Ten will gain 2 tricks instead of but 1, as follows:

♡ Q 7 3

♡ A J 5 4

```
N
W   E
S
```

♡ K 10 2

♡ 9 8 6

Now if you play the Ten, the Declarer cannot win a single heart trick. When the Ten holds the first round, you simply lead the King, and finally the deuce to the third round, which drops Dummy's Queen under your Partner's Ace. This gives your side a total of 4 heart tricks. But if you had played the King here—which is outwardly the same as all preceding combinations—Dummy's Queen would then be over your Partner's Ace and must therefore take a trick.

These last three combinations illustrate finessing against the Dummy, but they do not finesse against Partner. The fact that the Dummy contains an honor which may be set up if Third Hand plays high makes the play of the next lower card a finesse against the Dummy's hand.

Summary

When you play as Third Hand—which is to say, when you play the third card on Partner's opening lead (for only the first trick has been considered) against no-trump— you should generally, as has been shown, play your highest card.   But if the Dummy contains an honor which completes your broken honor sequence, or which may be set up if you play your highest card, you get a better percentage in tricks by playing your next lower card instead.

Also as Third Hand note this rule: When your highest cards of your Partner's led suit are in sequence, play the lowest of the sequence—not the highest.

You learned the application of the Rule of Eleven, which is based on the assumption that, until you learn otherwise, Partner's lead of a low card is his fourth best in the suit.

CHAPTER XIX

ELEMENTARY DEFENSE AFTER THE FIRST TRICK

THE reader may be amazed to observe that defensive play has taken up two chapters and not progressed beyond the first trick. As a matter of fact, however, the principles outlined for the first trick apply with practically equal force to the subsequent tricks. Except insofar as subsequent leads and plays may be modified by better knowledge of where the outstanding cards lie, the conventional leads and plays already explained for the opening trick apply just as much to any later trick.

As is true of play by the Declarer, not all the tricks won by the Defending Side can be secured with high cards. What may be regarded as the really important tricks will be won with low honors which have been promoted or with low cards which have been established. To secure these tricks should always be the primary object of every defensive lead and play.

As already pointed out, the Defending Side has one advantage. They gain one time unit from the privilege of making the opening lead. Except when a short suit is opened, this first lead is an attacking move, made for the purpose of establishing low-card tricks as quickly as possible. When the lead is a high honor (from a sequence), it will often turn out that the Declarer holds but one or two stoppers in the suit, and the high honor lead will drive out one of these stoppers without more ado. When the Defending Side succeeds in pulling a stopper out of the Declarer's hand, they have accomplished half their purpose. They need only one or two entry cards in order to regain the lead and run off their established low cards.

Naturally, when the Declarer holds two stoppers, one lead in that suit is not sufficient to achieve the aim of the Defending Side. When they regain the lead, it is necessary to revert to the original line of attack and lead this suit a second time—letting the Declarer take 2 tricks with his stoppers so that the suit will be cleared. To do this effectively, the Partners must coöperate. Nothing can be more wasteful—of both time and cards—than a policy of leading first one suit and then another. If the Declarer is a sound player, he will not have undertaken a no-trump contract without stoppers in all suits, so that to shift from one to another will not make the Declarer lose control of any of them.

The first principle of defensive play at no-trump may then be stated as follows: *Partner's suit should be returned at the first opportunity whenever there is reason to believe that it can eventually be established.*

The following deal illustrates this principle:

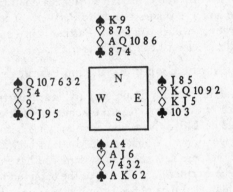

♠ K 9
♡ 8 7 3
◇ A Q 10 8 6
♣ 8 7 4

♠ Q 10 7 6 3 2
♡ 5 4
◇ 9
♣ Q J 9 5

♠ J 8 5
♡ K Q 10 9 2
◇ K J 5
♣ 10 3

♠ A 4
♡ A J 6
◇ 7 4 3 2
♣ A K 6 2

The contract is three no-trump, played by South. Your Partner (West) opens the six of spades, on which the nine is played from Dummy. You naturally play your Jack (Third Hand high) and the trick is won by the Ace. The Declarer thereupon leads a low diamond and finesses the Queen; you win with your King and must now select a return lead. Your own suit, hearts, looks more than tempting. However, the chances are that Declarer holds two stoppers in hearts. And you know that just one more lead is required for the Declarer to set up the rest of Dummy's diamonds. Consequently you cannot expect to regain the lead more than once. Your Partner opened the spade suit, showing some length in that suit. Of course, the King still remains in the Dummy, and this is the commanding card, but if this controlling card is driven out, your Partner will very likely be left with some high spades.

Your best clue to the proper play depends on applying the Rule of Eleven, which tells you that Declarer held originally one card higher than the six-spot. But he has already played it—the Ace on the first trick. Therefore, if you knock that King out of Dummy's hand,

all Partner's spades will be high. Surely you have no cause for hesitation—you return a spade.

The Declarer finds himself in quicksand. He can take his 2 club
tricks, his sure diamond trick, and his heart trick—giving him a total
of 6 tricks, since he has won that second round of spades, willy-nilly,
with Dummy's King. His best play in this desperate situation is to
lead the Ace of diamonds, hoping to drop the Jack. When this fails
to happen, he may as well concede you this diamond trick and pray
that you have no more spades to lead to Partner. You do have one
spade left, however, which you lead. Partner is in—and his 4 spade
tricks defeat the Declarer's contract by 2 tricks.

Choosing the Card in Returning Partner's Suit

Granted that it is vitally important to return Partner's opening
lead, the choice of the card to return is sometimes not easy to make.
In the example deal just given, you have a choice between the five-
spot and the eight-spot. Which should you lead back? You should
lead the eight, because it is the highest card you have and clears up
any doubt which Partner may have as to the outstanding high cards.
In this particular deal it is not very important, since Partner holds
all the high cards himself, but if he is confronted with the problem of
locating all the missing intermediate cards, he will know that he cannot count on you for anything higher—if you always follow the sound
principle, in returning Partner's suit, *always to lead back your higher
remaining card whenever you held three cards originally*. This is always important, but it has special significance when the combination
held by Third Hand is something like Ace-Queen-small, Ace-Jack-
small, or a similar tenace. With such a holding you must be very
sure to return the honor, not the low card, after winning the first
round with the Ace. In fact, to do this will very often embarrass the
Declarer exceedingly.

The play not only enables Partner to locate the missing cards higher
than your second highest, but it also serves to unblock the suit by
getting your high cards out of Partner's way. The unblocking is of
little consequence when your choice is between the eight and the
seven, but it is of great consequence when you hold two or more
honors.

With four cards of Partner's opening suit, however, the situation takes on a different hue. You do not need to hurry about unblocking, for you can do this later. Also, it is not so imperative to give your Partner information as to the missing high cards since, if Partner's lead indicates at least four cards in the suit (as it very likely does), you and your Partner hold most of the controlling cards together. But it *is* important that you tell your Partner that he has hit upon a fairly good length in your hand—such as four or more cards.

The following deal demonstrates the return lead from four cards:

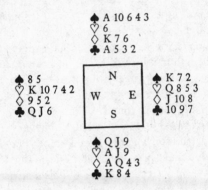

```
                    ♠ A 10 6 4 3
                    ♡ 6
                    ◇ K 7 6
                    ♣ A 5 3 2

    ♠ 8 5             ┌─────────┐        ♠ K 7 2
    ♡ K 10 7 4 2      │    N    │        ♡ Q 8 5 3
    ◇ 9 5 2           │ W     E │        ◇ J 10 8
    ♣ Q J 6           │    S    │        ♣ 10 9 7
                      └─────────┘
                    ♠ Q J 9
                    ♡ A J 9
                    ◇ A Q 4 3
                    ♣ K 8 4
```

Against South's three no-trump contract, your Partner opens the four of hearts. You naturally play your Queen, and Declarer wins with the Ace. By applying the Rule of Eleven on his own behalf, the Declarer can see that a hold-up in hearts will do him no good. His only hope is that you (East) have the Ten or the King. Declarer leads the spade Queen to the second trick, playing low in the Dummy. You win with your King, and decide to return Partner's suit without delay. The card to return is very important. If you lead the eight-spot, Declarer will play the nine (it so happens), and Partner will win with the Ten. He knows at once that the missing Jack is held by the Declarer. However, West cannot know whether the Jack is alone or accompanied by a small card. In other words, he will not know whether his best play is to put you in the lead again (if he can), so that you can lead through Declarer's hand a second time in hearts, or whether he should play his King immediately, hoping to drop the missing Jack.

The clue to the mystery—that is, mystery so far as Partner is concerned—lies in the card of his suit that you return. Since you held four hearts originally, you should not return the eight, but the *three*—the card that was originally your fourth best in the suit. When Declarer plays the nine your Partner will win with the Ten—and now he can tell that Declarer holds only one more heart, the lone Jack. Consequently he will promptly lay down his King and drop the unguarded Jack.

Two more interesting points characterize the deal just analyzed. The first is the question of your proper play on the third round of hearts. You still have remaining the eight- and five-spot, and you know that Partner originally held at least four hearts. His four must have included the seven-spot, or he would not have played the King immediately. If he held four, which card you play can make no difference; but if he held five, your play is very important. If you play the five-spot on the third round, your eight will be the highest outstanding heart and will win the fourth round. This will completely shut out Partner's fifth heart, which is good, and he will never be able to cash it in. To provide for the contingency that Partner may have held five hearts originally, you must play your eight on the third round. Then you can play the five on Partner's seven, and his deuce will be good for a trick. Thus, every heart you played was important—first the Queen, to make sure of driving out Declarer's stopper; second the trey, to tell Partner that you held originally four cards in the suit; and third the eight on the King, to unblock the suit. This is excellent defense—coöperating with Partner to give him the correct count on the hand, and getting out of his way.

The second interesting point is how West knew that the trey showed an original holding of four rather than only two hearts. After all, the trey might have been your only card. The answer is simple. If you had held only two hearts, the Declarer must have held five. Certainly if the Declarer had held five headed by Ace-Jack, he would have bid the suit some time during the auction. Since he did not ever call hearts, let us say, he must have held only three, and you had four.

Almost invariably a clue like this will enable Partner to read your return lead correctly—if you follow established conventions, as recommended here. If no clue is available, you must merely hope that your Partner guesses aright!

An Exception

Sometimes, to avoid blocking Partner's suit, it is necessary to return the highest card even from an original holding of four cards. But this happens only when an honor sequence is present. Take, for example, the following:

1. ◇ K Q J 3   **2.** ◇ Q J 10 2   **3.** ◇ J 10 9 4

In each situation, if Partner opens diamonds against a no-trump contract, you should play the bottom card of the sequence. Then, if you regain the lead, you cannot return your original fourth best because this is certain to block the suit if Partner held five cards originally. The play here is to lead back your top card and follow it on the next round with the next highest, reserving the low card to put Partner in the lead if he should hold one more diamond than you.

Holding Up in Defensive Play

You will recall that three forms of play were useful to the Declarer in the early chapters about no-trump play, namely, the hold-up, unblocking, and ducking. Every one of these is equally useful to the Defending Side.

The hold-up is the simplest. The Declarer holds up in order to shut off communication between the two Defending Hands and try to render one of them void of the suit they are trying to establish. The defensive player who employs the hold-up does it for exactly the same reason—to shut off communication between the Declarer's hand and Dummy's hand.

The following deal is an illustration:

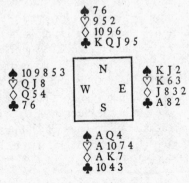

```
              ♠ 7 6
              ♡ 9 5 2
              ◇ 10 9 6
              ♣ K Q J 9 5
                  N
♠ 10 9 8 5 3              ♠ K J 2
♡ Q J 8        W    E     ♡ K 6 3
◇ Q 5 4                   ◇ J 8 3 2
♣ 7 6             S       ♣ A 8 2
              ♠ A Q 4
              ♡ A 10 7 4
              ◇ A K 7
              ♣ 10 4 3
```

Against South's three no-trump contract, your Partner (West) opens the five of spades. (He might have led the spade Ten, but here the choice is unimportant.) You play your King (Third Hand high), and Declarer wins with his Ace. Now Declarer must first attempt to set up his clubs, and leads the Ten from his hand to that end. Regardless of how he leads the clubs, *you must hold up your Ace until you are forced to play it on the third round*. The reason is not far to seek—obviously Dummy has no re-entries outside the club suit. By waiting until the third round to take your Ace, you succeed (as you hoped) in exhausting all the clubs from Declarer's hand so that the last two left in the Dummy will never be of any use to him. Upon taking the third round of clubs, you return the Jack of spades (your Partner's opening suit), and, whether or not Declarer wins this trick, he will have to lose several tricks eventually somewhere.

The hold-up is clearly unnecessary and futile when the Dummy has a re-entry. For example, look at the hand with a few cards changed:

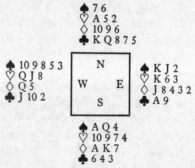

♠ 7 6
♡ A 5 2
◇ 10 9 6
♣ K Q 8 7 5

♠ 10 9 8 5 3   ♠ K J 2
♡ Q J 8   ♡ K 6 3
◇ Q 5   ◇ J 8 4 3 2
♣ J 10 2   ♣ A 9

♠ A Q 4
♡ 10 9 7 4
◇ A K 7
♣ 6 4 3

Here the first trick is the same as before, but the Declarer leads a low club toward Dummy. West plays low, and the Queen is played from Dummy. You can gain nothing by refusing to play your Ace now. If you hold it up, the later lead of a low club will pull out your Ace, and the Dummy still has an entry in the heart Ace. You must therefore win the first round of clubs and hope that your Partner holds a club trick. As it happens, he does hold the Jack-Ten in this deal, which will stop the run of the clubs later on. Had you held up the club Ace for no reason at all, in view of Dummy's sure re-entry, Declarer's losses in clubs (if he succeeded in guessing the situation aright) would have been only 1 trick instead of 2.

Unblocking in Defensive Play

Unblocking has already been mentioned in connection with the return of the second highest card in Partner's suit when holding but three originally. However, another unblocking principle is less evident. The following diagram illustrates it:

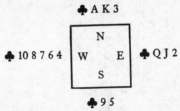

♣ A K 3

♣ 10 8 7 6 4   ♣ Q J 2

♣ 9 5

Partner opens the six (against South's no-trump contract), and the King is played from Dummy. On the King *you must play your Queen*, and never was a lady sacrificed for a better cause. You know that your Partner must be leading from a long suit since the four top honors are in plain sight. Consequently the Declarer can hold very few cards in that suit. If you play your deuce on the first trick, retaining your Queen-Jack, you will have to win the third round and you may not be able to put your Partner in the lead with any other suit. Therefore you should throw your Queen under the King and, as soon as the Ace is played, toss the Jack away under it. This leaves you with the deuce which, as soon as you get in the lead, you blithely lead to your Partner's commanding Ten.

This same unblocking principle comes into play with equal effect in the following situations, Dummy holding only two or three low cards:

1. ♡ Q J 10 8 2   ♡ A 5 or ♡ K 5   **2.** ♣ J 10 9 6 3   ♠ Q 4 or ♠ K 4

In No. 1, if Partner leads the Queen, you must play the Ace or the King, whichever you have. In No. 2, if Partner leads the Jack you must play the Queen or the King on it. You know that Partner's lead indicates a strong honor sequence, and you must therefore get out of his way as quickly as possible so that at a later time he will be able to run off his established tricks without hindrance.

An exception occurs when such an unblocking play will forfeit a trick, as in the following situation:

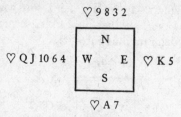

♡ 9 8 3 2

♡ Q J 10 6 4   W   E   ♡ K 5

♡ A 7

Here Partner opens the Queen, on which a low card is played from Dummy. Now it would be folly for you to play the King, since Declarer will win this trick with the Ace and eventually the nine-spot in Dummy's hand will be in line for a trick. Here you must play low, hoping that Declarer will refuse to win the first round. If he does, your Partner's lead of a low card will drive out your King and Declarer's Ace on the same trick, automatically unblocking the suit. Of course, a brilliant Declarer will take the first round, but every defending player must hope, occasionally, that the Declarer is not brilliant, or that he has been lulled into a false sense of security.

Ducking in Defensive Play

In defensive play, the use of the ducking strategy is usually confined to the hand of the Opening Leader. The purpose of the play is either to leave an entry card in Partner's hand (when the leader's hand lacks an entry) or to establish a tenace position over the Declarer.

The following deal is a case in point:

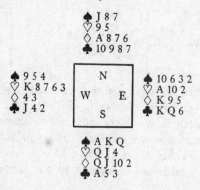

         ♠ J 8 7
         ♡ 9 5
         ◇ A 8 7 6
         ♣ 10 9 8 7

♠ 9 5 4   ♠ 10 6 3 2
♡ K 8 7 6 3   ♡ A 10 2
◇ 4 3   W   E   ◇ K 9 5
♣ J 4 2   ♣ K Q 6

         ♠ A K Q
         ♡ Q J 4
         ◇ Q J 10 2
         ♣ A 5 3

You now consider yourself in the West position. Opening the six of hearts against South's three no-trump contract, you watch the five played from Dummy and the Ace played by Partner, Declarer dropping the four-spot. At the second trick, your Partner returns the heart Ten, which immediately lets you know that he did not originally hold four hearts, and also locates the Queen and Jack in Declarer's hand. When Declarer covers the Ten with his Jack, therefore, you ponder a moment. If you win with the King and lead the suit back (with the eight), the hearts will be established, but what good will it do? Declarer wins the eight with his Queen, of course, and you have no entry—since Partner is exhausted and cannot lead hearts again.

Your only chance of getting the most out of your heart suit is to refuse to overtake the Jack at the second trick. You duck by playing the trey, hoping that your Partner will be able to obtain the lead once more and return his third heart. As it happens, Partner does regain the lead with his diamond King, and returns the deuce of hearts, which you win with the King, South having been forced to play his Queen. The heart suit is established with a vengeance, and you run off 2 more tricks. Had you overtaken the Jack at the second trick, you would have been held down to 2 heart tricks altogether.

The second application of ducking is very similar, with but one additional feature. A suit diagram only is sufficient to illustrate it, thus:

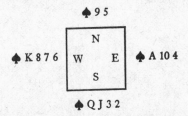

You open the six, on which Partner plays the Ace. When Partner returns the Ten, and Declarer covers with the Jack, you must duck by playing the seven, refusing to win the trick since you know that your King-eight becomes a perfect tenace over the Declarer's Queen-trey. Whenever your Partner regains the lead, he will return his last card (the four), and you will cover whichever card Declarer chooses to play.

In the following combination this ducking play is accentuated:

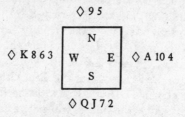

$\diamond$ 9 5

N
W   E
S

$\diamond$ K 8 6 3 $\diamond$ A 10 4

$\diamond$ Q J 7 2

By leading the trey, which your Partner wins with the Ace, you will be forced to pass up Declarer's play of the Jack on Partner's return of the Ten. You must do this because if you led a third round of the suit you would plunge right into Declarer's Queen-seven, losing 2 tricks in the suit instead of but 1.

SUMMARY

Subsequent defensive play follows, in general, the same principles as were laid down for the opening lead and the first trick. In returning Partner's opening suit, you learned always to return the highest card left in your hand from an original holding of three, but what was the fourth best from an original holding of four or more (except when an honor sequence is held, when the highest honor must be returned to guard against blocking the suit if Partner held five cards originally).

The application of the hold-up, unblocking, and ducking were tied up with defensive play, showing that they are as valuable to the Defending Side, on occasion, as to the Attacking Side, on other occasions.

CHAPTER XX

DEFENSIVE DISCARDS

O<small>NE</small> of the most complex aspects of defensive play is the proper handling of discards. Strictly speaking, a *discard* is the throwing off of an unwanted card—familiar in the common phrase "to throw into the discard," which means to abandon as worthless. In this sense, in Bridge, a card thrown off when the player is unable to follow to the suit led is a discard. But in the language we use in describing the play of the hand the term *discard* also includes the play of certain cards of the led suit. A discard, then, may be a card thrown off on a suit of which you are exhausted, or a card of the suit led played without any intention of taking the trick. For example, if you play the four of hearts on a heart lead, that is a discard in the wide meaning used here, and also if, lacking a heart, you throw off a spade (not a trump, of course), on a heart lead, that is a discard too.

Many "family" Bridge players who have made no study of the game think that discards are unimportant. If they cannot take the trick, they throw off any card that seems useless at the moment, failing entirely to take Partner into consideration or to consider very carefully what the future of the hand may have in store. This is lamentably unimaginative and may prove costly more often than not. *Every play* and *every card* are of importance. Even with what looks like a hopeless hand, you must not resign yourself to the rôle of a "dummy." The player who, because he holds no card above the Ten, sits back and pays attention only enough to follow suit when able—to avoid being penalized for a revoke—should take up some other game.

Discards, like leads, should tell a story. It may be a sad story, if you have a blank hand, but the story must be told nevertheless. In this way, discards become signals. Some are red lights telling Partner to stop; others are beckoning green lights telling him to make full speed ahead. There are thus discouraging discards and encouraging discards.

Discards, or signals, as they are sometimes called, fall into three main classes. Two have just been mentioned—encouraging and discouraging. The third class consists of what, for want of a better name, may be called "temporizing discards"—or "stalling," or "marking time." The encouraging discard is a signal to Partner that you desire a certain suit to be continued or to be led; the discouraging discard is a signal to Partner that you desire a certain suit to be discontinued or not to be led. The temporizing discard is perhaps the most important, and it indicates that you are not sure, at the moment, whether a certain lead is desirable or undesirable.

Encouraging and discouraging discards were once separated by a rather sharp line of demarcation—at the six-spot. Any card higher than the six was considered encouraging; any card lower than the six, discouraging. The only doubtful card was the six-spot itself. The limitations of this cut-and-dried system are at once apparent. What on earth could you do if your lowest card in a suit happened to be the seven, and you had to discard in this suit, and yet you wished to discourage your Partner? Or, holding A K 3 2 in a suit, you wanted to tell Partner to lead it, and yet had no encouraging card to discard? Certainly you would not throw off the Ace or King to encourage Partner, and the trey or deuce would be bound to tell him No.

The Echo and Its Uses

Mr. Joseph B. Elwell,* a famous Bridge authority, solved the problem by inventing a play which is now widely used in Contract Bridge. This play is known as the *echo*. It consists of discarding a card of any denomination whatsoever, either in following to Partner's led suit or in throwing off on a suit to which the player is unable to follow. Subsequently a lower card in the same suit is played, completing the echo. This is a definite signal—also dubbed the "high-low" signal—for Partner to continue the suit, if it is the one he is leading, or to shift to that suit at the first opportunity. This play has liberalized the iron-clad "six-spot" rule. A player could echo, you see, by playing as low a card as the trey, and later playing the deuce. Thus important cards could be conserved—an impossible thrift under the old régime. Today the echo has been considerably improved upon.

* Many readers will remember that Elwell was murdered, and that his slayer was never brought to justice. His name is thus famous not only in Bridge but also in the annals of unsolved murder cases.

Of course, the trouble with the echo is that sometimes it is not possible to complete the play. Holding $\diamondsuit$ Q 9 3, for example, the nine-spot must be played on Partner's lead of the King. Obviously the three-spot cannot be either led or discarded at a later time, as this will succeed only in blocking the suit. Under circumstances such as these, Partner must interpret the nine as an encouraging discard or, if he prefers, as the beginning of an echo which cannot be completed. Of course, with $\diamondsuit$ Q 9 7 3, it is easy to first play the nine-spot and discard the seven-spot later. Now the echo is completed.

Sometimes a card as high as the nine-spot is not available. For example, suppose that you held $\diamondsuit$ Q 5 3 and your Partner opens the Jack. You must play the most encouraging card available, namely, the five-spot. It is a little difficult for Partner to read this discard, but he may find the necessary clue from the fact that the three-spot is missing. This depends entirely on his judgment.

You will see, therefore, that there is some point in retaining a part of the old Whist convention. A card higher than a six-spot is more likely to be the beginning of an echo (whether it is subsequently completed or not) than a card lower than a six-spot. However, it is still true that a seven may on occasion be discouraging and a trey encouraging. Partner must watch each trick very carefully and form his opinion on the basis of the outstanding cards.

When to Encourage and When to Discourage Partner

The question of when to encourage and when to discourage Partner is rather simple when defending against a no-trump contract. If Partner leads an honor, the chances are that he holds a strong honor sequence. Therefore, if you also hold an honor in the suit, you must inform Partner of the good news, if possible, so that when he regains the lead he will have no qualms about continuing that suit.

The following rather elementary situation makes this clear:

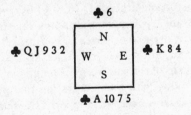

Your Partner (West) opens the Queen against South's no-trump contract. The Dummy's six is played, of course, and you are now faced
with a choice of cards. An unthinking player would automatically
drop the four-spot. If the distribution of the suit between Declarer's
hand and your Partner's is fairly normal, which you must take for
granted until you learn otherwise, you should not expect your Partner to have more than five clubs. If he held originally the Queen-
Jack-Ten or Queen-Jack-nine, Declarer will have either four to the
Ace-nine or four to the Ace-Ten. Therefore, you cannot afford to
unblock by plunking your King right on the Queen. And if you play
the four-spot, Partner will not know, when he regains the lead,
whether to continue clubs or shift to some other suit, for you can
never play a lower card than the four. You must do your best to be
informative, so your proper play is the eight. Contrary to a widespread belief, this does not immediately tell your Partner that you
have the King—it simply tells him that you want the suit continued.
If you play the four-spot, Partner must assume that you do not want
the suit continued, since you have not encouraged him. (He knows
that the four-spot must be your lowest card in the suit, as he holds
the trey and deuce himself.)

Take the following slightly more advanced case:

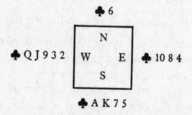

Again your Partner leads the Queen, and you should still play the
eight. Why? Because you know that against a no-trump contract,
Partner's Queen must mean either A Q J or Q J 9 (since you have the
Ten). In either instance, you must inform him that the continuation
of the suit seems advantageous. Even if you held 9 8 4, your play
would still be the eight on the first round, letting Partner know that
he can return a low card of the suit from his holding of Q J 10 (it must
be Q J 10 or A Q J now) with the expectation that you have a card
that will force out Declarer's second stopper. Of course, if Partner's

holding is as good as A Q J, he will continue with his high cards instead of a low one, but he is glad to know that you like the suit.

Even with echoing there must be a limit somewhere. If you hold 8 7 4 in the preceding situation, and Dummy still has only the six, you cannot encourage Partner—you cannot even temporize—but you must play the four. You realize that if Partner holds Q J 10 9 he will not care whether he receives any encouragement or not.

The proper play is more obvious when the Dummy has an honor:

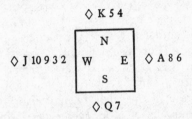

If Partner opens the Jack and Dummy plays low, you are naturally going to hold up your Ace as you must retain your tenace position over the Dummy, in order to keep that King from becoming the commanding card. However, you do not unthinkingly play the six, but you deliberately play the eight so that your Partner, when he regains the lead, can push his Ten through Dummy's King and render it worthless. Thus Declarer wins but 1 trick in this suit.

The question naturally arises as to what you should do when your lowest card is one which may easily be construed by Partner as encouraging. The answer is that your Partner is expected to be on the lookout for such situations and recognize them by examining his own and Dummy's low cards, to determine, if possible, whether your apparently high discard is likely to be your lowest in the suit.

Now suppose that, in the preceding situation, you hold only the eight and six (doubleton), instead of these two cards plus the Ace. Now you do not wish to encourage your Partner, so you play the six, and Declarer wins with his Queen. Could your Partner ever take that six as an encouraging card? Not on this deal, for he holds the trey and deuce himself and he can see the five and four in the Dummy. Consequently he knows that the six is your *lowest* card. Against a clever Declarer the true aspect of the suit may not be at once apparent if, for example, the Declarer holds the lower cards in the suit, for he may try to confuse the Defending Side by holding up those lower cards at first, in order to make a discard seem encouraging when it is really the lowest card the player has. But this is rather rare, and, furthermore, the dilemma can be escaped by the application of a little common sense.

Whenever you are the Opening Leader, you should watch your Partner's card very carefully. If there seem to be at least two cards lower than the one played, which are not visible, it is best for you to believe that your Partner intends to encourage you. If there is but one lower card missing, you must be wary and suspicious—your Partner may be encouraging you or the Declarer may possibly be laying a trap for you. Your decision must be based on the merits of the situation. If it is desperate, you had better be encouraged and take the consequences if any. Or perhaps you know your Declarer, and your knowledge of his psychology may help you. Do not let occasional errors demoralize you, for even experts often guess wrong.

As we have seen, the importance of the echo depends chiefly on the fact that it permits signalling with very low cards, as, for example:

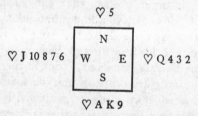

Your Partner opens his Jack, and you know that he must have held either A J 10 or K J 10, or something of the kind. Possibly he may have held only J 10 8. You like the suit, since you have four to the Queen, and you hope your Partner will continue it when he regains the lead. But certainly you cannot play your highest card—the Queen. Your best encouraging card is the four, and you therefore play it. Declarer wins the trick with his Ace. Partner reasons:

That four is probably encouraging, since both the trey and deuce are not to be seen and Partner may easily have one of them. The odds are in favor of this supposition, and the suit may be continued.

You, as East, must show Partner the trey or deuce of hearts at the first chance. This may be either on the second round of hearts (if you are in the lead), or, if a suit of which you are void is led, you must throw it off then. As soon as your Partner sees that lower heart he gets your message. Until you play the trey or deuce of hearts, your Partner must remain in doubt about your four-spot's meaning.

Echoing With an Honor

It is not impossible to echo with an honor, but the occasion for it is very rare. When such a play is made it is really not an echo in essence, but is the beginning of an unblocking play. For example, if your Partner leads a small card in a suit of which you hold the Jack-Ten and a small card, you naturally play the Ten if the Dummy plays low. However, if the Dummy plays a card higher than the Jack, you must encourage a continuation of that suit by playing your Ten or Jack under Dummy's commanding card. In this instance, your proper play is the Jack, which absolutely guarantees that you hold the Ten (unless the Jack is a singleton). Similarly, from a Queen-Jack combination, the discard of the Queen guarantees the Jack, and from a King-Queen combination, the discard of the King guarantees the Queen. As you will readily see, this is a combination of the echo and an unblocking play.

Echoing When Unable to Follow Suit

Encouraging discards can be effectively made when you cannot follow to the suit led, and the opportunity occurs rather often.

The following deal illustrates this play:

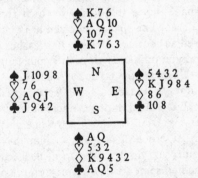

Your Partner (West) opens the spade Jack against South's three no-trump contract. The six is played from Dummy. Clearly you do not like this suit as a means of defense, so you discard your deuce—even though you hold four cards of your Partner's suit, you still do not wish to encourage him. Declarer wins with the Ace, deliberately concealing the fact that he also has the Queen, though his ruse will probably avail him nothing since East's deuce practically denies the Queen.

Now suppose the Declarer tries to take 4 club tricks, leading the Ace and Queen out of his own hand and winning the third round with Dummy's King. On this third round of clubs you have an opportunity to make a discard of some other suit. What card do you throw away? You should not hesitate, for you now have a chance to tell your Partner what suit of yours promises the best defensive hope. Hearts! And which heart? The nine, of course, which is so high that Partner cannot possibly mistake its significance. There is nothing to be gained by saving the nine and throwing off the eight, which may, once in a hundred times, mislead Partner. He *might* think the eight is your lowest heart, and the nine is a little more emphatic in its encouragement.

Declarer, having failed to make that fourth club trick (of course, he abandons the suit at the end of the third round when you make your high heart discard), now busies himself with diamonds, though they offer small hope. He will probably lead the Ten from Dummy and let it run around, your Partner winning with his Jack (the bottom card of his Queen-Jack). Your Partner, getting the message broadcast by your high heart discard, is under no misapprehensions about his lead. Your spade deuce told a story which the nine of hearts confirmed. You do not like spades, but you are crazy about hearts. Being thrifty as well as cautious, Partner first cashes in his good club Jack, of course, and you jubilantly throw off your four of hearts, completing the echo. There is now no doubt whatever—Partner leads a heart through Dummy's tenace. The Declarer probably will not go up with the Ace, but will attempt some sort of finesse. Whether he plays the Queen or Ten from Dummy, you win the trick.

Your best return is probably a spade. Though you do not particularly like the suit, you do not need to neglect it, since Partner's first lead showed he had some spades. Furthermore, you cannot lead hearts, and you are exhausted of clubs. Since the Declarer has been trying to establish diamonds, there is no reason for you to be so generous as to lead the suit for him.   The spade is led then, which Declarer wins.   Having little choice, Declarer continues his diamonds, giving your Partner another trick in this suit and the chance to lead his second heart.   Again the Declarer finesses, and again you win the trick. Your best return is again a spade.   At this point Declarer cannot help losing 2 more tricks to West—1 diamond trick and 1 spade trick.

The preceding hand is very elementary, and yet it exemplifies very well the proper way to signal Partner by means of discards.   If you did not hold both the King and Jack of hearts, or, in other words, if you did not hold 2 sure tricks in the suit, you could not make quite so emphatic a discard as the nine.   You would be better advised to temporize—a form of signalling soon to be explained.

The discouraging discard requires but a few words.   It is the reverse of the encouraging discard.   It tells Partner that, if he thinks a suit can be established, he must attempt it entirely on his own responsibility.   In other words, he cannot hope to find any aid in your hand.   The discouraging discard says, in effect, that if Partner cannot take full responsibility he must try some other suit in which you may possibly be able to help him—in short, he must shift to another line of defense.

You signal Partner to go warily, and to take the entire burden on his own shoulders, by playing your lowest possible card on his lead, whether the lead be a strong sequence lead or a plain length lead. By thus discouraging that particular suit, you indicate that you very likely have some assistance in one of the other suits.   If you have no assistance anywhere—if your hand is entirely blank—it is better to play some mildly encouraging or ambiguous card rather than to discourage Partner in his opening suit, for then the first suit may be as good as any defensive forces you have at your disposal.

TEMPORIZING DISCARDS

The necessity for a temporizing discard arises more often than for either a discouraging or an encouraging discard.   After all, Contract Bridge is not the sort of game in which the proper line of play is as plain as daylight from the start.   Even after a few tricks have been won or lost, it may not be entirely obvious which line of defense is likely to prove the best.   Therefore you have to make allowances, leaving some leeway for a change of mind later on, if desirable.

The following example of an encouraging discard will serve to show exactly how the temporizing discard works:

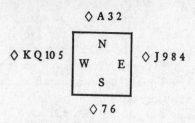

Your Partner (West) opens the King against South's no-trump contract. A low card is played from Dummy. You, as East, are eager to have the suit continued, since you know Partner's lead cannot be from anything other than King-Queen-Ten (you have the nine yourself, and the Ace is in the Dummy). As a matter of fact, you could throw off the Jack here without doing any damage, but this is not essential. Your play of the nine will tell your Partner the same story —that you hold the Jack and wish the suit continued.

Suppose, however, that the situation is as follows:

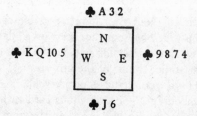

West makes the same King lead, and Dummy plays low. Now which card should you, as East, play? You have four cards in the suit; you know that your Partner is making a strength-showing lead—from either King-Queen-Jack or King-Queen-Ten—and yet you do not dare encourage him too strongly lest the Jack be in Declarer's hand. If you want to encourage him, you should play your eight; if you want to discourage him, you should play your four. Actually, you do not want to do either positively. You would much rather leave the decision to your Partner. Therefore, your proper play is the seven—to temporize.

You may ask, "How can Partner interpret this card?" The answer is that he may have trouble, but, allowing for the law of averages, he should decide that the seven may not be your lowest card. In fact, the Declarer will play the six-spot, leaving but one card lower than the seven missing—the four-spot. If Partner has no better lead, he will therefore feel that he had better continue this suit.

Consider Partner's reasoning somewhat further. He decides that the seven is not a downright discouraging discard, and that, in fact, it looks like a compromise. What holding can East have which induces him to make such a compromise? He cannot have four cards to the Jack, for then he would certainly want to be positively encouraging. If his seven-spot is neither his second highest nor his lowest card, East must have somewhat less than four to the Jack. If the holding were but three cards, he would have played his lowest beyond a doubt. His only possible holding, then, is four cards without the Jack. If this is true, the Declarer must hold the Jack alone, which can be caught under the Ace by the simple lead of the Queen.

A temporizing discard may occur when Declarer tackles a suit, thus:

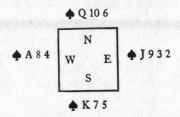

♠ Q 10 6

♠ A 8 4   N   ♠ J 9 3 2
          W   E
             S

♠ K 7 5

The Declarer leads low from Dummy (North) with the intention of playing his King. On Dummy's six what should you, as East, play? Should you casually follow suit with the deuce? No! You should play the trey. The King will still be played, and your Partner will win with the Ace. Of course, at this point your Partner cannot tell that you would like to have the suit led again. However, there will come a time later in the play when you will be able to discard on the lead of a suit of which you have no cards. Then you can complete your echo in spades by playing the deuce so that your partner will be absolutely certain that you hold the protected Jack over the Dummy, and he will lead the suit if he finds it necessary to the defensive campaign.

Sometimes early discarding prepares the way for plays made on the very last trick, as in the following deal:

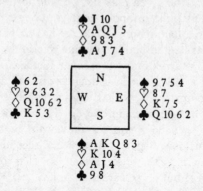

Suppose you and your Partner (East and West) are defending against South's contract of six no-trump. West opens a heart (the deuce). Difficulties present themselves at once. The Declarer will simply run off the first 9 tricks without stopping for breath—5 spade tricks and 4 heart tricks. If you and your Partner do not exchange some information, there is grave danger that you will both throw away the same suit. In other words, suppose that you, as East, decide to protect your King of diamonds by discarding clubs. Suppose that West should decide to do precisely the same thing—that is, keep his diamond Queen guarded by throwing off clubs. The result will be as follows at the end of the ninth trick:

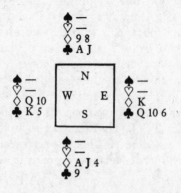

You may be sure that Declarer will have watched your discards. He will now simply lead a low diamond, conceding you the trick. You have to return a club, giving Declarer the lead with his Ace. He then plays his diamond Ace, on which West's Queen falls, and the Jack will be good for the last trick.

How can your partnership avoid the debacle? Looking at all four hands, you can easily see the answer. Your hand should hold on to the singleton King of diamonds, and three clubs to the Queen-Ten, just as you did before. But your Partner should retain the singleton King of *clubs*, and *three diamonds* to the Queen-Ten. Then, no matter how the Declarer plays, you will have both diamonds and clubs protected twice so that he cannot take more than 1 trick in either suit.

How can you exchange the necessary information to bring about this result without seeing all four hands? Simply by making a temporizing discard at the first opportunity. Let us say that after the opening heart lead, Declarer starts leading spades. On the fifth round, being exhausted of spades, you should discard the six of clubs. This discard will later show Partner the suit you are protecting. Meanwhile, your partner, after throwing off his worthless hearts, will have an opportunity to give you information. His first informative discard should be the six of diamonds. From now on the Declarer is doomed. You know that your Partner holds something in diamonds, and you can therefore afford to blank your King by throwing off your two little ones. Your Partner knows that you have something in clubs, and he can afford to blank his King of that suit. Thus your partnership secures command of the diamond and club situation by an exchange of signals.

Miscellaneous Discarding

Another rather important feature of discarding is the proper play after opening the highest card of Partner's bid suit. It is customary, under circumstances such as this, to *discard downward*. For example, if you hold 8 5 3 of the suit Partner has bid, and make the eight-spot your opening lead, the five should be played the next time the suit is led. This gives Partner a partial count on your hand, and enables him to place you definitely with a void in the suit whenever your second card is the lowest one outstanding. This conventional discarding downward, as a matter of fact, is of more importance against a suit contract than against a no-trump contract.

Another unusual discard occurs when Partner opens an Ace against a no-trump contract. This lead must be from a long and very strong suit. It requires you to unblock that suit and to give Partner as much information as possible regarding your own holding in it. You do this by playing your highest card first, regardless of its denomination, and following with your next highest. For instance, with 9 7 6, play first the nine and follow with the seven-spot.

Third Hand's Play to Partner's Short-Suit Leads

When you are sitting Third Hand, and Partner's opening lead is either the top of a short honor sequence or a pure desperation lead, the problem of what to do next is not by any means as difficult as it might appear.

When Partner's opening lead is an honor, you know immediately that he must also hold the honor directly below it in rank, but you cannot be very positive about the length of the suit. As a general rule, to be safe, you should assume that the suit probably contains at least four cards, but you must at the same time provide for the possibility that it contains only three cards—or even, occasionally, only two cards. The distribution of the suit is bound to show up more clearly after a few tricks have been played.

Naturally, when you yourself hold two cards headed by an honor, it is almost certain that Partner's lead is from four or five cards, and you must pave the way in your subsequent defense by unblocking immediately. When you hold three cards to an honor, you must encourage Partner by playing the middle card; when you hold four or more cards to an honor, the matter is even simpler, because you do not care whether Partner's lead is a short suit or not. With four low cards a temporizing discard is called for. In all other instances, the proper play is the lowest card you hold.

The desperation lead—top of a worthless short suit—does not require much comment. The only difficulty is how to tell Partner's desperation lead from a plain length lead. As a matter of fact, this dilemma is really your Partner's, not yours. He should avoid ever making a desperation lead with any card lower than the seven-spot, lest you mistake it for a length lead. If he simply cannot give you a desperation lead with a card higher than a seven, the application of the Rule of Eleven to Partner's lead will usually tell whether it is a length lead—or whether it can be a length lead. If the Rule of Eleven obviously does not fit the lead, the card may be taken as "top of nothing"—and usually it pays to assume that such a lead is being made from a three-card suit until later information tells you otherwise. In playing on such a lead, your own honor holdings should be handled as though Partner did not exist so far as that particular suit is concerned.

SUMMARY

This chapter has by no means told the whole story of defensive discards, but these elementals are always true:

The echo is the discard of a high card in a suit followed at a later time by a lower card of the same suit. The echo can be made by playing a trey first, later followed by the deuce—either in following suit or in throwing off on a suit of which your hand has no more cards. The echo, or "high-low" signal, is always encouraging. Until it is completed, Partner must take the first card—whether apparently encouraging or otherwise—with a grain of salt. The normal discarding of the lowest card followed by higher ones is discouraging. The temporizing discard, by far the most important because used the oftenest, consists of a card of a denomination such that, for the moment, Partner does not know whether it is encouraging or not. He has to decide for himself.

CHAPTER XXI

DEFENSIVE PLAYS BY SECOND HAND

T HUS far defensive play has been analyzed in fairly logical sequence, starting with the opening lead and continuing through the plays which are made later. A modern interpretation of leads and discards has been given. In all of these instances the Defending Side were attacking the Declarer, for the most part—either leading or making some preparation for a future lead. As a matter of fact, the Defending Side attack with comparative rarity. By far the greater part of the time the Defending Side are following suit to Declarer's leads and either winning or refusing to win these tricks.

The problem of the defensive player in the fourth position—that is, Fourth Hand in playing to a trick, after the other three players have already played—is not very difficult. Most of the time it is fairly easy for Fourth Hand to see when he should win the trick, if he can, and when he should refuse to win it.

The problem of the defensive player in the second position—he who plays Second Hand to a trick—is much less simple, for either the Dummy and Partner still have to play, or the Declarer and Partner still have to play. In other words, when you are Second Hand to a trick, there are still two chances left for someone else to win the trick after you play. The defensive play of Second Hand resolves itself into two categories: (1) the proper defensive plays when one is playing *before the Dummy*, and (2) the proper defensive play when one is playing *before the Declarer*.

PLAYING DEFENSIVELY BEFORE THE DUMMY

Playing defensively before the Dummy is no more difficult than playing before the Declarer, for you see not only your own cards but those in the Dummy. Nine times out of ten the Dummy's holding in the led suit will furnish the clue for Second Hand's proper play. Against no-trump contracts, particularly, it is no great problem for Second Hand to find the correct defense.

There is an old Whist maxim that Second Hand should play low— "Second Hand low"—which is analogous to that other one already discussed ("Third Hand high"). This saying has a lot of truth in it, in spite of the fact that it was at one time much overdone in the observance. The formula is still good, but it must be phrased somewhat differently, as follows: *Play low Second Hand unless there is some good reason for doing otherwise.*

The most obvious situation for playing Second Hand low occurs when the play of a high card will certainly sacrifice a trick. The following distribution illustrates the point:

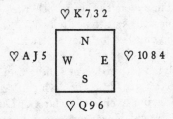

Declarer (South) leads the six-spot. You are Second Hand to this trick (West). Which of your three hearts should you play? Certainly you will not play the Jack, for this would be a purposeless waste of a possibly valuable card, as the Dummy will probably play the King anyway. Your choice, then, rests between the Ace and the five. If you play the Ace, the Dummy will play a small card and Declarer's Queen will be promoted to rank with Dummy's King and command the suit. In fact, since in this example hearts break 3-3 for the Declarer, he will be able to make 3 heart tricks if you go up with the Ace. The chances are that you cannot lose the Ace by holding it up for one round, so why not postpone cashing it in? Thus you decide that the five is your best play. If the Declarer goes up with Dummy's King, your Ace-Jack becomes a perfect tenace over Declarer, even if he should hold Queen-Ten, giving you 2 heart tricks if the suit is led again.

Even suppose the heart situation is as follows:

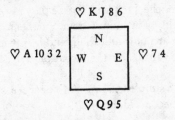

Suppose Declarer (South) leads the five-spot. You, as Second Hand (West), cannot see all four hands, but as you look at them now in the example above, you notice that if you play the deuce the Declarer can then win with the eight-spot. However, the Declarer cannot see all four hands! With both the Ace and Ten missing, he will probably lead his five with the intention of playing Dummy's Jack. When the Jack holds the trick, he will probably lead the six from Dummy and play his Queen. Then you can win with the Ace and hope that Declarer will later play the suit to be divided 3-3 (by leading his King) which will establish your Ten for another trick. Your proper play on the first round, then—since no one can see all four hands—is the deuce.

The point underlying all this discussion is that a defensive player should almost never try to win a trick which does not contain some honor originally belonging to either Declarer or Dummy. If you win a trick with an Ace on which everyone around the table has a chance to throw off small cards, the full value of that Ace is depreciated by half. You remember the promotional value of honors—that every time two honors fall on one trick an honor directly below becomes promoted in rank. This is what happens when, in the preceding example, you refuse to take your Ace until you can capture Declarer's Queen with it. Always play an Ace, if possible, in such a way that it will capture at least one opposing honor.

Look at the preceding example once again. The most foolish play of all would be the Ten. To be sure, the Ten will, you might say, force Dummy's Jack—but why do that? It is presumably the Declarer's *intention* to play Dummy's Jack when he leads his five-spot, and your play of a low card is not going to change his mind. Playing to "force out" a higher card for no reason at all is a weakness of some players. They feel that they have gained something if the Ten, in the last example, does force out Dummy's Jack, when actually they have succeeded only in losing the Ten. Besides, even supposing that, in a rare instance, the Jack will not be played from Dummy regardless of what you do, what about your Partner? He is likely to have at least one high card now and then, and he must be allowed full opportunity to take advantage of the situation if Declarer plays low from the Dummy also.

Following is another simple example of the necessity for playing low in the position of Second Hand:

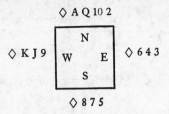

Here Second Hand (West) is in a finessing position when the Declarer leads the five. You, as West, must play your nine. The play of either the King or the Jack merely simplifies the Declarer's play—in fact, it will place for him all the missing honors in your hand. By playing the nine you may induce the Declarer to finesse Dummy's Queen on the first round, thereby making your King-Jack worth 1 sure trick.

A sequence changes the outlook, thus:

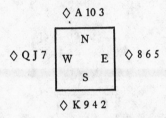

Here it is advisable, when West is Second Hand, to play for the certainty of making 1 trick. If Declarer leads low you, as West, should play the Jack, which forces the Ace and leaves you with a sure third round winner. Notice carefully the difference between this and the preceding situations. Here the play of the Jack is right because of the threatening Ten in the Dummy. Suppose the suit were distributed as follows:

◇ A 8 3 2

◇ Q J 7   N W E S

◇ 4 led

Now it would be dangerous for West to play the Jack, as the chances are against the Declarer's holding ◊ K 10 9 4. The danger in playing the Jack lies in the fact that to do so might conceivably force Dummy's Ace and drop Partner's singleton King. This would happen if the complete distribution were as follows:

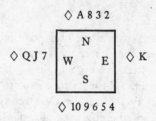

◊ A 8 3 2

◊ Q J 7   ◊ K

◊ 10 9 6 5 4

Put another way, with the Dummy holding ◊ A 8 3 2, the chances are pretty good that Partner holds either the King or the Ten, and to play low will force Dummy's Ace just as surely as to play the Jack— and is much safer.

Somewhat peculiar is the following specific instance in which Second Hand should also play low with a sequence:

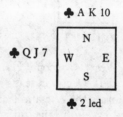

♣ A K 10

♣ Q J 7

♣ 2 led

With Declarer leading the deuce, you, as West, must play the seven even though you know that the Dummy's Ten may win the trick. Your only hope is that the Declarer will consider the possibility too remote that you have Queen-Jack and do not play one of them, and will simply, as a matter of safety first, go up with the Ace, hoping that the suit will ultimately break to his advantage. You see, to play the Jack here, flaunting it in the face of Dummy's powerful hold-ing, will give away the whole situation. The Declarer would win with Dummy's King, return to his own hand by way of another suit, and lead another low club. You would have to play low on this second round, which would practically tell the Declarer that you also have the Queen. He could not fail to finesse the Ten on the second round, preventing you from getting any tricks in clubs. Thus to play low on the first round is your only chance to make a club trick—by persuading the Declarer to play safe by not taking that double finesse of the Ten on the first round.

When Declarer leads low and Dummy lacks any high cards, Second Hand's decision becomes a matter of common sense. In the first place, ask yourself whether you want the lead or you wish your Partner to have it. If you want your Partner to get in the lead, you naturally play low and hope that Partner can overtake the Dummy; if you want the lead yourself, you naturally play higher than any card in the Dummy. But you cannot do this invariably. If you can win the trick cheaply—without the expenditure of a very high card— you should do so, generally speaking. Thus you would play the Jack from a King-Jack holding if the Dummy has no card higher than the Ten. But if you hold Ace-Queen, or only the Queen, you must be a bit circumspect.

Consider, for example, the following spade distribution:

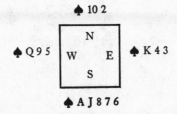

You are West. If Declarer leads the six, and you play the Queen, it will hold the trick. But the next time spades are led the Declarer will be able to lead a small card from Dummy and finesse through your Partner's King, rendering it worthless. By playing low on the first trick, you let Partner win with his King while you still retain your Queen as a certain winner for the third round.

The given situations take care of practically all low leads by the Declarer. When the Declarer leads a high card, and you are Second Hand to play before the Dummy, you have a real problem when the Dummy also holds a high card. You have undoubtedly heard the slogan to "cover an honor with an honor," which means that whenever a high card is led toward a hand which contains a higher honor, the intermediate hand (Second Hand) should play the middle honor in all cases so that the higher honor from Third Hand must be played to win the trick.   This is in direct contradiction to that other old saw that Second Hand should always play low!   Covering an honor with an honor, in Second Hand position, will very often prove to be the best play.

Note the following heart distribution:

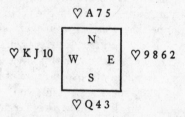

♡ A 7 5

♡ K J 10   N   W   E   S   ♡ 9 8 6 2

♡ Q 4 3

Here the decision is easy to reach.   If Declarer leads the Queen, you must of course cover with the King, which assures you of 2 tricks in hearts.   Against this you have the objection that if the Declarer knows much about Bridge he will not lead the Queen, for it is the height of folly to attempt such a finesse—as you already know.

Suppose that the hearts were distributed as follows, however:

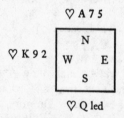

♡ A 7 5

♡ K 9 2   N   W   E   S

♡ Q led

Now Declarer leads the Queen, and what do you play?   You certainly hesitate about covering that Queen with your King, for Dummy's Ace will surely win.   But to cling to the King will do you no good, for if the Declarer also holds the Jack and Ten, he will continue to lead hearts until your King is caught eventually.   It is much better to "cover an honor with an honor," forcing the Dummy's Ace in the hope that Partner may have the Jack or Ten, which will be promptly promoted. If you hold up your King, you let Declarer's Queen win; if you cover the Queen, you reduce Declarer's Ace-Queen to 1 trick instead of 2.

Suppose the preceding distribution were as follows, complete:

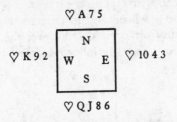

Now if West plays low on Declarer's Queen lead, and then does the same on the Jack, Declarer must eventually catch both King and Ten on the third round. Thus Declarer makes 4 heart tricks. But if West covers the Queen on the first round, the Ace goes up, the Jack wins the second round, and *Partner's Ten wins the third round*.

In the last example, if you, as West, lack that nine-spot with your King, you should reconsider covering an honor with an honor—especially against a good player. Any Declarer acquainted with the rudiments of the game will not lead the Queen unless he holds a lower honor with it. If Declarer does hold the Jack, however, together with the nine, he might attempt a secondary finesse, thus:

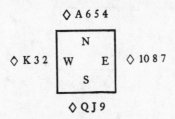

Here Declarer leads the Queen as before. If you, as West, cover with your King, Dummy's Ace will win and Declarer will lead a low card from this hand. If East plays the eight, Declarer can finesse his nine and catch the Ten with the Jack. Consequently, when you hold the King *and* the Ten or the nine, you should not hesitate to cover; but without one of these cards, you must weigh the issue. This does not mean that you should fail to cover the Jack if it is led subsequently, for then your only hope is that Partner holds the Ten and that your play of the King will establish a trick.

As to the question of covering honors other than the Queen, you need good judgment again. *Usually* it is a good play to cover the Jack with the Queen whenever the Dummy holds two dangerous cards, but to refrain from covering whenever the Dummy holds but one threatening card. Take the following situation, for example:

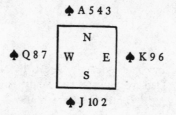

If Declarer leads the Jack and you cover with the Queen, the Declarer will win with Dummy's Ace and his Ten will now be sitting over* Partner's King. If you refuse to cover, Partner will win the trick with the King. Then if the Ten is led later, you can cover and establish Partner's nine.

Here is another Jack-Queen situation where there is only one threatening card in Dummy:

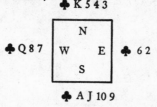

---

* To avoid any possible misunderstanding, it might be well to explain for those not used to Bridge parlance that "over" indicates a position *after* another player, and usually directly after, thus giving the "over" player the advantage; similarly, "under" means that the player must play *before* his left-hand Opponent, and hence is at a disadvantage. To say that a holding is "in back of" a hand, is equivalent to saying that it is "over" that hand. To be "behind" a player, is to be "over" him; to be "in front of" a player, is to be "under" him. More concisely, "over" indicates a player's position in relation to his right-hand Opponent; "under," in relation to his left-hand Opponent.

Here if you cover Declarer's Jack lead with your Queen, your Queen has been successfully "found" and captured. If you do not cover, the Declarer who (not being clairvoyant) was probably just probing, like as not will go up with the King and finesse against your Partner instead. Covering is just what he wanted you to do to save himself a guess.

The Jack lead should always be covered with Second Hand's Queen whenever it is apparent that, by not covering, Second Hand is establishing a tenace in the Dummy *against* the Defending Side. The following is the simplest situation of this nature:

```
              ◇ A 10 2
            ┌──────────┐
            │    N     │
  ◇ Q 8 3   │  W   E   │
            │    S     │
            └──────────┘
              ◇ J led
```

You (West) must cover with your Queen, for, if you do not, Declarer is certainly going to duck, and even if Partner wins with the King, your Queen-eight is bound to be helpless in front of Dummy's Ace-Ten. The only thing to hope for is that Partner holds—the nine-spot! Suppose he does:

```
              ◇ A 10 2
            ┌──────────┐
            │    N     │
  ◇ Q 8 3   │  W   E   │  ◇ K 9 6 4
            │    S     │
            └──────────┘
              ◇ J 7 5
```

By covering the Jack with the Queen, you force out Dummy's Ace, leaving you with the eight, which can be played before Dummy's Ten, thus making Partner's King-nine a perfect tenace over the Dummy.*

Carrying the principle further, sometimes Second Hand must cover

---

* Of course Declarer may be holding the King and this may turn out to be a simple search for a Queen, as in the previous example. In that case, you've been had. As mentioned, judgment is paramount.—S. F. Jr.

even a Ten to try to establish a tenace position in Partner's hand. Study the following diagram:

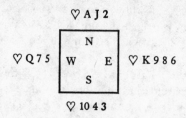

If the Ten is led, and you (West) play low, the Declarer makes 2 sure heart tricks. If you cover the Ten, Partner's King-nine are both bound to win if the suit is led again by the Declarer or yourself.

Still another problem is when to cover honors with honors when intermediate honors are missing, such as a Jack with a King, or a Ten with a King. The same principle holds true. If Dummy holds but one high honor, to cover is generally futile. If the Dummy holds two honors, and you foresee that you are going to be placed in a tenace position under the Dummy, you must sacrifice your honor bravely.

The following diagram illustrates an extreme instance of this:

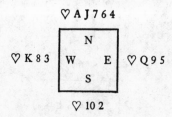

Declarer leads the Ten. You must play the King and let Partner's Queen-nine (which you hope he has) become a tenace over Dummy's Jack. The following is a variation:

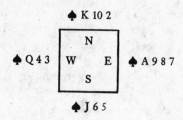

If the Jack is led, you (West) must cover with the Queen. The King is played, and Partner wins with the Ace. The Declarer is thereby held to 1 spade trick, as the Ten is the only card which can make. If you play low on the Jack lead, Partner will be forced to win with the Ace and the Dummy's King-Ten will be worth 2 sure tricks.

An exception to this method of covering occurs when Second Hand's King must be good anyway, as in this situation:

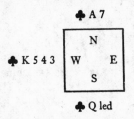

♣ A 7

♣ K 5 4 3

♣ Q led

The Queen being led, you (West) play small and the Queen holds. No more finessing can be done, and the Ace has to win the second round. Thus your King must win the third round no matter what happens.

Playing Defensively Before the Declarer

The fundamental principles of playing Second Hand before the Declarer—that is, on a card led from the Dummy—are exactly the same as those governing Second Hand's play before the Dummy. There is the obvious difference that in playing before the Declarer you cannot see the cards in the next hand to play, as you can see those in the Dummy. However, strange though it may seem, this lack of visibility sometimes makes your decision easier rather than more difficult.

The general rule is that, unless you hold many cards of the suit led, you should *always cover any bare honor led from the Dummy*. For example, with ◇ J 8 2 in the Dummy, and ◇ K 7 5 in your hand, you should not hesitate to plunk the King right on the Jack if it is led from Dummy. This cannot place your Partner in an embarrassing position because he will under no circumstances be playing before the Declarer, who holds the strong part of the suit. However, when the Dummy holds a sequence of two honors, and one of these is led, you must *practically never cover.*

Consider the following situations:

If the Queen is led in No. 1, or the Jack in No. 2, you must play low. If Partner can win the trick, all well and good. You can cover the *second* of Dummy's honors later. If Partner cannot win the trick, nothing is gained or lost for the result is the same no matter what Second Hand does in this case.

The only exception occurs when Second Hand holds a doubleton, thus:

$\diamondsuit$ Q J 8 4

```
        N
    W       E     ◇ K 3
        S
```

If the Queen is led, there is no sense in refusing to cover. If the finesse succeeds, a low card can catch your King later (if you do not cover at once), and Declarer will have used a minimum number of high cards to accomplish his aim. By playing the King at once you seize your one chance of making some gain, for there is a remote possibility that Partner may hold both Ten and nine.

SUMMARY

Defensive play by Second Hand means playing "Second Hand low" sometimes and "covering an honor with an honor" other times. Such rules as can be formulated are as follows:

When playing Second Hand before the Dummy—

Play low when to play high will certainly sacrifice a trick.

Try to capture an adverse honor whenever you play to win a trick.

Play low when you make the Declarer guess on a double finesse from Dummy.

With a sequence, play high to make sure of 1 trick (if Dummy has a threatening card).

With a sequence, play low when to do so may make Declarer consider safety first.

When Dummy has no high cards, use common sense.

With the King and the nine *or* Ten, cover Declarer's Queen lead.

Cover Declarer's Jack lead with the Queen whenever Dummy holds two threatening cards.

Do not cover Declarer's Jack lead with the Queen when Dummy holds only one threatening card.

Cover Declarer's Jack lead with the Queen whenever not to do so will place you under Dummy's subsequent tenace.

Cover Declarer's Jack, or even Ten, to try to establish a tenace over Dummy in Partner's hand.

Cover Declarer's Jack or Ten with even the King when Dummy holds two honors, and you foresee that not to cover may place you in a tenace position under Dummy.

Do not cover when your King must win the third round anyway.

When playing Second Hand before the Declarer—

Always cover a bare honor led from Dummy (except when you hold a great many cards of the led suit).

Do not cover when an honor is led from a sequence in the Dummy (except when your honor heads a doubleton).

CHAPTER XXII

CONTINUATION PLAYS

As already stated, defensive play is the most difficult aspect of Contract Bridge. Its difficulty lies in the fact that it is well-nigh impossible to classify or codify the different situations. Every hand requires special treatment. A principle which applies to one hand may not apply at all to another.

Doubtless you have been admonished to "lead through strength" in the Dummy, when the Dummy is on your left, and to "lead up to weakness" in the Dummy, when the Dummy is on your right. These principles are inherited from Whist, and they are quite sound, generally speaking. They are based on the fact, already demonstrated in this book, that it is more advantageous to play after an Opponent than to play before him, especially when tenace positions exist.

Actually, leading through strength and leading up to weakness amount to the same thing. They are given different names because, in the first, the play is made by an Opponent sitting on the right of the Dummy, and, in the second, by an Opponent sitting on the left of the Dummy. In other words, when you lead "through strength," you are leading through the Dummy so that Partner can play *after Dummy plays.* You hope that Partner holds strength in the suit and can make better use of it playing after the Dummy, which also shows strength in the suit. When you lead up to weakness, you are doing exactly the same thing, except that the Dummy is the weak hand in the suit and you are letting your Partner play *after the strong hand,* which happens to be the Declarer (who is presumably the strong hand, relative to Partner and the Dummy, though Declarer's cards cannot be seen, of course).

The following diagrams bring out these points:

You are sitting West, with the Dummy (North) the only hand you can see besides your own. If Partner leads the particular suit in each example, he will forfeit a trick. If Partner is to obtain the maximum possible number of tricks, in both situations, he must be allowed to play *after the Dummy*. The lead must come, that is, either from your hand or from Declarer's hand. If you are in the lead, there is no occasion to wait for Declarer to open the suit—for to do so would be disastrous for him, as he very well realizes. If you wait, Partner may be forced to lead later on and thus contribute tricks to the Declarer's score. In order to get the full advantage of such a suit distribution as in the foregoing situations, you should lead the suit promptly. The proper card is the highest—which is but an extension of the rule governing the proper card to choose when opening any suit.

A lead through strength should not be made when it appears that to do so may sacrifice a trick. Take, for example, the following situation:

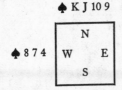

♠ K J 10 9

♠ 8 7 4

If you lead the eight of spades, it is true that you are leading through strength. But this play can do no good unless Partner holds both the Ace and Queen. If he holds the Ace but not the Queen also, he will surely win a spade trick anyway. If he holds the Queen but not the Ace also, Declarer must hold the Ace, and your play through strength simply traps Partner's poor Queen. It is true that the Dummy offers a finessing situation which Declarer can take advantage of himself, if left to his own devices, so you may figure that to lead through it will sacrifice nothing anyway. But it is also true that the Declarer, if allowed to lead spades himself, may not execute the finesse correctly. After all, he does not know where the Queen is, and he may decide to finesse against its being in *your* hand. If he does this, Partner's Queen will win anyway. Again the percentage is against such a lead through strength, for it risks the loss of a trick which might otherwise be made, under favorable circumstances.

To lead through strength in the following situation is even worse:

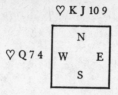

♡ K J 10 9

♡ Q 7 4

If you lead hearts at all you are committing suicide so far as this suit is concerned. You can gain nothing whatsoever, and you abandon your only chance for making 1 trick.

The point to remember is that you should lead through strength only when you do not risk losing a possible trick. Leads through strength are perfectly safe when everything depends on what Partner holds. If he can beat the Dummy, well and good; if he cannot, you simply let the Declarer take a trick with a high card which he must make in any event.

It is not necessary to analyze leads up to weakness in any detail, for they are but variations of leads through strength. The following simple illustrations will suffice:

◇ 8 6 4

1. ◇ Q J 5

◇ 8 6 4

2. ◇ J 10 3

◇ 8 6 4

3. ◇ 7 3 2

Suppose you are sitting East, with the Dummy (North) on your right. If you choose to lead this particular suit, you do so in the hope that Partner will hold some high card or cards in it which will enable him to play more advantageously after the Declarer than before him. Of course, the first situation is the best, and the third is the least desirable. However, they all offer a chance of rendering Partner's hand more effective by a lead up to Dummy's obvious weakness. In each instance, you should lead your highest card.

Applying Leads Through Strength and Up to Weakness

The proper handling of leads through strength or up to weakness, as the case may be, is indicated by the following deal:

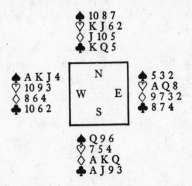

<pre>
                    ♠ 10 8 7
                    ♡ K J 6 2
                    ◇ J 10 5
                    ♣ K Q 5
  ♠ A K J 4   ┌──────────┐   ♠ 5 3 2
  ♡ 10 9 3   │   N   │   ♡ A Q 8
  ◇ 8 6 4   │ W   E │   ◇ 9 7 3 2
  ♣ 10 6 2   │   S   │   ♣ 8 7 4
                 └──────────┘
                    ♠ Q 9 6
                    ♡ 7 5 4
                    ◇ A K Q
                    ♣ A J 9 3
</pre>

Suppose you are sitting West and open the spade King against South's one no-trump contract. On your King, Partner plays the deuce, which tells you immediately that he does not hold the Queen (his discard was discouraging). The Queen being thereupon placed in Declarer's hand, it is apparent that you must try to get your Partner in the lead so that he can return a spade (leading through Declarer's strength and up to Dummy's weakness), thus enabling you to play after the Declarer. The only question you now have to consider is which suit to play next. By applying the principle of leading the suit which will give Partner's hand the best chance of winning, you choose a heart, and lay down your Ten. Dummy probably plays the Jack, and Partner's Queen holds the trick. Now Partner returns the five of spades, and, if South plays the nine, you win with the Jack. If South plays the Queen, you win with the Ace. But in either case you are certain of winning 4 spade tricks. When you are through taking these spades, you lead the nine of hearts, and, regardless of what Dummy plays, Partner is assured of 2 more heart tricks. All together you take 7 tricks, defeating the Declarer's contract by 1 trick.

The advisability of giving Partner a chance to play after the

Dummy is very important in defensive play that takes place after the opening lead. Sometimes, however, the play is not made blindly—that is, not simply because it is generally good policy to do so—but it is made because it offers the best chance of setting the Declarer.

Shifting to a Suit Other Than Partner's Lead

Thus far, the examples have shown that it is a good idea to return Partner's first suit rather than to shift to a suit of one's own. In general, this is the best line of defense, but occasionally some other procedure seems better. The shift to some other suit will be governed partly by the advisability of leading through strength or up to weakness, but this is by no means the whole story.

The following deal brings out the vital point:

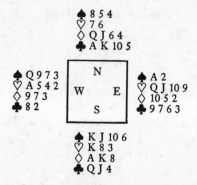

```
                    ♠ 8 5 4
                    ♡ 7 6
                    ♢ Q J 6 4
                    ♣ A K 10 5
      ♠ Q 9 7 3        N        ♠ A 2
      ♡ A 5 4 2                 ♡ Q J 10 9
      ♢ 9 7 3      W     E      ♢ 10 5 2
      ♣ 8 2          S         ♣ 9 7 6 3
                    ♠ K J 10 6
                    ♡ K 8 3
                    ♢ A K 8
                    ♣ Q J 4
```

You are sitting East, playing defensively against South's three no-trump contract. When Partner opens the three of spades, you win with the Ace and—though your first impulse is to return the suit, is this really the best line of defense? Stop and think a moment. By applying the Rule of Eleven, you discover that the Declarer holds as many spades as Partner. Of the three spades which Declarer must hold, two of them are almost certainly honors—as otherwise Partner would have led an honor from a sequence. This means that Declarer will obtain the lead almost immediately, and will probably be able to make his contract at once by means of his diamond and club tricks. Your *only chance of defeating the contract*, then, is to shift to some other suit. But what other suit? The only possible one is hearts, since diamonds and clubs are already pretty well controlled by Declarer, by the looks of the Dummy's hand. At the second trick, therefore, you lay down your heart Queen, leading up to Dummy's weakness (and consequently through whatever strength the Declarer has), and, as it happens, no matter how Declarer plays, your side must win 4 heart tricks. The shift to hearts defeats the contract by 1 trick. The spade return would have presented the game to the Declarer, for he could take 10 tricks before your side regained the lead (the time element).

The preceding deal is an interesting illustration of shifting from Partner's opened suit, but it does not mean that you should always shift to another suit. You must carefully weigh the chances of establishing Partner's suit, as against the chances of establishing your own suit. Whichever course offers the brightest hope is the course to follow.

When it is obvious that to establish your own suit will do no good, since your hand lacks entries and you *know* that you can never regain the lead, desperation tactics are necessary. The shift is clearly in order. You pray that you can strike gold by leading some other suit. Consider the following deal:

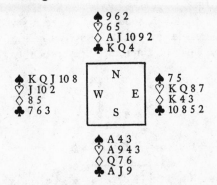

```
                    ♠ 9 6 2
                    ♡ 6 5
                    ◇ A J 10 9 2
                    ♣ K Q 4
                  ┌───────────┐
  ♠ K Q J 10 8    │     N     │    ♠ 7 5
  ♡ J 10 2        │           │    ♡ K Q 8 7
  ◇ 8 5           │  W     E  │    ◇ K 4 3
  ♣ 7 6 3         │     S     │    ♣ 10 8 5 2
                  └───────────┘
                    ♠ A 4 3
                    ♡ A 9 4 3
                    ◇ Q 7 6
                    ♣ A J 9
```

Sitting in the West position, you open the spade King against South's three no-trump contract. Declarer, applying the hold-up, refuses to win the trick, hoping to exhaust or strip the East hand of spades, so that he can never lead your suit back to you when he does get in the lead. You continue with your spade Ten, and again the Declarer holds up his Ace.

Declarer's play here is, as a matter of fact, poorly considered. He ought to know that if you held five spades originally, East can never return a third round. If you held but four originally, and East three, there is no danger in winning the second round either, because the Defending Side can then win but 3 spade tricks and 1 diamond trick at the most. We are supposing, for the sake of our illustration, that the present Declarer is not as good a player as he might be, and that he does hold up for two rounds of spades. You will run up against all kinds of players, so it is perfectly legitimate to assume now and then that your Opponent is not infallible.

Now it should be obvious that for your side to lead the third round of spades will do no good. You will establish two spades in your hand (West's hand), but you have no entries to regain the lead. You must therefore shift to another suit. What is more, this is no time to apply the principle of leading through strength, as Dummy's diamonds look far too potent to tamper with. Your only chance lies in hearts. You therefore lay down your Jack, on which Partner plays the eight (an encouraging discard), and Declarer is hamstrung. No matter how long he holds up his heart Ace, Partner (East) must eventually get in the lead with his diamond King and take enough tricks to defeat the contract.

Another occasion to shift to some other suit occurs when such a play will drive out a valuable entry from Dummy's hand, thus handicapping the Declarer. Of the three instances, probably the last is the most important.

The following deal shows the third type of suit shift:

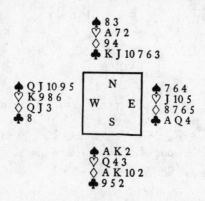

Sitting East, you are defending against South's three no-trump contract. Partner opens the spade Queen, which Declarer wins with the King (you play your four-spot). Declarer now leads a club and finesses Dummy's Ten. The finesse fails, for you win with the Queen. How do you size up the situation? If you return Partner's spades, the Declarer will probably be able to hold up and strip your hand of the suit. He will then certainly drive out your club Ace and you will not be able to put Partner in the lead. Whatever you play, at this point, Declarer will be able to enter the Dummy by means of the heart Ace and cash in his remaining clubs!

The heart Ace looms up as a vastly important card. Perhaps if you can drive it out of the Dummy immediately, Declarer will find the lack of it a sore trial. You therefore shift to hearts, laying down your Jack at the third trick. Whether or not Declarer plays the Queen, and whether or not he plays the Ace out of the Dummy, the entry will eventually be gone, for your Partner will cover the Queen. When Declarer tries to establish his clubs then, you simply hold up your Ace until the Declarer's own hand is stripped of the suit. He will then have to let you take whatever losing tricks he has left in his hand, for he can throw off none of them on Dummy's good clubs. A spade return, you see, would have allowed him to make his contract with ease.

The importance of driving out a vital entry from the Dummy is seen to be very well worth considering. Sometimes the principle develops into what is known as the Deschapelles Coup, which is described in a later chapter on advanced play.

SUMMARY

Generally speaking, when sitting on the right of the Dummy, you should lead a suit through Dummy's strength. Do not do so, however, if the play may sacrifice a trick. Leads up to weakness, when you sit on the left of the Dummy, are really leads made through presumed strength in the Declarer's hand, so that Partner can play after the strong holding. These leads during defensive play after the opening lead may have particular application when they offer the best chance of defeating the Declarer's contract, by shifting to some suit other than Partner's first lead, as indicated by the following general rules:

Shift to another suit—

When it seems to afford a better chance of establishing tricks than does Partner's suit.

When you hold no entries after your own suit will become established.

When you can drive out what looks like a vital entry in Dummy's hand.

CHAPTER XXIII

OPENING LEADS AGAINST A SUIT CONTRACT

T HE time has come to abandon temporarily the subject of defense against a no-trump contract and consider some of the aspects of defense against a suit contract. Of course, the majority of the principles taken up in discussing defensive play against no-trump apply with equal force to defensive play against suit contracts. However, some modification has occasionally to be made to fit the conditions when one suit (the trump suit) is of greater trick-taking power than the other three. Also, quite a number of new principles will be introduced.

The proper place to start is again with the opening lead. This is the first shot fired by the Defending Side, and the best possible effort should be made to have it take effect. Strangely enough, the opening lead against a suit contract does not greatly differ from that against no-trump. The same conventions, in general, are still effective. The lead of a Queen still tells Partner that the leader has the Jack, and the lead of a King promises the Queen or the Ace. Also, the lead of a low card is usually to be regarded as the fourth best from a long suit, so that the Rule of Eleven can be used by Partner. However, the order of preference in opening leads against a suit varies somewhat from that against no-trump, because the conditions of play differ.

The Most Desirable Leads Against a Suit Contract

The best opening lead of all is undoubtedly the lead of the King from an Ace-King holding. This lead is not only almost certain to win the first round, but it permits you to see the Dummy before you take your next step in planning your defense. Against no-trump, it is usually better to lead away from Ace-King combinations to facilitate development of long-suit tricks. Defending against a suit, however, you cannot waste time thinking about long-suit tricks, for by the time you develop any the Declarer or Dummy will be exhausted of the suit and able to trump in. Unlike no-trump defense, suit defense does not involve waiting around to take tricks. The best policy is almost always to grab what you can, and run—hoping, naturally, that what you can grab will be enough to set the contract.

Perhaps the next best lead against a suit is a singleton, or the top card of a doubleton, in the suit bid by Partner (if he bid a suit). This lead has several advantages. The fact that Partner has bid the suit indicates that he must have some strength in it, showing that he will either be able to win the first round or perhaps the second or third round. Furthermore, such a lead immediately shortens your own hand and puts you in the position of being able to ruff either the second or third round of that suit. The singleton lead is better than the doubleton because Partner need hold only the Ace to make the lead a strategic success.

The third best lead against a suit is already familiar to you. It is called, you remember, the honor-sequence lead, such as the King from King-Queen, the Queen from Queen-Jack or the Jack from Jack-Ten. Here again you perceive a difference between no-trump and suit defense. In no-trump defense the honor-sequence lead is most effective when the suit also has length; in suit defense, the lead is usually more likely to produce results when the suit contains only three cards. The reason for this is not far to seek. The more cards of a suit you hold, the fewer your Opponents will hold, and consequently the greater risk you run of being ruffed. The shorter your suit, the greater chance you have of making tricks before the Declarer can ruff.

There is another slight modification of the no-trump honor-sequence lead. Against no-trump it is customary to prefer the honor lead to a length lead only when three honors in sequence (or two honors in sequence with the third card only one step removed) are held. Against a suit, this is not true. Holding either K Q x x or Q J x x, your proper lead is the top honor—not the low card. The element of time is so much more important in suit defense that this is an important difference. You cannot afford to gamble on setting up a winner for the third or fourth round, because such winners exist only in rare distributions. Whatever tricks you win with high cards against a suit contract must be taken on the first or second rounds of the suit, as a rule. This also explains why the lead of the King from K Q x is desirable against a suit but undesirable against no-trump.

Other Good Leads Against a Suit Contract

Other good leads against a suit contract cannot be ranked in order of preference, since this is practically impossible, owing to the variety of conditions which may arise. The bidding is an important factor which cannot be allowed for in any set rule. The individual player will have to use his own best judgment, taking into consideration all the knowledge that he possesses.

There is the lead of Partner's bid suit when more than a doubleton is held. This may be a very good lead, in that it starts constructive defense. The only question is the choice of the particular card in that suit, which happens not to be very difficult. With four or more cards in Partner's bid suit, you should always lead the fourth best, the only exception being that the Queen should be led from Q J x x, and the Ace should be led from A x x x. With three cards the choice is less simple, and there is much difference of opinion among expert players which lead is likely to work out to the best advantage. If the three cards are headed by the Ten or some lower card, it is universally agreed that the highest of the three cards should always be led.[*] But if the tripleton in Partner's suit is headed by a card higher than the Ten, opinion is divided. The writer has found that the Jack from J x x and the Ace from A x x are good leads; and that the lowest card from K x x or Q x x seems the most desirable. The decision is a close one, but with K x x or Q x x it seems fairly evident that the honor should be retained, either for an entry later on or to kill any honor which may be held by the Declarer. Since the Jack in J x x cannot be expected to serve either purpose, it may as well be led. And to lead away from the Ace in A x x is far too dangerous a lead to toy with. Of course, when a doubleton is held originally, the higher of the two cards should be led, honor or no honor.

Short-suit leads against a suit are about the most paradoxical of all opening leads. If they succeed, they are crowned with glory, but if they fail, they deserve only ashes. When a short-suit lead fails to click, it may lose more than 1 trick, which is a dismal result. The advantage of a short-suit lead lies in the fact that the leader's hand is shortened and thereby is nearer to ruffing power. The chief disadvantage of such a lead lies in the fact that its significance is very easily read by the Declarer, so that he can immediately place all the missing honors in that suit in the hand of the leader's Partner. The card reading may do the Declarer no good, and if so the lead does no harm in that deal, but it may frequently be the very information the Declarer needs to enable him to make his contract.

[*] See Chapter XII, Part II, for a further discussion of this subject.—S. F. Jr.

Many players like to lead a low (worthless) singleton, or the top of a worthless doubleton.   Curiously enough, experience has shown that the worthless doubleton is a better lead than the worthless singleton. The reason is that the doubleton lead can be read with less facility by the Declarer, while it still offers almost as much of a chance of developing ruffing power in the leader's hand.   Futhermore, a small card is retained which may be of use in getting over to Partner's hand.

A player's trump holding is frequently the determining factor in choosing between an ordinary length lead and a short-suit lead. Strangely enough, the more trumps you hold the less inclined you should be to open a short suit.   With four or more trumps your object should be to try to reduce the number of Declarer's trumps, and so it is better to choose some long suit which may eventually compel him to ruff, thereby bringing him nearer your level.   This will be explained more fully in the chapter on Forcing the Declarer.

When you hold only two or three trumps, especially when they are headed by an honor which may easily turn out to be an entry, the short-suit lead is often a very successful maneuver.

A short-suit lead from any holding containing a single honor should usually be avoided.   Preserve as long as possible combinations like Ace-small, King-small, Queen-small, and Jack-small, as they are bound to prove more valuable if the suits in which they are held are first led by the Declarer.   Occasionally the Ace may be led from Ace-small in order to develop ruffing power when no other lead is available, but as a general rule it should be eschewed.   The Jack from Jack-small is also a possible lead on occasion, but the King-small and Queen-small combinations should be opened only when the situation is very desperate.

A lead of a singleton honor is just about as undesirable, with the possible exception of the singleton Ace.   To lead a singleton Ace gives you ruffing power in that suit immediately while you still retain the lead.   To lead a singleton King can only be described as dreadful, while a singleton Queen lead is not much better.   The latter may sometimes be led as a desperation lead, but the King can almost never be.   A singleton Jack, on the other hand, is sometimes a very desirable lead.

As for leading the top of two honors in sequence, this is really a pretty good lead. The King from King-Queen alone or the Queen from Queen-Jack alone are both very desirable, since they offer good foundations for later defensive play. The top card is usual, even from Ace-King alone, when the conventional opening is the Ace followed by the King on the second round. Whenever the opening lead of the Ace is immediately followed by the King on the next round, Partner knows that you hold no more cards of that suit, as this play is a reversal of the normal procedure when holding an Ace-King combination. He thus is informed of your ruffing power.

The simple or plain length lead, so common in no-trump defense, is also fairly common in suit defense, especially when no better lead is available. To lead fourth best from K x x x, Q x x x, J x x x or 10 x x x, at least stands a chance of promoting honors in Partner's hand, and may develop second- or third-round winners immediately. You may be surprised to see K x x x included here, for you have probably been told by some wiseacre that you should "*never* lead away from a King." Such advice is fantastic. Admittedly it is not usually a very desirable lead, but sometimes it is very necessary. The lead away from the lower honors is less dangerous, but the lead away from the lone King has the compensational advantage of the time element. A trick can be established with this lead more quickly than with any of the others if Partner holds but one high honor, namely, either the Ace or the Queen.

To lead fourth best from A x x x, however, is usually ill-advised, as to do so may lose a trick to Declarer's or Dummy's singleton King, especially when the leader holds more than four cards topped by the Ace. However, in certain desperate situations, such a lead must be made. These desperate cases will be described later.

You may also recall that the top card from a worthless tripleton was mentioned as a possible lead against no-trump. This lead is good against no-trump only when the leader's hand is otherwise quite worthless. Against a suit contract, such a lead—top of a worthless tripleton—is more advantageous when the rest of the hand is quite strong. The worthless suit is deliberately chosen to let the leader retain untouched his tenace combinations in the other three suits. Tenace combinations, which should not, as a rule, be led away from, include A Q x, K J x, A J x, A 10 x, and the like. For this reason, the lead of the top of a worthless tripleton is rather more common in suit than in no-trump defense.   In fact, such a lead is better than any card from A x, A x x, or A x x x.

Finally, there is the lead of the Declarer's trump suit.   When it is apparent from the bidding that the chief strength of the Declarer's hands depends on Dummy's ruffing power, the time element becomes of prime importance, and the Defending Side must make the most of the fact that they have the first move.   You might quite reasonably change your mind if you could see the Dummy first, but that first lead may very often be vital.   This trump lead is not common, but it must be mentioned here as a possibility, since it is sometimes imperative.   A later chapter is entirely devoted to the subject of killing Dummy's ruffing power.

The Declarer's trump suit may also be selected for the opening lead when the bidding has shown that the Declarer and Dummy hold all the strength in their bid suit.   This means that to lead a trump cannot possibly injure Partner's hand.   When no other desirable opening is available, the trump may be led under these circumstances.

As you gain in knowledge of suit defense, you will find it easier to judge which of all possible opening leads you have in your hand is the best.

Opening Leads Based on the Bidding

In our discussion of opening leads so far, we have not referred to a certain type of lead which occasionally proves very valuable.   This is the lead of a suit which has been bid on your left and denied on your right, and applies particularly to hands played at a suit contract. For example, let us suppose that the bidding has gone as follows:

SOUTH	WEST	NORTH	EAST
One Spade	Pass	Two Hearts	Pass
Two Spades	Pass	Two No-trump	Pass
Four Spades	Pass	Pass	Pass

You are sitting West and hold the following hand:

♠ Q 10 4
♡ 8 6
♢ K J 3 2
♣ Q 10 7 4

Obviously you cannot open the trump suit, as this will almost certainly sacrifice a trick.   Clubs and diamonds are both possible leads, but both run the risk of shooting right into an opposing tenace situation. It is true that hearts have been bid on your left, but they have not been supported—in fact, South showed little enthusiasm after hearing his Partner's heart take-out, but jumped to game over his second response. It would seem, therefore, as though South must not have much of a fit in hearts, and since North has never rebid the suit, the balance of strength must be with East. Your best opening, therefore, is a heart.

If you held an honor in the suit, such as the King or Queen, the principle would not apply. Then you would be better advised to open from one of your tenaces and hope for the best.

In no-trump contracts, a lead of this type should not be employed unless you are certain that the suit has been denied. A mere no-trump rebid does not imply a denial, as more often than not the opening bidder will hold a fit in his Partner's suit. Beware of bidding of this type:

South	West	North	East
One Spade	Pass	Two Diamonds	Pass
Two No-trump	Pass	Three No-trump	Pass
Pass	Pass		

If you are West and hold:

♠ Q 10 3 2
♡ K J 8 4
◊ 8 6
♣ Q 7 3

prefer the normal heart opening. A diamond lead will probably result only in trapping an honor of your Partner's. If your Partner should double three no-trump, however, then you must open a diamond. He is insisting on a lead through strength and telling you that he has the suit well under control.

Summary

The most desirable opening leads against a suit contract are the following:
1. The King from Ace-King and small cards.
2. A singleton or top of doubleton in Partner's bid suit.
3. The top of a sequence of two or more honors.

Other good leads (not in the order of preference, since to rank them is next to impossible) are the following:

Partner's bid suit—fourth best with four or more cards (except Q J x x, when the Queen shoul   be led, or A x x x, when the Ace should be led); the top of a tripleton headed by the Ten or lower; the Jack from J x x or the Ace from A x x; the lowest card from K x x or Q x x.

The top of a worthless doubleton, or, slightly less good, a worthless singleton.

The top of two honors in sequence, without lower cards in the same suit. This includes the Ace first from Ace-King alone, followed by the King on the second round.

The fourth-best card from a four-card or longer suit headed by a single honor (King, Queen, Jack or Ten).

Declarer's trump suit when the bidding has shown (a) dependence on Dummy's ruffing power, or (b) such trump strength that Partner's hand cannot be injured.

A lead of a suit which has been bid on your left and denied on your right.

The leader's hand should be scrutinized for all possible leads, and the lead finally selected should always be the best that the hand affords.

CHAPTER XXIV

DEFENSIVE SUIT PLAY BY THIRD HAND

AFTER the opening lead has been made, the defense devolves upon the leader's Partner, who is Third Hand in playing to the trick. The conventions learned for Third Hand defense against no-trump apply with full force to suit defense. You should still, as Third Hand, play high when the Dummy contains no high cards. You should still play the bottom card of your highest sequence when playing Third Hand high. You should still finesse against the Dummy when there seems to be a fair chance of gaining a trick by this means.

In finessing against the Dummy, you must modify your procedure to the extent of preventing the Declarer from winning a trick with a singleton honor. The following illustration shows what is meant:

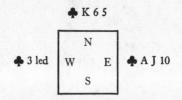

♣ K 6 5

♣ 3 led   ♣ A J 10

Partner opens the trey (of a suit not the trump suit). Assuming that a low card is played from Dummy, which card should you, in East's position, play here? If you play the Ten and Partner happens to have the Queen, you are obviously gaining a trick by finessing around the Dummy; but if the Declarer has the Queen, you are allowing him to take the first trick in the led suit. Is there any objection to letting the Declarer take this trick if he can? The answer to this question depends entirely on the distribution of the suit. By applying the Rule of Eleven you learn that Partner cannot hold more than five cards of the suit he opened—consequently the Declarer must hold at least two. Even if one of these two cards should happen to be the Queen, you still will not lose a trick by finessing the Ten against the Dummy's visible King, for the Declarer must still hold a loser and will probably have to concede it later. Put another way, one of two possible distributions probably exists:

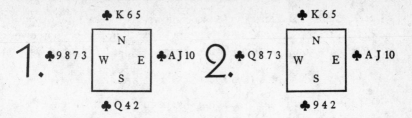

In No. 1, the play of the Ten by East lets the Declarer win a trick at once but leaves the Ace-Jack in perfect tenace position over the Dummy—to win the next two rounds.   The play of the Ace, on the other hand, concedes 2 club tricks to the Declarer.   In No. 2, it should be obvious that the play of the Ace allows Dummy's King to become a winner, while the play of the Ten places the King in a precarious position.

As a contrast with those preceding, consider the following club situation:

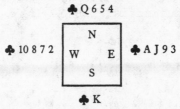

Partner opens the deuce and the Dummy plays low.   The Declarer must hold a singleton, which you learn by application of the Rule of Eleven.   That singleton may or may not be the King.   If you were defending here against no-trump, you would play your Jack—finessing it against the Dummy—in the hope that Partner holds the King, for, even if he does not, you can obtain 3 tricks in the suit later if Partner ever regains the lead.   Against a suit contract, it is risky to try this. If you finesse the Jack, and it loses to Declarer's singleton King, you probably will obtain no tricks in clubs at all—because of Declarer's control of the suit by ruffing. Even if your Ace captures only a low card, you have not lost much because your club tricks in this situation are limited by the threatening trump suit.   By playing high you assure your side of at least 1 trick, and you have time to map out your later defense.

Later defense by Third Hand also follows, in general, the defense against no-trump contracts—developing 1 or 2 tricks in your own suit, leading through strength or up to weakness, and similar plays.

DISCARDS (SIGNALS) IN SUIT DEFENSE

You should recall that discarding signals in no-trump defense were of three kinds, namely, encouraging, discouraging, and temporizing. The same three kinds of discards are used in defensive suit play, but with a slightly different application.

Against a no-trump contract, an encouraging discard usually shows an honor in the led suit plus some length also. Against a suit contract an encouraging discard shows an honor in the led suit but does not also promise length, which is more of a disadvantage than otherwise. Furthermore, the encouraging signal known as the echo is often used in suit defense to show shortness in the led suit.

The ensuing three deals (which are all variations of the same basic deal) illustrate these principles. The following is the first situation:

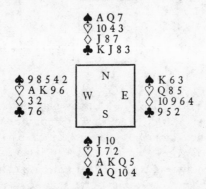

```
                    ♠ A Q 7
                    ♡ 10 4 3
                    ◇ J 8 7
                    ♣ K J 8 3
                 ┌─────────────┐
   ♠ 9 8 5 4 2   │      N      │   ♠ K 6 3
   ♡ A K 9 6     │             │   ♡ Q 8 5
   ◇ 3 2         │  W       E  │   ◇ 10 9 6 4
   ♣ 7 6         │             │   ♣ 9 5 2
                 │      S      │
                 └─────────────┘
                    ♠ J 10
                    ♡ J 7 2
                    ◇ A K Q 5
                    ♣ A Q 10 4
```

You are sitting East defending against South's four diamond contract. Partner opens the heart King. Your hand tells you that this King lead must show the Ace, for you yourself have the Queen. You see, then, that you can win the third round of the suit if the Declarer has three hearts. Certainly you must encourage your Partner to continue the suit, which you do by playing your eight. When Partner complies by leading the Ace on the second trick, you complete your echo by playing the five-spot. Partner again complies,

leading his six, which you win with your Queen. You need but 1
more trick to set South's contract, and you will make it in spades if
you never lead the suit to Declarer.

You may have noticed that in the example given, the Dummy contains tenaces in spades and clubs. Sometimes you should fail to
make an encouraging discard, even when your holding in the led suit
justifies it, in order to suggest to Partner that he lead through strength
by shifting to one of the suits in which Dummy has a tenace. In this
particular deal, however, you do not dare to give Partner the discouraging discard of the five-spot, because he would then be forced
to choose between spades and clubs. It happens to make no difference ultimately, but you cannot know this spontaneously, so your
best policy is to urge Partner to continue leading hearts, which is the
suit in which you stand the best chance of obtaining tricks quickly.

Now consider the following slight variation of the same deal:

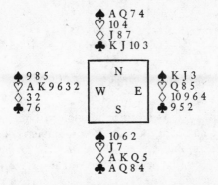

Again Partner (West) opens the heart King against South's contract
of four diamonds. You hold precisely the same heart combination
as before, but notice that the Dummy, instead of holding three hearts,
holds a doubleton. This means that your Queen cannot possibly
win the third round of hearts, because it will be ruffed in Dummy.
Consequently you do not want the suit continued, and you must
not make an encouraging discard. You play the five to suggest to
Partner that he will do better to shift to another suit. Confronted
with a choice between spades and clubs, Partner will probably lead a
spade. The club situation presents an undesirable combination for
leading through strength. West leads the nine of spades, on which

Declarer probably will play low from Dummy since a double finesse appears to be called for. You win with the Jack and return the eight of hearts to Partner's Ace. Another spade lead by West assures the defeat of the contract.

Note that, in the deal just given, if you had echoed in the heart suit, Partner would have led a third round which Dummy would have trumped. This would have enabled the Declarer to throw off one of his spades, and he would have then been able to keep his losers down to 3 tricks.

The following is a third variation of the same deal:

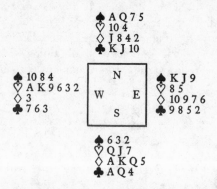

```
                ♠ A Q 7 5
                ♡ 10 4
                ◇ J 8 4 2
                ♣ K J 10
  ♠ 10 8 4          N          ♠ K J 9
  ♡ A K 9 6 3 2              ♡ 8 5
  ◇ 3            W     E      ◇ 10 9 7 6
  ♣ 7 6 3          S          ♣ 9 8 5 2
                ♠ 6 3 2
                ♡ Q J 7
                ◇ A K Q 5
                ♣ A Q 4
```

Now South's contract is only three diamonds, but West's opening lead is again the heart King. As in the preceding deal, the Dummy holds but two hearts, but this time you (East) also hold only two. Consequently you see that it is to your advantage to have the suit continued even through three rounds. On Partner's King lead, therefore, you play the eight (an encouraging discard), and on the lead of the Ace you play the five (completing the echo). The lead of a third heart at the third trick causes the Declarer acute embarrassment. If he simply discards a spade, you will ruff, and he can only follow suit from his own hand. If he ruffs with Dummy's eight or lower card, you will over-ruff. In either case two spades must be taken subsequently. If he goes up with Dummy's Jack, the situation is apparently the same, as he will establish a sure diamond trick in your hand, and the two spade tricks still seem available. However, at this point the contract can actually be made, as will be pointed out when this hand is used in the chapter on End Plays.

ANOTHER ECHO TO SHOW A SHORT SUIT

The following deal presents a situation which occurs very frequently in defending against suit contracts—the echo to show a short suit:

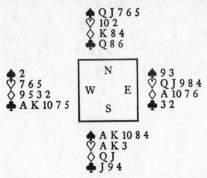

Your Partner (West) opens the club King against South's four spade contract. When a low club is played from Dummy, you play your *three-spot*, Declarer dropping the four. Your trey may not be very illuminating to Partner at this point, for he can hardly place any great hope on so low a card being encouraging. However, he has one glimmer of light in the fact that the deuce has not yet appeared. He reasons as follows: If the Declarer holds the deuce and is deliberately holding it up, the club Ace must surely win the second round; if Partner holds the deuce, the trey must have been the beginning of an echo to show ruffing power at the third round. Either way, the lead of the Ace seems wise. West lays down his Ace, and is overjoyed to see your deuce discarded on it, which shows that you held originally a club doubleton. The Declarer will probably play the Jack in an endeavor to confuse the issue, but Partner's reading has been so perfect that he should not be fooled. West's proper play is to lead a third round of clubs, letting you ruff. The diamond Ace sets the contract.

The echo can also be used in these situations:

1. ◇ A 7 6

    ◇ K led [N / W E / S] ◇ 8 4

2. ◇ A 7 6

    ◇ K led [N / W E / S] ◇ J 8 4

You are East in both situations. Partner opens the King of the suit, and, provided the Ace is played from Dummy, you must play the eight in both instances, because you want Partner to lay down the Queen the next time he is in the lead. Since you, as East in No. 1, have a doubleton, you can ruff the third round if you have a trump left. In No. 2, you at least can make an effort to win the third round with the Jack, if Declarer has three diamonds.

In the following diagram, however, East must not echo:

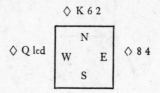

Your chances, as East, of obtaining a ruff on the third round are extremely slim. You must simply play the four-spot on the Queen. A continuation by Partner might easily sacrifice the third round of the suit to the Opponents.

DISCOURAGING AND TEMPORIZING DISCARDS IN SUIT DEFENSE

There is not much to be said about discouraging discards used in defensive suit play. Whenever you wish to discourage the continuation of a suit and suggest some sort of shift by Partner, you simply play the lowest card you have available in the led suit. Your Partner must interpret this kind of discard as a signal to shift his defense.

When it comes to temporizing discards in suit play, you run into a few snags. The following deal may help you to avoid them:

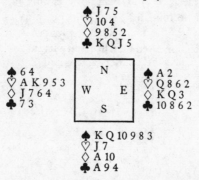

Partner opens the heart King against South's four spade contract. You notice Dummy's heart doubleton, which makes a continuation to the third round very unattractive in view of your own long holding in the suit. However, a second round will apparently do no harm. You therefore play the six-spot, knowing that this will urge Partner to lead out his heart Ace. He undoubtedly follows with this card on the second trick, and you then play the *eight-spot*, thus failing to complete the echo which your six-spot might have begun. This temporizing on your part should induce Partner to shift to another suit at the third trick. He will probably choose diamonds, since Dummy's clubs are patently too strong to lead through. Leading his fourth best diamond, Partner enables you to set up a trick in this suit before your spade Ace (trumps) is taken out. It should be clear that a third round of hearts or a shift to clubs at the third trick will permit the Declarer to make his contract.

THIRD HAND PLAY TO SHORT-SUIT LEADS

This is a much more important phase of the game against a suit contract than against a no-trump contract, partly because the short suit lead is more frequent but chiefly because of the ever-present importance of ruffing power. It is impossible to give any hard and fast rules for telling whether a lead which is obviously from a short suit is a singleton, a doubleton, or a tripleton, but experience has shown that it generally pays to assume a doubleton. When the card led is not an honor you must play whatever honor combinations you hold yourself, as though Partner were not involved in the hand at all, and merely strive to produce the maximum number of tricks in the specific suit without Partner's aid.

One rather interesting type of play must be described here. When Partner's opening lead is some card like an eight or seven and you hold four or five cards to the Ace, it generally pays to refuse to win the first round of the suit, contenting yourself with giving the most encouraging discard available. This play is based on the assumption that Partner's opening lead is a doubleton and that he will continue the suit when he next obtains the lead, allowing you to give him a third-round ruff. Naturally this applies only when the Dummy holds three or four cards of the suit led. When the Dummy holds two, together with some high trump honor, the play is useless because he can over-trump on the third round. If the Dummy holds five or six cards, the assumption of a doubleton no longer holds water and it is best to go right up with the Ace and return the suit in the hope that the lead was a singleton.

The following deal, which you will remember was used in the chapter on Ruffing Power, illustrates the hold-up of the Ace when Partner's lead appears to be a doubleton:

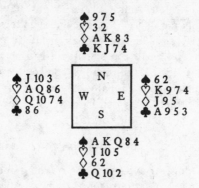

In our previous discussion, West opened the four of diamonds against South's contract of four spades. The trick was won in the Dummy and a heart led immediately in an attempt to develop Dummy's ruffing power. West won the trick with the Queen and shifted to a trump, but it was too late for this play to be successful, and the contract was made.

Actually West had a much better play at his disposal. After winning the Queen of hearts he should lead the eight-spot of clubs (the top card of his doubleton), on which East should play the *nine!* Now Declarer wins the trick with the Ten and lays down one round of trumps as a safety measure. He cannot afford to lead any more, however, and has to play another heart. Whether this trick is won by East or West is immaterial, as the clubs are continued and West trumps the third round for the setting trick.

It should be obvious why East cannot go up with his Ace on the first round of clubs and return the suit immediately. If he does so, Declarer will no longer try to establish a ruffing-trick in Dummy, as he has a perfectly good discard available on the fourth club in Dummy. He will simply draw trumps and fulfill his contract.

Summary

Third Hand no-trump defense applies equally well to suit defense. In particular, the echo in suit defense may have a wider variety of uses than in no-trump defense, for it may show the possession of an honor (to win the second or third round), or ruffing ability (at the third round). Also, failure to echo may indicate either the lack of a winning honor or the knowledge that Declarer or Dummy will be able to ruff the third round. A temporizing discard may be used to induce Partner to continue his opening suit through the second round, on which a higher discard fails to complete the echo, implying that he should shift to another suit at the third trick.

Third Hand play to short suit leads is more important in suit play than in no-trump play. It is usually good policy to assume that Partner's opening is a doubleton, and play low on his lead when holding the Ace so that he can retain his lower card for a subsequent lead.

CHAPTER XXV

THE POLICY OF SUIT SHIFTING

Unlike defense against no-trump contracts, when Partner's lead should almost always be returned, suit defense offers quite a field for the imagination of the individual player. At no-trump contracts you are almost always obligated to return the suit opened by Partner unless (1) you are fairly confident that your own suit can be established more rapidly, (2) it is very obvious that Partner's hand contains no entries, (3) you are desirous of eliminating an entry in Dummy, (4) it is clear that the whole suit is banked against you. Against suit contracts other considerations must be taken into account.

When one suit is predominant, or, in other words, when it is trump, the time element tends to militate against the Defending Side. At no-trump, tricks can very often be sacrificed immediately for the later good of the entire hand; at a suit, no sacrifice can be made without a reason which will prove important within a few tricks. The cause of this, of course, is the trump suit, which is always liable to take control of the whole hand. A shift to a suit other than Partner's, therefore, is frequently not only advisable but necessary, and any postponement of the play is liable to render it completely ineffective later.

Take, for example, the following deal, where a lead through strength must be made immediately because of the danger that the trump suit will interrupt future defensive activities:

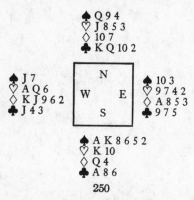

You are sitting East against a contract of four spades, played by South. Your Partner opens the six of diamonds, which you win with the Ace. If you were playing against a no-trump contract, you would be in no trouble in deciding on your proper return; you would simply lead back a diamond. Since spades are trumps, however, you see immediately that the diamond lead will accomplish nothing constructive, even if Partner can win the trick. He will be obliged to lead to the third trick and will not be able to play any card which can advance your combined cause in the slightest.

What is your best chance of defeating the four spade contract? Obviously Partner's spade or club tricks (if any) will make, no matter what you do or what you lead. Your one chance of capitalizing on the fact that you are in the lead lies in the heart suit—perhaps you can strike Partner with some combination of cards in this suit which must be led up to. You therefore abandon the diamond suit and switch to the deuce of hearts. This enables Partner to make both his Ace and Queen of hearts, in addition to his diamond King.

If you had continued the diamond suit, it is obvious that Declarer would have made his contract. Partner, unable to lead from the Ace-Queen of hearts, would probably have shifted to clubs, and Declarer would have been able to discard one of his heart losers on the long clubs in Dummy.

Sometimes a shift of the same type must be made when you know that Partner holds a second round winner in the suit opened and you do not dare trust him to shift suits immediately. For instance:

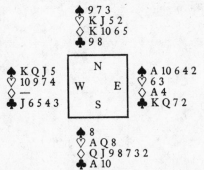

You are again East, defending against a contract of five diamonds, and Partner opens the King of spades. You must pause to consider the situation. Regardless of anything else you are bound to win a trick in trumps. One spade trick can probably be counted on, but can you make 2? If so, well and good, but if Declarer should happen to hold a singleton spade he will ruff your Partner's second lead. You may still obtain a club trick later, but there is a chance that Declarer holds only one club loser and, if so, the fourth heart in Dummy looks awfully dangerous and may easily be a card which can be used for discarding purposes.

You must therefore overtake Partner's King of spades with your Ace and shift immediately to the King of clubs. This insures the defeat of the contract, as you must regain the lead with your Ace of trumps and you can then cash in your good Queen of clubs. Note that, if you had failed to do this and Partner had continued a spade at the second trick, your Ace of diamonds would have been driven out before your club trick was established and the losing club in Declarer's hand would have been discarded on the fourth heart in Dummy. Thus the contract would have been made.

This overtaking play in order to shift can lose nothing. If it develops later that Declarer actually held another spade, this trick is still not lost; it can be cashed in after the setting trick (in clubs) has been taken.

The shift to another suit also occurs frequently when Third Hand sees a chance to develop ruffing power. The presence of a doubleton or a singleton in the hand should suggest immediately the chance of establishing a trick by shortening yourself. Take the following deal, in which you are sitting East, defending against a contract of four hearts played by South:

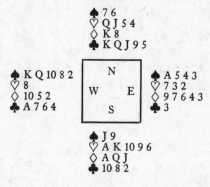

Ordinarily this would be a lay-down, as it seems as though the Declarer and his Partner can lose only 3 tricks—two in spades and one in clubs. However, proper defense will actually defeat the hand by 2 tricks.

Your Partner opens the King of spades, and you must *overtake with your Ace* in order to lead your singleton club. Your Partner should not mistake the meaning of such a lead, as he knows you will not deliberately establish this whole suit for Declarer without some good reason. He therefore returns a club, which you ruff. A spade lead from you puts him in the lead again and enables you to ruff the third round of clubs. You thus defeat an apparently impregnable contract by 2 tricks.

The same principle can also work out very well if applied to doubletons, as in this deal:

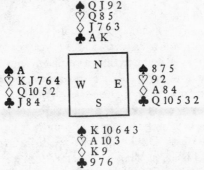

♠ Q J 9 2
♡ Q 8 5
◇ J 7 6 3
♣ A K

♠ A   ♠ 8 7 5
♡ K J 7 6 4   ♡ 9 2
◇ Q 10 5 2   ◇ A 8 4
♣ J 8 4   ♣ Q 10 5 3 2

♠ K 10 6 4 3
♡ A 10 3
◇ K 9
♣ 9 7 6

West opens the deuce of diamonds against South's contract of four spades. You (East) win this trick with the Ace. The futility of returning the suit strikes you at once, as Partner cannot possibly hold both King and Queen (if he did, he would have opened the King). The club situation is obviously hopeless and a trump lead is little short of senseless. There remains one chance. If you can shorten yourself sufficiently in hearts, you may be able to defeat the contract by developing a ruffing-trick.

You therefore return the nine of hearts (top of your doubleton), which Declarer allows West to win with the King. A heart is returned, won with Dummy's Queen, and the trumps started. Your Partner wins the first round with the Ace and leads a third round of hearts, which you, of course, ruff, for the setting trick. Note that this is the only line of defense which can defeat the contract.

Another time when Partner's suit should not be returned is when an honor in the Dummy threatens to become established for a discard. For example, take the following deal, in which you are again sitting East and defending against a four heart contract:

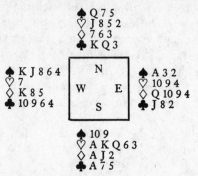

Your Partner (West) opens the six of spades and when Dummy plays low you win the trick with the Ace, as you have no finessing possibilities. You see at once that a return in this suit will establish Dummy's Queen, and so you look around for other means of defense. Of course the diamond suit is the most obvious, and so you shift to the Ten of diamonds. No matter what card Declarer plays, he can not avoid losing 2 diamond tricks and 1 more spade trick, and he is therefore set 1 trick. Obviously, the spade return enables him to get rid of one of his losing diamonds before his Ace is driven out.

There are many hands which call for but a temporary shift; that is to say, Partner's suit is actually continued but not until you have given him some information as to your hand. For example:

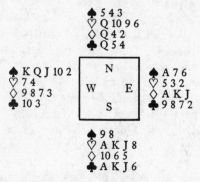

Your partner opens the King of spades against South's three heart contract. You should overtake with the Ace, in order to lay down the King of diamonds. Now you return a spade and Partner comes back with a diamond through Dummy's Queen. If the spade were returned immediately, Partner would be forced to guess whether to lead clubs or diamonds. If he happened to choose clubs, the contract would be made, as Declarer could get rid of a diamond in Dummy on the long club in his own hand.

Another similar case is the following:

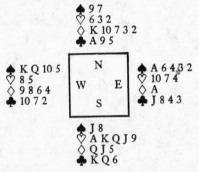

♠ 9 7
♡ 6 3 2
◇ K 10 7 3 2
♣ A 9 5

♠ K Q 10 5
♡ 8 5
◇ 9 8 6 4
♣ 10 7 2

♠ A 6 4 3 2
♡ 10 7 4
◇ A
♣ J 8 4 3

♠ J 8
♡ A K Q J 9
◇ Q J 5
♣ K Q 6

Your Partner (West) opens the King of spades against South's four heart contract. This card you must overtake with the Ace, and lay down the Ace of diamonds. Now when you return the spade, your Partner cannot mistake your meaning, and must return a second round of diamonds which you ruff for the setting trick.

These examples cover about all of the probable occasions for failing to return Partner's lead against a suit contract, which have not already been discussed under Continuation Plays. However, these opportunities will present themselves in many guises, and every situation must be weighed separately. Be sure to remember this— if the return of Partner's suit seems pointless, try to find some better lead. Nevertheless, make sure that to return Partner's lead really is pointless!

SUMMARY

In this short but important chapter you learned that it pays to shift suits at trump contracts more often than it does at no-trump contracts. Sometimes the reason may be that you must lead through strength immediately, and other times it may be because you wish control of the second lead yourself. You must also watch for any possible ruffing power, and be ready to develop it if you see a chance to do so.

CHAPTER XXVI

FORCING THE DECLARER TO RUFF

In no-trump defense, it was pointed out that it is usually very inadvisable to lead from tenace combinations, the reason being that such holdings are sure to prove more valuable when they are led up to than when they are led away from. This same principle applies to suit defense, with the one qualification that the *necessity* for attacking a suit headed by a tenace occurs slightly more often than in no-trump, because of the time element. Less time is available for developing a suit against a trumping Declarer.

As a general rule, it may be said that *it is good practice to throw the lead into the Declarer's hand whenever it is possible to do so.* The best way of accomplishing this is to lead some suit of which the Declarer's own hand is void. He will thus be compelled to exert his ruffing control by playing a trump, which reduces the number of trumps he holds and weakens his control to that extent. The fact that this sort of play has a negative aspect does not detract from its intrinsic value. It certainly loses nothing, and it very often gains something. It is of the greatest possible value when your own or Partner's hand (Defending Side) happens to hold a few trumps. If the Declarer is forced to ruff often enough, the time may come when one of the defending players will hold more trumps than he. When this happens, the Declarer has lost control of the hand and can no longer guide its destinies.

Because to lead a suit of which the Declarer has no more cards induces the Declarer to use one of his trumps for winning the trick, this play is called the *force* or "forcing the Declarer." The deals which follow illustrate how the force is used to gain tricks for the Defending Side. But the reader must bear in mind that these examples have been carefully chosen. In the great majority of hands in actual play the force will not succeed in accomplishing much. Sometimes it succeeds only in "passing the buck" to the Declarer, by obliging him to make the necessary guesses about the future course of the play. But, as stated before, the force loses nothing, and is a good defensive maneuver to annoy the Declarer with, even if it gains but little on some particular deal.

In the following deal the force succeeds in defeating an apparently easy contract of four hearts (played by South):

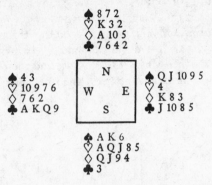

Holding the West hand, you should be immediately aware of the fact that you hold great defensive strength against four hearts. You have four trumps, which will certainly cause the Declarer some anxiety, and you also hold a long suit of your own that is practically established. With this type of defensive holding, it is always a good policy to lead out your strong suit. Even if the Declarer ruffs the first or second round, his trump holding is reduced and your own trump holding becomes more threatening.

To digress for a minute, a long and strong suit in a hand that also contains some length in the trump suit is a very powerful defensive weapon. Whenever you hold length in trumps—four or more—it is always best to open your longest suit, even if that suit is far from being solid. If you happen to catch your Partner with strength in the same suit, forcing the Declarer commences immediately and the value of your trump length mounts at once.

In the preceding deal, you select the club King for your opening lead. This card holds the trick, and you continue with the Queen. Declarer ruffs, and studies the situation. He sees at once that if the hearts are divided 3–2, his contract is safe. He can then take three rounds of trumps and try the diamond finesse. If the finesse fails, he will lose altogether only 1 diamond trick, 1 spade trick, and 1 club trick, as he will have one trump left with which to stop the run of the club suit. He therefore leads a low heart over to Dummy's King and returns a heart to the Ace in his hand. At this point, Partner fails to follow suit.   The Declarer sees that the hearts were not divided 3-2, as he had hoped, and cannot afford to draw your remaining trumps.   If he does draw the rest of the trumps, he will have none left himself, and will thus give up all protection against the club suit in the event that the diamond finesse does not go through as planned. He is therefore obliged to lead the diamond Queen first and play low from Dummy.   Partner wins with the King, and the business of forcing the Declarer shows an advantage.   The situation is as follows:

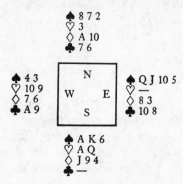

♠ 8 7 2
♡ 3
♢ A 10
♣ 7 6

♠ 4 3   N   ♠ Q J 10 5
♡ 10 9   W   E   ♡ —
♢ 7 6   S   ♢ 8 3
♣ A 9   ♣ 10 8

♠ A K 6
♡ A Q
♢ J 9 4
♣ —

If Partner should forget about the forcing play, and should blindly lead the spade Queen with the vague hope of developing a trick in that suit, Declarer will make his contract by winning the trick, drawing the last two trumps, and giving up a spade trick at the end.   However, Partner does not do this for the simple reason that the manner in which the Declarer has played the trump suit shows that you (West) hold enough trumps to be embarrassing.   East leads a third round of clubs, forcing the Declarer to ruff, and reducing his trumps to one less than you have.

From this point the Declarer is set.   His best play is to lead diamonds until you ruff.   You then lead a fourth round of clubs and he will probably discard a spade.   He then claims the balance of the tricks, but is defeated 1 trick.

An interesting point appears in connection with the above deal. You will notice that the Dummy contained four clubs, so that it was never able to trump the suit.   Had the Dummy ever become short in clubs, the suit should have been abandoned.

The reason for always forcing the long trump hand is obvious.   The

Declarer's long trumps are usually going to be winners eventually. If you force him to take these tricks immediately, you are hurrying his game and yet not giving up to him any tricks which he could not surely take later. If, on the contrary, you force the short trump hand to ruff, you obviously assist the Declarer in his development of ruffing-tricks. You know that part of Declarer's play consists of trying to win tricks with Dummy's otherwise worthless trumps. If, therefore, you lead a suit which Dummy can ruff, you simply aid the Declarer in his campaign. Indeed, this may cost your side a trick the Declarer could not otherwise make, for, if you should lead a suit which may be ruffed in either Dummy's or Declarer's hand, you are making the Declarer a free gift! With no cards of that suit in either hand, he cannot lead it himself; when you lead it, he can ruff in whichever hand he chooses and discard a loser from the other.

The following situation proves the last statement:

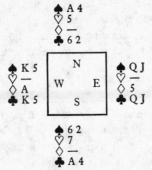

Hearts are trumps, and you are sitting West. It is your lead. If you lead the diamond Ace at this point, the Declarer can trump with the five of hearts in Dummy and discard either a spade or a club from his own hand, or he can discard either a spade or a club from Dummy and trump with the seven of hearts in his own hand. Whichever he does, he cannot lose more than 1 trick from this point on. If you lead a spade, however, or a club, no method of play yet discovered can prevent the Declarer from losing 2 more tricks. You must therefore come to the conclusion that the lead of a suit which can be ruffed in either opposing hand is bound to give up a trick to the Declarer unnecessarily (except, of course, when you have no other suit to lead, when you are forced to give up the trick).

A force can prove valuable even when you hold but three trumps. In the following deal, every factor militates in your favor, your chief advantage being the fact that the Dummy turns out to be long in the suit which you use to force with:

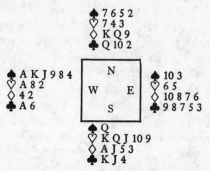

You, sitting West, open the spade King against South's contract of four hearts. You continue with the Ace. The Declarer ruffs the second round and starts drawing trumps. You refuse to take your Ace on the first round, but take the second, leading back another spade and thereby forcing the Declarer to ruff, which reduces his trump holding by one card. The Declarer then has one trump left, and so does the Dummy, and so do you. Declarer finds himself in a hopeless position. He can draw your last trump and cash in his diamond tricks, but you will then win the last 3 tricks with the club Ace and two good spades. Proper play by South, however, will enable him to keep his set down to 1 trick. He should disregard your last trump and allow you to win a trick with this card by ruffing a diamond, which saves him 1 trick, even though he still cannot make his contract. Needless to say, failure to continue forcing the Declarer by leading spades will result in the making of the contract.

Do not get the erroneous impression that it is always a good idea to force the Declarer. Forcing tactics will prove worth while as long as there is no danger that the Declarer will be able to take advantage of being in the lead by leading out an established suit for discarding purposes. You must be on the lookout for such a possibility, and if you see any danger signs you must abandon the forcing since it will put Declarer into the lead. Your better course is then to take whatever tricks seem winnable immediately.

Spotting a Danger Signal

The most usual danger signal is the presence of some long, almost solid suit in the Dummy. When you see a suit of this kind you must realize at once that you will not have time to reduce the Declarer's trump holding to your own level. The chances are that a force will simply give the Declarer more time to establish *his* suit and discard his losers. Consequently you must attack without hesitation and hope for the best.

The following deal shows how a danger signal may be spotted:

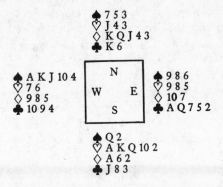

```
              ♠ 7 5 3
              ♡ J 4 3
              ◇ K Q J 4 3
              ♣ K 6
                 ┌─────────┐
♠ A K J 10 4     │    N    │     ♠ 9 8 6
♡ 7 6            │         │     ♡ 9 8 5
◇ 9 8 5          │  W   E  │     ◇ 10 7
♣ 10 9 4         │         │     ♣ A Q 7 5 2
                 │    S    │
                 └─────────┘
              ♠ Q 2
              ♡ A K Q 10 2
              ◇ A 6 2
              ♣ J 8 3
```

You are West, and open the spade King against South's contract of four hearts. Your Partner plays the six-spot, and, as soon as you see Declarer's deuce, you know that the six is a discouraging signal (because you know the whereabouts of all lower cards). Therefore you may as well lead the spade Ace, for if Partner holds three spades, the Declarer's Queen must fall. This happens, and at the third trick you are confronted with a chance to force the Declarer to ruff a third round of spades. Certainly such a play will not directly forfeit a trick, but at the same time you should be restrained from making it by the presence of the five-card diamond suit in the Dummy.

It should be apparent that if the Declarer has a solid heart suit plus the diamond Ace, he can run off enough tricks for his game contract before you can intercede. If Partner holds the diamond Ace, he will be sure to take it at a later time, and the fact that the suit is not led immediately will make no difference. The only suit left is clubs—and you must lead a club at the third trick. You select the

Ten—top of your tripleton—and, regardless of what Dummy plays, Partner must make both his Ace and Queen. If you had gone on with a third round of spades, the Declarer would have ruffed, it is true, but he would then have drawn the remaining trumps, taken his five diamonds, and scored his 10 tricks for game. The lead of a club at the third trick is your only way of stopping the game.

Not Forcing When It May Establish a Trick in Dummy

Another reason for refraining from forcing the Declarer is to avoid setting up a winner in the Dummy. This happens when the card you lead to force the Declarer is a high card which, when it falls, will promote a high card in the Dummy. As a matter of sober fact, it is usually bad policy to lead the highest outstanding card in a suit when the Dummy holds the next highest, whether or not it is likely that Declarer will ruff. Such a play merely takes a trick at once which would probably be won later on anyway, and may result in giving the Declarer the one discard he is looking for. In such cases, it is usually advisable to shift to some other suit, applying the principles of choice laid down in the chapter on Continuation Plays.

The following deal is an illustration:

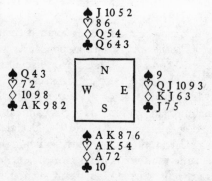

You open your club King against South's contract of four spades, and Partner plays the five while Declarer drops the Ten. You thus gain a fair amount of information about the distribution of the suit. Partner is certainly not starting an echo, and therefore he did not hold a doubleton originally. He may have held a singleton, or he may have held three cards. If he held the singleton, you can lead out your Ace and allow Partner to ruff the third round. If Partner held the tripleton, however, your club Ace will allow the Declarer to ruff and will leave the Queen in the Dummy available for a subsequent discard.

Clearly the club Ace is a dangerous lead and should be abandoned. The situation is not so desperate that such a risk is justified, as you must certainly make that Ace later if the Declarer should happen to hold three cards. Meanwhile, other lines of defense are open to you.

In deciding which suit to shift to, you come naturally and logically to diamonds. You hold a three-card sequence, such as it is, and Dummy holds an honor. That means that you will be leading through strength. If Partner should hold a tenace over the Dummy (which is quite possible), you may still defeat the contract by making the shift to diamonds. At the second trick, therefore, you abandon the club suit and lay down the diamond Ten. Declarer allows this card to come around to his Ace, and Partner drops the six—an encouraging card. Declarer thereupon leads out the Ace and King of spades, hoping that the suit will break 2-2. Of course, it does not break for him the way the cards lie, and you are left holding the good spade Queen. Declarer then leads the Ace and King of hearts, followed by a third round which he ruffs in the Dummy.

At this point, you must not make the major error of using your good trump to ruff the third round of hearts. If you do, the Declarer will simply discard a diamond from the Dummy, leaving him with but one loser in that suit. After ruffing the heart, the Declarer returns to his own hand by trumping a club and then ruffs his last heart with Dummy's last trump. Another club ruff puts him back in his own hand, and he is compelled to lead diamonds. Your Partner's King and Jack both take tricks, and the last trick is won with your good Queen of spades. The Declarer is defeated 1 trick. It is perfectly obvious that a club continuation would have allowed him to make his contract very easily.

The situation is not always as clear as it was in the preceding deal. Sometimes it is doubtful whether a continuation of the opened suit is not better than any shift will prove to be. In fact, sometimes you must go on with your original suit only to find that your sizing up of the situation was incorrect. Even in such instances, however, there are usually some means of repairing the damage which has been done.

Take, for example, the following deal:

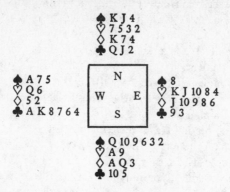

```
              ♠ K J 4
              ♡ 7 5 3 2
              ◇ K 7 4
              ♣ Q J 2

 ♠ A 7 5          N          ♠ 8
 ♡ Q 6                       ♡ K J 10 8 4
 ◇ 5 2        W       E      ◇ J 10 9 8 6
 ♣ A K 8 7 6 4    S          ♣ 9 3

              ♠ Q 10 9 6 3 2
              ♡ A 9
              ◇ A Q 3
              ♣ 10 5
```

South has reached a contract of four spades by somewhat ambitious bidding. Yet he has one chance of making it. You, sitting West, open your club King, and Partner starts an echo (to show ruffing potentiality) by playing the nine. Declarer plays the five. You are put at once into a quandary. Partner's nine shows either a doubleton or a singleton, which means that the Declarer must have held originally at least two clubs. Your club Ace will be certain to win the second round, then. However, if you lead it now and the ultimate distribution proves to be 2-2, the Dummy's Queen of clubs will be set up for discarding purposes. Therefore you should not continue with the club Ace <u>unless</u> you know the means you can take to prevent the use of Dummy's Queen as a third-round winner. If you see a later defense, you can play the Ace without any qualms.

Unfortunately, Partner and Declarer each had a doubleton originally. You must set about eliminating that club Queen in the Dummy. You know that Partner can ruff, but you also know that the Declarer can over-ruff. Does this do any harm? No, for whatever trumps your Partner holds must be negligible. Forcing Partner to ruff and Declarer to over-ruff will eliminate the Queen for discarding purposes. Nothing will have been lost, but the prevention of a discard from Declarer's hand will have been gained. You lead your third round of clubs, Partner ruffs with the eight of spades, and Declarer over-ruffs with the nine. The remaining play is unimportant; the Declarer must still lose 1 spade and 1 heart trick. He could have discarded that losing heart on Dummy's club Queen if you had not led the third round.

It is perfectly true that if you had shifted to the Queen of hearts at the second trick, Declarer's contract would still have been defeated. However, to make this play would give you no opportunity to find out whether Partner held a singleton club originally. By knowing that you could immediately kill the card set up in the Dummy, you were able to take advantage of *all* your defensive possibilities. A play of this kind is really a variation of the force.

FORCING THE DUMMY

In the early part of this chapter we stated that all forcing should operate on the strong trump hand. Like all Bridge rules, there is an exception to this principle. It is occasionally necessary to force *Dummy* to ruff, in order to eliminate an entry card. A situation of this kind can usually be recognized by the presence in Dummy of a long suit which threatens to become established. For example, take the following deal:

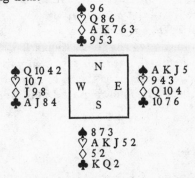

```
                  ♠ 9 6
                  ♡ Q 8 6
                  ◇ A K 7 6 3
                  ♣ 9 5 3

   ♠ Q 10 4 2        N        ♠ A K J 5
   ♡ 10 7                     ♡ 9 4 3
   ◇ J 9 8       W     E      ◇ Q 10 4
   ♣ A J 8 4                  ♣ 10 7 6
                     S

                  ♠ 8 7 3
                  ♡ A K J 5 2
                  ◇ 5 2
                  ♣ K Q 2
```

You are sitting East defending against South's contract of four hearts. Your Partner opens the two of spades and you win the first 2 tricks with the Ace and King. It is apparent that Declarer's plan of campaign will involve the establishment of the diamond suit in Dummy. Since you hold three diamonds yourself the suit will probably break and Dummy's Queen of hearts will serve as an entry. If possible, this plan of Declarer's must be circumvented.

At the third trick, therefore, you should lead another spade. (You know from partner's original lead of the deuce that Declarer holds one more spade). The Dummy is forced to ruff, and after this the diamond establishment does the Declarer no good. If he leads three rounds of diamonds, trumping the third round in his own hand, and then plays the Ace and another heart over to the Queen, you can ruff the next diamond lead and force him to eventually lose 2 club tricks.

Note what would happen if you simply returned a club. Your Partner's Ace would win Declarer's Queen, but Declarer would be in the lead with his King on the second round of the suit. He would then simply play three rounds of diamonds and then three rounds of hearts, winding up in the Dummy with the trumps all drawn. He would then discard his losing club on one of the established diamonds and fulfill his contract.

The above situation is not common, but the necessity for such a play does occur at times.

PREVENTING A DECLARER FROM DISCARDING

Another variation of the force on Declarer occurs when the Defending Side is faced with the problem of preventing a Declarer from obtaining discards in Dummy. As a general rule, it is safe to say that a player should always ruff, even though he knows that he is going to be over-ruffed. The trump sacrificed can be of little use and if the Declarer over-ruffs he is forced to retain whatever loser he is trying to get rid of. The following hand illustrates this principle:

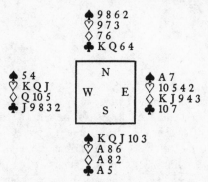

You are sitting East and South is the Declarer at a contract of four spades. West opens the King of hearts and Declarer wins with the

Ace. He can not afford to draw trumps immediately as then he will automatically lose 4 tricks. So he therefore leads three rounds of clubs in the hope of getting rid of one of his heart losers. On the third round of clubs you must ruff with the seven of spades and, from this point on, Declarer is helpless. He can either over-ruff or take his discard as he chooses, but nothing can prevent him from losing a total of 4 tricks.

Note that it makes a great deal of difference whether you ruff with the Ace or with the seven. If you ruff with the Ace, Declarer will simply discard his heart and will succeed in getting rid of two losers on 1 trick. If your holding were Ten-seven or Jack-seven, or even Queen-seven, however, you should prefer to ruff with the higher card, as this may develop a trick in partner's hand.* This is true even if you hold three cards headed by the Ten or Jack. With three cards headed by the Queen the situation is a little closer, as you may conceivably be giving up a trick by ruffing high. Your choice depends on your chance of obtaining a trick with that Queen later. However, do not make the mistake of thinking that you should preserve the Queen and the small cards too, for it is almost always better to use one of your trumps. Even if you sacrifice a possible trump trick, you are at least preventing the Declarer from obtaining a much-needed discard.

SUMMARY

Leading a suit of which the Declarer (but not the Dummy) is exhausted, and forcing the Declarer to ruff, is often an advantageous play, for it shortens the Declarer's trump holding often to the point of embarrassment. The force is particularly valuable when you have three or more trumps and a long, strong side suit.

The Declarer should not be forced when the Dummy has a long, almost solid suit, or when the force may set up a trick in the Dummy (unless the trick in Dummy can be eliminated later by some means which offers itself before the force is attempted).

---

* Umpteen years later this specific type of play was christened "the uppercut" by various and sundry experts.—S. F. Jr.

CHAPTER XXVII

TRUMP LEADS BY THE DEFENDING SIDE

As you know, one of the most advantageous aspects of Declarer's play at a suit contract is that certain otherwise losing cards can be ruffed in the Dummy (sometimes). This circumstance frequently increases the value of a hand by 2 or more tricks, and makes it to that degree unnecessary to hold so many high cards as would be required to make the same number of tricks at no-trump. Short suits and voids in the Responding Hand (the prospective Dummy) are always regarded as valuable assets, especially when three or four cards of Partner's bid suit (the prospective trump suit) are held.

The Defending Side, as you have already seen, busy themselves with trying to figure out how to best the Declarer. If the Declarer has certain assets, the Defending Side must try to depreciate those assets whenever possible. You have been told how the Defending Side try to establish high cards of their own before the Declarer can set up his for discarding purposes; how the Defending Side, on occasion, force the Declarer to ruff and thereby shorten his trump holding; and how the Defending Side may hold up in order to block the Dummy, or take an entry out of the Dummy to embarrass the Declarer, and so on.

The next step to learn is how to prevent the Declarer from making full use of Dummy's ruffing-tricks. Certainly the first method that should occur to anyone would be to reduce the number of trumps in Dummy's hand. This can be done the most easily by leading trumps yourself. If you see that the Dummy contains a short suit, and at the same time you perceive that the Declarer seems somewhat reluctant to draw trumps, it is a practical certainty that he is attempting to establish a few ruffing-tricks. If the Dummy does not contain any great number of trumps, you have a chance to foil the Declarer by leading the trump suit yourself—before the Declarer is ready to have it led. Of course this principle does not apply if the trump lead sacrifices a sure trick.

On the following deal you are sitting East, defending against South's contract of four spades:

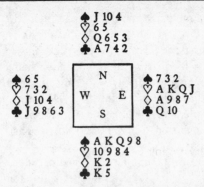

♠ J 10 4
♡ 6 5
◇ Q 6 5 3
♣ A 7 4 2

♠ 6 5   N   ♠ 7 3 2
♡ 7 3 2   ♡ A K Q J
◇ J 10 4   W   E   ◇ A 9 8 7
♣ J 9 8 6 3   S   ♣ Q 10

♠ A K Q 9 8
♡ 10 9 8 4
◇ K 2
♣ K 5

Partner opens the diamond Jack, on which a low card is played
from Dummy.   Your first problem is whether to play your Ace.   You
are practically certain that Partner does not hold the King, as a
lead from a King-Jack holding is fairly undesirable.   If the Declarer
holds the King, it may be a singleton or it may be guarded.   If it
should be a singleton and you play low, he will win the trick.   On the
other hand, even if you play the Ace and drop the King, the Queen in
Dummy will still permit a discard.   If the Declarer holds two diamonds, the play of the Ace gives him 2 diamond tricks, while the
play of a small card holds him to 1 diamond trick.   All in all, the
odds are in favor of passing Partner's Jack up to the Declarer.

You therefore play the nine, and the Declarer wins with the King.
Declarer leads the Ten of hearts, which you win with your Jack.
At this point you should see just what the Declarer is up to.   He is
trying to get rid of Dummy's low hearts so that he can eventually
ruff some losers with the low trumps there.   You must do your best
to thwart his plans, and your only means is the trump lead.   You
therefore return a trump, which Declarer wins in his own hand.   He
next leads another heart, which you win, and come right back with
another trump.   The Declarer will still have one trump left in
Dummy for ruffing, but one is not enough!   He will eventually be
forced to lose another heart in addition to the diamond Ace, which
will defeat him by 1 trick.

You will notice that in the preceding deal the *time element* is more
prominent than usual.   The entire play is a race between the Defending Side and the Declarer.   The Declarer did not have quite
enough time to establish Dummy's ruffing-tricks by leading hearts,

and you did not have quite enough time to prevent the Declarer from establishing 1 ruffing-trick. Your side could have eliminated all of Dummy's ruffing-tricks if your Partner had chosen a trump for his opening lead, but to do that he would have had to be a magician. This inspired opening would have permitted you to take all three trumps out of the Dummy before the Declarer could get around to ruff even a single heart. This is not a criticism of West's opening lead; the fact is mentioned here merely to emphasize the importance of the time element.

Another interesting point in the preceding deal is the play to the first trick. If you had played the Ace of diamonds, and by some chance returned another diamond, the Declarer would have made his contract, for the Queen of diamonds would have been available for the discard of his fourth heart. On the other hand, if you had played the Ace and immediately led a trump, the result would have been exactly the same as when you played low. You would have been able to take all three trumps out of the Dummy before the Declarer could ruff hearts. The Declarer would have lost the same tricks—three hearts and one diamond.

A SIMILAR BUT SIMPLER SITUATION

Sometimes it is easier to recognize situations when ruffing-tricks may be killed than at other times. The following deal is a fairly simple illustration:

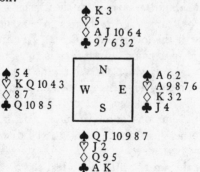

You are playing in the East position against South's contract of four spades. Partner opens the heart King. You see at once what you should do. You should overtake with your Ace, and immediately lay down the spade Ace and another spade. This takes all the trumps out of the Dummy and prevents the Declarer from ruffing his other heart. Eventually he will have to finesse the diamond, and let you get in the lead with your King, after which you can simply lead another heart to Partner's Queen. It is true that overtaking at the first trick is not entirely necessary, and that, if you play a low heart, Partner will probably know enough to lead trumps himself. However, you should never leave to your Partner a decision which you can determine rightly for yourself.

Killing Ruffing Power With the Opening Lead

Sometimes Dummy's ruffing power may be attacked immediately through the opening lead. This brings into consideration the bidding which precedes the play. Information gained during the auction often enables the Defending Side and the Declarer both to place certain key cards in certain hands, and to give some notion of what the distribution of the four suits approximates.

It is very difficult to lay down specific rules for the opening trump lead. However, it is usually indicated in one particular situation. Suppose that your right-hand Opponent, who eventually becomes the Declarer, has named two suits in his bidding. His Partner has denied one and indicated somewhat neutral support in the other. Let us further suppose that you hold a fairly strong tenace in the suit which has been denied but no strength of any importance in the other. It is apparent, then, that the success or failure of the final contract must depend almost entirely on whether the Declarer will be able to establish his side suit. Since you sit over him with a potential second- or third-round winner, you know that his only chance of doing this probably lies in ruffing his low cards in the Dummy. Under these circumstances, you must try immediately to diminish Dummy's ruffing power.

Suppose that the auction has gone as follows for the following deal (neither side vulnerable):

SOUTH	WEST	NORTH	EAST
One Spade	Pass	One No-trump	Pass
Two Hearts	Pass	Two No-trump	Pass
Three Hearts	Pass	Three Spades	Pass
Four Spades	Pass	Pass	Pass

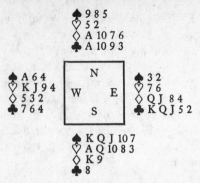

♠ 9 8 5
♡ 5 2
◇ A 10 7 6
♣ A 10 9 3

♠ A 6 4
♡ K J 9 4
◇ 5 3 2
♣ 7 6 4

♠ 3 2
♡ 7 6
◇ Q J 8 4
♣ K Q J 5 2

♠ K Q J 10 7
♡ A Q 10 8 3
◇ K 9
♣ 8

You are sitting West with the problem of leading against South's
four spade contract. South's bidding clearly marks him with at least
ten cards in spades and hearts combined. North's bidding has shown
that he does not particularly fancy either suit, but, if he must choose,
he prefers spades slightly. His rather weak one no-trump bid must
have shown maximum honor strength, because of his willingness to
bid two no-trump on the second round rather than sign off by bidding
two spades. The chances are therefore greatly in favor of North's
distribution being four diamonds, four clubs, three spades, and two
hearts. If this is true, the Declarer will probably be able to make
advantageous use of the spades in Dummy if he is allowed to do so.
You hold 3 almost certain heart tricks, provided this suit is led to
you enough times and also provided that the Dummy does not stand
over you with ruffing power in that suit. If you are to make these
3 heart tricks, you must start out with the intention of eliminating
Dummy's trumps. Your proper opening lead is therefore a low
spade.

Why should you lead a *low* spade? Why not the Ace? There are
two reasons for coming out first with a low spade. The first is that
by leading low you retain your Ace and consequently retain control
of the trump suit. If you should change your mind later as to your
best defense, you will still hold an absolutely certain entry. The
second reason is less abstruse. If the trump opening should prove to
be the best defense, and your Partner's original spade holding should
turn out to be a doubleton, the opening of the Ace followed by a low
card would eliminate Partner's two trumps immediately. Therefore,
if he should gain the lead in the early part of the hand he would not be

able to continue the trump attack, and only two rounds would be taken instead of three.   By leaving him with a small trump (which he quite possibly has), you give him the chance of continuing the attack with this card if he gets in the lead before you do, and then you can take your Ace and lead a third round of trumps (provided the trump continuation is indicated).

The important thing, however, is not really the choice of the card in the suit, but the choice of the trump suit itself.   The trump opening puts you a step ahead of the Declarer, a step which would be irretrievably lost if you choose any other suit.   See what happens.   You open a low spade and Dummy's eight holds the trick.   The Declarer probably leads a low heart out of the Dummy and finesses his Queen, which you win with the King.   By this time you are certain that your trump opening was the best defense, and you proceed to knock the remaining trumps out of the Dummy by leading the Ace and another. At this point the Declarer is tied hand and foot.   He will probably take another heart finesse, which must also lose, and the result will be that he loses 3 heart tricks and 1 spade trick—and the contract goes down one.

If you had not opened the spade suit, you would have been guilty of not making use of the one time unit that favored your side—the opening lead.   For the sake of argument, suppose that you opened a club instead.   The Declarer would win and take the heart finesse. By this time you would realize the necessity for killing Dummy's ruffing power, and would probably lead your Ace and another spade. But it would be too late.   The Dummy would still have a trump, and the Declarer would simply play the heart Ace and a low one, ruffing the latter.   Eventually he would have to lose another heart trick, but his total losers in this suit would be two instead of three.   In other words, he would make his contract because of your failure to make the time element work to your advantage.

The preceding example shows that a trump opening is usually indicated when the success of the Declarer's contract depends on the establishment of his side suit.   Of course, you must have a few trumps in order to make the trump opening effective, although at times you may depend on your Partner's ability to gain the lead, and continue this defense for you.   A moment's delay—that is, a delay of a round or two—may prove fatal.

SUMMARY

To kill Dummy's ruffing power you set about leading trumps. That is, you decide to draw trumps yourself, which will probably be much sooner than the Declarer wishes them drawn, for it will eliminate trumps from the Dummy which he is counting on for ruffing a few losers. That the Declarer is counting on Dummy's ruffing power can be perceived either during the play, by the fact that Declarer postpones drawing trumps, or by the fact that he is shortening a suit in the Dummy. Sometimes it can be guessed from the bidding, when it seems certain that the success of the Declarer's contract depends on setting up a side suit and that to do so he may have to ruff losers. Thus the trump lead may be indicated as early as the opening lead, or it may be suggested as the best line of defense any time during the play. You must keep your eyes open and your wits about you—as soon as you see what the Declarer's game is, you should try to block it.

CHAPTER XXVIII

OVER-RUFFING BY THE DEFENDING SIDE

Now that you know how important it often is to force the Declarer to ruff whenever your side holds any length in the trump suit, even though it may not do you any good, you are ready to discover how forcing the Declarer may become a specific means of obtaining more tricks. Generally, forcing can do the Defending Side no harm—you saw one or two instances, however, in which you should refrain from forcing. But now and then, when you lead a suit which Declarer can ruff, it not only does your side no harm but actually enables your Partner also to ruff, *when Partner is playing after the Declarer*. Thus Partner has an opportunity to over-ruff—both winning the trick and capturing one of Declarer's precious trumps.

Consider this a moment. You already know something about the strategic advantage of playing after another player, particularly when tenaces are held. This is just as true in the trump suit as in any other suit, and it is also true when you play after a ruffing player and you can ruff yourself. Thus trump honors increase in value whenever their holder can play them *after* the Declarer, especially when playing Third or Fourth Hand to the trick.

Take, for example, the following simple illustration:

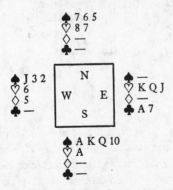

Spades are trumps; South is Declarer. It seems at first glance that Declarer must certainly win the rest of the tricks. However, he cannot win them all if East (your Partner) has the lead at this point.

East, who knows that he is the only player who has any clubs left, leads a club in the hope of letting you (West) do something. He succeeds. South must do one of two things: he must either trump the club with the Ten of spades or with the Queen of spades. If he trumps with the Ten, you over-ruff with the Jack; if he trumps with the Queen, you throw off your last diamond and you must eventually win a trick with your Jack, which has been promoted to a third-round winner. Note that, if Partner leads a heart, South will win the trick with his Ace and proceed to draw your trumps. Your Jack cannot possibly be turned into a trick unless Partner has the lead and leads a suit in which both the Declarer and you are lacking any cards.

The same sort of promotion occurs when you are able to over-ruff the Declarer no matter what he plays. In the preceding example, your Jack was really in tenace position over the Ace-King-Queen because it gained value from the fact that your hand played after the Declarer. The actual holding is, of course, not a tenace, but the principle can be seen more clearly if the relationship is understood.

The following example contains a combination which really looks like a tenace:

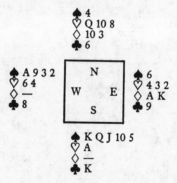

Spades are trumps; South is Declarer. Again both your hand (West) and South's are void in diamonds. Theoretically, your spade holding is worth only 1 trick, as the Declarer can simply lead his high honors until your Ace is driven out, and later pick up the rest of your low trumps. He holds four honors, while you hold but four cards in the suit, only one of which is higher than any of his. However, there is one way in which you can obtain 2 spade tricks—if Partner is in

,the lead at this point.   If Partner leads a diamond, the Declarer has to ruff with the Ten because he knows that you can over-ruff his five-spot with your nine.

You are now faced with the problem of whether to play your spade Ace immediately.   A moment's reflection will show that you should hold on to it.   If you win this trick with the Ace, you will have to return a spade, a heart, or a club.   Any of these cards can be won by the Declarer, who will then draw your remaining trumps and capture the rest of the tricks without hindrance.   By refusing to play the Ace, you promote your nine-spot.   Let us suppose that on this trick you throw off a low heart.   Declarer will probably continue with the spade Jack, which you then win with the Ace.   You return either a heart or a club, and Declarer's King-Queen of spades will pick up your trey and deuce.   This leaves the nine as the high trump and allows you to make 2 spade tricks rather than 1.

You thus see that the preceding example really illustrates the establishment of a tenace through a refusal to over-ruff.   This establishment was owing entirely to the fact that you were playing after the Declarer.   You will also see that the principle involved is the same as the one illustrated in the first example deal of this chapter.   Take the following deal:

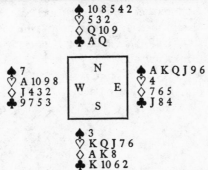

South is Declarer at a contract of four hearts, and you open your singleton spade from the West position.   This is not a violation of the rule not to lead short suits when length in trumps is held because in this instance your Partner has bid the suit.   A low card is played from Dummy and Partner plays the nine.   When this card holds the trick, he returns the Ace and South ruffs with the Jack of hearts. At this point, if you make the mistake of over-ruffing with the Ace, you will make a total of only 2 tricks in trumps, as South's King and Queen can pick up your eight and nine, leaving only the Ten as a winner. By refusing to over-ruff, you can win either the King or the Queen with the Ace later on, and return the Ten to knock out the other honor. In other words, you will make 3 trump tricks.

Do you see anything wrong with this deal? Is there any way in which the Declarer could make his contract? Yes, he could make his contract by going about it somewhat differently. South made a fatal mistake when he ruffed the second round of spades with one of his honors. If he had ruffed with the six-spot, there would have been no purpose in a refusal to over-ruff. You would have won the trick with the eight, but subsequently you would have been able to win only 1 more trump trick, as South would still hold the K Q J against your A 10 9, and Partner would never be able to regain the lead.

Leading a Low Card for Over-Ruffing

Sometimes the question of over-ruffing is not so simple, particularly for the player who forces the Declarer. This player, Partner of the one who is to over-ruff, very often faces the necessity of leading a card which both the Declarer and you (let us say) can ruff but which at the same time establishes a trick in the Dummy. Under these circumstances it is usually advisable for Partner to lead a low card. This play may or may not allow the Declarer a discard, but in most such instances the lead of a high card is sure to.

Take, for example, the following deal:

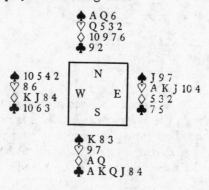

You are sitting East, playing against South's contract of five clubs. Partner chooses to open the eight of hearts, the top of a worthless doubleton (as you discover later, though you should see at once from applying the Rule of Eleven that the eight cannot be fourth best). Dummy plays low and you naturally play your Ten. You now play out the King, and, when everybody follows suit, you know that neither the Declarer nor your Partner holds any more hearts. It is apparent, therefore, that you are obliged to give your Partner a chance to ruff the third round. The only trouble is that, if you lead the heart Ace, the Dummy's Queen will be established for the fourth round and a discard. You should lead, not the Ace, but a low heart, knowing that the Declarer cannot afford to discard at this point, but must ruff. If he discards a loser, he loses this trick—his third—which defeats his contract forthwith. Now the Declarer cannot avoid, eventually, losing the Queen of diamonds. Had you led the heart Ace, Declarer would have ruffed with the Jack of clubs, drawn trumps, and used his heart Queen in the Dummy to discard his diamond Queen on. The lead of a low heart accomplishes the same aim—to give Partner a chance to ruff or over-ruff—and is safe.

Of course, the situation would be different if the Dummy contained no entry. Then, the lead of the Ace would be permissible.

Let us look at this matter of over-ruffing from the standpoint of the Declarer. In the preceding example, his best play was to ruff high, refusing to accept the chance to discard the diamond Queen. Generally speaking, this is not true, for if he holds some card which he must lose no matter what else happens, he may as well get rid of it.

Take the following deal as an example of this:

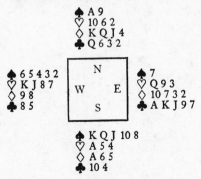

```
                    ♠ A 9
                    ♡ 10 6 2
                    ◇ K Q J 4
                    ♣ Q 6 3 2
                    ┌───────────┐
  ♠ 6 5 4 3 2      │    N      │      ♠ 7
  ♡ K J 8 7        │           │      ♡ Q 9 3
  ◇ 9 8         W  │           │  E   ◇ 10 7 3 2
  ♣ 8 5            │    S      │      ♣ A K J 9 7
                    └───────────┘
                    ♠ K Q J 10 8
                    ♡ A 5 4
                    ◇ A 6 5
                    ♣ 10 4
```

You are now the Declarer (South), playing a contract of four spades. West opens the eight of clubs, which East wins with the Jack (you playing low from Dummy). East now lays down his King, and follows with a small club. At this point, you are quite tempted to ruff with the eight of spades, since you know that you cannot be over-ruffed. However, what good will it do you? You hold in your hand 2 potential losing tricks in hearts. One of these you can discard on the extra diamond in the Dummy, but the other must be lost eventually. Why not lose it immediately? You retain at least your original length in spades, and know that after West has ruffed he can do no further damage. You therefore throw off a low heart on this trick, and let West ruff to his heart's content. The balance of the tricks now belong to you.

Note that if you had decided to trump in on the third round of clubs, you would have been reduced to four trumps against West's five. You would then have been sure to lose your contract. The trump distribution in the deal given is somewhat unlikely, but the good player must always be ready for such bad breaks.

Summary

The principles explained in this chapter have frequent application. Quite often they give rise to rather complex problems for both the Declarer and the Defending Side. In their connection, you should always remember three things, as follows: (1) never be reluctant, as Declarer, to throw off a card that is a sure loser anyway, even though to do so means you lose the current trick—one trick is as good as another, if you must lose it anyway; (2) never ruff blindly in a defending position, but look around to see whether your trump holding can be improved by refusing to over-ruff; (3) be very careful in giving your Partner a chance to over-ruff that you do not establish any tricks in the Dummy.

PART II

ADVANCED PLAY AND EXPERT TECHNIQUE

INTRODUCTION TO PART II

The Bridge player who has learned his fundamentals in the hard school of experience may, perhaps, dispense with a thorough-going study of the first part of this book, and make his beginning at this point—where explanation of advanced play and expert technique is comprehensively given. It is suggested to every reader, however, no matter how much experience he has had or how many books on the subject he has read, that he give Part I at least a brief survey before reading any portion of Part II. This is meant to be helpful, and not peremptory.

The diligent reader who has already made a careful perusal of Part I, and who is sure that he has its material well in hand, may proceed with the ensuing chapters with full confidence and anticipation.

CHAPTER I

THE LESS COMMON FINESSING SITUATIONS

In early chapters, the usual finessing situations were explained. The rarer situations were postponed until a later place, and now is the time to take them up.

You realize, of course, that a finesse can become established through an Opponent's lead, as in the following simple situation:

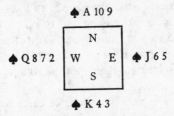

♠ A 10 9

♠ Q 8 7 2   ♠ J 6 5

♠ K 4 3

If you, as the Declarer (South), should be forced to lead this suit, you can obtain only 2 tricks at the most. However, if the suit is led by either East or West, a finessing position will be established for you which will enable you to make 3 tricks. For instance, if West leads the deuce, you play Dummy's nine and East will have to play the Jack. You win with the King and leave the Dummy in perfect tenace position over West's Queen-eight.

Again:

♡ J 10 9

♡ A 3 2

Similarly, if West leads this suit, you (South), are bound to get 2 tricks no matter how the other honors are distributed. It is true that you can finesse twice in this suit yourself, but if West should happen to hold both the Queen and the King, you could not help losing 2 tricks.

Here is a slightly more complex situation:

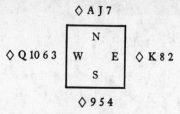

If you (South) have to lead this suit yourself, you can make only 1 trick in it. But if West should ever lead it, you can make 2 tricks if you guess right. Your best chance is not to finesse the Jack, in the hope that West holds both the King and the Queen, but to allow the trick to come around to your nine-spot. You should play the seven from Dummy, which forces East to win with the King (if he has it). This leaves your Ace-Jack in a very formidable position over West's Queen-Ten.

Changing the preceding combinations of cards around a little, you find that it is possible for you to make 2 tricks out of Ace-Jack-nine combinations even if the lead does not come from an Opponent, as, for instance, here:

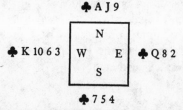

With the cards thus placed, you can lead low from your own hand and finesse Dummy's nine. This again establishes a second-round tenace. Or again:

Here you can lead the nine and pass it, since you also hold the eight. However, West can circumvent you by covering the nine with the

Ten. This forces Dummy's Jack, and the trick is won by East's King. On the second round, if you lead the eight, West should cover with his Queen. This establishes the seven-spot in East's hand as a third-round winner. Give South the nine-eight-seven instead of just nine-eight-three, however, and all the covering in the world by West will not harm South's play.

The following combinations are also fairly frequent:

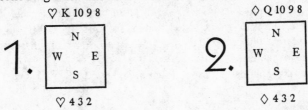

In No. 1, if your contract is such that you must win 2 tricks in this particular suit, your proper play is to lead low and finesse Dummy's eight-spot. This will probably drive out the Jack or the Queen, and on the second round you must hope that the finesse of the nine-spot will drive out the Ace. In other words, you hope that West holds either the Queen or the Jack. In No. 2, you must simply hope to find the Jack in the West hand. By leading low from your own hand, and finessing the eight and subsequently the nine, you may succeed in losing only 2 tricks to the Ace-King. This, of course, leaves 2 tricks in the suit for you.

These combinations will occur again and again, and you will not always be able to secure the maximum number of tricks by the plays just described. But that does not detract from the efficacy of the plays in the long run. Unfortunately, cards very often seem to take a perverse delight in being divided unfavorably, so that the most expert manipulation will not develop the desired tricks. However, as already said, these methods offer the best chance, and will gain tricks more often than any other method. This is not a matter of opinion; it is sound Bridge mathematics.

THE OBLIGATORY FINESSE

One particular type of finesse is called the Obligatory Finesse, for reasons which will appear. In some ways this play does not resemble a finesse at all, but it has become known as one because it is an attempt to take tricks with cards not in sequence. Recall for a moment the earlier discussion about combinations which lack the Ace and the Jack of a suit. You will remember that if you hold K x x in one hand and Q 10 x in the other hand, the proper play is to lead a low card up to the King. If the King holds the trick, you readily place the Ace in the hand on the left of the Queen-Ten and finesse the Ten on the return round. The Obligatory Finesse is really the same play, with the exception that the Ten is missing, and consequently the play is a finesse around five or six cards instead of but one! If you simply remember this characteristic you will have no trouble in recognizing the situation when it comes up.

To illustrate, consider the following deal:

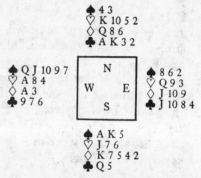

```
                ♠ 4 3
                ♡ K 10 5 2
                ◇ Q 8 6
                ♣ A K 3 2
♠ Q J 10 9 7                      ♠ 8 6 2
♡ A 8 4          N                ♡ Q 9 3
◇ A 3        W       E            ◇ J 10 9
♣ 9 7 6          S               ♣ J 10 8 4
                ♠ A K 5
                ♡ J 7 6
                ◇ K 7 5 4 2
                ♣ Q 5
```

You are South, playing a contract of three no-trump. The spade Queen is opened by West, placing you at once in an uncomfortable position, as spades are your most vulnerable suit. For the sake of safety, you decline the first trick, but you have to win the second round with the King. It is, by now, evident that the success of your contract depends on your early development of diamonds, but it is also as sure as sundown that if you lose 2 diamond tricks you cannot make three-odd (your contract). Since the Ace, Jack, Ten, and nine of diamonds are all missing, and the Opponents hold a total of five diamonds between them, it looks at first glance as though you are up against it and no mistake. However, there is one chance, and you must avail yourself of it without any fiddling around.

At the third trick you should lead a low diamond. West plays low and you win the trick with Dummy's Queen. This more or less places the Ace in West's hand. You now lead a low diamond from the Dummy, and East, who has previously dropped the nine, now drops the Ten. This means that only two key cards are missing, namely, the Ace and the Jack. The Ace is pretty well marked in the West hand, but the location of the Jack is still a dark secret. Yet you can be sure of one thing: if East has the Jack, West's Ace is alone! If this is true, you must play low, because you will then establish the next 3 diamond tricks for yourself. As a matter of fact, West's Ace does come out on your six-spot, and your troubles are ended. West can shift to a low heart, but even if you misguess the locations of the Ace and Queen, the Opponents can win at the most but 2 tricks in that suit, which gives them only 4 tricks altogether. If hearts are not led, you will still win 9 tricks—2 spade tricks, 4 diamond tricks, and 3 club tricks.

Note that the play just described can lose nothing. If West holds the Jack together with his Ace, he is sure of obtaining 2 tricks in the suit no matter what you do. Your only chance is to hope that his original holding consisted of Ace-small. Note also that this is your only chance of making the contract. Even if by some unforeseen chance you could win 3 heart tricks, this would give you only 8 tricks in all. And you really stood no chance of making 3 tricks in hearts.

This Obligatory Finesse—*obligatory* because it is the only way you can play the suit to hold the Opponents to 1 trick in it (provided the Jack is placed right for you)—would have been easier to recognize in the preceding deal if you had held the Ten of diamonds in your own hand. Actually, this card was of no importance, since everything depended, in this particular deal, on the location of the Jack. Incidentally, if the position of the King and Queen were reversed, the play would be exactly the same.

The same sort of play can be used with an Ace-Queen combination, although the choice is a little more difficult. Look at the following:

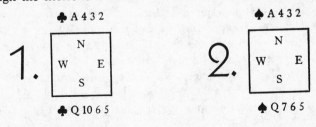

1. ♣ A 4 3 2

```
    N
  W   E
    S
```

♣ Q 10 6 5

2. ♠ A 4 3 2

```
    N
  W   E
    S
```

♠ Q 7 6 5

Obviously, you stand very little chance of accomplishing much with either of these holdings by leading the Queen to the Ace, for you do not hold the Jack. You must therefore lead out Dummy's Ace first, thereby reducing the outstanding cards to three. Assume that the three left against you include both the King and the Jack. You then lead low from the Dummy, and East also plays low. Now only the King and Jack are missing, and the result depends on where they are. Usually the bidding has given some sign of the whereabouts of the King, but if not, the problem becomes pure guesswork. In No. 1, your best play is probably the Ten on the second round, hoping that the Jack lies with East and the King with West. Of course, if the opposite is true, you will lose 2 tricks, but you have simply guessed wrong in finessing the Ten rather than the Queen. In No. 2, you have to choose between a simple finesse and an Obligatory Finesse. If you think the King lies with East, you must come up with the Queen, but if you think the King lies with West, you have a chance of catching it by playing low. In other words, you then hope that West's original holding consisted of King-small.

FINESSING TO ELIMINATE A GUESS

We now come to a type of finesse which has not been discussed at all as yet. It has no real name, but is used simply to eliminate a guess.

Suppose that your hand and Dummy's contain the following cards:

♡ A 7 4 2

♡ Q 10 9 8

You need 3 tricks in this suit. According to the preceding discussion, your best chance would seem to be to lead out Dummy's Ace and follow with a low card to the Queen-Ten. If East should also play low on the second round, however, you are forced to guess whether to finesse the Ten or the Queen. You may guess right, and then, on the other hand, you may not. There is a method of play which eliminates this guesswork and at the same time offers just as much chance of success. This consists of leading the Queen out of your own hand first. Obviously, if West holds the King your troubles are over without more ado, as, no matter whether he covers or not, one of the honors has been located. If West covers, you simply win with the Ace and eventually give up a trick to the Jack. If West does not cover, this leaves the Opponents with only three cards of the suit, so that you are certain that you will lose but 1 trick in it. Now suppose that East holds the King and wins the trick. Then the only card in which you are interested is the Jack, and you simply finesse for this card the next time the lead is in your own hand.

In other words, this mode of play is bound to win 3 tricks if West holds either one or both of the missing honors. It can lose if East holds both the King and the Jack, but it offers just as much chance of success as leading the Ace first, which must lose if West holds both honors. Its advantage lies entirely in the fact that the guess is eliminated. Of course, the play must not be used if the bidding seems to indicate that East holds both of the missing honors.

Strangely enough, the combination of cards just discussed can occasionally win 4 tricks, as in the following distributions:

In No. 1, if you lead out Dummy's Ace, West's King will fall, and all that you have to do is finesse against East's Jack twice. In No. 2, you can lead out your own Queen, and, if West covers with the King, the Ace will also capture East's lone Jack. Of course, if West does not cover, the Queen simply picks up East's Jack and you continue finessing through West's King until it falls. It is true that in each case you might decide on the losing play, but this is a question of human fallibility, for no Bridge player is clairvoyant. These particular combinations are highly improbable, but it is just as well for the reader to realize their possibility.

Suppose that the above combination is not quite so solid, as:

♡ A 9 3 2.

♡ Q 10 6 5

Now the Queen cannot be led safely because of the missing eight-spot. The best play is to lead low from Dummy at the first opportunity, and, if East also plays low, *guess* whether to play the Ten or the Queen. Even if you guess wrong, the fact that the Ace remains in Dummy gives you a second-round finesse.

The following example is slightly different:

A 6 5

Q J 4 3

With this combination the best way of playing for 3 tricks is to lead low from the Ace. If the King is in the East hand, your troubles are over, and if it is in the West hand you can still hope for a 3-3 break. Leading the Queen for a first-round finesse through West can *only* win 3 tricks on the 3-3 break.

AGAIN THE SIMPLE FINESSE IS NOT ENOUGH

We come now to handling such a combination as the following:

♠ Q 9 3

♠ A J 8 7 6

There are five cards missing in the suit, including the King and the Ten. Therefore more than a simple finesse is called for. Your best play is to lead low from Dummy and finesse your Jack. If the Jack holds, you are confronted with two possibilities. The Opponents' cards may have been divided originally in one of three ways, as follows:

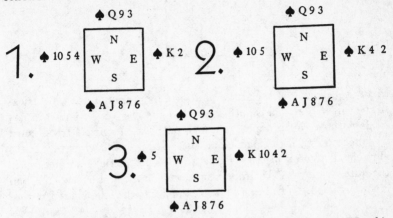

In all three instances, you first lead a low card from Dummy (North) and finesse your Jack, which holds the trick, West playing low. Of course, if West drops the Ten, you have a simple finesse left—by leading twice more through East's King.

In No. 1, you make sure of no losers by leading the Ace on the second round and dropping the King, as this makes your Queen high for the third around and also enables you to capture East's Ten. In No. 2, you cannot do this. To eliminate the losers you must get into the Dummy a second time and lead the Queen, which assures you of the balance of the tricks in the suit whether East covers or not, as West's Ten falls in any event. In No. 3, you must also lead the Queen on the second round, as the lead of the Ace gives East 2 tricks instead of 1.

It follows from the preceding discussion that the play of the Queen on the second round is generally the best. The play loses if the first division (No. 1) exists, and gains if the second or third divisions (Nos. 2 and 3) exist. The play is marked when the Ten drops on the first round. With such combinations as these, as with all others, the play offering the best chance of success is usually the one to choose. Incidentally, reversal of the Queen and Jack does not affect the manner of playing the suit for the best results.   Following is a similar situation:

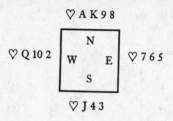

♡ A K 9 8

♡ Q 10 2   ♡ 7 6 5

♡ J 4 3

Here the lead of the Jack from your own hand is bound to win 4 tricks in the suit if West holds both the Queen and the Ten.   This is a play made without much hope of success, but is used when 4 tricks must be squeezed out of this particular suit.   It also wins when the Ten is alone or doubleton in the East hand.   If only 3 tricks are needed in the suit, the play for the drop of the Queen on the first or second round is equally good.   The same principle applies to the following situation:

◊ A K 9 4 3

◊ J 7 6

Your proper play is to lead out the King and, if neither the Queen nor the Ten falls, you have a choice of plays.   You can play the Ace and hope that the Queen will drop, or you can lead the Jack from your own hand and hope that East's original holding was Ten-small, as in this way you can drop two honors together.

The Backward Finesse

You are now ready to consider the very valuable type of finesse called the Backward Finesse.   Unlike other finesses, this play is not made to gain a trick, but is made to lose a trick immediately for the purpose of keeping one of the Opponents out of the lead.

We earlier discussed a combination of cards like the following:

♣ K J 10 9

♣ A 4 3 2

The finesse can be taken either one of two ways with equal likelihood of success. The way you choose must depend on which hand it is desirable to keep out of the lead—in the event that the finesse loses. Thus the precise purpose of the Backward Finesse comes to the front. It is called *backward* because it is taken in an unnatural way rather than in the way that most players would consider natural. Strangely enough, this unnatural or "backward" way sometimes results in gaining a trick which would have been lost by the natural approach.

The following hand is a good illustration:

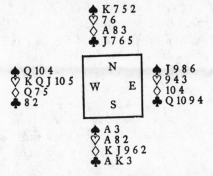

You are South, playing a contract of three no-trump. West opens the heart King and you naturally refuse to win the first two rounds of this suit. You win the third round, since you can hold up no longer, and you see immediately that you must establish the diamond suit if you are to make your contract. You also see that you do not need all 5 of the diamond tricks which are possible. If you can take only 4 diamond tricks, you will have the 9 tricks necessary for your contract. Therefore, you are perfectly willing to give up a trick immediately if such a course seems advisable. Obviously, it is not only advisable but necessary, because you realize the danger of allowing West to gain the lead on account of his established hearts. You therefore see that the natural method of finessing diamonds (leading over to Dummy's Ace and finessing the Jack on the way back) would lose your contract if the finesse loses. You must, then, play the Jack from your own hand with the intention of passing it if West plays low. You are perfectly willing to allow East to win the trick, since he presumably is exhausted of hearts.

What actually happens is rather remarkable. If West plays low you can take 5 diamond tricks instead of 4; if West covers, East's Ten drops on the second round and you still make 5 diamond tricks. Instead of giving up a trick, as you had intended and were quite willing to do, you wind up by making all the tricks in the suit.

Let us now consider the possible adverse diamond distribution to see why the Backward Finesse was so necessary.

To begin with, West might have Q 10 x, when no play will succeed. Of course, West could hold the Queen-Ten alone, and your play would then surely succeed, as the King would drop the Ten on the second round. At this point, you may say, "But we might have finessed the nine," and the answer is that you would not have done so because you were still trying to keep West out of the lead and you were still willing to give up the trick to East's Ten if he held it. Thirdly, East might have Q x, Q x x, or 10 x x. Fine! You lose but 1 trick in the suit—and that to East. The possible 4-1 distribution offers about an even break on chances. The Backward Finesse gains with some and loses with others. It is the tremendous advantage secured when the adverse distribution is 3-2 that makes the Backward Finesse so often a winning play—and the only winning play available.

SUMMARY

Finessing around more than one or two cards involves slightly different principles from those governing the simple and double finesses. Generally, the attempt with the more complex finesses is to give up tricks to as high outstanding cards as possible, so that later handling of the suit becomes less a matter of pure guesswork.

The Obligatory Finesse requires the play of a low card with the hope of finding the missing honors divided in the only way that will hold the Opponents to the fewest tricks (usually 1 trick, with the best division). Leading the Queen to the Ace, even without the Jack, if the Ten-nine-eight are also held, will eliminate the guess about the location of the missing King and Jack, for it should locate one of them immediately.

The Backward Finesse is similar, in that it consists of leading a card which can be finessed instead of leading up to it, with the intention of giving up a trick to keep the dangerous Opponent out of the lead if the finesse should fail.

CHAPTER II

SAFETY PLAYS

The main object of every Declarer is to fulfill his contract in the easiest and quickest way he can. Extra tricks can only be incidental; if he hopes by some spectacular elimination or squeeze play to eke out a trick above his contract, and at the same time overlooks a chance to make his contract as solid as Gibraltar, he may make the kibitzers crane their necks, but he runs serious danger of losing out on the score sheet—in the long run.

A *safety* play is exactly what its name implies: it is a play made to reduce to a minimum the risk of losing the contract. It is analogous to looking both ways before you cross a busy street, or to carrying a loaded rifle with the muzzle toward the ground, or to taking along an umbrella when there is a pretty good chance that it may rain. The nature of the safety play may clearly be seen when the two principal kinds are defined. One kind of safety play deliberately sacrifices a trick in order to run as little risk as possible of *losing 2 tricks*. This play is made, of course, when the contract is still safe if the sacrificed trick is given up. The other kind of safety play consists of handling honor combinations in such a way that the worst possible adverse distribution can be taken care of without losing the contract.

The execution of a safety play is not difficult. It does not require any special knowledge of card distribution, nor does it necessitate the ability to recognize certain specific situations (an ability required, for instance, to execute a squeeze play). You simply grasp the idea that a safety play is not card sense, but *card common sense*, and never forget to count the number of winning or losing tricks that a hand contains. In fact, certain elementary plays are really safety plays strictly considered. The hold-up is a safety play, as also is the refusal to draw trumps when it is not necessary to do so. The safety plays explained in the ensuing pages, however, are a degree more complex. But as you proceed from one example to another, you will see that it is always easy to recognize the place for a safety play *if you merely learn to count*.

REFUSING A TRUMP FINESSE

When the failure of a trump finesse may mean the loss of still another trick besides, a typical safety play may be in order, as in the following deal:

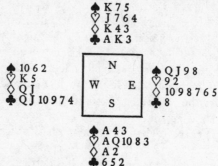

```
          ♠ K 7 5
          ♡ J 7 6 4
          ◇ K 4 3
          ♣ A K 3
♠ 10 6 2        N        ♠ Q J 9 8
♡ K 5                    ♡ 9 2
◇ Q J      W       E     ◇ 10 9 8 7 6 5
♣ Q J 10 9 7 4    S      ♣ 8
          ♠ A 4 3
          ♡ A Q 10 8 3
          ◇ A 2
          ♣ 6 5 2
```

With neither side vulnerable, the bidding has gone:

SOUTH	WEST	NORTH	EAST
One Heart	Two Clubs	Two No-trump	Pass
Three Hearts	Pass	Four Hearts	Pass
Pass	Pass		

West opens the club Queen, which North wins with the King, East dropping the eight and South the deuce. The four of hearts is now led from the Dummy, on which East plays the deuce, and South makes the *safety play* of the Ace of hearts—refusing the finesse. West plays the five. South's reason for his play is that he knows that West has several clubs—that non-vulnerable overcall of two clubs was not made on high cards, but on length (probably a six-card suit), and an outside entry. The outside trick is almost certainly the heart King. South cannot afford to take the heart finesse, then, because if it does lose to West, clubs will be continued and East will ruff Dummy's Ace. Having already lost 2 tricks, South would then lose 2 more by taking the trump finesse—a total of 4 tricks (1 heart trick, 2 club tricks, and 1 spade trick). He must play safe with the Ace of hearts and continue with a low heart, because this will either strip East's hand of trumps or will place East in the lead with no way of putting his Partner (West) back in the lead. Even if East should hold three hearts to the King, the contract is safe for West can never lead clubs for his Partner to ruff.

At the third trick South leads the trey of hearts, which West wins with the King, North dropping the six and East the nine. At this point all of the Opponents' trumps are gone, and South can lose only 2 more tricks—a spade and a club. South's contract is saved by avoiding that ruff on the Ace of clubs.

The time element has an important bearing in this deal. South cannot take the trump finesse because its failure means the loss of a ruffing-trick to the Opponents—2 tricks in all. The safe way is to refuse the finesse and give up a trick to the King, thus eliminating the probable ruff in clubs, and losing 1 trick instead of probably losing 2.

RENDERING AN ADVERSE RUFF USELESS

The following deal is a slight variation of the preceding one, but it contains a somewhat different type of safety play:

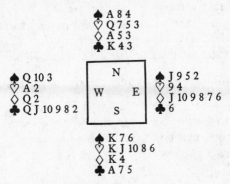

```
                    ♠ A 8 4
                    ♡ Q 7 5 3
                    ◇ A 5 3
                    ♣ K 4 3

    ♠ Q 10 3        ┌─────────┐        ♠ J 9 5 2
    ♡ A 2           │    N    │        ♡ 9 4
    ◇ Q 2           │ W     E │        ◇ J 10 9 8 7 6
    ♣ Q J 10 9 8 2  │    S    │        ♣ 6
                    └─────────┘
                    ♠ K 7 6
                    ♡ K J 10 8 6
                    ◇ K 4
                    ♣ A 7 5
```

With neither side vulnerable, the bidding has gone:

SOUTH	WEST	NORTH	EAST
One Heart	Two Clubs	Three Hearts	Pass
Four Hearts	Pass	Pass	Pass

West opens the club Queen, which North wins with the King, East dropping the six and South the five. The play of the club King from Dummy is a safety play, because the Declarer's greatest fear is again that East's club holding may be a singleton. This time South cannot avoid losing a trump trick immediately because the Opponents hold the Ace. West is almost certain to obtain the lead on the first round of trumps. Therefore, if South should obey his natural impulse and win the first trick in his own hand, West would be able to lead the Jack of clubs and East's trump would kill Dummy's King of clubs. By taking the King out of the Dummy immediately, South renders the ruff harmless, *as he can play low from both hands*.

At the second trick, the trey of hearts is played from Dummy, on which East plays the four, South the Ten and West wins with the Ace. West's return, as expected, is the club Jack, on which the trey is played from the Dummy, and when East ruffs with the nine of hearts, South is able to play the seven of clubs—retaining his Ace to win the third round of the suit. East is forced to ruff worthless clubs, but if the King remained in the Dummy till the second round, East's ruff would have killed it. Of course, East could refuse to ruff, but South's Ace would then win, and he would lose but 1 club trick anyway. By making the safety play of Dummy's King on the first trick, South is sure that his club losers will be held to 1 trick. He makes his contract without trouble this way.

This very important safety principle is frequently mishandled. Whenever the Declarer is in danger of a ruff, he should try to arrange his play so that the ruff does as little harm as possible.

Providing for the Worst Possible Distribution

You come now to a second kind of safety play, which consists of playing combinations of honors so that you are ready to handle the worst possible distribution of the outstanding cards. The following deal contains such a safety play:

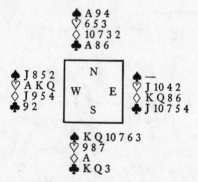

With East and West vulnerable, the bidding has gone:

SOUTH	WEST	NORTH	EAST
One Spade	Pass	Two Spades	Pass
Four Spades	Pass	Pass	Pass

West opens the heart King and the play to the first 5 tricks goes as follows:

Trick 1. West leads ♡ K, North plays ♡ 3, East plays ♡ J, and South plays ♡ 7. West's King wins the trick. East plays the heart Jack to show that he holds the Ten; this card also denies the Queen.

Trick 2. West leads ♡ Q, North plays ♡ 5, East plays ♡ 2, and South plays ♡ 8. West's Queen holds the trick.

Trick 3. West leads ♡ A, North plays ♡ 6, East plays ♡ 4, and South plays ♡ 9. West's Ace wins.

Trick 4. West leads ◊ 4, North plays ◊ 2, East plays ◊ Q, and South wins with ◊ A.

Trick 5. South leads ♠ K, West plays ♠ 2, North plays ♠ 4, and East discards ♣ 4.

The safety play is South's lead of the spade King at the fifth trick. South knows that there are four spades outstanding, including the Jack. If they are divided 2-2 or 3-1, they will fall on the Ace, King and Queen leads. However, if they are divided 4-0, the Jack may be set up for a fourth-round winner. The play of the King from the South hand (rather than the Ace from Dummy) eliminates this possibility. If the spades are actually divided 4-0, either East or West must fail to follow suit on the first round. If West is the one who has none, the second round will be won with Dummy's Ace, and South can finesse the Ten on the third round. If the void one should be East, as it is in this particular deal, South can lead a low spade at the sixth trick and finesse Dummy's nine-spot! Dummy's Ace can then be led out, South returning to his own hand with a club, and West's spade Jack is dropped on the lead of the Queen.

Note that the play of the spade King at the fifth trick protects South against any distribution. The play of the Ace at this point would permit him to make his contract under some circumstances—specifically, if the four spades are in East's hand. But if West has all four outstanding spades, the play of the Ace at the fifth trick means that South must lose a spade trick.

This same principle applies to all combinations of cards which permit "two-way" finesses if the distribution turns out to be unfavorable.

A two-way finesse may be taken either way, depending on which Opponent appears to have the missing honor. The safety play enables the Declarer to discover whether the adverse distribution is such that he can place the missing cards after the first round.

Providing Against a Special Kind of Adverse Distribution

This deal illustrates a reversal of the principle just given, owing to the fact that here a two-way finesse is impossible:

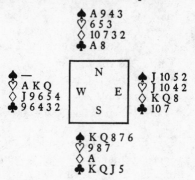

With both sides vulnerable, the bidding has gone:

South	West	North	East
One Spade	Pass	Two Spades	Pass
Three Clubs	Pass	Four Spades	Pass
Pass	Pass		

In the preceding example, it was shown to be good policy to start the lead of the trump suit—or, in fact, of any suit—from the hand containing a double honor combination, in order to provide for a two-way finessing position if the adverse distribution should turn out to be unfavorable. But sometimes deals occur in which no two-way finessing position is possible. Then the Declarer cannot provide against all kinds of unfavorable distribution, but must content himself with guarding against such bad breaks as he can. In other words, the safety play does not guarantee the contract against *any* adverse holding, but it provides insurance against *most* of the possible adverse holdings.

The first 5 tricks go as follows:

Trick 1.   West leads ♡ K, North plays ♡ 3, East plays ♡ J, and South plays ♡ 7.   West's opening lead wins the trick.

Trick 2. West leads ♡ Q, North plays ♡ 5, East plays ♡ 2, and South plays ♡ 8. Again West's lead wins.

Trick 3. West leads ♡ A, North plays ♡ 6, East plays ♡ 4, and South plays ♡ 9. West wins the third round of hearts, since the suit was distributed 4-3-3-3.

Trick 4. West leads ◇ 5, North plays ◇ 2, East plays ◇ Q, and South wins with ◇ A.

Trick 5. South leads ♠ 6, West discards ♣ 2, North plays ♠ A, and East plays ♠ 2. Dummy's Ace wins.

The play of the Ace of spades from Dummy at the fifth trick constitutes the safety play. South's only source of danger is the possibility that one Opponent may hold four spades headed by the Jack-Ten. If West holds these cards, no power on earth can prevent him from making a trump trick, as the Ten can force out the Ace at any time and leave the Jack as a certain fourth-round winner. If East holds the four spades, however, the situation is entirely different. South holds K Q 8, which, since the nine-spot is in the Dummy, constitutes a perfect tenace over East's J 10 5. Consequently the lead of the Ace provides against this distribution, while the lead of the King from the Declarer's own hand provides against no contingency of any kind.

The rest of the play goes as follows:

Trick 6. North leads ♠ 3, East plays ♠ 10, South plays ♠ Q, and West plays ◇ 4. South's Queen wins.

Trick 7. South leads ♣ 5, West plays ♣ 3, North plays ♣ A, and East plays ♣ 7. North's Ace wins.

Trick 8. North leads ♠ 4, East plays ♠ 5, South plays ♠ 7, and West discards ♣ 4. South's seven-spot wins.

Trick 9. South leads ♠ K, West discards ◇ 6, North plays ♠ 9, and East plays ♠ J. South's King wins, and the balance of the tricks clearly belong to South.

Note the difference between this deal and the preceding one. If you can provide against every possible adverse distribution, you should do so by all means, but if you cannot provide against *all* distributions, you should provide against as many as you can. Note particularly that the Ace, King, and Queen can be switched around and the proper play will remain the same. Note also that if South had held the spade Ten originally, the proper play would be the King first.

REFUSING A TRUMP FINESSE TO LOSE BUT ONE TRICK

Here is another kind of safety play. Here the Declarer deliberately refuses to take a finesse in the trump suit, because to do so he will risk more than he can afford. By refusing the finesse, he reduces to a minimum the chance of losing 2 trump tricks, thus:

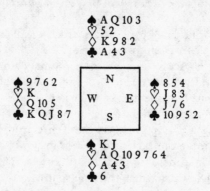

```
              ♠ A Q 10 3
              ♡ 5 2
              ◇ K 9 8 2
              ♣ A 4 3
♠ 9 7 6 2        N         ♠ 8 5 4
♡ K                       ♡ J 8 3
◇ Q 10 5    W       E      ◇ J 7 6
♣ K Q J 8 7     S         ♣ 10 9 5 2
              ♠ K J
              ♡ A Q 10 9 7 6 4
              ◇ A 4 3
              ♣ 6
```

With North and South vulnerable, the bidding has gone:

SOUTH	WEST	NORTH	EAST
One Heart	Two Clubs	Two Spades	Pass
Four Hearts	Pass	Five Clubs	Pass
Six Hearts	Pass	Pass	Pass

West opens the club King, which North wins with the Ace, East dropping the deuce and South the six. The deuce of hearts is now led from Dummy, on which East plays the trey, and South wins with the Ace, West's King falling.

The play of the Ace of hearts to the second trick is a safety play, and yet it has the simplest possible reasoning behind it. There are four trumps missing, including the King and the Jack. If West holds both honors and a small one, Declarer must lose 2 tricks no matter what. If West holds King-Jack alone, the Jack will drop and Declarer is faced with losing 1 trick (King of trumps). If West holds the Jack and a small one, two small ones, or a singleton, South can surely restrict his loss to 1 trick by entering the Dummy and leading a second round of hearts. In other words, the play of the Ace on the second trick provides for every adverse distribution except the one against which the Small Slam could not be made anyway.

In this particular deal, the safety play of the Ace brings greater reward than hoped for. The singleton King falls, and South need only enter the Dummy in order to finesse against East's Jack. The play which was made to prevent the loss of more than 1 trick actually succeeds in preventing the loss of any tricks at all. Though the safety play is required in any event, here it kept the Declarer from losing the trump finesse to a singleton King. In fact, if West's lone King had won, West would probably have returned a club, forcing Declarer to ruff. Entering the Dummy with a spade, Declarer would have led a second round of hearts on which East would have played the eight. Then South would be faced with a difficult guess. With only the Jack outstanding, he would have to choose between a finesse and playing for the drop, with the percentage slightly in favor of the drop. The safety play of the Ace on the second trick eliminates all this trial and tribulation.

If the hearts in this deal are divided 6-3 or 5-4 instead of 7-2, the safety play should still be made. Even if the distribution should be 5-3, the safety play is not a mistake. As a matter of fact, the play should always be made whenever the Declarer can safely give up 1 trick. If the contract were *seven hearts* instead of only six, in the example just given, the Declarer would probably be set 2 tricks.

A Safety Finesse

This safety play differs somewhat from those preceding in that it is concerned with the proper way of taking a finesse—that is, the way to take a finesse and at the same time insure the greatest degree of safety. The following deal is a good illustration:

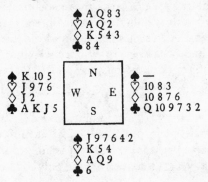

With North and South vulnerable, the bidding has gone:

SOUTH	WEST	NORTH	EAST
Pass	One Club	Double	Three Clubs
Four Spades	Pass	Five Spades	Pass
Six Spades	Pass	Pass	Pass

West opens the club King, which holds, North playing the four, East the Ten, and South the six. After his Partner's encouraging discard, West continues with the club Ace, on which North plays the eight, and East the nine, and South ruffs with the deuce of spades. Now South leads the spade Jack, on which West plays the five, and North the three, East throwing off the deuce of clubs.

The lead of the spade Jack by South is a safety finesse. With three trumps out the proper play is undoubtedly to take the finesse against the King. Therefore, if the Declarer decides to take this finesse, he must make provision for West possibly holding all three trumps (including the Ten). If South leads low from his own hand and finesses the Queen, and East should fail to follow suit, West must make a trump trick. The play of the Jack first permits a second finesse if West should cover.

Note that West does not cover South's Jack. From the bidding, West knows that South must hold all six outstanding spades (that strength bid of four spades shows a long suit plus honor strength somewhere). East's void shows up immediately, and will practically force the Declarer to return to his own hand to take the finesse against the Ten. West's only chance is to hope that the Declarer will go up with the Ace in Dummy and play to drop a singleton King in East's hand.

At the fourth trick, South leads the spade deuce, on which West plays the Ten, North winning with the Queen. At the fifth trick, North lays down the Ace of spades, on which East throws off the seven of clubs, and South plays the four as West's King now drops. The balance of the tricks are the Declarer's.

A SAFETY PLAY AGAINST THE QUEEN

This particular safety play is nothing more than a variation of the two preceding ones. It provides against an unfavorable distribution in the same way as that safety play made to provide "against a special kind of adverse distribution," the only difference being in the

combination of cards. The following deal illustrates a safety play
against the Queen:

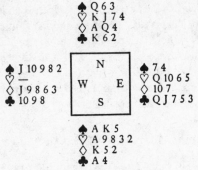

```
                  ♠ Q 6 3
                  ♡ K J 7 4
                  ◇ A Q 4
                  ♣ K 6 2

    ♠ J 10 9 8 2      N        ♠ 7 4
    ♡ —                        ♡ Q 10 6 5
    ◇ J 9 8 6 3   W     E      ◇ 10 7
    ♣ 10 9 8                   ♣ Q J 7 5 3
                     S

                  ♠ A K 5
                  ♡ A 9 8 3 2
                  ◇ K 5 2
                  ♣ A 4
```

With both sides vulnerable, the bidding has gone:

South	West	North	East
One Heart	Pass	Three Hearts	Pass
Four Clubs	Pass	Four Diamonds	Pass
Six Hearts	Pass	Pass	Pass

West opens the spade Jack, which North wins with the Queen, East
playing the four and South the five. Dummy's heart King is now
laid down on which East drops the five, South the deuce, and West
throws off the diamond trey. The play of Dummy's King of trumps
guarantees that no more than 1 heart trick can be lost even if the
outstanding hearts are all in one hand. Note also that the play of the
Ace allows East to make 2 trump tricks with his Queen-Ten holding.
The laying down of the King from Dummy is therefore a safety play
against the Queen.

The next 4 tricks go as follows:

Trick 3. North leads ♡ 4, East plays ♡ 10, South plays ♡ A,
and West discards ♠ 8. East must put up his Ten or South will
win the trick with the nine-spot.

Trick 4. South leads ♡ 3, West discards ♣ 8, North plays ♡ J,
and East wins with ♡ Q.

Trick 5. East leads ♠ 7, South plays ♠ K, West plays ♠ 9, and
North plays ♠ 3. South's King wins.

Trick 6. South leads ♡ 9, West discards ◇ 6, North plays ♡ 7,
and East plays ♡ 6. The rest of the tricks clearly belong to the
Declarer.

The play of this hand renders East perfectly helpless—he can make only 1 trick. However, he is certain to make 2 tricks if South errs by playing the Ace of hearts out of his own hand right away. The lead of the King of hearts also provides against finding four hearts in the West hand, for the Declarer can then simply lead a low heart over to his Ace on the second round, and lead the third round up to Dummy's Jack. West can then play either the Ten or the Queen, but he can never make more than 1 trick. The factor of safety requires that the King be laid down first.

PROVIDING AGAINST A 4-1 BREAK IN TRUMPS

The particular safety play illustrated in the following deal brings us back to fundamentals. Yet the hand must be included because it is an extremely common situation and one which is frequently muffed.

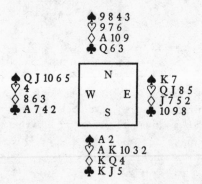

With neither side vulnerable, the bidding has gone:

SOUTH	WEST	NORTH	EAST
One Heart	One Spade	Pass	Pass
Double	Pass	Two Hearts	Pass
Three Hearts	Pass	Four Hearts	Pass
Pass	Pass		

The first 4 tricks go as follows:

Trick 1. West leads ♠ Q, North plays ♠ 3, East plays ♠ 7, and South wins with ♠ A.

Trick 2. South leads ♡ K, West plays ♡ 4, North plays ♡ 6, and East plays ♡ 5.

Trick 3. South leads ◇ 4, West plays ◇ 3, North plays ◇ A, and East plays ◇ 2. Dummy's Ace wins the trick, putting the lead on the table, for South enters the Dummy in order to lead the second round of trumps from that direction.

Trick 4. North leads ♡ 7, East plays ♡ 8, South plays ♡ 10, and West discards ♠ 5.

South is playing safe at the fourth trick by finessing the Ten of hearts; he has no idea of expecting it to hold the trick. If East holds all the remaining trumps, this finesse of the Ten is good insurance as a safety play. After one round of hearts, three trumps remain out, including the Queen and the Jack. Obviously, at least 1 trump trick must be lost. If West holds all the trumps, 2 tricks must be lost, but if East holds them all, the play of the Ten limits the loss to 1 trick. The play cannot possibly cost anything, for if West wins the Ten with either the Queen or the Jack the remaining honor is sure to drop on the Ace. In the deal just given, this safety play is absolutely necessary, because, if the Ace is led right out, East's Queen and Jack will become 2 tricks—a contingency which the safety play guards against.

East can do nothing to save himself. If he splits his equals by playing the Jack on the second round, South will win with the Ace, and Dummy's nine-spot will force out the Queen, leaving South's Ten to pick up the eight-spot.

This deal may seem a little simple in comparison with the others given in this chapter, but it illustrates a situation which occurs very often.

The rest of the play is cut and dried. At the fifth trick South cashes in the heart Ace, and has to lose just 3 tricks—a heart, a club, and a spade.

GIVING UP A TRICK WHEN IT IS SEEMINGLY UNNECESSARY

The play of the following deal shows the extremes to which it is sometimes necessary to go in order to insure absolute safety for the contract:

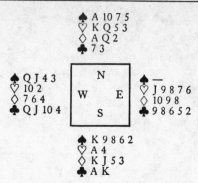

With North and South vulnerable, the bidding has gone:

SOUTH	WEST	NORTH	EAST
One Spade	Pass	Three Spades	Pass
Four Clubs	Pass	Four Diamonds	Pass
Four Hearts	Pass	Six Spades	Pass
Pass	Pass		

North and South could not have been severely criticized if they had reached a Grand Slam contract, as the making of 13 tricks depends only on a break in trumps. However, such a break is pretty much of a gamble, and here the safer Small Slam is preferable.

West opens the club Queen, which South wins with the King, North playing the trey and East the deuce. South leads the deuce of spades, which is won with Dummy's seven, West playing the trey and East throwing off the five of clubs.

One's first thought, on looking at this play, is that South has seen West's hand. Actually he has done nothing of the kind. This play is *absolutely marked.* It is obvious that the contract can be lost if one of the Opponents holds all four outstanding trumps. If the King is led right out, the contract is safe only if West holds all four spades, but is lost if East holds them. Similarly, the contract is safe if the Ace of spades is led and East holds the spades, but here again it will be lost if they lie with West. The immediate finesse of the seven-spot insures South against *both* possibilities of distribution. It is worth while to lose this trick, since it absolutely safeguards the remainder.

At the third trick, Dummy's spade Ace is cashed in, and at the fourth trick the spade King is laid down. Giving up a spade trick, South now makes his contract.

ESTABLISHING A TENACE FOR THE SAKE OF SAFETY

This particular safety play is interesting because it is a little harder to recognize than most safety plays. However, in essence it is really the same as the others. The following deal shows it clearly:

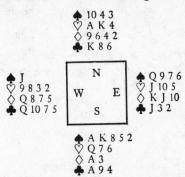

♠ 10 4 3
♡ A K 4
◇ 9 6 4 2
♣ K 8 6

♠ J
♡ 9 8 3 2
◇ Q 8 7 5
♣ Q 10 7 5

♠ Q 9 7 6
♡ J 10 5
◇ K J 10
♣ J 3 2

♠ A K 8 5 2
♡ Q 7 6
◇ A 3
♣ A 9 4

With both sides vulnerable, the bidding has gone:

SOUTH	WEST	NORTH	EAST
One Spade	Pass	One No-trump	Pass
Two Spades	Pass	Three Spades	Pass
Four Spades	Pass	Pass	Pass

The first 3 tricks are played as follows:

Trick 1. West leads ♣ 5, North plays ♣ 6, East plays ♣ J, and South wins with ♣ A.

Trick 2. South leads ♠ K, West plays ♠ J, North plays ♠ 3, and East plays ♠ 6.

Trick 3. South leads ♠ 2, West discards ♡ 2, North plays ♠ 10, and East wins with ♠ Q.

For the Declarer to play this way gives up a chance of dropping the Queen if West has blanked it (that is, if he held Queen-Jack alone originally). But South can well afford to give up a spade trick, as his only other losers are a club and a diamond. He cannot, however, afford to lose 2 spade tricks, and he *will* lose 2 spade tricks if he bangs down the Ace of spades at trick 3. The lead up to the Ten forces East to win with the Queen and leaves South's Ace-eight in tenace position over East's nine-seven.

The play proceeds as follows:

Trick 4. East leads ♣ 3, South plays ♣ 4, West plays ♣ 10, and North wins with ♣ K.

Trick 5. North leads ♠ 4, East plays ♠ 7, South plays ♠ 8, and West discards ♡ 3. South's eight wins the trick.

Trick 6. South leads ♠ A, West discards ◇ 5, North discards ◇ 2, and East plays ♠ 9. It is now only necessary for South to give up 1 club and 1 diamond trick, and he makes his four spades.

UNBLOCKING AS A SAFETY MEASURE

The following deal contains a somewhat different type of safety play. The principle involved is encountered quite frequently, and shows how it is often necessary to refuse a finesse for fear that to take it may block the suit. Though we are not concerned in this book with the subject of bidding beyond its effect on the subsequent play, it might be mentioned that North's three no-trump jump is decidedly open to question on this particular deal.

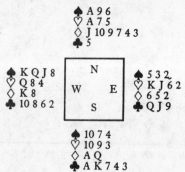

```
                    ♠ A 9 6
                    ♡ A 7 5
                    ◇ J 10 9 7 4 3
                    ♣ 5
                 ┌──────────┐
  ♠ K Q J 8      │    N     │      ♠ 5 3 2
  ♡ Q 8 4        │          │      ♡ K J 6 2
  ◇ K 8        W │          │ E    ◇ 6 5 2
  ♣ 10 8 6 2     │    S     │      ♣ Q J 9
                 └──────────┘
                    ♠ 10 7 4
                    ♡ 10 9 3
                    ◇ A Q
                    ♣ A K 7 4 3
```

With East and West vulnerable, the bidding has gone:

SOUTH	WEST	NORTH	EAST
One Club	Pass	One Diamond	Pass
One No-trump	Pass	Three No-trump	Pass
Pass	Pass		

The play goes as follows:

Trick 1. West leads ♠ K, North plays ♠ 6, East plays ♠ 2, and South plays ♠ 4. West's opening lead holds the trick.

Trick 2. West leads ♠ J, North plays ♠ A, East plays ♠ 3, and South plays ♠ 7. Dummy's Ace wins. Declarer cannot afford to hold up twice in the spade suit, because he fears that West may shift to hearts.

Trick 3.   North leads ♢ 3, East plays ♢ 2, South plays ♢ A, and West plays ♢ 8.

South deliberately refuses the diamond finesse in order to avoid blocking the suit. He knows very well that if the finesse should happen to lose, West's first move will be to drive the heart Ace out of the Dummy. This will leave the Declarer with a singleton Ace of diamonds in his own hand, which will prevent the run of Dummy's good diamonds. By refusing the finesse, the Declarer hopes that whichever Opponent holds the King has it guarded only once, when it will have to win the second round. The finesse would win if East held the King and one small card, but the finesse wins *only in this situation*, whereas the safety play of refusing the finesse wins *if either hand* holds the King and a small card. Remember that only 5 diamond tricks are needed to fulfill the contract.

Trick 4.   South leads ♢ Q, West plays ♢ K, North plays ♢ 4, and East plays ♢ 5.   West's King wins.

Trick 5.   West leads ♠ Q, North plays ♠ 9, East plays ♠ 5, and South plays ♠ 10.   West's Queen holds the trick.

Trick 6.   West leads ♠ 8, North discards ♡ 5, East discards ♡ J, and South discards ♡ 3. West's eight of spades wins, but the rest of the tricks clearly belong to South, for he has at his command 4 established diamond tricks, the Ace of hearts, and the Ace-King of clubs.

If an aside may be permitted at this point, the preceding deal has considerable interest from the point of view of the Defending Side. If West could only read the Declarer's hand, he would abandon spades at the second trick and lead a heart—when the contract will be defeated. The Declarer must stay off of two rounds of hearts in order to strip the West hand of this suit, but if he does this the defense should shift back to spades. The second shift will make South's defeat a certainty.

The deal offers another interesting point. If at the third trick, South actually takes the diamond finesse and West wins with the King, West would cash in the Queen of spades, on which everyone must follow suit. If West thereupon led the thirteenth spade, South would discard the diamond Ace and unblock the suit! West, if this situation develops, must refrain from taking his thirteenth spade at this point and shift instead to hearts.

Besides the points mentioned, and its illustration of a safety play, the deal is also a nice example of timing. The reader will find it worthy of study from all angles.

A Safety Play in a Side Suit

The play in the following deal which insures a factor of safety for South's spectacular contract is interesting chiefly because it is very simple:

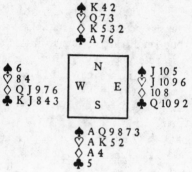

```
                ♠ K 4 2
                ♡ Q 7 3
                ♢ K 5 3 2
                ♣ A 7 6

  ♠ 6            ┌─────────┐         ♠ J 10 5
  ♡ 8 4          │    N    │         ♡ J 10 9 6
  ♢ Q J 9 7 6    │ W     E │         ♢ 10 8
  ♣ K J 8 4 3    │    S    │         ♣ Q 10 9 2
                 └─────────┘
                ♠ A Q 9 8 7 3
                ♡ A K 5 2
                ♢ A 4
                ♣ 5
```

With North and South vulnerable, the bidding has gone:

SOUTH	WEST	NORTH	EAST
One Spade	Pass	Two No-trump	Pass
Three Hearts	Pass	Three Spades	Pass
Four No-trump	Pass	Five Diamonds	Pass
Five No-trump	Pass	Six Hearts	Pass
Seven Spades *	Pass	Pass	Pass

The play proceeds as follows:

Trick 1. West leads ♢ Q, North plays ♢ 2, East plays ♢ 8, and South wins with ♢ A.

Trick 2. South leads ♠ 3, West plays ♠ 6, North plays ♠ K, and East plays ♠ 5. Dummy's King wins. Note that the Declarer plays the King from the Dummy first, to be prepared for the possibility that East has all four spades to the Jack-Ten.

Trick 3. North leads ♠ 2, East plays ♠ 10, South plays ♠ Q,

---

* South has located the necessary Ace and two Kings via Blackwood. His seven bid still has to gamble on finding an acceptable heart holding in Dummy. Justifiable, say we, in view of North's original two no-trump response.

and West discards ♣ 8. South's Queen wins, and the Declarer is a bit disappointed.

If the spades had broken 2-2, the Declarer could have laid down his hand, for his extra heart could be ruffed in the Dummy with the long trump. To attempt this play is now extremely dangerous, for there is one outstanding trump, but it is still the best play the Declarer has at his disposal. Once the trumps do not break right, it is apparent that everything depends on the heart suit. If the hearts are divided 3-3, the contract is made very easily, but if they are divided 4-2, a trick must be lost if the last trump is taken out of Dummy. However, there is still a chance that if the hearts break 4-2, *the hand which holds the extra trump will also hold the four hearts.*

Trick 4. South leads ♡ A, West plays ♡ 4, North plays ♡ 3, and East plays ♡ 6.

Trick 5. South leads ♡ 2, West plays ♡ 8, North plays ♡ Q, and East plays ♡ 9. Dummy's Queen wins.

Trick 6. North leads ♡ 7, East plays ♡ 10, South plays ♡ K, and West discards ♣ 4. The Declarer now knows that he is safe, for East has the high heart and also the high trump.

Trick 7. South leads ♡ 5, West discards ◇ 6, North ruffs with ♠ 4, and East plays ♡ J. North's ruff wins after all, as South knows after the sixth trick.

Trick 8. North leads ♣ A, East plays ♣ 2, South plays ♣ 5, and West plays ♣ 3. North's trick.

Trick 9. North leads ♣ 6, East plays ♣ 9, South ruffs with ♠ 9, and West plays ♣ J. South's ruffing-trick.

Trick 10. South leads ♠ A, West discards ◇ 7, North discards ◇ 3, and East plays ♠ J. The rest of the tricks belong to the Declarer.

As already stated, the principle involved in this deal is really quite simple. If the hearts are divided 3-3, well and good. They may just as well be led first if they are so divided, because the hand with the trump cannot make any use of it. The method described adds considerable safety to the play of the hand, since the hearts may be divided 4-2.

The Acme of Foresight in a Safety Play

The safety play in the following deal is considerably more complex than any given thus far—it represents the acme of foresight:

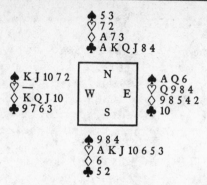

♠ 5 3
♡ 7 2
◇ A 7 3
♣ A K Q J 8 4

♠ K J 10 7 2   ♠ A Q 6
♡ —   ♡ Q 9 8 4
◇ K Q J 10   ◇ 9 8 5 4 2
♣ 9 7 6 3   ♣ 10

♠ 9 8 4
♡ A K J 10 6 5 3
◇ 6
♣ 5 2

With both sides vulnerable, the bidding has gone:

SOUTH	WEST	NORTH	EAST
Three Hearts	Pass	Four Clubs	Pass
Four Hearts	Pass	Pass	Pass

West opens the diamond King, which Dummy's Ace wins, East playing the four and South the six. The deuce of hearts is now led from Dummy, on which East plays the four, and Declarer *finesses the Ten!* This is certainly a spectacular finesse in view of the fact that there are only four outstanding trumps. Yet this play is absolutely necessary to safeguard the contract against a very bad break. South has 3 losing tricks in spades, and he will surely lose all of them if the trumps are taken out of the Dummy. If the Declarer plays his trumps in the hope that the adverse ones break 2-2, and they fail to break, he must make an attempt to run off his clubs. If the hand with the missing trump also had a club singleton originally, the Declarer's contract goes up in smoke.

The finesse of the heart Ten on the second trick is an absolute safety measure. Only one thing can spoil it—an original void in clubs on the Declarer's right. But such a void is very unlikely and should not be considered. The Declarer does not care if the finesse loses, for he can pick up all the trumps later and the Dummy, meanwhile, still retains its potential ruffing power for the third round of spades.

DESTROYING AN ENTRY CARD TO PLAY SAFE

The following deal shows another very unusual safety play which takes place at a defensive bid:

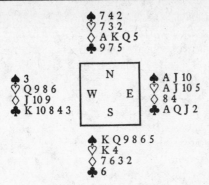

```
                    ♠ 7 4 2
                    ♡ 7 3 2
                    ◇ A K Q 5
                    ♣ 9 7 5
        ♠ 3                          ♠ A J 10
        ♡ Q 9 8 6          N         ♡ A J 10 5
        ◇ J 10 9      W        E     ◇ 8 4
        ♣ K 10 8 4 3       S         ♣ A Q J 2
                    ♠ K Q 9 8 6 5
                    ♡ K 4
                    ◇ 7 6 3 2
                    ♣ 6
```

With East and West vulnerable, the bidding has gone:

SOUTH	WEST	NORTH	EAST
Pass	Pass	Pass	One Heart
One Spade	Two Hearts	Two Spades	Three Clubs
Three Spades	Pass	Pass	Three No-trump
Pass	Four Clubs	Pass	Four Hearts
Four Spades	Pass	Pass	Double
Pass	Pass	Pass	

In order to appreciate the play of this deal, the reader must study the bidding carefully. The bids do not conform entirely to recognized sound methods, for North's spade raise is made without adequate trump support. However, the Ace-King-Queen of diamonds seem to require some sort of action, and the bid of two spades is perhaps the best at North's disposal. The point here is that the bidding by East and West tells a plain story, so crystal clear that the Declarer can all but count the Opponents' hands, especially after he sees West's opening lead. The play proceeds as follows:

Trick 1. West leads ♡ 6, North plays ♡ 2, East plays ♡ A, and South plays ♡ 4. West's lead is obviously fourth best, and South is thereby enabled to mark East with an original holding of only four hearts. This means that he can have at the most four clubs. His bid of three no-trump seems to indicate that he has a double stopper in spades, and that gives him three spades and two diamonds. If this is his actual distribution, South has a chance of fulfilling his contract.

Trick 2. East leads ♡ J, South plays ♡ K, West plays ♡ 8, and North plays ♡ 3. East cannot tell whether his Partner's lead was away from the King or the Queen, until he sees South win the trick with the King.

Trick 3.   South leads ◇ 2, West plays ◇ 9, North plays ◇ Q, and East plays ◇ 8.   The Declarer enters the Dummy with the diamond Queen in order to lead spades from that direction.   At the same time, East starts an echo to show that he originally held a doubleton diamond.

Trick 4.   North leads ♠ 2, East plays ♠ 10, South plays ♠ Q, and West plays ♠ 3.   At this point, South stops to consider.

It is obvious that South must lead trumps from the Dummy a second time, but it is also obvious that if he does so by leading diamonds for entry purposes, East will be exhausted of this suit. It will then be a simple matter for East to go up with the Ace of spades on the second round, underlead his Ace of clubs and put his Partner in the lead, so that a diamond can be led for East to ruff with his last trump.   This must be prevented in some way.

Trick 5.   South leads ♣ 6, West plays ♣ 10, North plays ♣ 5, and East wins with ♣ J.

Trick 6.   East leads ♣ A, South ruffs with ♠ 5, West plays ♣ 3, and North plays ♣ 7.

Trick 7.   South leads ◇ 3, West plays ◇ 10, North plays ◇ K, and East plays ◇ 4.   Dummy's King wins.

Trick 8.   North leads ♠ 4, East plays ♠ A, South plays ♠ 6, and West discards ♣ 4.   East goes up with his Ace, but it now does him no good.   As East and West can win no more tricks, the Declarer makes his contract.

Suppose we go back to the fifth trick and see what would have happened if South had blindly led a second round of diamonds.

Trick 5.   South leads ◇ 3, West plays ◇ 10, North plays ◇ K, and East plays ◇ 4.   Dummy's trick.

Trick 6.   North leads ♠ 4, East plays ♠ A, South plays ♠ 5, and West discards ♣ 10.

Trick 7.   East leads ♣ 2, South plays ♣ 6, West plays ♣ K, and North plays ♣ 7.   West's trick.

Trick 8.   West leads ◇ J, North plays ◇ A, East ruffs with ♠ J, and South plays ◇ 6.   Obviously this trick sets the contract, and yet, as was shown, it could be easily prevented.

South's lead of the six of clubs effectively destroyed the only way that East could put his Partner in the lead.   It destroyed all the lines of communication for the Opponents, and enabled the Declarer to fulfill a contract which he embarked upon rather unwillingly to start with. This safety play is rather rare, for the reason that it is unusual for the proper play to be the deliberate leading out of a sure losing trick.

Summary

The expert takes chances—chances which may mean the loss of his contract—only when he has to. If there is any way of avoiding the risk, or if he can make any play that will give a modicum of safety to his contract, he will surely seize the opportunity gladly. That, after all, is the way an expert player rises from the ranks to a position of importance among champions.

There are two principal varieties of the safety play. One is executed by giving up 1 trick in order to reduce to a minimum the possibility of losing 2 tricks. The other consists of manipulating honors (when possible) in such a way that the worst possible adverse distribution (if it turns up) can be taken care of.

Thus a finesse may be refused, and a trick given up to the outstanding honor, in order to avoid the loss of an additional trick if the finesse should fail. Similarly, when faced with an adverse ruff in a suit of which he holds command, the Declarer can sometimes render the ruff useless by maneuvering so that he plays a commanding card *after* the ruff, and can substitute a lower one if the ruff occurs. When playing a trump suit, the worst possible distribution of the outstanding trumps should always be considered, and the best way found to play the holding so that the worst break will be met at least with your eyes open.

In general, the safety play is really an application of common sense and foresight. As you plan your play, you consider every possibility—every snag which may lie ahead—and you plan to handle your cards in the best way possible to meet the contingencies that may arise. And you should always choose to play safe, for in Contract Bridge it may safely be said that discretion is always the better part of valor.

CHAPTER III

END PLAYS

THE *end play** is perhaps the most interesting of the advanced plays in Contract Bridge. For this reason it has often been written about, and very often maltreated and given an air of complexity which it really does not deserve. Broadly speaking, the end play is but another application of a principle which is described in the elementary section (Part I) of this book—namely, that it is usually more advisable to force an Opponent to lead up to your tenace holdings than it is to lead away from those holdings yourself. This is really all there is to an end play, except that to execute this more advanced form of the situation a certain amount of preliminary sparring must be done to secure the right opening. Furthermore, the true end play, properly executed, does not give the Opponents any chance of protecting themselves.

The end play has been given many names. It has been called *the elimination play, the strip play, the throw-in play, the forced-lead play,* etc. These names are mostly variants of the same thing, and they are quite unnecessary. Some end-play situations require elimination of side suits, but others do not, and such a variation can be taken care of very easily when it comes along. After all, it does not matter what the play is called just so long as the player knows how to execute it.

The following is a simple illustration:

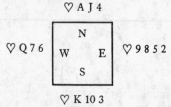

$\heartsuit$ A J 4

$\heartsuit$ Q 7 6   N W E S $\heartsuit$ 9 8 5 2

$\heartsuit$ K 10 3

---

* It would appear that an end play, if properly named, must occur toward the *end* of a hand—say at the 10th trick or later. Broadly speaking, any strategic play which takes place at the 10th trick or later might be called an end play. But the term *end play,* by virtue of its long use in a particular sense, has come to mean just one form of play toward the end of a hand—that form of play which forces an Opponent to lead as desired, by putting him in the lead when he can lead back only to the Declarer's advantage. The preparation for an end play, of course, may begin at the first trick, and, as a matter of fact, the climax may on occasion occur in the very middle of the hand.

The heart distribution shown here offers South (Declarer) a two-way finesse. If you, as South, decide that West has the missing Queen, you should finesse the Jack against West, but if you think it more likely that East has the Queen, you must finesse the Ten. In other words, the whole decision rests on guesswork—which means accident. Sometimes you will be right, and sometimes wrong. But if it should happen that either Opponent has the lead and must lead a heart, before any hearts have been played at all, your troubles are over. As soon as either East or West leads a heart, you no longer care which one of them has the Queen, for it is sure to be picked up. Clearly, then, it is to your advantage to place one of the Opponents in the lead —if you can do so.

Perhaps the remaining cards in the deal are as follows:

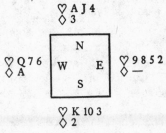

Suppose you are sitting South and the lead is in the Dummy (North). Unwilling to guess which Opponent has the missing Queen of hearts, you simply lead your low diamond and force West to win with his Ace. Any heart which he now leads will assure you of 3 tricks in the suit, and you are not even curious to know whether West has the Queen or whether East has it.

Naturally, the example just given is an invented, artificially set up situation. Yet you could plan from the beginning, or fairly early in the hand, so that such a situation might develop. You could actually make sure that the Opponents hold no more cards in any of the other suits, so that a heart lead will be the only one available to them. This requires careful planning, of course, but that is all it takes.

Frequently an end play *must* be made when it is not a question of dodging an issue at all. Sometimes the result is a certainty, and at other times some risk is involved. Consider the following situation at the end of the tenth trick:

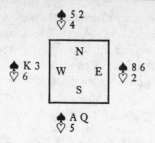

Suppose that the lead is now in the Dummy (North) and that you (South) must win 2 out of the 3 remaining tricks. It is true that the spade finesse offers about a fifty-fifty chance of success, but if you can avoid this chance of *losing* you must certainly do so. If you have studied the cards already played, you know, let us say, that West must hold the high heart (six-spot) and two spades. You know that you can place West in the lead and force him to lead back a spade. This takes care of the possibility that the spade finesse will not work. In other words, here you have a mode of play which will work 100 times in 100 trials, as against a finesse which can work only 50 times in 100 trials (on the average). Why take a chance when you have a sure thing?

A certain amount of preliminary work is necessary, as a rule, to develop an end-play situation. This is planned by the Declarer, and comes about as an accident only on rare occasions. Look at the following diagram:

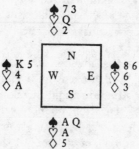

This is substantially the same situation as in the preceding example, except that now the tenth trick has not been played and everyone holds at least one card in three suits instead of only two suits. You can lead a diamond (from the South position) and force West into the lead, but he will not have to lead back a spade. He still has a heart which he can throw to the four winds, and thus put the lead right back in your hand—and you will be forced *to lead spades to him*. West will thus have the advantage—not you. The first thing you must do at this stage (at the tenth trick), then, is to get rid of that heart all round. You take your Ace of hearts, therefore, before throwing West in the lead. You lead your low diamond at the eleventh trick, and West is caught. He has to lead back a spade.

This play of the heart suit first is the elimination or strip play which is preparing for the end play. Before you can *force* West to lead spades, you must make sure that he holds no cards of any other suit to lead back to you. As soon as you have *eliminated* all other suits, the rest of the play is as easy as falling off a log.

You may think it is much more difficult when an entire hand has to be stripped in preparation for an end play. It is somewhat more difficult, of course, but not really much more difficult. All that you need is enough imagination to recognize the fact that certain card combinations are bound to be more valuable to you if the Opponents can be induced to lead into them. Once you have this fact well learned, it is not such a hard matter to start the preparations for an end situation in which you leave a luckless Opponent with no choice but to lead the suit you wish. Imagination plus the ability to count up to thirteen—scarcely more than this is required to execute end plays with the touch of a master.

The following deals illustrate different types of end plays, but they are all of the same fundamental character.* They all involve reaching a situation in which an Opponent can be thrown in the lead at a moment when he can lead back only what the Declarer desires.

Before taking up the first example, it must be emphasized that any understanding of end plays requires very careful watching of all the cards as they are played. End plays are made, as a rule, to avoid

---

* Some writers have divided end plays into two or more classes or groups. This seems rather pointless, since there is essentially no difference between them in principle. To classify merely for the sake of classifying in Bridge is about as idle a pastime as one can imagine, though when classification aids the student there is some value to it. It is true that elimination at no-trump, in preparation for an end play, means leading out high cards, and that elimination at a suit means ruffing outside suits—but this difference is not a characteristic of end plays, but a characteristic of no-trump as contrasted with suit play.

taking finesses, because they offer a better chance of success than a finesse. However, a finesse is sometimes the better play; sometimes the hand which you can throw in the lead will be one holding nothing but good tricks, and one which will never be forced to lead the suit you wish. Under such circumstances, you must prefer the finesse.

A Simple End Play

The following deal shows a simple end play in which the preparatory process brings about the desired result of a lead into a heart tenace as surely as two and two make four.

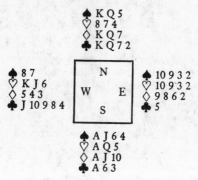

With North and South vulnerable, the bidding has gone:

South	West	North	East
Two No-trump	Pass	Six No-trump	Pass
Pass	Pass		

The play goes as follows:

Trick 1. West leads ♣ J, North plays ♣ 2, East plays ♣ 5, and South wins with ♣ A. South immediately comes to the conclusion that West is probably long in clubs. Nevertheless, he makes a mental reservation that West may be leading from a short suit.

Trick 2. South leads ♠ 4, West plays ♠ 7, North plays ♠ Q, and East plays ♠ 2. Dummy's trick. The Declarer may just as well cash in his spade tricks.

Trick 3. North leads ♠ K, East plays ♠ 3, South plays ♠ 6, and West plays ♠ 8.

Trick 4. North leads ♠ 5, East plays ♠ 9, South plays ♠ J, and West discards ◊ 3. South's trick. By now South knows something more—West held but two spades originally, which increases the chances of his being long in clubs.

Trick 5. South leads ♠ A, West discards ♣ 4, North discards ♡ 4, and East plays ♠ 10.

Trick 6. South leads ♣ 3, West plays ♣ 8, North plays ♣ Q, and East discards ♢ 2. Dummy's trick, on which East shows out of clubs, and the Declarer knows that West held five clubs originally. Already seven of the cards originally held by West are known.

Trick 7. North leads ♢ 7, East plays ♢ 6, South plays ♢ A, and West plays ♢ 4. The lead is back in the South hand.

Trick 8. South leads ♢ J, West plays ♢ 5, North plays ♢ Q, and East plays ♢ 8. Again Dummy's trick.

Trick 9. North leads ♢ K, East plays ♢ 9, South plays ♢ 10, and West discards ♡ 6. The pattern of distribution is now complete in the Declarer's mind, as follows:

West has already thrown off a diamond, has followed suit on two diamond leads, and has failed to follow suit on the third round. Therefore he held originally three diamonds—and it was previously shown that he originally held five clubs and two spades. That means that his original hand contained three hearts, of which he has discarded one. Therefore he still holds two hearts. Furthermore, South *knows* that West's remaining cards consist of two clubs—exactly the Ten and nine—and two hearts (denomination unknown). The possible end play is no longer a shot in the dark.

Trick 10. North leads ♣ K, East discards ♡ 2, South plays ♣ 6, and West plays ♣ 9.

The situation at this point is as follows:

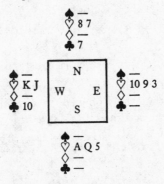

The last 3 tricks are played as follows:

Trick 11.   North leads ♣ 7, East discards ♡ 3, South discards ♡ 5, and West wins with ♣ 10.   Here West is thrown in the lead, when South knows that he has only two hearts left and nothing else.

Trick 12.   West leads ♡ J, North plays ♡ 7, East plays ♡ 9, and South wins with ♡ Q.

Trick 13.   South leads ♡ A, West plays ♡ K, North plays ♡ 8, and East plays ♡ 10.

This end play, which took place at the eleventh and twelfth tricks, was absolutely sure to work, because South's count on West's hand was perfect.   Even if West did not hold the King of hearts, the contract was sure to be made, as West would have to lead the heart suit anyway.   It is equally apparent that a heart finesse would have lost the contract, as South needed 2 heart tricks to complete his required total of 12.   At the beginning of the hand he could see 4 sure spade tricks, 1 sure heart trick, 3 sure diamond tricks and 3 sure club tricks, 11 tricks in all.   The heart Queen offered the only chance of making the twelfth trick.   Finessing would have meant losing the card altogether, as East and West also held the Jack, Ten, and nine.

Before leaving this example deal, it should be added that West might have made things very trying for South.   If, instead of discarding a club, West had thrown off the Jack of hearts, a different result might have come about.   West's last three cards would then have been the Ten and nine of clubs, and the singleton King of hearts.   This would put the Declarer in a terrific dilemma.   He would know that West held only one heart, but he would have no way of telling it was the King.   The discard of the Jack might indicate that West had blanked the King of hearts, but this would not be conclusive.   South would have to reach a decision from what he knew of the psychology of the West player.*

Throwing the Lead in the Suit Desired as the Return

The following deal is an interesting example of an end play in clubs. It is normal except that the Opponent is thrown in the lead in the same suit in which the return lead is desired:

---

* It should be clear that with West holding two clubs and one heart at the eleventh trick, the end play is out. If South leads a club, West makes 2 club tricks. The dilemma South faces is whether to finesse his Queen or lay down the Ace of hearts for the drop.

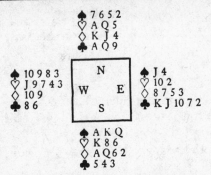

```
              ♠ 7 6 5 2
              ♡ A Q 5
              ◇ K J 4
              ♣ A Q 9

♠ 10 9 8 3      ┌─────────┐      ♠ J 4
♡ J 9 7 4 3     │    N    │      ♡ 10 2
◇ 10 9          │ W     E │      ◇ 8 7 5 3
♣ 8 6           │    S    │      ♣ K J 10 7 2
                └─────────┘

              ♠ A K Q
              ♡ K 8 6
              ◇ A Q 6 2
              ♣ 5 4 3
```

With North and South vulnerable, the bidding has gone:

SOUTH	WEST	NORTH	EAST
One No-trump	Pass	Four No-trump	Pass
Six No-trump	Pass	Pass	Pass

The bidding is unusual, but perfectly logical. Neither North nor South have a suit really worth mentioning, but they have a plethora of high cards. North feels that if South is strong enough to open with one no-trump when vulnerable, he is strong enough to withstand a Slam invitation, and results bear him out. The play then proceeds as follows:

Trick 1. West leads ♡ 4, North plays ♡ Q, East plays ♡ 2, and South plays ♡ 6. Dummy's Queen wins.

Trick 2. North leads ♠ 2, East plays ♠ 4, South plays ♠ Q, and West plays ♠ 3. Winning with the Queen, South is going to try to establish his fourth spade in the Dummy.

Trick 3. South leads ♠ K, West plays ♠ 8, North plays ♠ 5, and East plays ♠ J.

Trick 4. South leads ♠ A, West plays ♠ 9, North plays ♠ 6, and East discards ◇ 3. The plan fails, for West is left with the high spade.

Trick 5. South leads ◇ 2, West plays ◇ 9, North plays ◇ J, and East plays ◇ 5. Winning with Dummy's Jack, South has attacked the diamond suit in an endeavor to obtain some sort of count on the Opponents' hands.

Trick 6. North leads ◇ K, East plays ◇ 7, South plays ◇ 6, and West plays ◇ 10.

Trick 7. North leads ◇ 4, East plays ◇ 8, South plays ◇Q, and West discards ♡ 3. The lead is back with South.

Trick 8. South leads ◇ A, West discards ♣ 6, North discards ♠ 7, and East discards ♣ 2. Declarer throws off Dummy's now useless spade. He also finds that East originally held four diamonds and two spades. Note particularly East's throwing off of the deuce of clubs on this trick. East fears the end play which he sees coming and is trying to befuddle the Declarer.

Trick 9. South leads ♡ 6, West plays ♡ 7, North plays ♡ A, and East plays ♡ 10.

Trick 10. North leads ♡ 5, East discards ♣ 7, South plays ♡ K, and West plays ♡ 9. East now shows out of hearts. He has already failed to follow on both diamonds and spades, and so he has nothing left now but clubs! The next play is as compulsory as obeying a military command.

Trick 11. South leads ♣ 3, West plays ♣ 8, North plays ♣ 9, and East wins with ♣ 10.

Trick 12. East leads ♣ J, South plays ♣ 4, West discards ♠ 10, and North wins with ♣ Q.

Trick 13. North leads ♣ A, East plays ♣ K, South plays ♣ 5, and West discards ♡ J.

Nothing could be more simple than this play. Once South knows that East has nothing but clubs, he knows that his contract is made. The play is a sure thing no matter how the clubs are divided. Even if West held either the Jack or the Ten, and played this card, it would make no difference. Suppose, for instance, that West played the club Ten. The Queen would be played from the Dummy, and if East won with his King, he would still be forced to lead away from the Jack into Dummy's Ace-nine tenace.

Note also that a simple finesse of the Queen of clubs will cost the Declarer his contract.

An Elimination End Play

The club end play in this deal differs from the preceding principally in the fact that the honors which the Declarer must lead in preparation are all placed in the same hand.

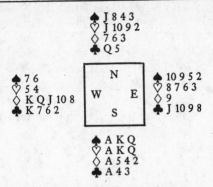

♠ J 8 4 3
♡ J 10 9 2
◇ 7 6 3
♣ Q 5

♠ 7 6
♡ 5 4
◇ K Q J 10 8
♣ K 7 6 2

♠ 10 9 5 2
♡ 8 7 6 3
◇ 9
♣ J 10 9 8

♠ A K Q
♡ A K Q
◇ A 5 4 2
♣ A 4 3

With neither side vulnerable, the bidding has gone:

South	West	North	East
Three No-trump	Pass	Pass	Pass

The play proceeds as follows:

Trick 1. West leads ◇ K, North plays ◇ 3, East plays ◇ 9, and South plays ◇ 2. West wins, because South holds up his Ace, partly to make sure that the East hand will be exhausted of this suit, and partly to obtain some information as to the adverse distribution. Incidentally, he sees that his chief difficulty is the lack of a sure entry into the Dummy's hand.

Trick 2. West leads ◇ Q, North plays ◇ 6, East discards ♡ 3, and South plays ◇ 4. Though East shows out of diamonds, South continues to hold up—he has formed a plan.

Trick 3. West leads ◇ J, North plays ◇ 7, East discards ♡ 6, and South wins with ◇ A.

Trick 4. South leads ♠ A, West plays ♠ 6, North plays ♠ 3, and East plays ♠ 2.

Trick 5. South leads ♠ K, West plays ♠ 7, North plays ♠ 4, and East plays ♠ 5.

Trick 6. South leads ♠ Q, West discards ♣ 2, North plays ♠ 8, and East plays ♠ 9. South has now stripped West of spades.

Trick 7. South leads ♡ A, West plays ♡ 4, North plays ♡ 2, and East plays ♡ 7.

Trick 8. South leads ♡ K, West plays ♡ 5, North plays ♡ 9, and East plays ♡ 8.

Trick 9. South leads ♡ Q, West discards ♣ 6, North plays ♡ 10, and East discards ♠ 10. The West hand is now stripped of hearts also, and the stage is set if West holds the King of clubs.

Trick 10. South leads ♢ 5, West plays ♢ 8, North discards ♡ J, and East discards ♣ 8. West wins with the eight-spot.

Trick 11. West leads ♢ 10, North discards ♠ J, East discards ♣ 9, and South discards ♣ 3. West is completely helpless and is forced to lead away from his King of clubs at the twelfth trick.

Trick 12. West leads ♣ 7, North plays ♣ Q, East plays ♣ 10, and South plays ♣ 4.

Trick 13. North leads ♣ 5, East plays ♣ J, South plays ♣ A, and West plays ♣ K.

The manner of playing this hand—hoping right along that West holds the club King—is common with expert players. It is colloquially termed "playing for the best chance," which means to play the hand in a way that will make the contract if the adverse cards are placed right. In this deal, if East should hold the club King, the contract cannot be made anyway. South loses nothing, and has everything to gain, therefore, by playing as though the club King were placed in the West hand. His optimism was rewarded; such optimism—playing for the best chance—is really good Bridge, for it is playing to win some of the time as against always losing.

Choosing Between an End Play and a Finesse

In the next deal, a finesse in spades would be quite as successful, it happens, as the end play in the same suit. But, since the Opponents' hands cannot be seen, the direction of the finesse must be guessed, while the end play is practically a certainty.

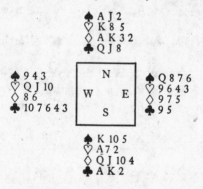

```
                    ♠ A J 2
                    ♡ K 8 5
                    ♢ A K 3 2
                    ♣ Q J 8
                        N
    ♠ 9 4 3                         ♠ Q 8 7 6
    ♡ Q J 10                        ♡ 9 6 4 3
    ♢ 8 6        W         E        ♢ 9 7 5
    ♣ 10 7 6 4 3                    ♣ 9 5
                        S
                    ♠ K 10 5
                    ♡ A 7 2
                    ♢ Q J 10 4
                    ♣ A K 2
```

With neither side vulnerable, the bidding has gone:

SOUTH	WEST	NORTH	EAST
One No-trump	Pass	Six No-trump	Pass
Pass	Pass		

The play proceeds as follows:

Trick 1.   West leads ♣ 4, North plays ♣ 8, East plays ♣ 9, and South wins with ♣ K.

Trick 2.   South leads ◇ Q, West plays ◇ 6, North plays ◇ 2, and East plays ◇ 5.

Trick 3.   South leads ◇ J, West plays ◇ 8, North plays ◇ 3, and East plays ◇ 7.

Trick 4.   South leads ◇ 4, West discards ♣ 3, North plays ◇ K, and East plays ◇ 9.   Dummy's trick.

Trick 5.   North leads ◇ A, East discards ♡ 3, South plays ◇ 10, and West discards ♣ 6.   West is shedding his clubs madly as it is obvious that this suit, though he opened it, can never be established. He thinks his best play is to get rid of them while he has the chance, though it will appear later that these were not his best discards (but there is almost no way for West to know this soon enough to do him any good).

Trick 6.   North leads ♣ J, East plays ♣ 5, South plays ♣ 2, and West plays ♣ 7.

Trick 7.   North leads ♣ Q, East discards ♡ 4, South plays ♣ A, and West plays ♣ 10.   South notes with satisfaction that both Opponents have now been stripped of clubs and diamonds.   He also notes that East has thrown off two hearts, which leaves only five hearts outstanding.

Trick 8.   South leads ♡ 2, West plays ♡ 10, North plays ♡ K, and East plays ♡ 6.

Trick 9.   North leads ♡ 5, East plays ♡ 9, South plays ♡ A, and West plays ♡ J.   Now there is only one heart remaining—the Queen.   South has available a two-way spade finesse, but he does not know in which direction to take it, as both Opponents have assiduously refrained from discarding any spades lest they give a clue.   However, South does know that whichever hand wins the third round of hearts will win it with the Queen, and that this hand will be absolutely forced to lead spades.

Trick 10.   South leads ♡ 7, *West wins* with ♡ Q, North plays ♡ 8, East discards ♠ 6.

The situation at the beginning of the eleventh trick is as follows:

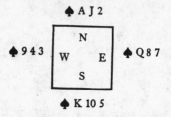

♠ A J 2

♠ 9 4 3   W   N   E   ♠ Q 8 7
                       S

♠ K 10 5

West, thrown in the lead on the tenth trick, must lead one of his three spades—whichever he chooses, the Declarer makes the 3 last tricks.

Of course, it may be contended that South could have guessed the finesse right—but what of that?   The end play by throwing West in with a heart is much surer—in fact, it is a dead certainty.   Incidentally, note West's discards.   If he had only known, he might have kept an extra club, and Declarer would not then have dared to throw him in with a heart.   However, in this particular deal, he would have been forced to discard a spade instead of the club, which would probably have enabled the Declarer to mark East with the Queen.

MAKING AN END PLAY FOR AN EXTRA TRICK

One more example of an end play at a no-trump contract, and then we go on to the much more frequent use of end plays at a suit declaration.   In the following deal an end play is used to secure an extra trick in the spade suit after the contract has been made secure.

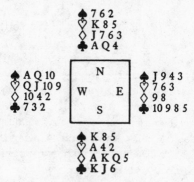

♠ 7 6 2
♡ K 8 5
◇ J 7 6 3
♣ A Q 4

♠ A Q 10   N   ♠ J 9 4 3
♡ Q J 10 9   W   E   ♡ 7 6 3
◇ 10 4 2   ◇ 9 8
♣ 7 3 2   S   ♣ 10 9 8 5

♠ K 8 5
♡ A 4 2
◇ A K Q 5
♣ K J 6

With neither side vulnerable, the bidding has gone:

SOUTH	WEST	NORTH	EAST
One Diamond	Pass	Two Diamonds	Pass
Two No-trump	Pass	Three No-trump	Pass
Pass	Pass		

The play proceeds as follows:

Trick 1. West leads ♡ Q, North plays ♡ 5, East plays ♡ 3, and South wins with ♡ A. South immediately sees 9 tricks in sight, and decides that he may as well take them before something unforeseen occurs.

Trick 2. South leads ◇ A, West plays ◇ 2, North plays ◇ 3, and East plays ◇ 8.

Trick 3. South leads ◇ K, West plays ◇ 4, North plays ◇ 6, and East plays ◇ 9.

Trick 4. South leads ◇ Q, West plays ◇ 10, North plays ◇ 7, and East discards ♡ 6.

Trick 5. South leads ◇ 5, West discards ♣ 2, North plays ◇ J, and East discards ♠ 3. Dummy's trick.

Trick 6. North leads ♣ 4, East plays ♣ 5, South plays ♣ K, and West plays ♣ 3. South's trick.

Trick 7. South leads ♣ 6, West plays ♣ 7, North plays ♣ Q, and East plays ♣ 8. Again Dummy's trick.

Trick 8. North leads ♣ A, East plays ♣ 9, South plays ♣ J, and West plays ♠ 10.

Trick 9. North leads ♡ K, East plays ♡ 7, South plays ♡ 2, and West plays ♡ 9. This makes the ninth trick won by South—his contract is made. But he sees a way of making a trick with his King of spades if West holds the remaining hearts, which is probable.

Trick 10. North leads ♡ 8, East discards ♣ 10, South plays ♡ 4, and West wins with ♡ J.

Trick 11. West leads ♡ Q, North discards ♠ 2, East discards ♠ 4, and South discards ♠ 5.

Trick 12. West leads ♠ A, North plays ♠ 6, East plays ♠ 9, and South plays ♠ 8.

Trick 13. West leads ♠ Q, North plays ♠ 7, East plays ♠ J, and South wins with ♠ K.

It should be obvious that if the Declarer blindly led spades up to his King in the vague hope of stabbing at a finesse, he would have lost all 4 of the last tricks instead of losing but 3 of them.   The end play gives him an overtrick.

The End Play at a Suit Contract

Contrary to the general belief, the execution of an end play at a suit contract is comparatively simple, requiring only an average amount of knowledge of fundamentals.   This type of play is not difficult to recognize.   Whenever you see a combination of cards in your hand that will gain in trick-taking value if led up to, that is the time to look around for a chance to eliminate the other suits in preparation for an end play.   The following deal contains a particularly clear situation, with J 10 9 in one hand and A x x in the other, which is one of the most common combinations leading eventually to end plays.

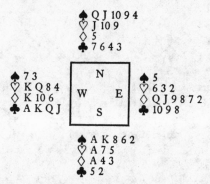

With both sides vulnerable, the bidding has gone:

South	West	North	East
One Spade	Double	Three Spades	Pass
Four Spades	Pass	Pass	Pass

The play proceeds as follows:

Trick 1.   West leads ♣ K, North plays ♣ 3, East plays ♣ 8, and South plays ♣ 2.

Trick 2.   West leads ♣ Q, North plays ♣ 4, East plays ♣ 9, and South plays ♣ 5.

Trick 3.   West leads ♣ J, North plays ♣ 6, East plays ♣ 10, and South ruffs with ♠ 2.

Trick 4.   South leads ♠ A, West plays ♠ 3, North plays ♠ 4, and East plays ♠ 5.

Trick 5. South leads ♠ K, West plays ♠ 7, North plays ♠ 9, and East discards ◇ 2. All the adverse trumps are now drawn, and South sees that a perfect end-play situation can be created if both clubs and diamonds are removed from his own hand and the Dummy's.

Trick 6. South leads ◇ A, West plays ◇ 6, North plays ◇ 5, and East plays ◇ 7.

Trick 7. South leads ◇ 3, West plays ◇ 10, North ruffs with ♠ 10, and East plays ◇ 8. Dummy's ruffing-trick.

Trick 8. North leads ♣ 7, East discards ♡ 2, South ruffs with ♠ 6, and West plays ♣ A. South's ruffing-trick.

Trick 9. South leads ◇ 4, West plays ◇ K, North ruffs with ♠ J, and East plays ◇ 9. Again Dummy's ruffing-trick—the deadly cross-ruff is being used for elimination purposes.

At this point, neither the Declarer's nor the Dummy's hand contain any suits but spades and hearts. The situation is as follows:

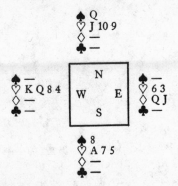

Trick 10. North leads ♡ J, East plays ♡ 3, South plays ♡ 5, and West wins with ♡ Q.

At the eleventh trick, West must lead back a heart, for he holds nothing else. It makes no difference whether he leads the King or a small card. Even if he held a club or a diamond, he could still not make any tricks. If he held a club or a diamond, and led it, Declarer could retaliate in one of two ways: he could discard a heart from the Dummy and ruff in his own hand, or he could ruff in the Dummy and discard his own losing heart. In other words, the lead of a suit in which both his hands are blank, permits the Declarer to use both of two remaining trumps separately and make 2 tricks instead of 1. It is apparent that the possible play of taking two finesses in hearts will fail, as West holds both the King and the Queen.

Another End Play When There Is a Trump Suit

The end play in clubs in the following deal belongs in the same category with the one just preceding, the only difference being in the card combinations involved:

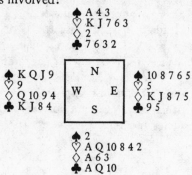

♠ A 4 3
♡ K J 7 6 3
◇ 2
♣ 7 6 3 2

♠ K Q J 9
♡ 9
◇ Q 10 9 4
♣ K J 8 4

♠ 10 8 7 6 5
♡ 5
◇ K J 8 7 5
♣ 9 5

♠ 2
♡ A Q 10 8 4 2
◇ A 6 3
♣ A Q 10

With both sides vulnerable, the bidding has gone:

South	West	North	East
One Heart	One Spade	Three Hearts	Three Spades
Six Hearts	Pass	Pass	Pass

The play proceeds as follows:

Trick 1. West leads ♠ K, North plays ♠ A, East plays ♠ 5, and South plays ♠ 2. Dummy's trick.

Trick 2. North leads ♡ 3, East plays ♡ 5, South plays ♡ A, and West plays ♡ 9. Declarer's trick.

Trick 3. South leads ◇ A, West plays ◇ 4, North plays ◇ 2, and East plays ◇ 5.

Trick 4. South leads ◇ 3, West plays ◇ 9, North ruffs with ♡ 6, and East plays ◇ 7. Dummy's ruffing-trick.

Trick 5. North leads ♠ 3, East plays ♠ 6, South ruffs with ♡ 2, and West plays ♠ 9. Declarer's ruffing-trick.

Trick 6. South leads ◇ 6, West plays ◇ 10, North ruffs with ♡ 7, and East plays ◇ 8. Dummy's ruffing-trick—the value of the cross-ruff in stripping down the hands is clearly seen here.

Trick 7. North leads ♠ 4, East plays ♠ 7, South ruffs with ♡ 4, and West plays ♠ J. South finishes his elimination of diamonds and spades from his own and Dummy's hands. However, the club lead must come from Dummy's hand, so he is forced to waste a trump.

Trick 8. South leads ♡ 8, West discards ♣ 4, North plays ♡ J, and East discards ♠ 8.

The situation is now as follows:

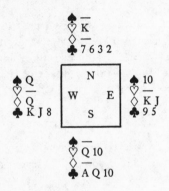

West is now to be thrown in the lead.

Trick 9. North leads ♣ 2, East plays ♣ 5, South plays ♣ 10, and West wins with ♣ J. In taking this double finesse, South is not particularly interested in which card wins the trick. West is now in the lead and has a choice of three suits for his return—anything but a trump (hearts). Certainly a club is out of the question, for it will plunge right into Declarer's Ace-Queen tenace. A spade or a diamond amounts to the same thing—that is, they are the same in effect —so let us suppose that West returns his spade Queen.

Trick 10. West leads ♠ Q, North ruffs with ♡ K, East plays ♠ 10, and South discards ♣ Q. The Declarer ruffs in the Dummy and discards his losing club from his own hand. He now holds two trumps and the Ace of clubs—clearly the rest of the tricks are his.

Notice one thing—the Declarer must discard the club from his *own* hand. To discard a club from the Dummy will avail him nothing, as, even with the discard, the Dummy would still hold two clubs, one of which must lose.

You have probably observed by this time that the elimination or stripping which takes place in preparing for an end play at a suit contract occurs in both Declarer's and Dummy's hands—so that the suits which, at no-trump, it would be undesirable for the Opponent to lead, can be controlled by Declarer's or Dummy's remaining trumps. In this way, if the player forced to lead to the Declarer chooses to avoid the suit in which the Declarer holds a tenace over him, he must lead a suit of which the Declarer and Dummy are void, thereby enabling the Declarer to ruff in one hand and to throw off from the other hand that subordinate part of the tenace which a lead in that suit would have enabled him to win. In other words, an end play at a suit contract is slightly more complex only in that it permits the Declarer to benefit even when the tenaced suit is not led. The player thrown in the lead has to lead into a tenace or lead a suit which will give the Declarer a ruff and a discard.

A Throw-in With Another Suit

The following deal illustrates the same principle as that just preceding, except that the player forced to lead is thrown in a side suit.

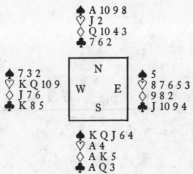

With North and South vulnerable, the bidding has gone:

South	West	North	East
Two Spades	Pass	Three Spades	Pass
Four Diamonds	Pass	Five Diamonds	Pass
Six Spades*	Pass	Pass	Pass

The play proceeds as follows:

Trick 1. West leads ♡ K, North plays ♡ 2, East plays ♡ 3, and South wins with ♡ A.

---

* An overbid.

Trick 2. South leads ♠ K, West plays ♠ 2, North plays ♠ 8, and East plays ♠ 5.

Trick 3. South leads ♠ Q, West plays ♠ 3, North plays ♠ 9, and East discards ♡ 5.

Trick 4. South leads ♠ 4, West plays ♠ 7, North plays ♠ 10, and East discards ♡ 6. Dummy's trick.

Trick 5. North leads ◇ 3, East plays ◇ 2, South plays ◇ A, and West plays ◇ 6. South's trick.

Trick 6. South leads ◇ K, West plays ◇ 7, North plays ◇ 4, and East plays ◇ 8.

Trick 7. South leads ◇ 5, West plays ◇ 7, North plays ◇ Q, and East plays ◇ 9. The lead is back in the Dummy.

Trick 8. North leads ◇ 10, East discards ♡ 7, South discards ♣ 3, and West discards ♡ 9. The stage is now set for the end play. West's lead of the King of hearts showed that he had the Queen (the Declarer himself had the Ace), and can be put in the lead.

Trick 9. North leads ♡ J, East plays ♡ 8, South plays ♡ 4, and West wins with ♡ Q. Now in the lead, West must return either a heart, permitting Declarer to ruff in the Dummy and discard the Queen of clubs from his own hand; or a club, allowing Declarer to make 2 club tricks.

An End Play by Giving Up a Trick That Might Be Saved

The end play to avoid a club finesse in this deal involves giving up a trick which does not necessarily have to be lost.

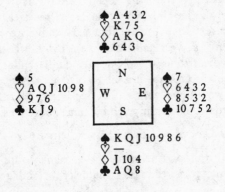

With East and West vulnerable, the bidding has gone:

SOUTH	WEST	NORTH	EAST
One Spade	Two Hearts	Three Spades	Pass
Four Hearts	Pass	Five Diamonds	Pass
Six Spades	Pass	Pass	Pass

The play proceeds as follows:

Trick 1. West leads ◇ 9, North plays ◇ Q, East plays ◇ 2, and South plays ◇ 4. North's trick.

Trick 2. North leads ♡ 5, East plays ♡ 2, South ruffs with ♠ 8, and West plays ♡ 8. Note that the Declarer starts stripping hearts even before drawing trumps. This is not absolutely necessary, but by doing this he makes sure that he will not lose his tempo.

Trick 3. South leads ♠ K, West plays ♠ 5, North plays ♠ A, and East plays ♠ 7. Dummy's trick.

Trick 4. North leads ♡ 7, East plays ♡ 3, South ruffs with ♠ 6, and West plays ♡ 9. South's ruffing-trick, continuing the elimination of hearts.

Trick 5. South leads ◇ 10, West plays ◇ 6, North plays ◇ K, and East plays ◇ 3. The diamond King puts the lead back in the Dummy.

Trick 6. North leads ◇ A, East plays ◇ 5, South plays ◇ J, and West plays ◇ 7.

Trick 7. North leads ♡ K, East plays ♡ 4, South discards ♣ 8, and West wins with ♡ A. This is the important play, throwing West in the lead.

Declarer could, of course, ruff the heart King, but if he does so the success of his contract will still depend on the club finesse. He therefore throws off the club which he most lose later anyway, in order to make sure that West will have to lead up to him. Note that this play renders West as helpless as a baby. To lead a heart permits South to discard his losing Queen of clubs, while the club lead eliminates the club loser since it enables South's tenace to win. Of course, the play would not work if the Declarer did not first remove the low hearts from the Dummy. This is absolutely essential.

AN OPTIMISTIC TRY FOR AN END PLAY

The end play in this particular deal is extremely rare, and it is a little harder to recognize than the majority of similar situations.

It takes a good deal of optimism to attempt this play, since it can succeed only against certain distributions.

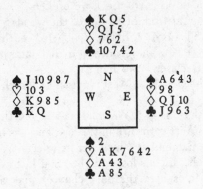

```
                    ♠ K Q 5
                    ♡ Q J 5
                    ◇ 7 6 2
                    ♣ 10 7 4 2
♠ J 10 9 8 7          N           ♠ A 6 4 3
♡ 10 3                            ♡ 9 8
◇ K 9 8 5       W         E       ◇ Q J 10
♣ K Q                            ♣ J 9 6 3
                     S
                    ♠ 2
                    ♡ A K 7 6 4 2
                    ◇ A 4 3
                    ♣ A 8 5
```

With both sides vulnerable, the bidding has gone:

SOUTH	WEST	NORTH	EAST
One Heart	Pass	One No-trump	Pass
Three Hearts	Pass	Four Hearts	Pass
Pass	Pass		

The play proceeds as follows:

Trick 1. West leads ♠ J, North plays ♠ Q, East plays ♠ A, and South plays ♠ 2. East wins the trick.

Trick 2. East leads ◇ Q, South plays ◇ 3, West plays ◇ 9, and North plays ◇ 2. Against East's diamond attack, South holds up his Ace. By thus deliberately letting East retain the lead, he begins somewhat craftily the process of elimination which he earnestly desires.

Trick 3. East leads ◇ J, South plays ◇ A, West plays ◇ 5, and North plays ◇ 6. South takes the second round of diamonds.

Trick 4. South leads ♡ 2, West plays ♡ 3, North plays ♡ J, and East plays ♡ 8. Dummy's trick.

Trick 5. North leads ♠ K, East plays ♠ 3, South discards ◇ 4, and West plays ♠ 7. In shifting to spades, South does not draw the second round of trumps. He leaves the heart Queen in the Dummy to serve as an entry.

Trick 6. North leads ♠ 5, East plays ♠ 4, South ruffs with ♡ 6, and West plays ♠ 8. South's ruffing-trick.

Trick 7. South leads ♡ 7, West plays ♡ 10, North plays ♡ Q, and East plays ♡ 9. That Queen puts the Declarer back in the Dummy. What is more, the adverse trumps have broken 2-2, which is a help, but the Declarer is far from being out of the woods yet.

Trick 8. North leads ◇ 7, East plays ◇ 10, South ruffs with ♡ 4, and West plays ◇ 8. The spades and diamonds have now been eliminated from Declarer's two hands.

Trick 9. South leads ♣ A, West plays ♣ Q, North plays ♣ 2, and East plays ♣ 3.

Trick 10. South leads ♣ 5, West plays ♣ K, North plays ♣ 4, and East plays ♣ 6. West is thrown in the lead and has no choice but to lead a spade or a diamond. Whichever he selects, South will ruff in the Dummy and discard his losing club. South, by playing for the best chance (which is here the only chance) makes his contract.

It may be true that the situation in this deal, is a little far-fetched. The trumps must break 2-2, and the clubs must be divided in such a way that the Opponent who obtains the lead on the second round cannot continue them. However, the play is the only one that has a chance of fulfilling the contract, and consequently should be tried.

ANOTHER END PLAY AS THE ONLY CHANCE*

It is quite true that some end plays are attempted when there is perhaps very little hope of their succeeding—that is to say, the preparatory plays leading up to the end play itself may not work out as hoped. However, such a play is often the only chance of making the contract, as in this deal:

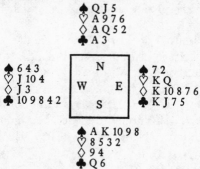

```
              ♠ Q J 5
              ♡ A 9 7 6
              ◇ A Q 5 2
              ♣ A 3
                ┌─────────┐
♠ 6 4 3         │    N    │      ♠ 7 2
♡ J 10 4        │         │      ♡ K Q
◇ J 3         W │         │ E    ◇ K 10 8 7 6
♣ 10 9 8 4 2    │    S    │      ♣ K J 7 5
                └─────────┘
              ♠ A K 10 9 8
              ♡ 8 5 3 2
              ◇ 9 4
              ♣ Q 6
```

___
* This is one of those rare end plays that occur as early as the seventh trick.

With North and South vulnerable, the bidding has gone:

South	West	North	East
Pass	Pass	One Diamond	Pass
One Spade	Pass	Two Spades	Pass
Three Spades	Pass	Three No-trump	Pass
Four Spades	Pass	Pass	Pass

The play proceeds as follows:

Trick 1. West leads ♣ 10, North plays ♣ 3, East plays ♣ K, and South plays ♣ 6. East wins the trick. South's first hope fails to materialize, namely, that the King of clubs was on his left.

Trick 2. East leads ♣ 5, South plays ♣ Q, West plays ♣ 2, and North wins with ♣ A. The club is as good a return lead as any East can make. As a matter of fact, any return at this point would work out in the same way.

Trick 3. North leads ♠ Q, East plays ♠ 2, South plays ♠ 8, and West plays ♠ 3.

Trick 4. North leads ♠ 5, East plays ♠ 7, South plays ♠ 9, and West plays ♠ 4.

The Declarer now stops to consider. He has lost 1 trick already, and is sure to lose at least 2 more tricks (in hearts). The contract therefore seems to depend on a diamond finesse, as the one trump which is still outstanding seems to prevent any elimination play. However, he sees one chance and goes after it.

Trick 5. South leads ♡ 2, West plays ♡ 4, North plays ♡ A, and East plays ♡ Q. Dummy's trick.

Trick 6. North leads ♡ 6, East plays ♡ K, South plays ♡ 3, and West plays ♡ 10. Here East is thrown in the lead for an end play at the seventh trick. He holds no more spades and no more hearts. A diamond lead eliminates the finesse in this suit and a club lead permits the Declarer to discard a diamond.

South really did not think he would succeed when he made this play, but he simply took advantage of this extra possibility. The hearts have to be lost anyway, so why not lose them at once? The missing trump is not at all dangerous and can just as well be left alone for a while.

A Brilliant End-Play "Coup"

The brilliance of the end play in the next deal gives it a good many aspects of the coup. Certainly it is spectacular. It is really an end play, and not a coup, since a certain amount of elimination is necessary for its operation. It aims to capture an apparently impregnable King of spades, and is indeed a rare situation.

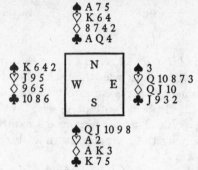

```
                    ♠ A 7 5
                    ♡ K 6 4
                    ♢ 8 7 4 2
                    ♣ A Q 4
    ♠ K 6 4 2          N           ♠ 3
    ♡ J 9 5                         ♡ Q 10 8 7 3
    ♢ 9 6 5      W         E        ♢ Q J 10
    ♣ 10 8 6                        ♣ J 9 3 2
                    S
                    ♠ Q J 10 9 8
                    ♡ A 2
                    ♢ A K 3
                    ♣ K 7 5
```

With North and South vulnerable, the bidding has gone:

South	West	North	East
One Spade	Pass	Two No-trump	Pass
Four No-trump	Pass	Five Spades	Pass
Six Spades	Pass	Pass	Pass

The play proceeds as follows:

Trick 1.   West leads ♢ 9, North plays ♢ 2, East plays ♢ 10, and South wins with ♢ K.

Trick 2.   South leads ♠ Q, West plays ♠ 2, North plays ♠ 5, and East plays ♠ 3.   It becomes apparent at once to South that he must lose 1 diamond trick. The success of the hand therefore depends upon the trump finesse. South is very pleased to see that it is successful.

Trick 3.   South leads ♠ J, West plays ♠ 4, North plays ♠ 7, and East discards ♡ 3.   At this point South receives a jolt. The spade King is correctly located, but it still cannot be caught by any ordinary means. The only chance now is to try an elimination play.

Trick 4.   South leads ♣ K, West plays ♣ 6, North plays ♣ 4, and East plays ♣ 2.

Trick 5.   South leads ♣ 5, West plays ♣ 8, North plays ♣ Q, and East plays ♣ 3.   Dummy's trick.

Trick 6.   North leads ♣ A, East plays ♣ 9, South plays ♣ 7, and West plays ♣ 10.

Trick 7. North leads ♡ 4, East plays ♡ 7, South plays ♡ A, and West plays ♡ 5.

Trick 8. South leads ♡ 2, West plays ♡ 9, North plays ♡ K, and East plays ♡ 8.

Trick 9. North leads ♡ 6, East plays ♡ 10, South ruffs with ♠ 8, and West plays ♡ J.

Trick 10. South leads ◇ A, West plays ◇ 5, North plays ◇ 4, and East plays ◇ J. The situation is now as follows, with South in the lead:

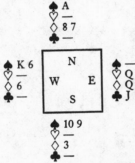

Trick 11. South leads ◇ 3, West plays ◇ 6, North plays ◇ 7, and East wins with ◇ Q. East is thrown in the lead and must return either a heart or a club, either of which will bring about the result desired by the Declarer.

What happens here is that, no matter what card East leads back, South simply ruffs with the nine of spades and West must either overtrump or undertrump—and either way his King cannot make a trick. A seemingly uncatchable King has been nicely trapped!

The principal characteristic of this end play, which also has something of the glamour of the coup, is that the player thrown in the lead, instead of being forced to lead into Declarer's tenace or to lead a suit providing Declarer with a ruff and a discard, is forced to lead a suit of which both Partner and Dummy are void, so that poor West is obliged to ruff under the Dummy's Ace of trumps.

ANOTHER END-PLAY "COUP"

This example is very much like the preceding one, in that in some respects it resembles a coup more than it does an end play. But the fact that certain suits are eliminated first casts the ballot in favor of calling it an end play. In this hand two apparently certain trump losers are reduced to one.

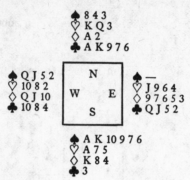

With both sides vulnerable, the bidding has gone:

South	West	North	East
One Spade	Pass	Three Clubs	Pass
Three Spades	Pass	Three No-trump	Pass
Five Spades	Pass	Six Spades	Pass
Pass	Pass		

The play proceeds as follows:

Trick 1. West leads ♢ Q, North plays ♢ 2, East plays ♢ 3, and South wins with ♢ K.

Trick 2. South leads ♠ A, West plays ♠ 2, North plays ♠ 3, and East discards ♢ 5. The blow falls. West seems to hold 2 spade tricks that belong to him as naturally as his skin. However, an elimination play is possible.

Trick 3. South leads ♣ 3, West plays ♣ 4, North plays ♣ A, and East plays ♣ 2. Dummy's trick.

Trick 4. North leads ♣ 6, East plays ♣ 5, South ruffs with ♠ 6, and West plays ♣ 8. South's ruffing-trick.

Trick 5. South leads ♢ 4, West plays ♢ 10, North plays ♢ A, and East plays ♢ 6. The lead is back in the Dummy.

Trick 6. North leads ♣ 7, East plays ♣ J, South ruffs with ♠ 7, and West plays ♣ 10. In the lead again, South re-enters the Dummy by ruffing there also.

Trick 7. South leads ♢ 8, West plays ♢ J, North ruffs with ♠ 4, and East plays ♢ 7.

Trick 8. North leads ♡ 3, East plays ♡ 4, South plays ♡ A, and West plays ♡ 2.

Trick 9. South leads ♡ 5, West plays ♡ 8, North plays ♡ Q, and East plays ♡ J. Back in the Dummy again.

Trick 10. North leads ♡ K, East plays ♡ 9, South plays ♡ 7, and West plays ♡ 10.

The situation is now as follows, with North still in the lead:

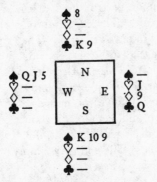

West can now be thrown in the lead and his 2 natural spade tricks reduced to 1, thus:

Trick 11. North leads ♠ 8, East discards ◇ 9, South play ♠ 9, and West wins with ♠ J. West can do nothing but kiss his second spade trick goodby, for he has to lead into Declarer's King-Ten.

An End Play in Trumps

Consider the following deal:

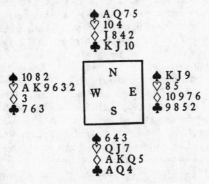

You will remember this hand as occurring in Part I, Chapter XXIV. It was used there as an example of a reverse discard by East and it was pointed out at the time that Declarer could actually fulfill his contract of three diamonds by means of an end play.

West wins the first 2 tricks with the Ace and King of hearts and continues the suit. Declarer, noticing East's echo should now go up with the Jack of diamonds in Dummy. East's best discard is a club. Now three rounds of trumps are led disclosing the unfortunate break in the suit. Three rounds of clubs follow, Declarer taking care to wind up in his own hand. The last trump is then led, throwing East into the lead with the Ten of diamonds and forcing him to lead into Dummy's Ace-Queen of spades. East obtains the last spade trick but the contract of three diamonds is nevertheless made.

Note that this course involves no danger as East is marked with holding the last trump and has already shown out of hearts. Note also that if East discards a spade instead of a club at the third trick the situation is the same. The end play simply occurs at the twelfth trick instead of at the eleventh trick.

Summary

All end plays have one characteristic in common—they occur toward the end of a hand, seldom earlier, indeed, than the tenth trick. An end play, as the term is used by the majority of writers on Bridge and related games, occurs when an Opponent is put in the lead at a time when he can lead back only to the Declarer's advantage. The "Declarer's advantage" may be any one of a number of situations. The Opponent may be forced to lead into a tenace, thus destroying the value of his own guarded honor or honors, or he may be forced to lead a suit which the Declarer can ruff in one hand and throw off on in the other. Only the first type of end play—that which forces an Opponent to lead into a tenace—is possible at a no-trump contract. At a suit contract, both kinds just mentioned are possible, and one or two variations. One rare sort of end play occurs when an Opponent is forced to lead a suit of which both his Partner and one of the Declarer's hands is void, so that Partner is forced to trump under the Declarer's commanding trumps.

A certain amount of preparation is necessary for most end plays. This preparation consists of eliminating those suits which it is not desirable for the Opponent to return when he is thrown in the lead. Often, when the end play is designed to give the Declarer a ruff and a discard, the elimination is from the Declarer's partnership hands instead of from the hand of the Opponent who is to be thrown in.

The beauty of an end play is that it frequently offers a practical certainty in place of a doubtful finesse, or, at best, a finesse which depends on a fifty-fifty chance. Not all end plays are dead certainties, of course; in fact, the Opponents may occasionally circumvent the Declarer as he tries to approach an end play.

CHAPTER IV

DEFENSE AGAINST END PLAYS

Some end plays, once envisioned, are as inevitable as the impact o a falling body once it has started to fall. They can no more be prevented, even by the most astute defending player, than the attraction of gravity can be annihilated. But *all* end plays are not so surely predictable in their outcome, for against many types of end plays there is available certain more or less effective defensive strategy. If a player on the Defending Side is alert enough to see that the Declarer is preparing for an end play, he can quite frequently perceive at just what vulnerable spot the end play is to be directed and perhaps escape the trap by failing to do as the Declarer wants him to do. Just as the preparation for an end play must often start very early in the hand—sometimes at the very first trick—so the defense against an end play must also begin early. If the defense does not get under way in time, at the moment the defending player is thrown in the lead it may be entirely too late to do anything about the situation. By that time the end play has been consummated.

The advice given for defensive play, in the chapters dealing with fundamentals (in Part I of this book), applies equally well to advanced defensive play against the advanced technique of an expert Declarer. The advice was this: always try to figure out what the Declarer is attempting to do, and prevent him from carrying out his plans, if you can. There is a tactical advantage in this method of defending a hand, and there is also a psychological advantage. Many a Declarer, when he suddenly discovers that his Opponents have been "wise to him" all along, is for the moment thrown off his balance. Sometimes his surprise is so great, particularly if he has underestimated the caliber of his adversaries, that he never regains his *savoir faire*, and becomes an easy victim to Opponents who are merciless now that they have caught him.

In essence, the defense against end plays is but an extended application of playing the Declarer's game mentally in order to out-maneuver him in the end. But there are certain tactics—certain mechanical methods, if they may be so called—which you must know. These are set forth in the following deals, all of which illustrate successful defense against a threatening end play.

Escaping an End Play by Unblocking

The defending player, perceiving that the Declarer is going to throw him in the lead at a time when he must lead back a suit the Declarer wishes to have led, can sometimes escape the fate that threatens him by getting rid of the high card with which the Declarer expects to put him in the lead. The following deal, for example, is exactly the same as one in which a successful end play was executed (in the preceding chapter), except that West has been given the trey of clubs in place of the Queen, and the Queen has been placed in the East hand. The cards are otherwise exactly the same. But now West has a chance to evade the end play by nice side-stepping at the ninth trick. Watch closely!

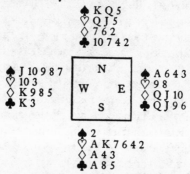

```
                    ♠ K Q 5
                    ♡ Q J 5
                    ◇ 7 6 2
                    ♣ 10 7 4 2

   ♠ J 10 9 8 7       N        ♠ A 6 4 3
   ♡ 10 3                      ♡ 9 8
   ◇ K 9 8 5     W       E     ◇ Q J 10
   ♣ K 3                       ♣ Q J 9 6
                     S
                    ♠ 2
                    ♡ A K 7 6 4 2
                    ◇ A 4 3
                    ♣ A 8 5
```

With both sides vulnerable, the bidding has gone:

South	West	North	East
One Heart	Pass	One No-trump	Pass
Three Hearts	Pass	Four Hearts	Pass
Pass	Pass		

The first 8 tricks go as follows, as the Declarer lays the groundwork for an end play:

Trick 1. West leads ♠J, North plays ♠Q, East plays ♠A, and South plays ♠2.

Trick 2. East leads ◇Q, South plays ◇3, West plays ◇9, and North plays ◇2.

Trick 3. East leads ◇J, South plays ◇A, West plays ◇5, and North plays ◇6.

Trick 4. South leads ♡2, West plays ♡3, North plays ♡J, and East plays ♡8.

Trick 5.   North leads ♠K, East plays ♠3, South discards ♢4, and West plays ♠7.

Trick 6.   North leads ♠5, East plays ♠4, South ruffs with ♡6, and West plays ♠8.

Trick 7.   South leads ♡7, West plays ♡10, North plays ♡Q, and East plays ♡9.

Trick 8.   North leads ♢7, East plays ♢10, South ruffs with ♡4, and West plays ♢8.

The stage is now set for the end play. At this point South leads the Ace of clubs and follows with a small club, to put West in the lead—he hopes!—with the King of clubs. In the preceding chapter West was forced to win with his King, for he held King-Queen doubleton originally. Holding the King and small originally, however, West can prevent the end play by simply unblocking himself out of the projected throw-in, thus:

Trick 9.   South leads ♣A, West plays ♣K! North plays ♣2, and East plays ♣6.

Now that West has thrown off his King under South's Ace, keeping the trey instead, the Declarer's plans are completely frustrated. Declarer knows he is beaten the minute he sees that King flung out. To lead a small club to the tenth trick will be futile, for it will throw East in the lead, who can take 2 more club tricks. If only West had held on to his King and played the trey on the Ace—then, at the next trick, West would have paid the penalty for his gluttony by being forced to lead back a suit that would give the Declarer a ruff and a discard.

The principle embodied in this example is a most important one for avoiding being thrown in the lead at an awkward moment. Whenever a high card or cards appear to be dangerous, it is a good idea to begin unblocking by throwing them off at the earliest chance. Sometimes the need for unblocking will not materialize, and if it does not, you can always change your mind at the last minute. In the preceding deal, the throwing off of West's King may cost 1 trick, but it is the only chance of setting the contract.

How does West know that South has an end play in view? Simply by *counting*—counting the cards that have been played. He knows that South has no more spades, and he can see that the Dummy has no more. His count of diamonds tells him that all are gone except the King he has left.   No clubs have been played.   The Declarer has lost 2 tricks already, and he stands to lose the King of clubs and possibly another club trick, for West knows that only two hearts remain unplayed, which means that Declarer must have them (Ace-King), and that his other three cards are clubs.   Even if the Declarer has both Ace and Queen of clubs, he must lose 2 club tricks—unless he can give up 1 club trick and force an Opponent to lead him a spade or a diamond, which he can ruff in one hand and discard a club from the other.   West sees that his King of clubs will do just this for the Declarer on the second round of the suit, and he therefore unblocks by flinging it on the Ace.   Declarer's lead of the Ace tells West that he has decided not to attempt the finesse, and that the end play offers better chances.   The way to circumvent him is to throw off the King in the chance that the Declarer does not have the Queen.

PROPER AND IMPROPER DEFENSE CONTRASTED

Here is a deal in which South becomes the Declarer at a Small Slam contract in spades.   Certainly the bidding is highly optimistic, and the North and South partners reach a contract they have no right to, but it so happens, in spite of that, that the cards lie in such positions that only the most expert defense can defeat the Slam.   The end play that South attempts would work with a great many average players sitting in the West position on this deal:

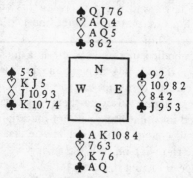

With North and South vulnerable, the bidding has gone:

SOUTH	WEST	NORTH	EAST
One Spade	Pass	Three Spades	Pass
Six Spades	Pass	Pass	Pass

West leads the Jack of diamonds, and the Dummy goes down. The outlook for South does not seem very bright, as two finesses appear to be necessary. Yet there may be a way of avoiding the club finesse. Assuming that West holds the King of hearts, South can strip the hand down, take the heart finesse, and throw West in the lead with the King of hearts, forcing him to lead back into the club Ace-Queen tenace. Declarer decides to try this, and the play proceeds as follows:

Trick 1. West leads ♢J, North plays ♢Q, East plays ♢2, and South plays ♢6. Dummy's trick.

Trick 2. North leads ♠Q, East plays ♠2, South plays ♠4, and West plays ♠3.

Trick 3. North leads ♠6, East plays ♠9, South plays ♠K, and West plays ♠5. The lead shifts to the South hand.

Trick 4. South leads ♢7, West plays ♢3, North plays ♢A, and West plays ♢4. Again Dummy wins.

Trick 5. North leads ♢5, East plays ♢8, South plays ♢K, and West plays ♢9. The lead is back with South, and the stage has been set for the proposed end play. The end play succeeds if West fails to defend against it properly, as follows:

Trick 6. South leads ♡3, West plays ♡5, North plays ♡Q, and East plays ♡2. Dummy's trick.

Trick 7. North leads ♡A, East plays ♡8, South plays ♡6, and West plays ♡J.

Trick 8. North leads ♡4, East plays ♡9, South plays ♡7, and West wins with ♡K.

Here West is thrown in the lead, as South planned, and he must now lead either a diamond (which permits the Declarer to ruff in the Dummy and discard the Queen of clubs from his own hand) or a club (which plays right into the Declarer's Ace-Queen tenace). Thus South makes a contract at which he arrived by what was really preposterous bidding.

But West, with his wits about him, should have anticipated this! He should foresee that the Declarer will try to throw him in the lead in order to avoid taking the gamble that the club finesse offers. Certainly the Declarer must have something in his hand to justify his highly optimistic bidding, and he is therefore practically certain to hold the Ace-Queen of clubs. In the first 5 tricks, if West has counted the hand as he should, he knows that Declarer has stripped his own hands of diamonds, and has also drawn all the adverse trumps, having two left in Dummy and three in his own hand. West can see that the heart finesse will work, but that Declarer may easily have a losing heart to boot, and a club tenace to worry about. West should see that his only chance of defeating the contract depends on whether he can keep an exit card* in his hand.

After such reasoning, West's play after the fifth trick should go:

Trick 6. South leads ♡3, West plays ♡J, North plays ♡Q, and East plays ♡10. Note West's spectacular discard of the Jack. Seeing what the Declarer is up to, he starts to unblock immediately. Note also East's play of the Ten—East has his eyes open, and plays the Ten to show that he has the nine—further to encourage his Partner in the unblocking procedure.

Trick 7. North leads ♡A, East plays ♡2, South plays ♡6, and West plays ♡K! West completes his unblocking. South cannot throw him in the lead with a heart, for West knows that his Partner controls the third round.

Trick 8. North leads ♡4, East plays ♡8, South plays ♡7, and West plays ♡5. East's trick!

Trick 9. East leads ♣3, South plays ♣Q, West plays ♣K, and North plays ♣2.

The club lead coming from the wrong direction, South is obliged to finesse his club Queen at the ninth trick. The finesse loses—and there goes his contract! This manner of defense against end plays comes up rather frequently, especially when two honors are held. With combinations such as King-Jack-small, Queen-Jack-small, and Queen-Ten-small, it is usually advisable *to play the middle card first* in order to give yourself a chance to complete the unblocking play if such a course seems necessary, or else change your mind.

PROTECTING PARTNER FROM AN END PLAY

Frequently situations arise where it should be apparent to a player on the defense that the Declarer is planning to throw his partner into the lead in order to force a favorable return. At times such as these it behooves him to find some way to block these plans. He can often do this by attempting to gain the lead himself.

---

* An exit card is a card used to get out of one's hand with.

In the following deal South can make his contract by means of a diamond end play on East if West is not alive to the possibilities of the situation.

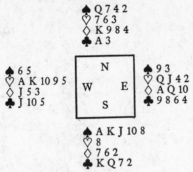

♠ Q 7 4 2
♡ 7 6 3
◇ K 9 8 4
♣ A 3

♠ 6 5
♡ A K 10 9 5
◇ J 5 3
♣ J 10 5

♠ 9 3
♡ Q J 4 2
◇ A Q 10
♣ 9 8 6 4

♠ A K J 10 8
♡ 8
◇ 7 6 2
♣ K Q 7 2

With neither side vulnerable, the bidding has gone:

SOUTH	WEST	NORTH	EAST
One Spade	Two Hearts	Two Spades	Three Hearts
Four Spades	Pass	Pass	Pass

West opens the King of hearts. Declarer at once sees that the contract can be made easily if the Ace of diamonds is in the West hand. Even if it is not he sees a chance to develop an end play on East.

The play proceeds as follows:

Trick 1. West leads ♡K, North plays ♡3, East plays ♡2, and South plays ♡8.

Trick 2. West leads ♡A, North plays ♡6, East plays ♡Q, and South trumps with ♠8.

West should not continue hearts after receiving the discouraging deuce from his Partner. He could shift to the diamond Jack and defeat the contract immediately. However, he has a chance to redeem himself later.

Trick 3. South leads ♠A, West plays ♠5, North plays ♠2, and East plays ♠3.

Trick 4. South leads ♠K, West plays ♠6, North plays ♠4, and East plays ♠9.

Trick 5. South leads ♣2, West plays ♣5, North plays ♣A, and East plays ♣4. North's trick.

Trick 6. North leads ♣3, East plays ♣6, South plays ♣Q, and West plays ♣10.   South's trick.

Trick 7.   South leads ♣K, West plays ♣J, North discards ◊4, and East plays ♣8.

Trick 8.   South leads ♣7, West discards 5♡, North trumps with ♠7, and East plays ♣9.   North's trick.

Trick 9.   North leads ♡7, East plays ♡4, South trumps with ♠10, and West plays ♡9.   The elimination of clubs and hearts has now been completed and Declarer is ready to try his diamond end play. He plans to lead low and play the eight-spot from Dummy if West plays low.   This will force East into the lead and compel him to lead into the diamond King or give Declarer a ruff and discard. However—

Trick 10.   South leads ◊2, and West plays ◊J!

Declarer is now helpless.   It is immaterial at this point whether he goes up with the King or not, as he must lose 3 diamond tricks in any event.

Superior Attack Met by Superior Defense

The following deal is one of the most brilliant examples of superior attack met by superior defense that is to be found in the annals of Contract Bridge.   The brilliant defense was played by Mr. Waldemar von Zedtwitz, a champion player who has no superior as a strategist, sitting in the East position.   The detailed trick-by-trick play of this deal shows how Mr. von Zedtwitz was able to put to naught the deeply laid plan of the master player who was the Declarer.

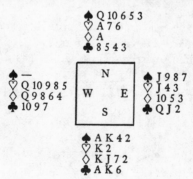

                    ♠ Q 10 6 5 3
                    ♡ A 7 6
                    ◊ A
                    ♣ 8 5 4 3

    ♠ —   ♠ J 9 8 7
    ♡ Q 10 9 8 5   N   ♡ J 4 3
    ◊ Q 9 8 6 4   W   E   ◊ 10 5 3
    ♣ 10 9 7   S   ♣ Q J 2

                    ♠ A K 4 2
                    ♡ K 2
                    ◊ K J 7 2
                    ♣ A K 6

With neither side vulnerable, the bidding has gone:

SOUTH	WEST	NORTH	EAST
One Spade	Pass	Three Spades	Pass
Four No-trump	Pass	Five Hearts	Pass
Six Spades	Pass	Pass	Pass

Ordinarily this hand would be a lay-down. All that is necessary to make the success of the contract absolutely certain is a 3-1 break in spades. Since the spades are actually divided 4-0, 1 trump trick must be lost, and possibly 1 club trick. The Declarer saw one chance of making 12 tricks, however, and he proceeded to play for that "only chance," as follows:

Trick 1. West leads ♡10, North plays ♡6, East plays ♡3, and South wins with ♡K.

Trick 2. South leads ♠A, West discards ♡5, North plays ♠3, and East plays ♠7. West's failure to follow suit tells South that 1 trump trick must be lost.

Trick 3. South leads ◇2, West plays ◇4, North plays ◇A, and East plays ◇3.

Trick 4. North leads ♣3, East plays ♣J, South plays ♣K, and West plays ♣10. East's Jack shows that already, at the fourth trick, he sees danger coming and begins to unblock. His Partner assists him, and corroborates the move, by playing the Ten (thereby showing possession of the nine, which can control the third round of the suit).

Trick 5. South leads ◇7, West plays ◇6, North ruffs with ♠5, and East plays ◇5.

Trick 6. North leads ♡A, East plays ♡4, South plays ♡2, and West plays ♡8.

Trick 7. North leads ♡7, East plays ♡J, South ruffs with ♠2, and West plays ♡9.

Trick 8. South leads ◇K, West plays ◇8, North discards ♣4, and East plays ◇10.

The stage is now almost set for the big scene. The hand has been stripped, and it begins to look as though the throw-in play may succeed.

Trick 9. South leads ◇J, West plays ◇Q, North ruffs with ♠Q, and East undertrumps with ♠8. A trick glittering with two brilliant plays!

At this, the ninth trick, the Declarer cannot afford to ruff low in the Dummy, for he thinks East is probably exhausted of diamonds, and if East overtrumps there will later be a club trick lost also. Hence the ruff with the Queen of trumps, by which the Declarer hopes to induce East to throw off a club. If Mr. von Zedtwitz had done this, the Declarer would have cashed in his Ace and led a third round of the suit so that, having nothing but trumps left, East would have been forced to ruff his Partner's good trick and then lead a trump away from his guarded Jack. Mr. von Zedtwitz foresaw this end-play possibility and deliberately undertrumped to foil the Declarer.

Trick 10. North leads ♣5, East plays ♣Q, South plays ♣A, and West plays ♣7.

The Declarer did not give up hope until the tenth trick had been completed. If Mr. von Zedtwitz had failed to play the Queen of clubs, he would have been thrown in on the third round of this suit and still forced to lead into the trump tenace. But Mr. von Zedtwitz played his Queen, and the situation became:

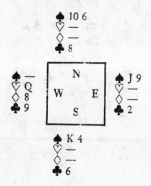

The Declarer faces defeat, and knows it. If he leads a club, the trick will be won by West. If he leads a trump, East's Jack-nine represents a sure trick. Of course, if East could be made to lead— but Mr. von Zedtwitz has evaded all possibility of being thrown in the lead now.

The Declarer's play of this particular hand was little short of inspired, and it really deserved to succeed. But it was his hard luck to be opposed by a most perspicacious player on his right—an Opponent truly worthy of his steel. The fact that Mr. von Zedtwitz was able to sense the possibility of the end play at the fourth trick and retain an exit card in his hand in spite of everything, confirms his standing as one of the world's greatest players.

Making the Declarer Guess

One form of defense against end plays involves playing in such a way that the Declarer is forced to *guess*. The moment the Declarer is not quite sure where the adverse cards lie—which is to say, the moment that he doubts his original assumption of the distribution—the Defending Side have a fifty-fifty chance of saving themselves, for the Declarer may guess wrong! The following deal is a good illustration:

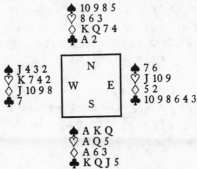

```
              ♠ 10 9 8 5
              ♡ 8 6 3
              ◇ K Q 7 4
              ♣ A 2
♠ J 4 3 2        N        ♠ 7 6
♡ K 7 4 2    W     E      ♡ J 10 9
◇ J 10 9 8               ◇ 5 2
♣ 7              S        ♣ 10 9 8 6 4 3
              ♠ A K Q
              ♡ A Q 5
              ◇ A 6 3
              ♣ K Q J 5
```

With neither side vulnerable, the bidding has gone:

South	West	North	East
One Club	Pass	One Diamond	Pass
Three No-trump	Pass	Four No-trump	Pass
Six No-trump	Pass	Pass	Pass

The play proceeds as follows:

Trick 1. West leads ◇J, North plays ◇4, East plays ◇2, and South wins with ◇A.

Trick 2. South leads ♠A, West plays ♠2, North plays ♠5, and East plays ♠6.

Trick 3. South leads ♠K, West plays ♠3, North plays ♠8, and East plays ♠7.

Trick 4. South leads ♠Q, West plays ♠4, North plays ♠9, and East discards ♣3. Declarer sees his first hope flying out of the window. The Ten of spades in the Dummy cannot be established.

Trick 5.   South leads ♣5, West plays ♣7, North plays ♣A, and East plays ♣4.

Trick 6.   North leads ♣2, East plays ♣6, South plays ♣J, and West discards ♡2.

Trick 7.   South leads ♣K, West discards ♡4, North discards ♠10, and East plays ♣8.

Trick 8.   South leads ♣Q, West discards ♡7, North discards ♡3, and East plays ♣9.   West deliberately blanks his King of hearts, for he has a reason.

West thinks he sees what is going to happen.   He must retain all his diamonds in order to keep protection in this suit.   His only other available discard is the good Jack of spades.   It is true that the Declarer has thrown off Dummy's spade Ten, and the Jack can therefore be thrown off too without losing anything.   But if West does this, he knows that the Declarer can put him in the lead on the fourth round of diamonds and force him to lead away from his King of hearts.   On the bidding, Declarer undoubtedly holds the Ace of hearts.   The location of the Queen is doubtful, but if West's Partner holds this card, the fact that the King is blanked can make no difference.

Trick 9.   South leads ♢3, West plays ♢8, North plays ♢Q, and East plays ♢5.

Trick 10.   North leads ♢K, East discards ♣10, South plays ♢6, and West plays ♢9.

The Declarer is now up the well-known tree.   He knows that West has the high spade and the high diamond, and that his third card is a heart.   But he does not know which heart it is!   West, the Declarer reasons, may have foreseen the end play and deliberately blanked his King, but he may never have held the King at all.   The guess is very difficult for the Declarer. Probably, everything considered, the finesse is his best play at this point.

Trick 11.   North leads ♡6, East plays ♡9, South plays ♡Q, and West wins with ♡K.

The last 2 tricks belong to West, for he has the high spade and the high diamond.   Declarer never makes his Ace of hearts, and is set 2 tricks.

It is easy enough to say that the Declarer could make his contract by playing the Ace of hearts on the eleventh trick and dropping West's King.   In actual play, however, it is very difficult to do this, in view of all the possibilities, and for this reason the Declarer cannot be criticized for taking the finesse. West simply took advantage of his opportunity to throw sand in the Declarer's eyes. But the Declarer did make an earlier mistake on the hand—he should never have thrown off Dummy's Ten of spades. By keeping this card in the Dummy he had a perfect squeeze on West—but we have not yet taken up squeeze plays, so this cannot be discussed now.

Summary

As in practically all plays at Contract Bridge, the most essential thing about defending against possible end plays is counting the cards as they fall. This will enable you very often to see what the Declarer is up to, in time for you to take some steps to defend yourself against his scheme. Once you have an idea of what the Declarer is trying to do, it is a comparatively simple matter for you to find any defensive tactics that the gods of distribution may have placed at your disposal.

Perhaps the most common defense against an end play is to unblock in the suit which the Declarer seems likely to use for throwing you in the lead. You defeat his purpose by getting rid of the high card so that he cannot throw you in. This defense works perfectly whenever your Partner is able to retain a card for controlling the third or fourth round of the suit—which means that your Partner instead of you will be thrown in. You perceive, of course, that you are the one the Declarer wishes to have in the lead, by noticing that it may help the Declarer to lead into a tenace he holds, or to lead a card which will give him a ruff and a discard. Other times it is necessary to go up with a high honor in order to try and prevent your partner from being thrown into the lead.

Another mode of defense is to play in such a way that the Declarer is forced to guess. If you raise a doubt in the Declarer's mind as to the location of a key card, he may be misled into what he thinks is a better play—to his sorrow.

Of course, you cannot always evade an end play. Nor can you always be right in your appraisal of the situation. But you will find it one of the great thrills of the game to outwit a clever Declarer, even if you succeed in doing it only once in a great while.

CHAPTER V

COUNTING

Throughout the pages of this book it has been emphasized that a knowledge of the fundamentals of play is not enough to make you a good card player. Even if you know the proper treatment which even the rarer situations require, you will still not make all the contracts that you should make, unless you learn to take advantage of every little bit of information which falls your way. All hands involve a certain amount of competitive bidding, all of which is informative in some degree,* and if you become the Declarer, you have at least some knowledge of the distribution of the Opponents' hands, however vague it may be. You may know only that one Opponent holds a five-card suit, or something resembling it, but even this sparse information should be noted mentally.

In addition to information gleaned from the bidding, there is the story told by the opening lead, and the cards immediately located when the Dummy's hand is exposed. Every player at the table knows the whereabouts of twenty-six cards—his own hand and the Dummy's. As soon as the opening lead is made, the Declarer and leader's Partner know the location of *twenty-seven* cards, and they have some glimmering of the *probable* location of certain other cards. By studying the Dummy and the opening lead in connection with his own hand, the Declarer and leader's Partner can figure out pretty well what the lead means. If it happens to be a Queen, and if the Jack of the same suit is not among the twenty-seven visible cards, the leader is almost certainly marked with the Jack. The conventions governing opening leads, as given in an earlier chapter (in Part I), enable the other two players to deduce a fair amount of information from the denomination of the card led to start the play.

Then it is of the greatest value to watch each card that falls on every trick. Every card, no matter how seemingly insignificant its

* Curiously enough, some of the earlier bidding conventions were described as "informative" when they were intended primarily for conveying information to Partner, such as the informative double, though any bid whatever, or any call, including a pass, must by its very nature be informative. The fact that a player passes instead of making a bid, or that he doubles (whether for a penalty or to be taken out by Partner), is certainly indicative in some degree of the sort of hand he has—or thinks he has.

denomination, tells a story all its own. You may think that it does not matter when some player drops the deuce on your lead. It does matter. It may be a discouraging signal to his Partner and may even show his willingness to stand some other lead his Partner is bound to make later. Even if it has no particular meaning, a mental reservation of possible future importance should be made.

You begin your counting by noting mentally the number of certain winners you hold, or the number of certain and probable losers. Thus you get immediately some notion, when you are Declarer, of whether your contract is likely to be easy or difficult to fulfill. At any rate, you have the basis for planning a campaign—you know whether you can take your tricks and be done, or whether you must maneuver to develop a trick or two somewhere that does not manifest itself at the start. You may later change your mind, of course.

But what is really meant by *counting* is the habit of keeping a mental tally on the number of cards of each suit that have been played as soon as each successive trick is quitted. Not only that, but the *denomination* of the cards that have been played, so that outstanding higher cards are known to you. A good player *knows*, at the tenth trick, for example, that his seven of diamonds is high, or that an Opponent still holds the eight-spot.

Counting also means the noting of each Opponent's hand distribution, as it is revealed, first, by the bidding, and, later, by the fall of the cards in the play. If you are on the Defending Side, you count the Declarer's hand and also your Partner's hand. You pounce upon each bit of information to fill in the blanks—you learn, finally, that another player held four spades originally, and that he has two hearts left, and so on. This placing of the cards in the other hands is absolutely essential to the success of such maneuvers as end plays, squeeze plays, and the like.

Counting, in fact, is really an intrinsic part of every family of plays that exists. To execute an end play consciously and successfully—or, for that matter, to execute a squeeze, a coup, or any other play, elementary or advanced—some sort of count, something approaching a count, of the Opponents' hands is invariably essential. Because of this fact, the subject of counting has already been frequently mentioned and somewhat explained in earlier chapters, and, for this reason, the present chapter is naturally shorter than it would

otherwise be.   The ability to count and the imagination to interpret the counting are indispensable to every Bridge player.

Curiously, however, *teaching* would-be players to count is practically an impossibility. Since "counting" in Bridge is somewhat
more than one, two, three, etc., being applied to each of the four
suits and also to each of the four hands, it requires a logical mind, a
great deal of patience (or what might be called dogged determination),
and a certain amount of imagination. Without these qualities, a
person can never become a great player anyway, so that it may also
be said that without these qualities, a person cannot learn to *count*.

Take the following deal as an example. The Declarer should
be able to tell the distribution of *all four hands*—almost as soon
as the first trick has been played.   Only by this counting of the hands
can he make his contract, for to fulfill his bid he has to use a double
end play.   Lest the reader think this hand is a pure invention, note
that this hand was actually dealt at Crockford's Club, New York
City, and was played by Mr. Oswald Jacoby, one of the outstanding players of the world, who sat in the South position as the Declarer.

COUNTING MAKES POSSIBLE A DOUBLE END PLAY

Mr. Jacoby, by brilliant analysis, is able to mark with great accuracy the adverse distribution at the end of the first trick.   With the
knowledge thus derived, he is able to make a series of plays—consti-
tuting a double end play—which guarantees his contract against any
possible defense.   Without this counting, the hand would have to
be played in what might be called "ordinary" fashion, when the
Declarer would almost certainly be set at least 1 trick.

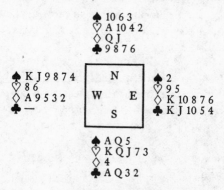

With both sides vulnerable, the bidding has gone:

SOUTH	WEST	NORTH	EAST
One Heart	One Spade	Two Hearts	Three Clubs
Four Hearts	Pass	Pass	Pass

West's opening lead is the Ace of diamonds.

First, what did Mr. Jacoby (Declarer) learn from the bidding? With his own powerful hand, it seemed impossible that the Opponents could bid so strongly when vulnerable. Mr. Jacoby decided at once that the bidding must be based chiefly on distribution.

Take East's bid of *three clubs*—a pretty strong bid, vulnerable. Declarer's and Dummy's hands contain eight clubs. To justify his bid, East obviously requires all remaining five clubs. Even then the suit is not very strong, headed by only King-Jack-Ten. Surely he must have an escape suit to turn to if doubled. There is only one possible suit available to him for escape. It cannot be spades, for Mr. Jacoby holds Ace-Queen, and there was a spade overcall on his left. The only possible suit is diamonds. Consequently East probably holds five diamonds besides his five clubs. Since West cannot have any high cards to amount to anything (other than the Ace of diamonds), he is practically certain to have six spades besides his club void (East had all the outstanding clubs, you remember). This gives East a singleton spade, and East's two other cards must be hearts (small ones, for the Declarer and Dummy have all the honors).

Thus the distribution of the Opponents' cards is practically marked after the opening lead. West is almost certain to have six spades, two hearts, five diamonds, and no clubs. East must hold one spade, two hearts, five diamonds, and five clubs. With these facts in front of him, Mr. Jacoby went about making his contract as follows:

Trick 1. West leads ♢ A, North plays ♢ J, East plays ♢ 8, and South plays ♢ 4.

Trick 2. West leads ♢ 3, North plays ♢ Q, East plays ♢ K, and South ruffs with ♡ 3.

Trick 3. South leads ♡ K, West plays ♡ 6, North plays ♡ 2, and East plays ♡ 5.

Trick 4. South leads ♡ 7, West plays ♡ 8, North plays ♡ 10, and East plays ♡ 9. Mr. Jacoby notices that his count of the hearts is correct, for both Opponents followed suit on two rounds.

Trick 5. North leads ♠ 10, East plays ♠ 2, South plays ♠ 5,

and West wins with ♠ J.   This is end play the first.   West is immediately forced to lead a diamond or a spade, either of which gives
Mr. Jacoby an extra trick.   West led back a diamond.

Trick 6.   West leads ◇ 2, North discards ♠ 6, East plays ◇ 6,
and South ruffs with ♡ J.   One loser eliminated!

Trick 7.   South leads ♠ A, West plays ♠ 4, North plays ♠ 3,
and East discards ◇ 7.

Trick 8.   South leads ♠ Q, West plays ♠ K, North ruffs with ♡ 4,
and East discards ♣ 4.

Trick 9.   North leads ♣ 6, East plays ♣ 10, South plays ♣ Q,
and West discards ♠ 8.

Trick 10.   South leads ♣ 2, West discards ◇ 5, North plays ♣ 7,
and East wins with ♣ J.   This is end play the second.   East is
thrown in the lead with the Dummy holding the nine and eight of
clubs, Mr. Jacoby the Ace and trey of clubs, and East the King and
five of clubs.   If East returns a club, Mr. Jacoby makes 2 club tricks;
if East returns a diamond, Mr. Jacoby can discard his losing club.

Mr. Jacoby lost 3 tricks—a spade, a diamond, and a club.

Giving such a complicated example of counting to start off with was
done deliberately, in order to impress the reader with its importance.
Sometimes the counting is quite simple, and making use of it does not
involve any great amount of mental work.

GIVING UP LOSERS TO GET A COUNT

The deal which follows illustrates getting a count at the very end of
a hand.   The Declarer has to give up his losers before he can reach
any conclusion as to his proper play.

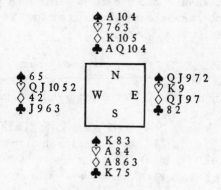

♠ A 10 4
♡ 7 6 3
◇ K 10 5
♣ A Q 10 4

♠ 6 5   ♠ Q J 9 7 2
♡ Q J 10 5 2   ♡ K 9
◇ 4 2   ◇ Q J 9 7
♣ J 9 6 3   ♣ 8 2

♠ K 8 3
♡ A 8 4
◇ A 8 6 3
♣ K 7 5

With neither side vulnerable, the bidding has gone:

South	West	North	East
One Diamond	Pass	Two Clubs	Pass
Two No-trump	Pass	Three No-trump	Pass
Pass	Pass		

West's opening lead is the Queen of hearts. The bidding having gone uncontested, the Declarer has no information from his Opponents' bids. Obviously he must hold off in hearts, since the Ace is his only stopper. He can surely count 2 spade tricks, 1 heart trick, 2 diamond tricks, and 3 club tricks—a trick short of his contract. The needed trick can be found in two ways. The fourth club in the Dummy may be set up if the suit breaks 3-3, or if the Jack falls, and there is also a possibility of establishing a long diamond trick.

The play proceeds as follows:

Trick 1. West leads ♡ Q, North plays ♡ 3, East plays ♡ K, and South plays ♡ 4. East's trick; the Declarer holds up his Ace.

Trick 2. East leads ♡ 9, South plays ♡ 8, West plays ♡ 10, and North plays ♡ 6. Declarer holds up again, and West wins.

Trick 3. West leads ♡ 2, North plays ♡ 7, East discards ♠ 2, and South wins with ♡ A. Now the Declarer knows that East held only two hearts originally, which means that West must have held five (and has two left).

Trick 4. South leads ◇ 3, West plays ◇ 2, North plays ◇ 10, and East wins with ◇ J. Declarer is now making an attempt to establish the thirteenth diamond, as the club play can be made at any time. Naturally he takes care to lose the trick to East, since this player has no more hearts. So far he has received very meager information about the adverse hands.

Trick 5. East leads ♠ Q, South plays ♠ 3, West plays ♠ 5, and North plays ♠ 4. Letting East win this trick is a brilliant stroke by the Declarer. Although he has two spade stoppers, he lets East's Queen ride through in order to get as much data as he can on the rest of the adverse cards.

Trick 6. East leads ♠ 7, South plays ♠ 8, West plays ♠ 6, and North wins with ♠ A.

Trick 7.   North leads ◇ K, East plays ◇ 7, South plays ◇ 6, and West plays ◇ 4.

Trick 8.   North leads ◇ 5, East plays ◇ 9, South plays ◇ A, and West discards ♡ 5.   Now South knows more about the distribution of West's hand, though his hoped-for fourth diamond trick has failed to materialize.   West originally held five hearts, and only two diamonds, with at least two spades.

Trick 9.   South leads ♠ K, West discards ♡ J, North plays ♠ 10, and East plays ♠ 9.   The count of the hands is now complete. West was dealt two spades, five hearts, two diamonds, and four clubs; East had five spades, two hearts, four diamonds, and two clubs. Since West has four clubs, South knows that he can make his contract whether West has the Jack or not.

Trick 10.   South leads ♣ 5, West plays ♣ 3, North plays ♣ Q, and East plays ♣ 2.

Trick 11.   North leads ♣ 4, East plays ♣ 8, South plays ♣ K, and West plays ♣ 6.   Note that Declarer is being cautious.   He plays first to see whether the Jack is one of East's two clubs.   Since it has not dropped, he can now finesse against it in West's hand, for he still has Ace-Ten in Dummy.

Trick 12.   South leads ♣ 7, West plays ♣ 9, North plays ♣ 10, and East discards ♠ J.

Trick 13.   North leads ♣ A, East discards ◇ Q, South discards ◇ 8, and West plays ♣ J.

Observe how simple the count was on this hand.   Yet it would have been impossible without giving up that spade trick on the first round of the suit.   If South had won East's Queen, West would have followed suit on the two rounds South controlled, and South would never have learned that West had only two spades originally.   Then he would have had to make an unaided guess at the end as to whether to take the club finesse or hope for a 3-3 break in the suit.

A Simple and Common Method of Counting

In this particular deal you find yourself back with elementary principles.   The counting here is extremely simple, but deals of this type frequently occur.

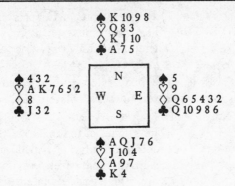

♠ K 10 9 8
♡ Q 8 3
♢ K J 10
♣ A 7 5

♠ 4 3 2   ♠ 5
♡ A K 7 6 5 2   ♡ 9
♢ 8   ♢ Q 6 5 4 3 2
♣ J 3 2   ♣ Q 10 9 8 6

♠ A Q J 7 6
♡ J 10 4
♢ A 9 7
♣ K 4

With East and West vulnerable, the bidding has gone:

South	West	North	East
One Spade	Pass	Three Spades	Pass
Four Spades	**Pass**	Pass	Pass

The play proceeds as follows:

Trick 1. West leads ♡ K, North plays ♡ 3, East plays ♡ 9, and South plays ♡ J.

Trick 2. West leads ♡ A, North plays ♡ 8, East discards ♢ 2, and South plays ♡ 4.

Trick 3. West leads ♡ 2, North plays ♡ Q, East ruffs with ♠ 5, and South plays ♡ 10.

Trick 4. East leads ♣ 10, South plays ♣ K, West plays ♣ 2, and North plays ♣ 5.

Trick 5. South leads ♠ A, West plays ♠ 2, North plays ♠ 8, and East discards ♢ 3. The Declarer now knows nine of West's cards, or that West originally held six hearts and three spades.

Trick 6. South leads ♠ 6, West plays ♠ 3, North plays ♠ 9, and East discards ♣ 6.

Trick 7. North leads ♠ K, East discards ♢ 4, South plays ♠ 7, and West plays ♠ 4. The adverse spades are now all drawn, and the hand seems to depend on the diamond finesse. First, however, South must find some way of obtaining more information before he decides which way to take his two-way finesse. This can be done with comparative ease.

Trick 8. North leads ♣ A, East plays ♣ 8, South plays ♣ 4, and West plays ♣ 3.

Trick 9. North leads ♣ 7, East plays ♣ 9, South ruffs with ♠ J, and West plays ♣ J.   A ray of sunlight!   West has shown up with three clubs, which, with six hearts and three spades already accounted for, make twelve cards.   Therefore he can hold but one diamond, and, if this is not the Queen, the finesse must be taken through East.

Trick 10.   South leads ◇ 7, West plays ◇ 8, North plays ◇ K, and East plays ◇ 5.   The next play is absolutely marked.

Trick 11.   North leads ◇ J, East plays ◇ 6, South plays ◇ 9, and West discards ♡ 5.   The balance of the tricks are the Declarer's.

Surely the business of counting the adverse distribution now seems less mysterious.   Sometimes it is comparatively easy, and sometimes rather difficult.   But always in the Declarer's mind—if he is a good player—is the questing effort to find out how many cards of each suit each of his adversaries was originally dealt.   When he knows that, he has won a goodly portion of his battle against the unknown.   You should try to habituate yourself to count automatically—and always, no matter how simple the hand as a whole may be.

The examples which follow do not introduce any more difficult instances of counting, but they do involve different methods of obtaining information.   After all, as with so many accomplishments, to count well it is necessary chiefly to practice patiently and carefully. Superficial counts may be obtained on practically every hand after a few well-chosen tricks have been won or lost.   The seemingly more complicated counts should then come about in the same way that skill at playing the piano finally follows suddenly upon hours of arduous drills.

Using a Percentage Play When the Count Is Doubtful

When counting a hand or trying to locate cards from the bidding, it is not always possible to obtain the exact adverse distribution.   Certain cards can be placed rather definitely in every hand, but two or three cards will always be doubtful in most hands.   In such situations, there is available a kind of play known as a *percentage play*.   The basis of it is that there seems to be more chance of finding a specific card in one hand than in the other, and the Declarer gambles on this percentage of expectancy.   It may involve playing for a drop when the finesse seems like the more natural play, or vice versa.   The following deal illustrates the "vice versa."

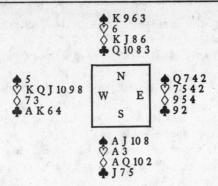

♠ K 9 6 3
♡ 6
◇ K J 8 6
♣ Q 10 8 3

♠ 5   ♠ Q 7 4 2
♡ K Q J 10 9 8   ♡ 7 5 4 2
◇ 7 3   ◇ 9 5 4
♣ A K 6 4   ♣ 9 2

♠ A J 10 8
♡ A 3
◇ A Q 10 2
♣ J 7 5

With East and West vulnerable, the bidding has gone:

SOUTH	WEST	NORTH	EAST
One Spade	Two Hearts	Two Spades	Pass
Three Diamonds	Three Hearts	Three Spades	Pass
Four Spades	Pass	Pass	Pass

The play proceeds as follows:

Trick 1. West leads ♣ K, North plays ♣ 3, East plays ♣ 9, and South plays ♣ 5.

Trick 2. West leads ♣ A, North plays ♣ 8, East plays ♣ 2, and South plays ♣ 7.

Trick 3. West leads ♣ 4, North plays ♣ 10, East ruffs with ♠ 2, and South plays ♣ J.

Trick 4. East leads ♡ 2, South plays ♡ A, West plays ♡ K, and North plays ♡ 6.

South can now see how to win the rest of the tricks if he can but locate the Queen of spades. Since East has already trumped a club, only four trumps remain out, and that makes it look as though the lead of the Ace followed by the King is the natural play. However, South recalls the bidding. West, being vulnerable, would hardly venture to bid *three hearts* all by himself without having at least six cards of the suit. (Furthermore, East's return of the deuce of hearts at the fourth trick is almost certainly a fourth best.) West has already shown up with four clubs, and therefore he holds only three cards in spades and diamonds. East must then hold six cards in spades and diamonds, which makes the chances slightly in favor of the Queen of spades being in the East hand. Under these circumstances, the finesse offers a slightly better percentage for the Declarer, particularly if a high trump is led first.

Trick 5.   South leads ♠ J, West plays ♠ 5, North plays ♠ K, and East plays ♠ 4.

Trick 6.   North leads ♠ 3, East plays ♠ 7, South plays ♠ 8, and West discards ♡ 8.

Note that the Declarer eliminates one of West's unknown cards before he takes the finesse—this is a kind of safety play. The finesse might easily prove unsuccessful, but it offers a slightly better chance of success, when all the factors are taken into consideration, than to play for the drop.

PLACING CARDS FROM THE BIDDING

Key cards can often be placed from inferences drawn from the bidding. This card-placing is not quite the same thing as card-counting, but it is likewise an endeavor to learn what the Opponents hold, and it has a definite place in the play of every hand in which the Opponents have done anything except pass. The following deal is a case in point:

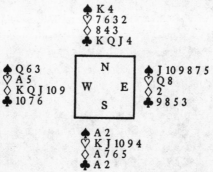

```
                    ♠ K 4
                    ♡ 7 6 3 2
                    ◇ 8 4 3
                    ♣ K Q J 4
    ♠ Q 6 3              N          ♠ J 10 9 8 7 5
    ♡ A 5          W         E      ♡ Q 8
    ◇ K Q J 10 9                    ◇ 2
    ♣ 10 7 6             S          ♣ 9 8 5 3
                    ♠ A 2
                    ♡ K J 10 9 4
                    ◇ A 7 6 5
                    ♣ A 2
```

With East and West vulnerable, the bidding has gone:

SOUTH	WEST	NORTH	EAST
One Heart	Two Diamonds	Two Hearts	Pass
Four Hearts	Pass	Pass	Pass

The play proceeds as follows:

Trick 1.   West leads ◇ K, North plays ◇ 3, East plays ◇ 2, and South wins with ◇ A.

Trick 2. South leads ♣ A, West plays ♣ 6, North plays ♣ 4, and East plays ♣ 3.

Trick 3. South leads ♣ 2, West plays ♣ 7, North plays ♣ J, and East plays ♣ 5.

Trick 4. North leads ♣ K, East plays ♣ 8, South discards ◇ 5, and West plays ♣ 10.

Trick 5. North leads ♣ Q, East plays ♣ 9, South discards ◇ 6, and West ruffs with ♡ 5.

Declarer decided at the fourth trick that he might as well continue leading clubs. He must lose 2 diamond tricks anyway, and he eliminates them early by throwing them off here. By letting West ruff the fifth trick, he gets rid of one adverse trump. In fact, there was a possibility that the Opponent who wished to win this trick might have to use a trump honor to ruff with.

Trick 6. West leads ◇ Q, North plays ◇ 4, East discards ♠ 5, and South plays ◇ 7.

Trick 7. West leads ◇ J, North plays ◇ 8, East discards ♠ 7, and South ruffs with ♡ 4.

Trick 8. South leads ♠ 2, West plays ♠ 3, North plays ♠ K, and East plays ♠ 8.

The problem of the Declarer is now to locate the heart honors. He plans to lead low from Dummy, but he must guess whether to play the Jack or the King of hearts from his own hand if East plays low. This seems like a pure guess, but actually it is not. South recalls West's vulnerable overcall of *two diamonds*, and yet West, as South now knows, held only five diamonds originally. West did not have the Ace and King of spades, nor the Ace and King of clubs. But he must have had some high-card strength, and the only card he could have to justify his vulnerable overcall is the Ace of hearts. Of course, he might also hold the Queen of hearts but, if he does, nothing can be done about it.

Trick 9. North leads ♡ 2, East plays ♡ 8, South plays ♡ J, and West wins with ♡ A. The Queen of hearts is now the only outstanding trump, and so the Declarer loses no more tricks.

The foregoing deal is interesting because it shows how easy it is, in this particular situation, to locate the Ace of trumps. It is interesting also for another reason. South's diamond discards were absolutely essential, and if he had led trumps immediately he would have been defeated. If at the second trick he had gone over to the King of spades and taken the heart finesse right away, West would have won the trick with the Ace and would then have cashed in 2 diamond tricks instead of the 1 he finally made. With three rounds of diamonds gone, he would have led a fourth diamond, and East's Queen could have over-ruffed any trump in the Dummy, while the Declarer would have to follow suit. However, this Declarer had the foresight to realize this, and get rid of his diamonds before doing anything else.

Counting by the Defending Side

Counting is just as important to the Defending Side as it is to the Declarer. By watching the fall of the cards very carefully, noting each denomination and counting the number of cards played in each suit, it is often a simple matter to deduce the entire distribution of a hand. The following play was actually made by Mr. Walter Malowan of New York City, an expert player famous for his ability to drop singleton Kings. Mr. Malowan sat East on this deal:

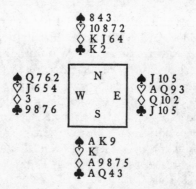

With North and South vulnerable, the bidding proceeded as follows:

South	West	North	East
One Diamond	Pass	Two Diamonds	Pass
Two No-trump	Pass	Three No-trump	Pass
Pass	Pass		

South's bidding was perhaps unusual, but cannot be criticized.

West opened the spade deuce, and Declarer won Mr. Malowan's Ten-spot with the King. He now laid down the diamond Ace and another diamond and on finding that the suit did not break conceded the trick to East. Mr. Malowan began to count.

His partner had opened the deuce of spades, showing that he held no more than four originally. He had also shown up with a singleton diamond, which marked him with eight cards in hearts and clubs. It seemed unlikely that either of these suits could be of five-card length, as otherwise he would have opened it rather than spades. Therefore, they were probably each of four-card length.

The situation was beginning to clear up. If West held four hearts, Declarer must hold a singleton, as the Dummy also held four and so did Mr. Malowan. The proper play was not even close. The Ace of hearts was laid down, felling Declarer's lone King; a small heart was led to West's Jack and the return through Dummy's Ten enabled both the Queen and nine-spot to make. The contract was thereby defeated 1 trick, while an ordinary return of Partner's suit would have permitted it to be made.

MATHEMATICAL TABLES

The mathematics of card distribution is not an exact science. The fact that the various published tables of distribution differ somewhat from each other tends to prove this. Even assuming such tables to be accurate, the percentages or conclusions would be too general for practical use at the Bridge table except as a valuable adjunct for use when more specific clues are not available.

More specific information about distribution can be obtained most of the time by close application to the bidding and by watching the cards as they fall on each trick. All the knowledge of hand patterns in the world is much less important or useful than this common-sense method of counting.

SUMMARY

The principal thing to remember about counting is how absolutely necessary it is. It should become a habit. Any player who cannot learn to count, habitually, on every hand, can never progress very far in the game. It is not particularly difficult, so no one should become discouraged. Keep at it, trying it on every deal you play, and it will gradually become easier and easier, until it seems as natural as following suit.

No hard-and-fast rules can be given for counting. It is always important to remember any bids the Opponents may have made. Vulnerable bids are usually especially revealing, since very few players will run any great risk with shaded bids when vulnerable—the possible penalties are too great. The bidding enables certain cards to be placed tentatively in a certain hand, and you can proceed on this basis until the fall of the cards gives you good reason to alter your first diagnosis.

By coördinating the adverse bids with the later fall of the cards, a great deal of insight into the Opponents' holdings can usually be obtained. As soon as one player shows out of a suit, the entire suit becomes placed, since the fourth player must have held the remainder originally. The opening lead frequently shows length, as well as something about honor strength. A player's signals to his Partner—by means of discards and echoes—also help the Declarer, though he must often be wary and not place absolute reliance upon them.

The whole secret of accurate counting depends on the factor 13. There are only *thirteen* cards of a suit, and there are always *thirteen* cards in each original hand. This seems too obvious to require statement, and yet it is true that many otherwise good players fail to utilize the fact.

CHAPTER VI

COUPS

THE word "coup," from the French use of it in *coup d'etat*, suggests a strategic stroke, a brilliant move, whether in defense or in attack. But the word has been carelessly applied to so many widely different types of plays that it is impossible to give a definition of the word "coup" itself which will include all the plays that have been honored with the name. Practically all of these plays have come down from the days of Whist, and have merely been adapted to Bridge with its exposed Dummy hand.

The more famous coups include those plays called the Bath Coup, the Deschapelles Coup, the Grand Coup, and the Vienna Coup. Two of these were named for the places in which they supposedly first occurred, namely, Bath (England) and Vienna (Austria). One, the Deschapelles, is named after the great French player who is reputed to have discovered it in the days of Whist. The Grand Coup is so called because it is a highly spectacular play in which a winner is ruffed in order to capture eventually an opposing trump honor. Various coups are treated together in this chapter because they have happened to be called coups, though they vary widely in their structure. A quadruple Grand Coup is possible, for instance, but the combination of cards necessary for its execution, and the bidding necessary to reach a contract in which it may be utilized, are almost as unlikely as the collision of the earth and a comet.

THE BATH COUP

The Bath Coup is an extremely elementary play wholly undeserving of the high-sounding name it bears. The Bath Coup is nothing more nor less than a hold-up with a tenace combination. The following situation explains it:

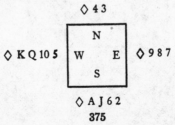

$\Diamond$ 4 3

$\Diamond$ K Q 10 5   W   E $\Diamond$ 9 8 7

$\Diamond$ A J 6 2

West leads the King. The "coup" consists in South's holding up the Ace, hoping thereby to induce West to continue the suit. South must take care, however, to play the six and not the deuce, so that West may be led to believe that his Partner's seven-spot starts an echo. If West does continue the suit, South makes 2 tricks, when otherwise he can make only 1.

It might be said that the Bath Coup seldom works against good opposition. The smaller cards are very seldom so distributed that the leader can be led to believe that his Partner is starting an echo. However, it is very frequently a highly successful maneuver, in fact a *must* play, to this extent: Even if the Defense doesn't continue the suit and sacrifice a trick, the very fact that they must abandon the suit and thus lose a valuable time unit may result in the salvaging of Declarer's contract.

THE DESCHAPELLES COUP

In sharp contrast to the Bath Coup, the Deschapelles Coup is a very brilliant and effective play available to the Defending Side on occasion. Indeed, there are two varieties of this coup. In one, a high card is deliberately sacrificed in order to knock an entry out of the Dummy and prevent the run of an established suit. In the other a high honor is deliberately sacrificed in order to create an entry in Partner's hand.

The following deal illustrates the first type of coup:

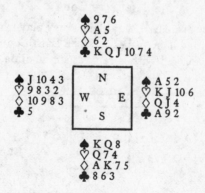

With neither side vulnerable, the bidding has gone:

SOUTH	WEST	NORTH	EAST
One Diamond	Pass	Two Clubs	Pass
Two No-trump	Pass	Three No-trump	Pass
Pass	Pass		

West opens the three of spades, and East wins the trick with the Ace. Looking the situation over, East sees that the Declarer will probably be able to make his contract as soon as he establishes clubs. Since East holds the Ace of clubs, he can hold off for two rounds, and perhaps eliminate all the clubs from Declarer's own hand. But this will do no good so long as the Ace of hearts remains in the Dummy for an entry. Therefore, the success or failure of the contract may depend on whether the Ace of hearts can be knocked out of the Dummy.

Obviously the lead of a low heart will not accomplish the purpose. The time element enters very strongly here, too, for East will not have a second opportunity to bring about the desired result. South's *two no-trump* bid must certainly mean that he has the Queen of hearts, so that for East to play a low heart will not frustrate his plans. The Jack or the Ten would meet the same fate—they would be captured by the Queen, and the Ace would be left in the Dummy. In spite of the fact that East's King is a sure winner if he holds on to it (provided Declarer leads the suit twice), East must play this card now—sacrificing it deliberately—in order to make sure that Dummy's hand will be shut out of the later play.

Of course, this play of the heart King is a refusal to return Partner's suit, but a moment's consideration will show why this return should not be weighed in the balance. South opened the bidding and rebid without an honor in clubs, with only the Queen in hearts, and, at the most, the Ace and King of diamonds. He must therefore hold at least the King and Queen of spades, which precludes the possibility of the spade return being at all constructive. Note what happens in the first 6 tricks, assuming that East finally decides in favor of the King of hearts' return.

Trick 1. West leads ♠ 3, North plays ♠ 6, East plays ♠ A, and South plays ♠ 8.

Trick 2.   East leads ♡ K, South plays ♡ 4, West plays ♡ 2, and North wins with ♡ A.   This lead of the King by East constitutes the Deschapelles Coup   The Declarer cannot refuse to win with the Ace, for, if he does, the suit will be continued.

Trick 3.   North leads ♣ K, East plays ♣ 2, South plays ♣ 3, and West plays ♣ 5.   East now employs the hold-up in clubs.

Trick 4.   North leads ♣ Q, East plays ♣ 9, South plays ♣ 6, and West discards ♡ 3.   It is obvious that East's play will work.

Trick 5.   North leads ♣ J, East plays ♣ A, South plays ♣ 8, and West discards ♡ 8.

Trick 6.   East leads ♠ 5, South plays ♠ Q, West plays ♠ 4, and North plays ♠ 7.

The rest of the play is not important.   Certainly the Declarer is shut out of the Dummy, and must win whatever tricks he gets from now on with the cards in his own hand.   He has already lost 2 tricks and must still lose 2 diamond tricks and 1 heart trick.   Note that if East had made any other lead but the heart King at the second trick, the Declarer must make at least 10 tricks at no-trump.

The other form of the Deschapelles Coup is less obvious, involving, as it does, the deliberate sacrifice of a high card in the hope of establishing an entry in Partner's hand.   The following deal illustrates its use:

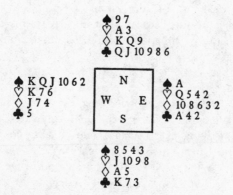

With East and West vulnerable, and North the Dealer, the bidding has gone:

SOUTH	WEST	NORTH	EAST
		One Club	Pass
One No-trump	Pass	Two Clubs	Pass
Two No-trump	Pass	Three No-trump	Pass
Pass	Pass		

The bidding is rather unusual, if not downright mad.* North's opening bid is a minimum as far as high cards are concerned, but he is nevertheless compelled to take out *one no-trump* with *two clubs*. South's *two no-trump* bid is perfectly logical in view of the fact that his *one no-trump* was far above a minimum hand for that response. It is North's *three no-trump* bid which is incomprehensible. He should, of course, bid *three clubs* to sign off. However, as the cards lie South can be beaten only by expert defense.

West opens the King of spades. At the beginning of the hand, he was rather hoping that North and South would reach a game contract, and for this reason he refrained from bidding his spades, but he almost wished he had bid the suit as events developed. East wins the first trick with the Ace, and curses softly under his breath because he cannot lead a spade back to his Partner. If West happens to hold either the Ace of diamonds or the King of clubs (a remote possibility), he is pretty sure to get in the lead anyway, but if his only possible entry should happen to be the King of hearts, the Ace of hearts has to be driven out of Dummy's hand pronto. Furthermore, East cannot afford to lead a low heart, as this will kill Partner's King (if he has it). Therefore he must lead the heart Queen, in the hope that Partner has the King, which will be set up for an entry when the heart Ace is forced out of the Dummy. This play is the Deschapelles Coup.

After the lead of the heart Queen by East, the Declarer must go down 4 tricks, while any other lead to the second trick will enable him to make his contract without the slightest trouble.

By way of clinching this matter of the Deschapelles Coup, one more example of it is included here. The following deal was actually played in the National Challenge Team-of-Four Championship (1932), in which Mr. Oswald Jacoby sat West, being the Partner of the author. Mr. Jacoby's play of the Deschapelles Coup in this deal stands on record as one of the finest defensive plays ever made:

---

* Louis understated his case as to the bidding. Even in 1934 South should have responded with one heart on the first round. But Louis had to get South as the declarer at three no-trump by hook or crook.—S. F. Jr.

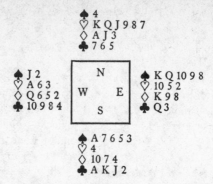

♠ 4
♡ K Q J 9 8 7
◇ A J 3
♣ 7 6 5

♠ J 2   ♠ K Q 10 9 8
♡ A 6 3   ♡ 10 5 2
◇ Q 6 5 2   ◇ K 9 8
♣ 10 9 8 4   ♣ Q 3

♠ A 7 6 5 3
♡ 4
◇ 10 7 4
♣ A K J 2

With both sides vulnerable (North, Dealer), the bidding has gone:

SOUTH	WEST	NORTH	EAST
		One Heart	One Spade
Double	Pass	Two Hearts	Pass
Two No-trump	Pass	Three No-trump	Pass
Pass	Pass		

Mr. Jacoby, sitting West, opened the Jack of spades, which South allowed to hold the trick. South feared that Mr. Jacoby may have held two spades originally (which was the fact).

The opportunity for the Deschapelles Coup now presented itself. If Mr. Jacoby continued the spades, the contract would easily be made. However, he analyzed the situation correctly, and figured that Dummy's Ace of diamonds was a very necessary entry for the heart suit. Acting upon this perception, he laid down his Queen of diamonds at the second trick, a noble sacrifice to Dummy's Ace. From this point on it was impossible for Mr. Stearns to preserve his entry, and the heart suit was successfully and completely blocked from all further play. You notice that the lead of a low diamond does not accomplish the same purpose, and, of course, Mr. Jacoby's play cannot succeed if his Partner does not have the King.

THE TRUMP COUP

The Grand Coup is the most publicized—the most widely talked about—of all the trump coups. The play has gained a reputation that it does not deserve, for it is far from being a very useful play. Actually, the mechanics of it are fairly simple, for it is merely a trump-shortening play with the additional feature that the shortening is brought about by the deliberate ruffing of 1 or 2 *winners*.

To make the Grand Coup clear, it is first necessary to explain the simple coup. The opportunity to make a simple coup occurs when the Declarer holds a finessing position in the trump suit over the player on his right, but cannot finesse because of the lack of trump cards in the Dummy. His play must therefore be to reduce the number of his own trumps to the same number as held by his right-hand Opponent, meanwhile arranging the lead so that, at the proper time, the Dummy's hand will be in the lead to come through the Opponent's trumps. The way of shortening Declarer's own trumps is to ruff some of Dummy's cards, as in the following situation:

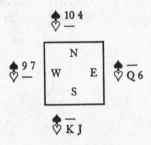

Hearts are trumps. If the lead is in the Declarer's (South's) hand at this point, he will have to lose a trick to the Queen of hearts on his right. However, if the lead is in the Dummy hand at this point, the Declarer need but lead a spade, thereby forcing East to ruff, and South can then over-ruff, catching East's remaining trump on the final lead. Throughout the earlier part of the hand in which this end situation came about, Declarer's purpose must have been to develop the hand so that just this position was arrived at. For instance, if one more card is added, putting the situation back 1 trick:

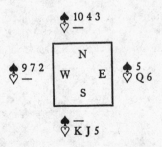

Now if a spade is led from the Dummy, nothing is accomplished. The spade is high, but, when East plays his small spade, South is forced to ruff the trick, since he has nothing but trumps in his own hand. (Even if East lacks a spade, but has a small card of some suit other than trumps, he must discard the side card on this card—not attempt to ruff it.) On the lead of the Ten of spades, in other words, both Opponents imperturbably follow suit, but the trick must still be won in the Declarer's own hand. This means that the Declarer will be forced to lead a trump at the eleventh trick, thereby giving up a trick to East's Queen. This is because the cards are not in the true coup position; in other words, the Declarer holds one more trump than East. Suppose one more card is now added, placing the play at the tenth trick:

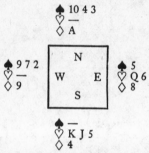

If the Declarer is in the Dummy at the tenth trick, he can pave the way for the coup by leading a spade and ruffing it in his own hand. The Ace of diamonds then serves as a re-entry to put him back in the Dummy, whereupon his King-Jack of trumps is in tenace position over East's Queen-six, and the lead is coming from the right direction. It is only necessary to lead another spade—East now has to ruff, and South can over-ruff.

Here is a good chance to point out the slight difference—a technical difference only—between the *simple* coup and the *Grand* Coup.* In the preceding diagrams, if the Declarer should choose to lead a

---

* The trump coup, simple or Grand, is further dubbed single, double, triple, etc., according to the number of cards ruffed for the purpose of shortening Declarer's own trump holding. If Declarer has one more trump than his right-hand Opponent, and shortens his holding by one ruff, the play is a single coup; if he shortens himself twice, it is a double coup. The triple coup, simple or Grand, is extremely rare. As was stated earlier, a Quadruple Grand Coup can be set up artificially, but such a hand will probably never be dealt in actual play.

low spade (lower than West's nine-spot) from the Dummy for the purpose of ruffing it in his own hand, the play is a simple coup, since he ruffs a trick that would otherwise be lost to an Opponent. But if he chooses to ruff the Ten of spades (which is good), the play is the Grand Coup, because he deliberately ruffs a winning card in order to get into the proper coup position. The difference is really of small import, since the principle is the same.

A good sense of timing is very essential for the successful execution of a trump coup. Each card must be played at just the right moment. Foresight is necessary if the right hand is to be in the lead when the *denouement* finally takes place. A single error in timing—a mistake in the order in which the cards should be played—may mean the loss of the whole hand.

A DOUBLE SIMPLE COUP

The following example shows a simple coup in which the Declarer ruffs two losing cards in order to shorten his own trump holding by two cards; the play is therefore a double coup.

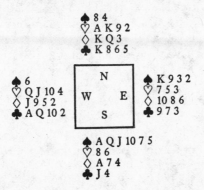

With North and South vulnerable, the bidding has gone: [*]

SOUTH	WEST	NORTH	EAST
One Spade	Pass	Three Hearts	Pass
Four Spades	Pass	Five Spades	Pass
Six Spades	Pass	Pass	Pass

---

[*] "That's actually how they got there, so help me!" Louis said to me when I was first shown the hand.—S. F. Jr.

The play proceeds as follows:

Trick 1. West leads ♡ Q, North plays ♡ K, East plays ♡ 3, and South plays ♡ 6.

Trick 2. North leads ♠ 4, East plays ♠ 2, South plays ♠ 10, and West plays ♠ 6.

Trick 3. South leads ♡ 8, West plays ♡ 10, North plays ♡ A, and East plays ♡ 5.

Trick 4. North leads ♠ 8, East plays ♠ 3, South plays ♠ J, and West discards ♣ 2. At this point, South learns that East still holds the King of spades, guarded. The Dummy holds no more trumps, and so the only way in which the King of trumps can be captured is through a coup. The Declarer must try to reduce his four trumps to two (the number East holds), and wind up at the twelfth trick with the lead in the Dummy.

Trick 5. South leads ♣ 4, West plays ♣ A, North plays ♣ 5, and East plays ♣ 3.

Trick 6. West leads ◇ 2, North plays ◇ Q, East plays ◇ 6, and South plays ◇ 4.

Trick 7. North leads ♡ 2, East plays ♡ 7, South ruffs with ♠ 5, and West plays ♡ 4. This is the first trump-shortening ruff, and South has accomplished half his purpose.

At this point, a new danger looms ahead of South. Hearts have been led three times, which means that East is almost certain to be exhausted of the suit. If East is permitted to discard when another heart is led, he will undoubtedly throw off a card from his shortest suit. The chances are that he holds only two more diamonds, and he consequently must be prevented from getting rid of any of these. South must therefore strip the hand of diamonds so that the third round will not be ruffed later.

Trick 8. South leads ◇ A, West plays ◇ 5, North plays ◇ 3, and East plays ◇ 8.

Trick 9. South leads ◇ 7, West plays ◇ 9, North plays ◇ K, and East plays ◇ 10. One more obstacle has now been overcome.

Trick 10. North leads ♡ 9, East discards ♣ 7, South ruffs with ♠ 7, and West plays ♡ J. The King of clubs cannot be led and the third round of clubs trumped for the simple reason that the Declarer needs the club King for a re-entry.

Trick 11. South leads ♣ J, West plays ♣ Q, North plays ♣ K,

and East plays ♣ 9.   South is back in the Dummy, and his contract
is as good as made, for the situation is now as follows:

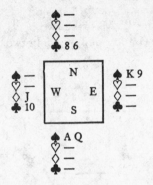

   The position of these cards is practically the same as those given in
the preliminary coup diagrams a few pages back.   Either club that
Declarer chooses to lead from the North hand will produce the same
result.   East is forced to ruff ahead of South, and South holds a tenace in trumps which enables him to over-ruff and draw the last trump.
Thus East's guarded King is roped in, in spite of the fact that Declarer
had no small trumps in Dummy which would let him take a finesse.
   Although the preceding deal is really quite simple, a certain amount
of careful timing is required.   South had several chances to go wrong,
particularly when he began to shorten himself in trumps.   If at the
eighth trick he had led a small diamond instead of the Ace, winning
with Dummy's King, and then led his last heart, West would have
thrown off a diamond and would have ruffed the third round of this
suit, had Declarer led it again at the tenth trick.   For this reason, a
coup situation resembles, in a vague sort of way, a cross-ruff situation,
in that the side suits must be led out first so as not to give the Opponents any chance to throw off losers.   At the same time, the side
suits cannot be eliminated too quickly, for they may be needed for
communication purposes—their high cards serve as needed entries.
All in all, it is impossible to execute a coup successfully without looking ahead and planning exactly what is going to happen at each trick.
If you do not see ahead of you the precise position you wish to bring
about at the twelfth trick, you may just as well not bother with the
coup at all.

The Double Grand Coup

It is a comparatively simple matter to change the preceding double simple coup into a Grand Coup. In order to prove that there is practically no difference between the two plays, the following deal is given to illustrate the Grand Coup, yet only two cards are changed:

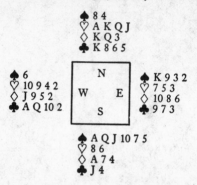

♠ 8 4
♡ A K Q J
♢ K Q 3
♣ K 8 6 5

♠ 6
♡ 10 9 4 2
♢ J 9 5 2
♣ A Q 10 2

♠ K 9 3 2
♡ 7 5 3
♢ 10 8 6
♣ 9 7 3

♠ A Q J 10 7 5
♡ 8 6
♢ A 7 4
♣ J 4

The bidding is much the same as before, South playing the hand at a contract of six spades.

West opens the Ace of clubs and then shifts to a heart. This leaves the Declarer with the same number of entries to the Dummy, and he should play the hand in exactly the same fashion as the preceding one, the only difference being that when he shortens himself by trumping hearts, he is trumping *winning* cards instead of *losing* (small) cards. In spite of the fact that the principle of play in both hands is the same, the former is correctly called the double simple coup, and this play is given the name of Double Grand Coup.

Defense Against the Trump Coup

The following deal is very much like the two preceding; in fact, only three cards are differently placed. The Queen of diamonds has been transferred to the South hand, and North and West have exchanged two hearts. What does this change of the diamond Queen do? It removes one of the Declarer's essential entries from the Dummy and consequently prevents him from shortening himself in trumps and at the same time ending up in the Dummy for the coup lead. He cannot possibly do all these things *unless the Opponents assist him.* First look at the deal, and then consider the possibilities:

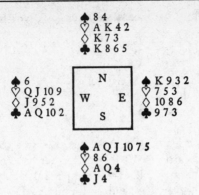

The contract is still six spades, played by South.

West's opening lead is the heart Queen, which Dummy wins with the King. The spade finesse is now taken against East, and holds. The Dummy is re-entered with the heart Ace, and the spade finesse taken a second time, which holds, but shows West to have had only one trump originally. South now leads a club, which West wins with the Ace.

The crucial point for the Defending Side comes right here. West should know that South is hoping to execute a coup, and he should therefore try to prevent him from shortening himself in trumps. The temptation to lead a heart is very great, as it seems to be a very safe lead. But the heart is one lead which will let the Declarer accomplish his purpose, since it will give him a ruff, thereby shortening him in trumps, *without wasting one of the precious re-entries*. After the heart ruff (if West leads the heart) the Declarer will take three rounds of diamonds, winding up in the Dummy, and then trump the last heart in his own hand. This will reduce him to two trumps, and a low club led to the King serves as his final re-entry to the Dummy. If West leads some card other than a heart, however, the Declarer will not be able to shorten himself and retain his last entry at the same time.

Let us suppose that West returns a diamond at the sixth trick, and the play proceeds as follows:

Trick 6. West leads ◇ 2, North plays ◇ 3, East plays ◇ 10, and South wins with ◇ Q.

Trick 7.   South leads ♢ A, West plays ♢ 5, North plays ♢ 7, and East plays ♢ 6.

Trick 8.   South leads ♢ 4, West plays ♢ 9, North plays ♢ K, and East plays ♢ 8.

Trick 9.   North leads ♡ 2, East plays ♡ 7, South ruffs with ♠ 5, and West plays ♡ 10.

Trick 10.   South leads ♣ J, West plays ♣ Q, North plays ♣ K, and East plays ♣ 9.

Trick 11.   North leads ♡ 4, East discards ♣ 9, South ruffs with ♠ 7, and West discards ♣ 10.   Declarer has succeeded in shortening himself, and he now holds two trumps and East also holds two. Unfortunately, however, the lead is not in the Dummy, but in his own hand, and he must therefore give up a trick.

Thus you see, that by making a few minor changes, the simple coup, the Grand Coup and a coup in which the Declarer must rely on an Opponent to help him, can all be illustrated with much the same deal.   The importance of timing is just as great to the Defending Side as to the Declarer.

An Unnecessary Finesse in Preparing for a Coup

The following deal shows a hand actually played, in which a seemingly unnecessary finesse becomes necessary in order to keep the tempo of the hand at the right pace for the successful execution of the trump coup:

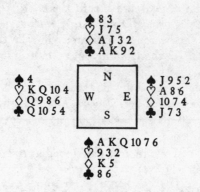

With both sides vulnerable, the bidding has gone:

South	West	North	East
One Spade	Pass	Two No-trump	Pass
Three Spades	Pass	Three No-trump	Pass
Four Spades	Pass	Pass	Pass

It is at once apparent that South can make the hand if he takes the finesse against the Jack of spades. But it would take a mind reader to be sure of the distribution.

Trick 1. West leads ♡ K, North plays ♡ 5, East plays ♡ 8, and South plays ♡ 2.

Trick 2. West leads ♡ 4, North plays ♡ 7, East plays ♡ A, and South plays ♡ 3.

Trick 3. East leads ♡ 6, South plays ♡ 9, West plays ♡ Q, and North plays ♡ J.

Trick 4. West leads ♣ 4, North plays ♣ K, East plays ♣ 3, and South plays ♣ 6.

Trick 5. North leads ♠ 3, East plays ♠ 2, South plays ♠ Q, and West plays ♠ 4.

Trick 6. South leads ♠ K, West discards ♡ 10, North plays ♠ 8, and East plays ♠ 5. The bad news is out. Having already lost 3 tricks, East's Jack of spades must somehow be rendered trickless if the contract is to be made.

The only way of getting the better of East's Jack of trumps is for South to shorten himself twice. Now there is always one point that all coup situations have in common: the number of entries which are needed into the Dummy *is always one more than the number of times one must shorten himself*. In this hand, then, three entries into the Dummy must be found.

Unfortunately, the Dummy appears to have only two entries, namely, a club and a diamond. This permits South to get through the shortening process all right, but he will not wind up with the lead in the proper hand. The only chance therefore depends on finding an extra entry, and the Jack of diamonds pops up as an immediate possibility. If West happens to have the Queen, the Jack can be finessed, and the coup is in the bag. Of course, if East has the Queen of diamonds, taking this finesse will mean that South is set 2 tricks instead of 1, but this is negligible in comparison with the chance of making game.

Therefore the play proceeds:

Trick 7. South leads ♣ 8, West plays ♣ 5, North plays ♣ A, and East plays ♣ 7.

Trick 8. North leads ♣ 2, East plays ♣ J, South ruffs with ♠ 6, and West plays ♣ 10. The crucial moment has now arrived.

Trick 9. South leads ◇ 5, West plays ◇ 6, North plays ◇ J, and East plays ◇ 4. The finesse holds.

Trick 10. North leads ♣ 9, East discards ◇ 7, South ruffs with ♠ 7, and West plays ♣ Q.

Trick 11. South leads ◇ K, West plays ◇ 8, North plays ◇ A, and East plays ◇ 10.

South now holds the Ace-Ten of spades over East's Jack-nine, and the lead is in the Dummy. The coup is successful. *

TRUMP COUPS IN GENERAL

The trump coup is not confined to situations in which only one honor is missing. Even what seems like a rather innocuous combination of cards, such as that in the following diagram, may present a coup situation:

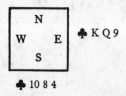

The lead is in the Dummy (North)—let us assume that to have the lead there at this point was prearranged by the Declarer, Dummy of course holding no trumps. The hand has actually been "couped," for in this situation South must make a trick with his Ten (the Ace and Jack already having been played). If the lead is in the South hand at this point, no tricks at all can be obtained in this suit (trumps).

The trump coup is applicable to any combination of cards resembling a tenace, whenever a finesse is impossible. It depends, of course, on learning that the right-hand Opponent holds the missing honors *under* your own tenace, and on being able to lead from the Dummy at a time when he must play before you—or ruff before you,

---

* Yes, Louis knew, too, that if East spectacularly puts up the diamond Queen at trick 9, Declarer's coup will be foiled.—S. F. Jr.

to be more exact.   Two things must always be remembered, namely, that the Opponents must be prevented from discarding if possible, and that the number of entries to the Dummy must be one more than the number of times it is necessary for the Declarer to shorten himself in trumps.

The *Vienna Coup*, since it is really the preparation for a squeeze play, is taken up in the next chapter.

SUMMARY

The principal coups, so called, are as follows:

The Bath Coup.—Holding up an Ace-Jack combination on the lead of the King, hoping that the Opponent will continue the suit.

The Deschapelles Coup.—Sacrificing a high card (a sure winner if held on to) in order (1) to set up an entry in Partner's hand, if possible, or (2) to knock an entry out of the Dummy, to shut out the play of a long suit.

The Simple Coup.—A trump-shortening play in which the Declarer reduces his own trumps to the number held by his right-hand Opponent in order to place his own holding in tenace position over the Opponents', with the lead finally in the Dummy so that the Opponent will be forced to ruff before the Declarer.   In the simple coup the trump-shortening is accomplished by the ruffing of small cards (losers) from the Dummy.

The Grand Coup.—Exactly like the simple coup, except that the trump-shortening is accomplished by ruffing winners led from the Dummy.

The Vienna Coup.—A play preparatory to a squeeze, explained in the chapter on squeeze plays.

CHAPTER VII

SQUEEZE PLAYS

THE squeeze play is undoubtedly the most fascinating and the most exciting of all the so-called advanced plays. To the average player the squeeze seems so complex that he will frequently make no attempt to understand the true meaning and the inner workings of the play. Contracts which could easily be made by a squeeze, if the Declarer only knew how to apply it, are allowed to go up in smoke. Yet the mechanics of the squeeze are by no means beyond the ability of the average person to grasp, particularly if the reader of this book has progressed from the first page to this, and absorbed all the pages in between. Certainly by now the operation of many hitherto obscure plays has become clear and understandable.

A *squeeze play* is an attempt by the Declarer to force one of his Opponents to discard either a winning card or the guard to a winning card, so that by such a discard the Declarer is able to make a trick which is virtually created by the Opponent's discard. Sometimes both Opponents are squeezed—that is, each Opponent is put in a situation such that he has no choice but to unguard a winner or throw off the winner itself. Thus squeezes may be classified in two groups, simple squeezes and double squeezes.* In the simple squeeze, one Opponent is forced to discard unwillingly; in the double squeeze, both Opponents are obliged to throw off a card each very much wants to keep.

There are two obvious varieties of the simple squeeze. That applied to the Opponent on the left of the Declarer is a *direct* squeeze, and that applied to the Opponent on the right of the Declarer is a *backward* squeeze.

THE SIMPLE SQUEEZE END-PLAY SITUATION

The best way to introduce the simple direct squeeze is to give the end-play situation first, as follows:

---

* Some writers on Bridge refer to a "triple squeeze." If by "triple" squeeze is meant a squeeze in three suits, the simple or "single" squeeze must, to be consistent, refer to a squeeze in one suit, which is manifestly impossible. The only sensible differentiation appears to be between a squeeze on one Opponent (a simple or single squeeze) and a squeeze on two Opponents (a double squeeze). Since no squeeze can operate upon more than two Opponents, in three suits, the term "triple squeeze" is superfluous and misleading.

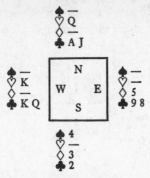

Spades are trumps, and South is in the lead at the eleventh trick. South must make all 3 of the remaining tricks, yet West has the high heart, East has the high diamond, and West has a cast-iron club trick in the King-Queen doubleton. Declarer has 2 certain tricks—his last trump, the only one left, and the club Ace.

A squeeze becomes effective as soon as the Opponent squeezed cannot follow suit and has no worthless card to throw off. To squeeze an Opponent, then, it is first necessary to lead a card on which he must make a discard from another suit, and, second, the Opponent must be reduced only to cards which he needs, so that the discard is literally *squeezed* out of him against his will.

In the end-play situation above, South has but to lead the four of spades. West cannot follow suit, and must discard something. What is more, West must discard *before* the Dummy, so that the Declarer can adjust Dummy's discard to whatever West throws off. West has very little choice—he must throw away his heart King or the Queen of clubs. If he throws the club, South will discard the Queen of hearts from the Dummy, and the Ace-Jack of clubs will win the last 2 tricks. If West throws the heart King, South will discard the Jack of clubs from the Dummy, and win the last 2 tricks with the heart Queen and the club Ace. In short, West is absolutely helpless. There is no way on earth for him to avoid unguarding his clubs or giving up his commanding heart.

Note carefully that if South led anything but the trump at the eleventh trick the squeeze vanishes. Only the lead of the trump at that point can enable South to win the last 3 tricks. Such is the simple direct squeeze in essence.

The following end-play situation shows the simple backward squeeze.   Only a few cards are changed from the preceding example:

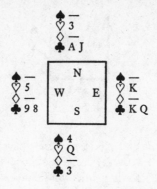

Again South leads the four of spades (trumps), but this time it is not West's discard he is interested in.   He throws off Dummy's three of hearts (having the Queen still in his own hand), and *East* is squeezed. East is obliged to throw off his high heart or give up his club protection—as Declarer well knows from the preliminary play of this deal. Whichever card East throws away, he loses a trick by so doing— yet he cannot help it.   This is the simple backward squeeze, which differs from the direct squeeze only in that the Opponent on the Declarer's right is the one squeezed.

Against either the direct or backward simple squeeze there is no defense.   By the time the squeeze situation is reached, the Opponent is as helpless as an automaton.

WORKING TOWARD THE SQUEEZE

The completion of the simple squeeze is easy enough to see.   Two preliminary steps, namely, card placing and hand preparation, are necessary to bring about the situation in which the squeeze becomes effective.   Card placing is merely the counting of the Opponents' hands as the play progresses, so that the Declarer can see that a squeeze is possible.   Application of the principles already laid down for counting will take care of this first step.   The hand preparation, however, requires some further explanation.

The following complete deal will help to clarify the points involved:

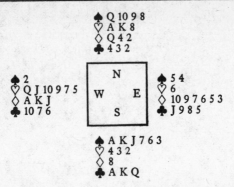

♠ Q 10 9 8
♡ A K 8
◊ Q 4 2
♣ 4 3 2

♠ 2
♡ Q J 10 9 7 5
◊ A K J
♣ 10 7 6

N
W   E
S

♠ 5 4
♡ 6
◊ 10 9 7 6 5 3
♣ J 9 8 5

♠ A K J 7 6 3
♡ 4 3 2
◊ 8
♣ A K Q

Both sides are vulnerable; North and South reach a contract of six
spades, with South the Declarer. The bidding is not pertinent to
the play, beyond the fact that the final contract was *six spades*,
West having at one point overcalled with *two hearts*.

West's opening lead is the diamond King, which holds the trick.
At the next trick West shifts to the Queen of hearts, fearing that
Declarer may have held a singleton diamond, judging from the
Slam contract undertaken. Declarer looks the hands over specula-
tively, and sees 11 tricks sure enough, but the twelfth must be probed
for. There is a losing heart which cannot be got rid of in any simple
manner. But if South knows the mechanics of the squeeze, he can
see a squeeze on West in the offing.

First, he knows from West's diamond King lead that West also has
the Ace, and the vulnerable heart overcall marks West with at least
five hearts, of which he has just led one. South thus knows five of
West's remaining cards—four hearts and the Ace of diamonds. Now
South can take the next 11 tricks, and on the first 10 of these West
must play ten cards—which means that at the eleventh trick West
will be reduced to three cards. These will be the Ace of diamonds,
unquestionably, and two hearts. When South leads to the eleventh
trick, West will have to relinquish either his high diamond or one of
his hearts. This is as sure as ice in zero weather. And it is all
nothing more than simple arithmetic.

South therefore wins the second trick with Dummy's heart King,
and immediately takes five rounds of spades and three rounds of clubs.
It does not matter how West's clubs and spades are divided; at the
eleventh trick the situation *must* be as follows:

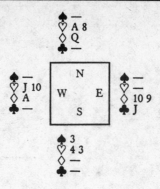

On the fifth round of spades, South threw off Dummy's extra diamond, which is obviously of no use.   Now, on the lead of the sixth round of spades (South's trey), West is relentlessly squeezed.   If he throws a heart, Dummy's diamond Queen will be thrown off; if he throws the diamond, Dummy's eight of hearts will go by the board.

You have just seen all three stages of the simple squeeze, as follows: (1) the counting of West's hand; (2) the preparation for the squeeze at the eleventh trick by leading out trumps and solid side tricks; and (3) the completion of the squeeze by leading the last trump, forcing West to make a discard that ruins his hand.

THE BACKWARD SQUEEZE

The following deal illustrates the execution of a backward squeeze:

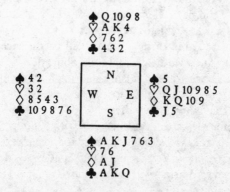

The situation is practically the same, except that here it is East, instead of West, who will be squeezed. North and South reach a somewhat ambitious Grand Slam contract of seven spades. West's opening lead is the Ten of clubs.

Adding up his tricks, South sees that he can be sure of only 12; there is an extra diamond which looks like an almost certain loser. The only way the diamond can be saved is through a squeeze play of some kind. On South's first 8 tricks, each Opponent must play 8 cards. These 8 tricks will be the first five rounds of spades and three rounds of clubs. Now if one Opponent is able to keep three hearts to the Queen, and the other is able to keep the King or Queen of diamonds protected, the squeeze will be impossible. However, if the *same* Opponent has the King-Queen of diamonds *and* six hearts to the Queen, the squeeze will be possible. The reason for this is that, if one Opponent has six hearts, the other can have only two hearts, which means that Dummy's Ace-King will eliminate those two hearts anyway. But with Dummy's little four-spot, if one Opponent has a diamond honor and the other has three hearts, he can always keep that third heart over Dummy's four-spot. In other words, the squeeze works only when it is up to one Opponent to keep both hearts and diamonds.

Since the squeeze possibility is South's only chance, he must play for it. He therefore leads his five rounds of trumps and three rounds of clubs, reducing the hand to the following situation:

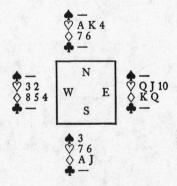

South knows the situation at this point, for West followed suit on two rounds of spades, discarded two clubs and a diamond on the next three rounds, and followed suit on three rounds of clubs. This means that East, who had only a singleton spade and a doubleton in clubs originally, must still hold three hearts and two diamonds. If only these diamonds are the King and Queen, the backward squeeze is a certainty.

South leads his last trump (trey), and West's play is immaterial. The six of diamonds is discarded from the Dummy (since two diamonds are retained in Declarer's own hand), and East is mercilessly squeezed. If East throws off the Ten of hearts, all three of Dummy's hearts will be good; if he throws off a diamond, South's Ace-Jack will romp home as winners. There was no way that East could have prevented this situation. If the adverse cards lie right, the workings of the squeeze are inexorable.

THE PSEUDO-SQUEEZE

No discussion of the simple squeeze could be complete without an explanation of its half-brother, the pseudo-squeeze. The prefix "pseudo-" is simply ancient Greek for "false." The pseudo-squeeze is not really a squeeze at all, but is an attempt by the Declarer to make his Opponents *think that they are being squeezed*, so that they will have to guess which discard they should make. Sometimes, when the Opponents are thus made to guess, they will guess wrong, and those are the times when the Declarer will make his contract—in spite of the fact that no inescapable squeeze situation exists at all.

The following deal illustrates the workings of the pseudo-squeeze:

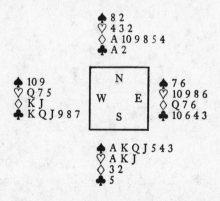

South is the Declarer at a contract of six spades. West opens the club King, which Dummy wins with the Ace.

South has 11 sure tricks, and the twelfth appears to depend on the heart finesse. A squeeze is practically impossible, chiefly for the reason that the Declarer has no way of running any suit but spades. It is true that if the adverse spades break 2-2, South can force both Opponents to find five discards, but they will probably be able to retain the guarded Queen of hearts in one hand and the King of clubs and guarded diamond honor in the other. But there is a distinct possibility of fooling the Opponent who may have the key cards. At any rate, the heart finesse can be postponed until the pseudo-squeeze is tried.

The Declarer therefore leads out seven rounds of spades, and West is somewhat embarrassed in choosing his discards, since he is all in the dark about South's hand. He does not know that the Declarer had a singleton club originally, and he has no inkling of the location of the Queen of diamonds. He follows suit on the first two rounds of spades, of course, and discards four clubs on the next four rounds. On the last round of spades, however, he is up against the following blind situation:

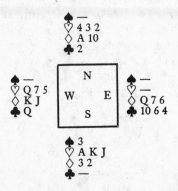

When South leads the last spade, West is in a tough spot. He has nothing to help him, but must guess which card to throw off. After all, he does not know but that Declarer may hold the following:

♠ —
♡ A K J
◇ Q
♣ 10

If this is true, West is actually squeezed, and it makes no difference which card he throws off. Since he does not know, he may accidentally throw off a heart, and the pseudo-squeeze will have enabled the Declarer to make 3 heart tricks.

Of course, if West throws away anything but a heart, the Declarer has no choice but to take the heart finesse. It so happens that it will not work on this deal, but the Declarer has done his best and must solace himself with the thought that he *tried* the pseudo-squeeze, at least.

As a matter of fact, the pseudo-squeeze should be attempted even when there seems to be no chance of success. When a contract is assured, and the Declarer holds a number of good trumps and other established cards in his hand, it does no harm to play these out before conceding his losing tricks. Frequently the Opponents will not discard as well as they might, and will either throw some commanding card or unguard some protected suit. The Declarer will then find himself presented with an entirely unexpected trick or tricks.

The Progressive Squeeze

A variation of the simple squeeze occurs when one Opponent is squeezed in more than two suits; this is not, strictly speaking, a double squeeze, since only one Opponent is involved. The variation happens rather often, and is called by some authorities a *progressive* squeeze.

The following deal illustrates this play:

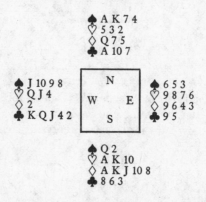

```
              ♠ A K 7 4
              ♡ 5 3 2
              ◇ Q 7 5
              ♣ A 10 7
                  ┌─────────┐
  ♠ J 10 9 8      │    N    │    ♠ 6 5 3
  ♡ Q J 4         │         │    ♡ 9 8 7 6
  ◇ 2             │  W   E  │    ◇ 9 6 4 3
  ♣ K Q J 4 2     │    S    │    ♣ 9 5
                  └─────────┘
              ♠ Q 2
              ♡ A K 10
              ◇ A K J 10 8
              ♣ 8 6 3
```

North and South, let's assume, were far behind in the game or else there's no real excuse for their reaching a contract of *seven* diamonds. However there they are with South as Declarer, West having over-called dangerously in clubs. The play proceeds as follows:

Trick 1. West leads ♠ J, North plays ♠ 4, East plays ♠ 3, and South wins with ♠ Q.

Trick 2. South leads ◇ 8, West plays ◇ 2, North plays ◇ Q, and East plays ◇ 3. The outlook is far from hopeful, but South sees one chance. West's overcall must have been based, at the very least, on practically all of the missing honors. If this is so, West must be caught in a progressive squeeze.

South knows from the bidding that West must have at least five clubs, and he knows from the opening lead that he probably had four spades to the Jack-Ten-nine. He has already played a diamond, which accounts for ten cards, leaving only three hearts to the Queen-Jack, at best. Certainly the vulnerable overcall must have been based on a short suit somewhere, and the singleton diamond seems very likely. This being so, West must find four discards on the next four rounds of diamonds, which will put him rather in a spot.

Trick 3. North leads ◇ 5, East plays ◇ 4, South plays ◇ 10, and West discards ♣ 2. West's first discard.

Trick 4. South leads ◇ A, West discards ♣ 4, North plays ◇ 7, and East plays ◇ 6. This reduces West to the King-Queen-Jack of clubs, the Ten-nine-eight of spades, and Queen-Jack-small of hearts. If he wants to make a spade trick, he must keep all three of his spades; if he wants to make a heart trick, he must keep all of his hearts; and if he wants those 2 good-looking club tricks, he must keep all the clubs. But he cannot do all of these things. He has made his last available discard. After this, every discard will cause him severe pain.

Trick 5. South leads ◇ K, West discards ♣ J, North discards ♡ 2, and East plays ◇ 9.

Twelve tricks are now a certainty, for South can see that West is no longer able to hold on to all his protecting cards.   However, there is even a chance now that South can make his contract, winning all 13 tricks.

Trick 6.   South leads ♢ J, West discards ♡ 4, North discards ♡ 3, and East discards ♡ 6.   West decides to abandon his heart protection.

Trick 7.   South leads ♡ A, West plays ♡ J, North plays ♡ 5, and East plays ♡ 7.   Relentless, South now proceeds to strip West of his remaining hearts.

Trick 8.   South leads ♡ K, West plays ♡ Q, North discards ♣ 7, and East plays ♡ 8.

The situation is now as follows:

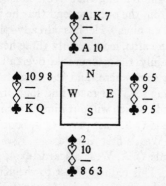

West has already been squeezed so that he had to give up his heart stopper.   But the very giving up of that precious heart has placed him in a situation such that the third round of hearts will squeeze him again, and he will have to give up either a spade or a club. Either way, he presents the Declarer with a trick, as can easily be seen.   (If the club is thrown, Dummy's spade will be discarded and the Ace-Ten of clubs will win 2 tricks.)   Thus the progressive squeeze moves forward like an avenging fate.

Trick 9.   South leads ♡ 10, West discards ♠ 8, North discards ♣ 10, and East plays ♡ 9.   Since West elected to throw the spade, the Ten of clubs is discarded from the Dummy, leaving 3 good spade tricks and the Ace of clubs to clean up the hand.

By the use of this progressive squeeze, the Declarer was able to make 13 tricks on a hand which, in top cards alone, promised him only

11. As soon as West was squeezed into unguarding one suit, this very suit was played right at him, forcing him to unguard another.

A Squeeze to Obtain a Count

Sometimes forcing the Opponents to discard is not done for the purpose of eventually obliging them to give up the commanding card of a suit. It is often done simply to compel them to give up enough cards so that the Declarer can *place* a specific honor. In other words, with a choice between a finesse and playing for a drop this guess can sometimes be eliminated by means of a squeeze which is not really a squeeze at all. Take for example the following illustration:

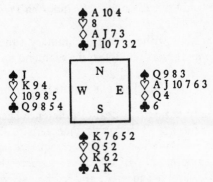

```
               ♠ A 10 4
               ♡ 8
               ◇ A J 7 3
               ♣ J 10 7 3 2
    ♠ J                          ♠ Q 9 8 3
    ♡ K 9 4          N           ♡ A J 10 7 6 3
    ◇ 10 9 8 5    W     E        ◇ Q 4
    ♣ Q 9 8 5 4     S            ♣ 6
               ♠ K 7 6 5 2
               ♡ Q 5 2
               ◇ K 6 2
               ♣ A K
```

With neither side vulnerable the bidding has gone:

South	West	North	East
One Spade	Pass	Two Clubs	Two Hearts
Two Spades	Pass	Four Spades	Pass
Pass	Pass		

West opens the King of hearts and continues with the nine. Declarer ruffs in Dummy and returns to his own hand with the King of clubs. He now ruffs his last heart and follows by leading out his Ace of spades. When the Jack drops from the West hand he is immediately fearful that the spades will not break. This suspicion is confirmed when he returns to his own hand with the King of liamonds, and then leads out the King of trumps. Having already lost 1 heart trick he must obviously also lose 2 spade tricks, and so the contract seems to be dependent on the diamond finesse—unless he can in some way locate the position of the Queen.

The King of clubs is played and East ruffs. East then leads out his other high trump and follows with a high heart which is ruffed by Declarer. Now the last trump is led and the situation begins to clear up. West has followed suit on one diamond lead and has been forced to discard another diamond. At this point he must let go a third card of the suit as he must retain his Queen of clubs. As soon as this discard is made Declarer throws the now-worthless Jack of clubs from Dummy, leaving that hand with nothing but the Ace-Jack of diamonds. Now when Declarer leads the diamond and East follows with the Ten, Declarer knows that the Queen must fall on the Ace, because there is only one diamond left and *West's other card is known to be the Queen of clubs*.

It is apparent that without this preliminary squeeze to obtain a count Declarer must resort blindly to the diamond finesse.

The Double Squeeze

There is actually not a great deal of difference between the simple and the double squeeze. The double squeeze is really nothing more nor less than a combination of a direct squeeze and a backward squeeze in the same hand. In the direct squeeze the Opponent on the left of the Declarer is squeezed, and in the backward squeeze the Opponent on the right of the Declarer is squeezed. Both of these simple squeezes happen at the same time. The play also resembles the progressive squeeze, in that the same play of the Declarer which forces one Opponent also forces the other—both are squeezed simultaneously.

Summarized briefly, the double squeeze works like this:

The Declarer leads a card to which neither Opponent can follow suit, and such that it immediately squeezes his left-hand Opponent. This Opponent chooses to discard protection in a suit rather than a high card. Now Dummy makes the proper discard to fit the left-hand Opponent's discard, and immediately, on the same trick, the right-hand Opponent is also squeezed, and must choose between two discards, both unfavorable to him.

The following end-play situation shows this in skeleton form:

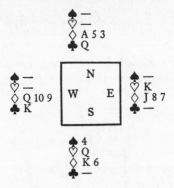

Spades are trumps and South (Declarer) has to win the rest of the tricks.

When South leads his four of spades, the last trump, West is squeezed. If he throws off the King of clubs, Dummy's Queen is promoted. He must therefore throw away his nine of diamonds, giving up his protection in this suit; he does this in preference to throwing off the club King, because he knows that up to the moment East has retained the Jack twice guarded. Seeing West's diamond discard, Declarer throws off Dummy's now useless club, *and East is squeezed*—the pressure swings backward! If East throws off the King of hearts, he establishes Declarer's Queen; if he throws off a diamond, he gives up protection in that suit. Having little choice, but hoping against hope that the diamond situation is not as bad as it looks, he plays the diamond seven. The double squeeze is completed, and Declarer can now lead the King and another diamond to clear the suit, winning the last trick with Dummy's *trey*.

The build-up for the double squeeze comes about in much the same way as for the simple squeeze. The Declarer, utilizing his count on the hand, sees that the direct squeeze on his left-hand Opponent may be possible, and also that a backward squeeze on his right-hand Opponent may work at the same time. The double squeeze requires somewhat closer attention than the simple squeeze on one Opponent, but otherwise there is nothing mysterious about it.

A squeeze becomes possible when the Declarer is in a position to eliminate one or two suits from one or both Opponents' hands, and can continue to lead cards to which the *squeezed* player cannot follow suit, so that that player is obliged to make a costly discard. No squeeze can be planned, of course, without counting of some sort.

The following deal, which was actually played by Mr. Edward Hymes, Jr., one of the most brilliant card players the game of Contract Bridge has developed, contains a very pretty double squeeze:

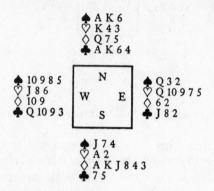

With North and South vulnerable, the bidding has gone:

South	West	North	East
One Diamond	Pass	Four No-trump	Pass
Six Diamonds	Pass	Seven Diamonds	Pass
Pass	Pass		

Mr. Hymes played the Grand Slam from the South position, as Declarer. The play proceeded as follows:

Trick 1. West leads ♠ 10, North plays ♠ K, East plays ♠ 3, and South plays ♠ 4.

From the opening lead, Mr. Hymes was up against it, as he stood a chance to make the hand immediately by playing low in Dummy in the hope that West held the Queen. However, he knew that West was not a player who opened from Queens against a Grand Slam contract, and that East almost surely had the Queen. He decided, at any rate, to place the spade Queen in East's hand (mentally) and hope that a double squeeze might be developed.

Trick 2. North leads ◇ 5, East plays ◇ 2, South plays ◇ A, and West plays ◇ 9.

Trick 3. South leads ◇ 3, West plays ◇ 10, North plays ◇ Q, and East plays ◇ 6. This finishes the drawing of trumps.

Trick 4.   North leads ♣ A, East plays ♣ 2, South plays ♣ 5, and West plays ♣ 3.

Trick 5.   North leads ♣ K, East plays ♣ 8, South plays ♣ 7, and West plays ♣ 9.

Trick 6.   North leads ♣ 4, East plays ♣ J, South ruffs with ◇ 4, and West plays ♣ 10.   South is stripping the Opponents of clubs, a play absolutely necessary in preparation for the squeeze position. Mr. Hymes knew that both Opponents probably held club stoppers. It was therefore urgent that three rounds be led to eliminate all but one club.

Trick 7.   South leads ♠ 7, West plays ♠ 5, North plays ♠ A, and East plays ♠ 2.   This is a very important play.*

Mr. Hymes deliberately established the Queen of clubs in the West hand (presumably) so as to create a possible squeeze.   Then he similarly set up the Queen of spades in the East hand (according to his mental placing of the cards, for the purposes of his campaign).   Without this preparation, the squeeze will not exist, as will appear.

Trick 8.   North leads ◇ 7, East discards ♡ 5, South plays ◇ J, and West discards ♠ 8.

Trick 9.   South leads ◇ K, West discards ♠ 9, North discards ♠ 6 and East discards ♡ 7.   The screws of the rack now begin to tighten. The situation is as follows:

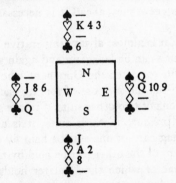

The cards are in the proper position for the double squeeze.

Trick 10.   South leads ◇ 8, West discards ♡ 6, North discards ♣ 6, and East discards ♡ 9.   West cannot discard the club Queen,

---

* Technically called the Vienna Coup, explained more fully later in the chapter.

as to do so will establish Dummy's six-spot. Therefore, when West throws off a heart, Declarer discards the now useless six from the Dummy. The backward squeeze now presses hard against East, who cannot throw off the spade Queen without setting up Declarer's Jack, and therefore also sacrifices his heart protection.

The last 3 tricks now belong to Mr. Hymes; he takes them all in hearts.

Note the preparation necessary to execute this squeeze. First, the clubs had to be led three times in order to leave but one card outstanding in this suit, and, next, the high spade had to be taken out of the Dummy to give Mr. Hymes an available discard and also to prevent the squeeze from working on the Dummy as well as on East. (If this is not clear, the reader should lay out the hand with actual cards and try to make the squeeze work without first making these preliminary plays; he will then see why they are necessary.) The last bit of preparation is particularly interesting; in fact, it has been called a coup—the Vienna Coup, to be exact, from a variation of it played in a Whist Double Dummy problem by a great Viennese expert many years ago. The Vienna Coup, as will appear in later examples, is simply a variation of the squeeze.

The Essentials of a Squeeze Situation

To recognize a squeeze play ahead it is necessary to know certain things.

In the first place, it is almost always imperative for the Declarer to hold a long suit which can be led again and again after neither Opponent can follow suit—or after the Opponent who is to be squeezed cannot follow suit—for the purpose of forcing each Opponent to relinquish control of one of two other suits. In the second place, when the squeeze exerts pressure in three suits, it is absolutely essential that the commanding card of one suit be held by one Opponent and the commanding card of the other suit be held by the *other* Opponent. The third suit is one of which the Declarer holds the commanding cards, so that both Opponents are obliged to keep protection (stoppers) in it as long as possible. When the squeeze becomes effective, each Opponent will hold on to his commanding card in one of the three suits, but will then have to give up his protection in the untouched suit—always in the hope that Partner can hold on to *his* protection in that suit. If the double squeeze actually develops, the Partner cannot keep his protection either.

The third requirement is that in the third suit, of which both Opponents have control for the third round (until they are forced to relinquish it by the relentless workings of the squeeze), both the Dummy's and Declarer's hands should contain entries. This enables the Declarer to pass from one hand to the other, as the results of the squeeze may demand—so that, if either Opponent decides to keep his protection and throw off the commanding card in one of the other suits, Declarer can benefit without being blocked.

Thus, in the end-play situation just given, Mr. Hymes has the Ace of hearts to serve as an entry to his own hand, and the King of hearts as an entry to the Dummy.

Finally, no double squeeze can be executed unless the number of top tricks (sure winners) is within 1 trick of the number required for the contract. That is to say, the double squeeze provides only 1 additional trick.

The Vienna Coup

The Vienna Coup is a play made in preparation for a squeeze play. The play is made by leading out a high card—cashing it in—so that one of the Opponents is deliberately given the controlling card in that suit. In other words, the Vienna Coup establishes a card for an Opponent, so that he may eventually be squeezed by having to choose between throwing off this good card or unguarding another suit.

The following deal illustrates the ordinary Vienna Coup:

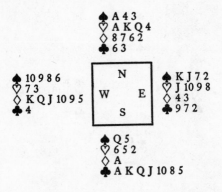

South becomes the Declarer at a contract of seven clubs. Obviously, this contract is a lay-down if the hearts break 3-3. But if the hearts do not break evenly (and they do not), the hand can be made by means of a squeeze if East holds four hearts and the King of spades. To make the squeeze operative, it is necessary for the Declarer to take the Ace of spades out of the Dummy early in the hand. If he fails to do this, the situation will develop to this point:

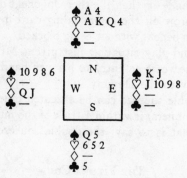

Declarer now leads the five of clubs, his last trump, in an attempt to squeeze East. But what happens? Declarer must discard something from Dummy. If he throws off a spade, East does the same and wins the fourth round of hearts. If a heart is thrown off from Dummy, East again does the same, and wins the last trick with the King of spades. In other words, the squeeze fails to materialize.

Notice the quite different situation when the Ace of spades is removed early in the hand. The situation then develops to the following:

```
              ♠ 4
              ♡ A K Q 4
              ◇ —
              ♣ —
  ♠ 10 9 8   ┌─────────┐   ♠ K
  ♡ —        │    N    │   ♡ J 10 9 8
  ◇ Q J      │ W     E │   ◇ —
  ♣ —        │    S    │   ♣ —
             └─────────┘
              ♠ Q
              ♡ 6 5 2
              ◇ —
              ♣ 5
```

Now, when the club is led, the spade can be discarded from the Dummy, and East is unable to find any harmless discard. Throwing the King of spades will establish the Declarer's Queen, and throwing a heart makes the Dummy's hearts all good.

THE VIENNA COUP PAR EXCELLENCE

Mr. Oswald Jacoby, whose brilliance at the Bridge table is well known, contends that the true Vienna Coup is much more complex than the mere establishing of a high card in an Opponent's hand for squeeze purposes. His Vienna Coup is still a preparation for a squeeze, but it is certainly much more subtle. The following deal is an example of it:

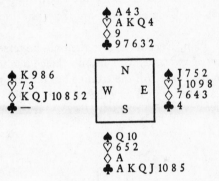

```
                    ♠ A 4 3
                    ♡ A K Q 4
                    ◇ 9
                    ♣ 9 7 6 3 2
  ♠ K 9 8 6                         ♠ J 7 5 2
  ♡ 7 3            ┌─────────┐      ♡ J 10 9 8
  ◇ K Q J 10 8 5 2 │ N       │      ◇ 7 6 4 3
  ♣ —              │ W     E │      ♣ 4
                   │    S    │
                   └─────────┘
                    ♠ Q 10
                    ♡ 6 5 2
                    ◇ A
                    ♣ A K Q J 10 8 5
```

With both sides vulnerable, the bidding has gone:

South	West	North	East
One Club	Four Diamonds	Six Clubs	Pass
Seven Clubs	Pass	Pass	Pass

The Declarer's first reading of the hand is based on the bidding. The vulnerable overcall of *four diamonds* must indicate a hand of strong playing strength and few high cards. But the King of spades, the only important missing card outside the diamond suit, must certainly be in the West hand too, as otherwise that player would hardly venture such a strong vulnerable overcall.

West opens the diamond King, which Declarer wins with the Ace. The contract is in the bag if the hearts break 3-3, but if they do not, some other means must be found to make the hand. In fact, the chances are much in favor of an uneven distribution of hearts, in view of West's overcall of *four diamonds*.

The fourth heart or a second spade can be made by a squeeze play—perhaps. But will the sort of Vienna Coup used ordinarily work in this instance? No, for if East holds four hearts he cannot be squeezed as long as West holds the commanding spade (the King), since he can discard all his spades and keep his heart protection. If only East had the control of spades as well!

Now let's see. If West holds the King of spades *without the Jack also*, perhaps East's Jack can be promoted to the control of the spade situation. The high spade may thus be *transferred* from one hand to the other. If this can be done, the squeeze will succeed; or at least, it looks possible. The Declarer bases his campaign, then, on the hope that West has the King of spades and East the Jack of spades, with four hearts.

Carrying out his plan, Declarer draws the only adverse trump and *lays down the Queen of spades*. West has no choice but to cover, and Dummy wins with the Ace. All the trumps but one are now led out, and the situation is as follows (West's discards are really immaterial):

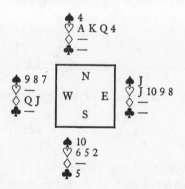

The lead of the last club now squeezes East, for he cannot retain both his commanding spade and his heart protection.

The result is the same as with the ordinary Vienna Coup, but here a very subtle play was made to set up the high card *in the hand the Declarer preferred*. The whole play involves a very nice piece of card-placing. As soon as the Declarer saw that East could not be squeezed by normal methods, he set about finding a way of giving East the winner he wanted him to have—and he did it by eliminating the controlling cards, not only from his own hands, but from the hand of East's Partner as well! The essence of the squeeze thus appears once more—a player is squeezed only when he has to choose between giving up a trick in either of two suits, both equally to his disadvantage.

Choosing Between a Squeeze and a Finesse

Occasionally the Declarer finds himself facing the somewhat despairing situation of having to decide whether an invisible squeeze has worked or whether he should take a finesse. The choice must largely depend on the psychology of the Declarer. Take the following partnership hands:

♠ K 5
♡ Q 4 3
♢ 7 6 5
♣ A Q 9 7 6

♠ A Q J 10 7 6
♡ A J 8
♢ 9 4 2
♣ 5

With neither side vulnerable, and North the Dealer, the bidding has gone:

South	West	North	East
		Pass	One Heart
One Spade	Pass	One No-trump	Pass
Three Spades	Pass	Four Spades	Pass
Pass	Pass		

West opens the Queen of diamonds, receives an encouraging discard from his Partner, and continues the suit. East wins the second and third tricks with the Ace and King of diamonds, and now shifts to a trump, which is won with Dummy's King. The Queen of hearts is led from Dummy, covered by East with the King, and the trick won by Declarer's Ace. Five rounds of trumps follow, and the Jack of hearts is cashed in. The situation is now as follows:

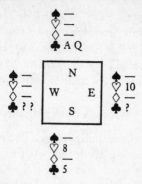

The lead is in the Declarer's own hand. He knows that East holds the good heart (having earlier discarded two hearts) and one club. But he does not know *which* club East holds. Perhaps East has been squeezed and perhaps he has not. East opened the bidding, it is true, but he has already showed up with the Ace and King of diamonds, and the King of hearts. He may still have the King of clubs, but not necessarily. What is the right play for South to make? Frankly, it is impossible to say; it depends entirely on the character of the Opponents South is playing against.

Making an Adversary Squeeze His Partner

Sometimes an adversary can be made to squeeze his Partner—to the Declarer's advantage. Usually an alert Opponent can evade this, but it is not always easy for him to perceive what is going to happen.

The following deal is a good illustration:

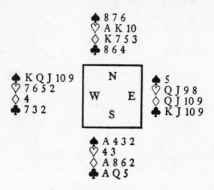

South becomes the Declarer at a contract of three no-trump, and the play proceeds as follows:

Trick 1.   West leads ♠ K, North plays ♠ 6, East plays ♠ 5, and South plays ♠ 2.

Trick 2.   West leads ♠ Q, North plays ♠ 7, East discards ♣ 9, and South plays ♠ 3.

Trick 3.   West leads ♠ J, North plays ♠ 8, East discards ♡ 8, and South wins with ♠ A.

Trick 4.   South leads ♠ 4, West plays ♠ 9, North discards ◇ 3, and East discards ◇ 9. The squeeze now begins to operate—East has to discard a diamond.

Trick 5.   West leads ♠ 10, North discards ◇ 5, East discards ♣ 10, and South discards ♡ 3. The squeeze has oozed the life out of East's hand. East has to give up his club stopper.

Trick 6.   West leads ♡ 2, North plays ♡ A, East plays ♡ 9, and South plays ♡ 4.

Trick 7.   North leads ♣ 4, East plays ♣ J, South plays ♣ Q, and West plays ♣ 2.

Trick 8.   South leads ♣ A, West plays ♣ 3, North plays ♣ 6, and East plays ♣ K.

Trick 9.   South leads ♣ 5, West plays ♣ 7, North plays ♣ 8, and East plays ?.

At this point, East is under the gun and must give up either his heart stopper or diamond stopper. Whichever he does, the balance of the tricks belong to the Declarer. When West was persuaded to go on with his spades, he mercilessly squeezed his Partner to the point where South's last club could squeeze him again. This was really a progressive squeeze, in which the first pressure was applied in one suit and then in another suit.

Summary

Aside from the number of suits or the number of Opponents concerned in a squeeze play, there may be said to be *sure* squeezes and *attempts* at squeezes. The sure squeeze appears when, from the bidding or otherwise, the Declarer is able to get a fairly accurate count on the Opponents' hand from the start, and can see at once that there is a squeeze and that it must work. This does not happen very often. A squeeze play is frequently *attempted*, however, when it is *possible* or perhaps even *probable* that the adverse cards lie right for the squeeze, and the Declarer proceeds on that assumption, often when it is his only chance to make his contract, and sometimes to avoid the alternative of some more risky play. He may, of course, be reduced at the end to taking the risky play after all, if the squeeze fails to come out as planned. In the pseudo-squeeze, a squeeze play is not actually attempted, since the Declarer knows what his Opponents do not know—that he does not hold the necessary equipment to effect a squeeze. But in the pseudo-squeeze the Declarer hopes to throw dust in the eyes of his Opponents and make them *think* that they are being squeezed, so that one of them may make the wrong discard.

The preparation for a squeeze takes three steps, as follows: (1) counting the Opponents' hands to perceive the squeeze possibility, (2) stripping down the hands so that all harmless discards will be eliminated, and (3) leading the final "squeeze" card on which the luckless Opponent must throw away a trick against his wishes. Sometimes a single Opponent may be squeezed so that he will have to throw off a card which will put him in a position to be squeezed by the lead of *that* suit later—this is the progressive squeeze. It is even possible, occasionally, to induce that Opponent's Partner to lead cards to which he cannot follow suit, thereby effecting the first blow of the progressive squeeze.

The equipment the Declarer needs to effect a squeeze, aside from his ability to count and think ahead, must include a long suit on which the Opponents are obliged to discard, first, all their worthless cards, and, at last, some valuable card which sets up a trick for the Declarer. If the squeeze is to be double—in three suits, effecting pressure in two suits on one Opponent, and in two suits on the other Opponent, one suit being the same in both hands—the commanding card of one suit must be in one Opponent's hand, and the commanding card of the other Opponent's suit must be in the *other* Opponent's hand. The third suit is one that the Declarer has not touched, but in which he holds control, as a rule, of the first two rounds, thereby obliging his Opponents each to try to keep control of the third round. When the double squeeze becomes effective, each Opponent finds it impossible to keep both his commanding card in one suit and his protection in the other. In the third suit, common to both Opponents, the Declarer must have entries into both hands, to maintain his communications if one Opponent should decide to throw off his commanding card instead of abandon his protection.

A squeeze is effective only when the Declarer has sure tricks within 1 trick of his contract. Other factors being present, the squeeze may gain the needed trick.

The Vienna Coup is a form of preparation for a squeeze play, in which the Declarer sets up a high card in an Opponent's hand so that, when the squeeze is applied, the only choice will be between throwing off that high card and some other valuable card.

CHAPTER VIII

TWO UNUSUAL ECHOES

I~N~ addition to the ordinary echo given along with the other fundamental principles (in Part I), there are two other interesting and
occasionally useful echoes, or conventional discards. They consist
of a trump echo and a no-trump echo.

In Auction Bridge, the trump echo was known as "the three-card
peter,"* and was always used to inform Partner of the fact that three
trumps were held. For example, if a defensive player held, in the
trump suit, the eight, five and deuce, he would play the five-spot
on the first lead of trumps, and follow with the deuce on the second
round, to convey the information that an additional trump was held.
If he failed to use this echo, his failure told his Partner that he held
originally either two trumps or four.

The experience of Contract players has modified this convention
to make it more useful. At Contract Bridge, a player should not echo
in trumps simply because he held three of them originally, but he
should confine his echoing to show ability to ruff some side suit.

THE TRUMP ECHO

Following are two complete deals which illustrate the trump echo:

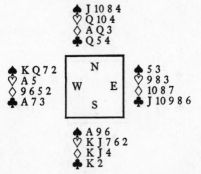

```
              ♠ J 10 8 4
              ♡ Q 10 4
              ◇ A Q 3
              ♣ Q 5 4
                  ┌─────────┐
  ♠ K Q 7 2       │    N    │       ♠ 5 3
  ♡ A 5           │         │       ♡ 9 8 3
  ◇ 9 6 5 2       │  W   E  │       ◇ 10 8 7
  ♣ A 7 3         │         │       ♣ J 10 9 8 6
                  │    S    │
                  └─────────┘
              ♠ A 9 6
              ♡ K J 7 6 2
              ◇ K J 4
              ♣ K 2
```

---

* The word *peter* as used here has no relation to the masculine name Peter. The
origin may be traced back to the *blue peter*, a trump signal (calling for a trump lead
from Partner) used in Whist, which was so called from the nautical term *blue peter*,
a corruption of "blue repeater," used in signalling with flags. The "three-card
peter" was merely a loose modification of the original Whist term, to indicate a signal
made *in* the trump suit, but not to induce Partner to lead trumps.

With neither side vulnerable, the bidding has gone:

SOUTH	WEST	NORTH	EAST
One Heart	One Spade	Two Hearts	Pass
Four Hearts	Pass	Pass	Pass

West opens the King of spades, on which East plays the five and South the Ace. This leaves West in something of a quandary, for he does not know whether his Partner is starting an echo in spades or not. At the second trick, South leads a heart, which—we will assume for the sake of argument—West ducks. Dummy plays the Ten, and *East plays the eight.* Now the Queen of hearts is led, and *East plays the three.* West wins this trick with the Ace, and he now knows, through the trump echo used by East, that East has one more heart. He also knows that East wants to ruff something, and the only possibility is spades. He therefore lays down his Queen of spades and East is enabled to complete his echo in that suit by playing the trey. West follows with a third round of spades, which East ruffs. Of course, West must also make his Ace of clubs, and the contract is defeated.

If this convention of the trump echo were not used in the foregoing example, West would be forced to guess whether to continue spades or shift to diamonds. It is true that he might now and then guess correctly, but the trump echo convention eliminates the uncertainty.

The following deal illustrates the reverse of the principle:

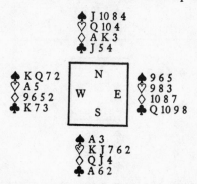

```
                    ♠ J 10 8 4
                    ♡ Q 10 4
                    ◇ A K 3
                    ♣ J 5 4
♠ K Q 7 2        ┌──────────┐      ♠ 9 6 5
♡ A 5            │    N     │      ♡ 9 8 3
◇ 9 6 5 2        │  W   E   │      ◇ 10 8 7
♣ K 7 3          │    S     │      ♣ Q 10 9 8
                 └──────────┘
                    ♠ A 3
                    ♡ K J 7 6 2
                    ◇ Q J 4
                    ♣ A 6 2
```

The bidding is the same as on the preceding example, neither side vulnerable.

West opens the spade King, and East still plays the five (not starting an echo this time, though his Partner does not yet know it), and South wins the trick with the Ace. Now the heart lead proceeds in the same fashion, but this time East plays the *three* of hearts on the first round and the *eight* on the second. Therefore, when West gets in the lead, he will know that East does *not* want to trump spades, and consequently West will shift to some other suit. West, guessing that a diamond trick cannot be established in time, shifts to clubs, and East and West thereupon make 2 club tricks, 1 heart trick, and 1 spade trick. On this deal the negative inference was even more valuable than the positive inference in the preceding example.

THE NO-TRUMP ECHO

The no-trump echo is another interesting little gadget for signalling purposes. It is used to show the possession of only two cards of a suit when a long suit in the Dummy threatens to become established. It enables the hand holding the controlling cards to count the distribution of this particular suit with unerring accuracy, and frequently stops him from making an unnecessary hold-up. The no-trump echo may, like the trump echo, also be used negatively, which makes it an extremely valuable convention.

The following deal shows the positive use of the no-trump echo:

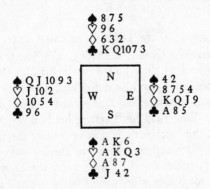

With neither side vulnerable, the bidding has gone:

SOUTH	WEST	NORTH	EAST
Two No-trump	Pass	Three No-trump	Pass
Pass	Pass		

West opens the Queen of spades, and South wins the trick with the King—as South does not want a shift to diamonds. He now leads the Jack of clubs and *West should play the nine*. The nine-spot starts an echo, telling Partner that he has only two clubs. East can therefore count South's hand as containing two more clubs (when West's next play is the six), and consequently should refuse to take the Ace of clubs until the third round. This effectively shuts the Dummy out of the play, and South must go down 1 trick, for he can then take only 2 club tricks, 1 diamond trick, 3 heart tricks, and 2 spade tricks. Without this convention, East would be hard put to it to guess how many clubs Declarer held originally in his own hand.

The negative inference of the no-trump echo is illustrated in the following deal:

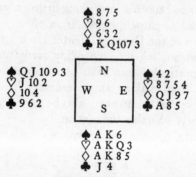

```
                  ♠ 8 7 5
                  ♡ 9 6
                  ◇ 6 3 2
                  ♣ K Q 10 7 3
                  ┌─────────────┐
♠ Q J 10 9 3      │      N      │      ♠ 4 2
♡ J 10 2          │             │      ♡ 8 7 5 4
◇ 10 4            │  W       E  │      ◇ Q J 9 7
♣ 9 6 2           │             │      ♣ A 8 5
                  │      S      │
                  └─────────────┘
                  ♠ A K 6
                  ♡ A K Q 3
                  ◇ A K 8 5
                  ♣ J 4
```

Assume South again to be the Declarer at three no-trump.

West again opens the Queen of spades, and South wins with the King, leading the Jack of clubs to the second trick. West plays the deuce, Dummy goes in low, and East holds off with his Ace *for the first round only*. West's discouraging (low) card (followed by a higher one—the six) tells East that his Partner holds *more than two clubs*, which means that the Declarer could have had at the most only two in his own hand. East can therefore win the second round of clubs with perfect safety, automatically shutting off the Dummy. This is very worth while, for if Declarer is allowed to make 2 club tricks on this deal, he will make his contract.

<h3 align="center">SUMMARY</h3>

The trump echo—the play of a high trump on the first round of the suit, followed by a lower trump on the next round—indicates the possession of at least one more trump and also the possession of ruffing power in a side suit. Acting upon this signal, Partner may be instructed to play in a way that will defeat the Declarer's contract. Failure to echo in trumps indicates that no ruffing power in another suit is held.

The no-trump echo—the play of a high card on the first round of the suit, followed by a lower card on the next round—indicates the possession of a doubleton in a suit of which the visible Dummy holds practically all the high cards, and thereby gives Partner an accurate count on the number of cards held by the Declarer. When the Dummy has no outside entries, this echo tells Partner whether to hold up, and, if so, for how many rounds. Failure to employ the echo tells Partner that more than two cards are held in the suit. *

* See Chapter XIII for a modern corollary to this convention.—S. F. Jr.

CHAPTER IX

MISCELLANEOUS ADVANCED PLAYS

THIS miscellany of advanced plays and playing principles is thrown together here because the examples included do not fit into any other category. They illustrate situations that occur rather frequently and that require special treatment. The reader must not get the notion that this chapter is not important; the situations dealt with here are vital, but the fact that they cannot be grouped logically with other types of plays simply goes to show that the subject of the play of the hand is peculiarly difficult of classification and codification.

HOLDING UP WITH KING-QUEEN AND WITH QUEEN-JACK

When the elementary form of the hold-up was considered (in Part I), it was mentioned that this very useful play has other forms.

In the following deal the King-Queen hold-up is illustrated:

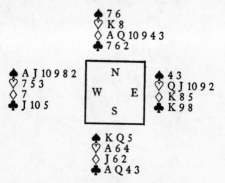

♠ 7 6
♡ K 8
♢ A Q 10 9 4 3
♣ 7 6 2

♠ A J 10 9 8 2   ♠ 4 3
♡ 7 5 3   ♡ Q J 10 9 2
♢ 7   ♢ K 8 5
♣ J 10 5   ♣ K 9 8

♠ K Q 5
♡ A 6 4
♢ J 6 2
♣ A Q 4 3

With neither side vulnerable, the bidding has gone:

SOUTH	WEST	NORTH	EAST
One Club	One Spade	Two Diamonds	Two Hearts
Two No-trump	Pass	Three No-trump	Pass
Pass	Pass		

West, not forgetting that his Partner has bid hearts, still decides to open his own suit, and comes out with the Jack of spades. The whole point of the hand occurs right away: *South must allow the Jack to hold the first trick.* He knows that by so doing he abandons all chance of making 2 spade tricks, but he also saves himself from being set if East has only two spades and the King of diamonds.

After the hold-up, West can either continue spades or shift to hearts. It makes no difference which, as his hand is shut out of the play completely from this point on. Note that if South wins the first trick with his Queen of spades, he is forced to allow East to get in the lead later with the King of diamonds, and East would then return his other spade, enabling West to take 5 spade tricks. This hold-up, or ducking of the first trick, is really a sort of safety play, for it is made to protect the Declarer against a possible spade doubleton plus the King of diamonds on his right.

The following deal illustrates the Queen-Jack hold-up:

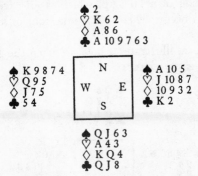

```
                    ♠ 2
                    ♡ K 6 2
                    ◇ A 8 6
                    ♣ A 10 9 7 6 3

  ♠ K 9 8 7 4           N           ♠ A 10 5
  ♡ Q 9 5                            ♡ J 10 8 7
  ◇ J 7 5        W         E         ◇ 10 9 3 2
  ♣ 5 4                              ♣ K 2
                        S

                    ♠ Q J 6 3
                    ♡ A 4 3
                    ◇ K Q 4
                    ♣ Q J 8
```

With neither side vulnerable, the bidding has gone:

SOUTH	WEST	NORTH	EAST
One No-trump	Pass	Three No-trump	Pass
Pass	Pass		

The opening lead by West is the seven of spades, won by East with the Ace. The Ten of spades is returned, and South must hold up— or duck, whichever you want to call it. If he plays the Jack, West will play the four, thereby establishing a tenace over the Declarer, so that, when East regains the lead (with the club King) and leads back another spade, West will run off 3 spade tricks.

For Declarer to hold up here can do no harm and it may save the contract. After the Ten of spades is allowed to hold the second trick, it makes no difference whether West later holds off or not, as East will be exhausted of the suit. In other words, the Declarer, by holding up on the second trick, will lose only 3 spade tricks and 1 club trick.

The hand just given also has another interesting point. If East had played the Ten of spades instead of the Ace on the first trick, South would have been put in a bad spot. If South thought East was deliberately holding back either the Ace or the King, he should duck, of course. However, if both the Ace and the King should be in the West hand, the duck will be a losing play as East can come through the Declarer twice. However, the Ten of spades on the first trick is an almost impossible play for East to make, since West might be leading from the King-Jack, when the Ten simply loses a trick to an unguarded Queen. Taking everything into consideration, the play of the Ten by East is a little far-fetched, but with the play of the Ace on the first trick the subsequent play by the Declarer was marked.

Another variation of a hold-up, which is an exception to a rule learned in Part I, occurs when you are desirous of keeping a certain hand out of the lead.

The following deal illustrates a hold-up when the King and Queen are divided between two hands:

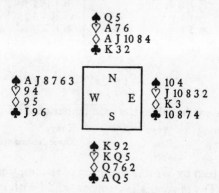

The seven of spades is opened by West, against South's contract of three no-trump.

As explained in Part I, Declarer's best chance of obtaining 2 tricks in spades lies in going up with the Queen in Dummy. In this particular case, however, he is not interested in 2 spade tricks. All he wants to do is to keep West out of the lead. If he plays the Queen and East eventually obtains the lead with the King of diamonds, the King in his own hand will be led through and captured. He should therefore play low from the Dummy and also play low from his own hand, when East plays the Ten. This effectively shuts the West hand out of the play entirely.

AN ACE-KING HOLD-UP TO AVOID A GUESS

The following deal illustrates still another variation of the hold-up:

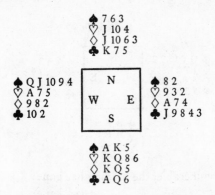

```
                    ♠ 7 6 3
                    ♡ J 10 4
                    ◇ J 10 6 3
                    ♣ K 7 5
     ♠ Q J 10 9 4         N         ♠ 8 2
     ♡ A 7 5                         ♡ 9 3 2
     ◇ 9 8 2          W       E      ◇ A 7 4
     ♣ 10 2                          ♣ J 9 8 4 3
                         S
                    ♠ A K 5
                    ♡ K Q 8 6
                    ◇ K Q 5
                    ♣ A Q 6
```

With neither side vulnerable, the bidding has gone:

SOUTH	WEST	NORTH	EAST
Two No-trump	Pass	Three No-trump	Pass
Pass	Pass		

West's opening lead is the spade Queen, and South must refuse to win this trick for a very good reason. If the spades against him are divided 4-3, he can lose only 2 spade tricks and two Aces. If they are divided 5-2, he may be in danger of losing his contract. In order to make 9 tricks, he must establish both diamonds and hearts, and he must therefore guess which Ace is held by which Opponent. If he should win the first spade trick, and decide in favor of starting diamonds, East will be able to return the spade suit and West will eventually obtain the lead with the Ace of hearts and set the contract.

It is true that if South should start to establish hearts first, he can still make his contract, but this is nothing but a guess, pure and simple. The hold-up on the first trick can lose only if West held five spades originally and *both* Aces, in which case the hand cannot be made anyway.

ESTABLISHING A TRICK IN A SHORT SUIT FIRST

The ensuing deal shows the occasional necessity of establishing a trick at no-trump in a short suit before the long suit is tackled at all. In this deal, this must be done in order to make sure that the hand with the established tricks can never obtain the lead:

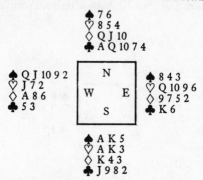

```
                ♠ 7 6
                ♡ 8 5 4
                ◇ Q J 10
                ♣ A Q 10 7 4
  ♠ Q J 10 9 2    ┌─────────┐   ♠ 8 4 3
  ♡ J 7 2         │    N    │   ♡ Q 10 9 6
  ◇ A 8 6       W │         │ E ◇ 9 7 5 2
  ♣ 5 3           │    S    │   ♣ K 6
                  └─────────┘
                ♠ A K 5
                ♡ A K 3
                ◇ K 4 3
                ♣ J 9 8 2
```

With both sides vulnerable, the bidding has gone:

SOUTH	WEST	NORTH	EAST
One No-trump	Pass	Two No-trump	Pass
Three No-trump	Pass	Pass	Pass

West opens the Queen of spades and South allows this card to hold the trick. This sort of hold-up can do no harm, and may strip the East hand of spades. When a spade is continued, South wins the second trick with the King. His first impulse is to take his club finesse, but a simple count of the tricks which are available to him will show him that such a precipitate course is wrong. If the club finesse works, he can run off 9 tricks without even bothering about the diamond suit, but if the club finesse loses, he will have only 8 tricks, and the spades will be established against him before the Ace of diamonds is put out of the fight. If East holds the diamond Ace, all will still be well, but if it should lie in the West hand and if West held five spades originally, the diamond Ace will defeat the Declarer. The point is that Declarer must make sure of 1 diamond trick at once.

At the third trick, therefore, South leads a low diamond, and the trick will probably be won with Dummy's Ten. Having the ninth trick tucked safely away, South can return to the Ace of hearts and take the club finesse. This will lose, but the Declarer need not worry now, since he can make his contract with a total of 2 spade tricks, 2 heart tricks, 1 diamond trick, and 4 club tricks.

Note that the play cannot possibly lose. Leading the diamond first simply provides against a 5-3 distribution of spades. If the spades are adversely divided 4-4, the Declarer cannot lose more than 4 tricks anyway. Note also that immediately taking the club finesse allows East and West to set the contract, as East can knock out South's last spade stopper upon obtaining the lead with the club King, and West will simply retain two good spades and his Ace of diamonds for the last 3 tricks.

Leading into a Tenace—The Time Element

The following deal illustrates a very pretty play:

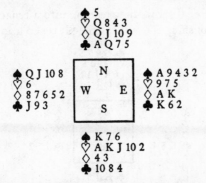

With East and West vulnerable, the bidding has gone:

South	West	North	East
One Heart	Pass	Three Hearts	Pass
Four Hearts	Pass	Pass	Pass

East was rather disappointed because he could hardly get into the bidding at the range of three-odd, but he is amply repaid later.

West opens the Queen of spades, and East wins the trick with the Ace. He immediately sees that his Partner will never be able to regain the lead, and consequently that his short diamond suit can be of no value (South's opening bid marked him with at least the Ace-King of hearts and the King of spades). There are in sight 3 sure tricks, but where is the fourth one necessary to set the contract? East sees one chance. He leads a low club away from his King into the Ace-Queen tenace in the Dummy. Declarer plays low, and West's nine forces the Dummy's Queen.

The Declarer then draws trumps and puts East in the lead with the King of diamonds. Another low club is led by East, and West's Jack forces Dummy's Ace. Declarer now cannot help giving up 1 more club trick and 1 diamond trick.

Note the importance of the time element in this example. An instant's delay will give the Declarer time to establish his diamonds and discard his losing clubs. If delayed, the play is worthless.

LEADING INTO A TENACE TO ESTABLISH A SUIT

The following deal shows how leading into a tenace may, on occasion, aid in establishing the suit for the player so leading:

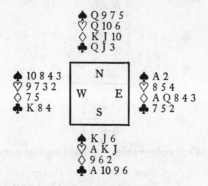

♠ Q 9 7 5
♡ Q 10 6
♢ K J 10
♣ Q J 3

♠ 10 8 4 3
♡ 9 7 3 2
♢ 7 5
♣ K 8 4

♠ A 2
♡ 8 5 4
♢ A Q 8 4 3
♣ 7 5 2

♠ K J 6
♡ A K J
♢ 9 6 2
♣ A 10 9 6

With both sides vulnerable, the bidding has gone:

SOUTH	WEST	NORTH	EAST
One No-trump	Pass	Three No-trump	Pass
Pass	Pass		

West's opening lead is the three of spades, which East wins with the Ace. It is apparent at once to East that the return of the suit is quite meaningless. The only chance left is diamonds, and East must underlead his Ace-Queen. This trick is won with Dummy's Ten. Declarer now counts his tricks and finds that he has but 8 available. He must therefore take the club finesse, and West, upon obtaining the

lead with the King, returns a diamond through Dummy's now useless
King-Jack.   This lead defeats the contract by 2 tricks.

If East had waited for his Partner to lead diamonds, South's contract would have been made without interference.

THE TIME ELEMENT AND THE OPENING LEAD

The following deal   shows the time element at the height of its
power and influence:

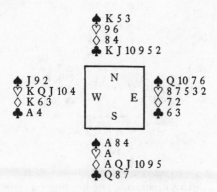

```
                        ♠ K 5 3
                        ♡ 9 6
                        ◇ 8 4
                        ♣ K J 10 9 5 2

        ♠ J 9 2          ┌─────────┐         ♠ Q 10 7 6
        ♡ K Q J 10 4     │    N    │         ♡ 8 7 5 3 2
        ◇ K 6 3          │  W   E  │         ◇ 7 2
        ♣ A 4            │    S    │         ♣ 6 3
                         └─────────┘
                        ♠ A 8 4
                        ♡ A
                        ◇ A Q J 10 9 5
                        ♣ Q 8 7
```

With both sides vulnerable, the bidding has gone:

SOUTH	WEST	NORTH	EAST
One Diamond	One Heart	Two Clubs	Two Hearts
Five Diamonds	Pass	Pass	Pass

From the bidding, West decided that his Partner's raise must be
based entirely on length in hearts.   He is pretty sure of obtaining a
diamond trick and a club trick, but he does not have much faith in
the heart suit as a trick-producer.   The Opponents seem to have all
the high cards except those in West's hand, but West finally comes to
the conclusion that there is a chance that his Partner may hold the
Queen-Ten of spades.

On this assumption, West opens the deuce of spades, and continues
with the nine when he gets in later with the diamond King.   This
makes it impossible for the Declarer to shut out his spade trick, and
so he is defeated 1 trick.   With the normal opening of the heart

King, the spades cannot be brought in in time and the clubs are bound to afford ample discards. This appreciation of the time element in the opening lead is most important in a great many contracts.

Unnecessarily Giving Up a Trump Trick

The following deal shows how a trump trick, given up apparently without having to relinquish it, can mean a great deal as a judicious sacrifice:

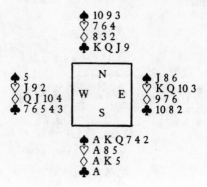

```
              ♠ 10 9 3
              ♡ 7 6 4
              ◇ 8 3 2
              ♣ K Q J 9

  ♠ 5              N              ♠ J 8 6
  ♡ J 9 2                        ♡ K Q 10 3
  ◇ Q J 10 4    W       E        ◇ 9 7 6
  ♣ 7 6 5 4 3      S             ♣ 10 8 2

              ♠ A K Q 7 4 2
              ♡ A 8 5
              ◇ A K 5
              ♣ A
```

With North and South vulnerable, the bidding has gone:

South	West	North	East
Two Spades	Pass	Three Clubs	Pass
Three Spades	Pass	Four Spades	Pass
Six Spades	Pass	Pass	Pass

South's opening bid is forcing to game, but the bidding after that seems a bit optimistic. North may perhaps be excused for bidding *three clubs* in view of the honors he holds in addition to what South's opening bid must show, but he should certainly bid *three no-trump* in response to Partner's *three spades*. As North responds, South cannot be blamed for undertaking the Slam.

West's opening lead is the diamond Queen, won by Declarer's King. The six-odd contract would be secure, sure enough, if the Dummy only had a sure re-entry. But, unfortunately, the only chance of getting into the Dummy seems to be in the trump suit. If the adverse trumps are divided 2-2, the Ten will prove to be an entry, but if either Opponent holds three spades to the Jack, the Dummy will be completely shut out of the play.

On the second trick, Declarer should lay down the Ace of spades in the hope that the Jack will fall. When the Jack does not appear, he should lay down the Ace of clubs in order to unblock the suit. Then he should lead a low spade to the nine in Dummy, deliberately allowing the missing Jack to win the trick. With only one spade left among the missing, the Ten becomes a sure entry, and the Declarer can discard his own 3 losing tricks on the three high clubs in Dummy.

Had South simply led out his high spade, the Jack would not have fallen, and he would have gone down 2 tricks. Of course, the Opponents can defeat this hand by opening the heart suit at the first trick, but West can hardly be expected to be clairvoyant enough to know it.

Choosing Between Two Re-entries

The deal below involves a choice between two re-entries. It so happens that the choice is important, for on the re-entry selected depends the success of the contract.

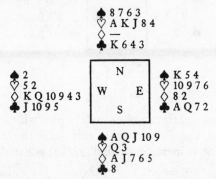

♠ 8 7 6 3
♡ A K J 8 4
◇ —
♣ K 6 4 3

N
W E
S

♠ 2
♡ 5 2
◇ K Q 10 9 4 3
♣ J 10 9 5

♠ K 5 4
♡ 10 9 7 6
◇ 8 2
♣ A Q 7 2

♠ A Q J 10 9
♡ Q 3
◇ A J 7 6 5
♣ 8

With North and South vulnerable, the bidding has gone:

South	West	North	East
One Spade	Two Diamonds	Two Hearts	Pass
Two Spades	Three Diamonds	Four Diamonds	Pass
Four Spades	Pass	Five Spades	Pass
Six Spades	Pass	Pass	Pass

West's opening lead is the club Jack, on which the King is played from the Dummy. East wins the trick with the Ace and returns the Queen, which Declarer ruffs. South must now get into the Dummy in order to take the spade finesse. He must enter the Dummy by means of the diamond void. He does so by ruffing a diamond, taking the spade finesse, and going over to Dummy by ruffing another diamond, taking the spade finesse a second time. Then he leads out his Ace of spades, and then lays down the Queen of hearts. In this way he cannot fail to make his contract.

Notice, however, that if South decides to enter the Dummy by means of hearts, leading a low heart first for the purpose, he will subsequently be blocked and he will have to overtake the Queen of hearts with a higher card in the Dummy, thereby establishing East's Ten. In such a situation, with the entries by means of ruffing available, the better play is to risk a possible over-ruff.

Keeping the Dangerous Hand out of the Lead

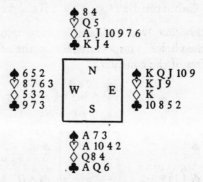

This hand involves a variation of the safety play which is used to try and keep the hand with an established suit out of the lead.

With neither side vulnerable, the bidding has gone:

South	West	North	East
One No-trump	Pass	Three No-trump	Pass
Pass	Pass		

West, on lead and faced with a choice of nothings, finally guesses the spade suit, selecting the six. East plays the nine. Declarer holds off for two rounds, but is forced to win the third. It is at once apparent that the success or failure of the contract depends on the diamond suit, and that the finesse against the King seems to be the only chance. However, does the actual finesse really matter? If West holds the King and is allowed to take a trick with it he will not be able to lead spades to his Partner's established suit, as was proved by his opening of the six-spot (this marks East with K Q J 10 9, and three rounds have been played).   If East holds it the contract is lost anyway—unless he holds it alone!

The proper play, then, is for the Declarer to lead a low diamond and go right up with the Ace in Dummy.   As it happens the King drops and four no-trump is made.   What if it had failed to drop?   A low diamond would be led in the hope that West still held the King. Then three no-trump would still be made.   The slight additional margin of safety turns out in this case to be very important.

TRUMPING YOUR PARTNER'S ACE

Of all famous Bridge jokes, the best known probably concerns the man who trumped his partner's Ace and thereafter underwent all the agonies of the dunce in the country schoolhouse.   Strange as it may seem, such a play may turn out to be a brilliant piece of strategy, as witness the following deal:

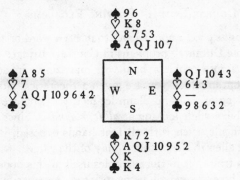

```
                    ♠ 9 6
                    ♡ K 8
                    ♢ 8 7 5 3
                    ♣ A Q J 10 7

    ♠ A 8 5            N            ♠ Q J 10 4 3
    ♡ 7                             ♡ 6 4 3
    ♢ A Q J 10 9 6 4 2  W    E     ♢ —
    ♣ 5                 S          ♣ 9 8 6 3 2

                    ♠ K 7 2
                    ♡ A Q J 10 9 5 2
                    ♢ K
                    ♣ K 4
```

With both sides vulnerable, the bidding has gone:

WEST	NORTH	EAST	SOUTH
One Diamond	Two Clubs	Pass	Four Hearts
Five Diamonds	Pass	Pass	Five Hearts
Pass	Pass	Pass	

West opens the Ace of diamonds and East must reflect before he decides what card to play.   His partner has bid five diamonds all by himself, even though vulnerable, and obviously lacks the King of this suit, as he has opened the Ace.   It would seem, then, as though he must hold *eight* diamonds in order to justify this bid, together with some outside trick.   This outside trick can only be a spade honor.

If East discards either a low spade or a low club, the Ace will drop Declarer's lone King, but thereafter East and West can win nothing but the Ace of spades, and even this card must be cashed immediately! Otherwise Declarer can discard all his spade losers on the long clubs in Dummy after he has drawn trumps. There is one chance, and East must take it. He must trump his Partner's Ace and return the Queen of spades in the hope that Declarer holds the spade King and his Partner the Ace. This is his only chance to obtain the lead in order to come through the spades, and he must take advantage of it.

Of course the play succeeds and the contract of five hearts is defeated 1 trick. The play seems difficult, but actually involves only an intelligent piece of deduction. If West has eight diamonds it is essential, and even if he holds only seven all is not lost if he still holds the Ace of spades. All in all, it represents the best chance of defeating the contract.

"Double Dummy" Playing Problems

This is perhaps as good a spot as any to insert a word or two about so-called "Double Dummy" problems in Contract Bridge. You will frequently run across problem hands in magazines, in advertising matter, and so on, in which you are given a theoretical situation requiring the making of a Grand Slam, let us say. You are supposed to solve the problem while looking at *all four hands*. Since the problem is really difficult, even with all four hands exposed, it becomes something quite alien to the ordinary play of the game.

Although it is true that in the examples used in this book the four hands are usually exposed, all being printed, necessarily, in plain sight on the page, there are no real "Double Dummy" problems* among them. Every hand presents a situation which can be logically analyzed by a player who sees only his own cards and those in the Dummy that are exposed in regular Bridge.

---

* The "Double Dummy" problem came to be so called from the Whist game of Double Dummy, a variant of ordinary Whist, intended for two persons, each with an exposed or dummy hand for a partner. In the actual Double Dummy Bridge problem, there are really four dummies, or, if you like, one player and three dummies, for the one player manages all the hands to arrive at a solution which will work against any possible defense by the opposing side. Many difficult Double Dummy problems involve fantastic squeeze plays, discards, etc., which could not by any stretch of the imagination ever be planned by the world's most masterly player if he could not always see all four hands.

A Double Dummy problem hand really does not teach Bridge tactics at all. It is on a par with an end game in chess, or with a problem in algebra. You can manipulate the cards any way you like to reach a solution, the only requirement being that you lead and follow suit as in the actual game of Bridge. Otherwise the Double Dummy problem does not even remotely resemble Bridge. Such tactics as safety plays, deception, and counting have no possible place.

A careful line must be drawn, then, between the Double Dummy problem, as such, and the printed Bridge hand which, for lack of any other way of presenting the deal to a single reader at a time, shows all four hands also. The Bridge hand intended as an example of actual play requires wholly different approach on the part of the reader. In seeking to get the greatest benefit from an example hand, such as those printed in this book and those printed in daily newspaper articles on Contract Bridge, the reader should look only at his own hand, putting himself in the place of but one player at the table, and try to deduce from his own thirteen cards and the Dummy (as soon as it is exposed—after the opening lead has been made) what *he* would do if he were confronted with this situation in actual play. To this end it may prove advantageous to cover the two hands which would be concealed in normal play. After a plan of play has been made in this fashion, the reader's perspicuity can then be checked with reference to the covered hands, and to the explanatory text.

This note on Double Dummy or exposed hands is appended here chiefly to dispel a prevalent notion that Bridge experts claim to be miracle workers. Many average players have seen certain Double Dummy hands, and have been frankly skeptical that even the greatest player in the world could solve them—without seeing all the cards. If the hand is really a Double Dummy problem, and correspondingly intricate, the skeptical readers are perfectly right. In fact, there are many expert Bridge players who are not at all adept at working out Double Dummy problems, and who, if the truth must be told, do not care to become any better at it, for the very good reason that the technique is entirely different from actual play. There are also a number of good Double Dummy experts, who are "puzzle solvers" at heart, but who are about average when it comes to the contest of wits in an honest-to-goodness rubber.

DUPLICATE STRATEGY

The differences between play at Duplicate Bridge and play at Rubber Bridge are not as great as the differences in bidding.

Play at team-of-four matches, which are always scored at total points, is approximately the same as at Rubber Bridge, but match point play for pairs, either by the Howell or the Mitchell method, is sometimes quite different. For example, a player who has reached a contract of four spades might on occasion risk getting set when his bid is assured, merely for the sake of obtaining an extra trick. This extra trick, which counts only 30 points in regular Bridge, can very easily give him a top score on the board.

This is not generally good policy, however, and a play of this type should not be made unless the percentages are very much in favor of its success, or unless the pair has so bad a score at the moment that very desperate measures are required. With a good score, the tendency should be to play for average and let the other pairs worry about the tops.

The other main difference revolves around the fact that a pair is often liable to get into the wrong contract. For instance, suppose that you found yourself at one no-trump and saw immediately that the hand was a lay-down for three hearts. If it seemed that most other teams would play the hand at hearts, you would then be forced to try desperate means to make—not two no-trump, as this would count only 70 as against the 90 produced by three hearts—but three no-trump! Even if you went down in the process, this loss would probably involve very few match points. However, if the hand were such that it seemed likely that most pairs would reach four hearts and go down one, then the best thing to do would be to play safe and assure yourself of a plus score.

So far as technique—attack or defense—is concerned, it is the same in Duplicate Bridge as in Rubber Bridge.

SUMMARY

Not much can be said in summarizing this chapter, since the points involved depend so greatly on the specific instance. You were told that a hold-up of a King-Queen or a Queen-Jack suit might occasionally prove profitable, when there is a specific reason for so doing. You were shown the advantage, or rather the necessity, sometimes, of establishing a trick in a short suit, at no-trump, before proceeding to the more lucrative business of setting up a long suit. You were informed that an Ace-King suit should be held up under certain circumstances, to eliminate a guess. And, contrary to the rules laid down in Part I, you had demonstrated to you the occasional value of deliberately leading into an adverse tenace—to prevent the Declarer from establishing a suit before your own setting trick was in sight, or to establish a suit which otherwise could not be set up. The time element was a vital factor in practically all of these situations. You were also shown a rather spectacular example of trumping your partner's Ace, and a less spectacular, but perhaps more valuable case, where a chance of dropping a singleton King was taken just for a little bit of extra safety.

The principal lesson of the chapter should be that a good player always looks about him before he plunges ahead with his play. He tries to see whether normal play will make his contract, and, if not, he casts about for something which, even if a departure from the normal, may give him a chance. Very often playing for the only chance will not result in victory, but the fact that it fails is no worse a blow than certain defeat without such an attempt being made, and the fact that it occasionally succeeds is ample reward for perceiving the possibility.

CHAPTER X

PSYCHOLOGICAL STRATEGY

ALL the knowledge of cards in the world, and even the highly perfect ability to count accurately, will not necessarily make you a great Bridge player. If you know all the principles of sound play, and even all of the involved situations which require special treatment, you cannot rise to the heights until you have learned how to *deceive*. This necessity for deception—of one's adversaries, of course, and not of one's Partner (except when it cannot be helped)—has led to the many analogies drawn between Bridge and warfare. Camouflage, the masking of batteries, the bluff show of strength not possessed, the feint attacks, the ambushes, the covered retreats, the drawing of the enemy's fire, all are forms of deception used in military strategy. They do not all have exact counterparts in Contract Bridge strategy, but deceptive tactics certainly have their vital place.

Deception in the bidding has been widely publicized as "psychic" bidding. When bluff bids were first introduced, they were extremely effective because no one knew quite how to cope with them. They were like the first use of poison gas in warfare, because they came without warning. Also like poison gas, they might be blown back against their maker by an adverse breeze caused by Partner's confusion, and this was both their drawback and their fascination. To make a bluff bid has the allure of trying to run unscathed through a rain of bullets. However, everyone is now on the alert for a psychic bid, and much of the effectiveness of such bidding tactics has been lost, while a great deal of their danger remains. Many players, thinking they are being cleverly deceptive, make what are only suicidal bids, deceiving everybody at the table, including themselves.

Even if bluff and surprise bids go entirely by the board, however, there is still plenty of room for deception in the play of the hand. Deceptive and startling plays are quite as effective as deceptive and startling bids, and very often more so, while they usually lack the dire consequences of a bluff bid unwisely made. Such deceptive plays may take the form of a high card unnecessarily thrown off, a discard made at a time when it will greatly confuse an Opponent, a trick refused for a reason the Opponent can only guess, or a trump played when it apparently sacrifices a trick. Such plays often succeed in implanting incorrect impressions in the minds of those you are striving to defeat.

Lack of imagination is to be deplored in any activity, but it is particularly pathetic in Bridge playing. A player who lacks imagination can only be described as wooden; he plays like an automaton, and can be relied upon with as much confidence as a chemist can be sure of a chemical reaction under any given conditions. Such woodenness makes the player's moves an open book to his Opponents, and he becomes easy prey. And it is just as wooden to make unnatural plays often, as it is never to make them at all. Certainly it is just as harmful to gain a reputation for always false-carding, as it is to be ticketed as a player who never false-cards. If a deceptive play is injected when it is least expected, however, it may become the means of making a contract or the means of defeating an apparently unbeatable hand.

In this chapter are presented a number of deceptive plays and maneuvers:

FALSE-CARDING

False-carding is simply the play of a card which is the unnatural one for the player to select under the circumstances. False-carding by the Defending Side is much more risky and consequently much less common than false-carding by the Declarer. The reason for this should be obvious. The Declarer's Partner is the Dummy in name and in fact. Any deceptive play made by the Declarer can deceive only his Opponents. But a deceptive play made by an Opponent of the Declarer, and designed to deceive the Declarer, may also deceive that player's Partner. Consequently a player on the Defending Side has to weigh the possible result of misleading his Partner as well as the Declarer. A defending player should, as a matter of fact, confine his deceptive plays to those times when it makes no difference whether his Partner is deceived or not.

As a general thing, the trump suit offers the most frequent means for a defending player to fool the Declarer, both because this suit is usually the one that is disposed of first and also because Partner's reactions are not of any great importance.

Take, for example, the following deal:

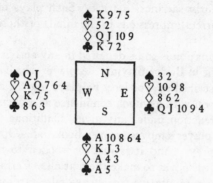

```
                    ♠ K 9 7 5
                    ♡ 5 2
                    ◇ Q J 10 9
                    ♣ K 7 2
    ♠ Q J              N            ♠ 3 2
    ♡ A Q 7 6 4                     ♡ 10 9 8
    ◇ K 7 5      W         E        ◇ 8 6 2
    ♣ 8 6 3            S            ♣ Q J 10 9 4
                    ♠ A 10 8 6 4
                    ♡ K J 3
                    ◇ A 4 3
                    ♣ A 5
```

With East and West vulnerable, the bidding has gone:

SOUTH	WEST	NORTH	EAST
One Spade	Pass	Two Spades	Pass
Two No-trump	Pass	Four Spades	Pass
Pass	Pass		

It is apparent from the bidding that South's contract cannot be defeated by any ordinary defense. With his high-card strength, West knows that his Partner probably does not have even a single trick. If West is very lucky, he may take 3 tricks himself, with his Ace-Queen of hearts and his King of diamonds, but this will not defeat the contract. A fourth trick must be found somewhere if the Declarer is to be stopped from making the game. The only chance appears to be in spades—the trump suit. The most strategic opening lead, therefore, appears to be the Jack of spades! According to the conventions of leads in general use, the Jack denies possession of the Queen, and this false lead, therefore, may induce the Declarer to place the Queen in the East hand. If the Declarer falls for the ruse, he will go up with Dummy's King on the first round, and return a low spade toward his Ace-Ten, finessing the Ten against the Queen which he presumes is with East. Believing West's opening lead to be genuine, the Declarer will thus be misled into losing to West's Queen, which will cause him to lose an otherwise sure contract. If the Declarer guesses that West's lead is false, he will play for the drop—assuming that the only reason for West to open a trump honor is that he holds the Queen also—and make his contract.

No one would be so fatuous as to claim that such a play as this will always prove effective. At least it does create a situation which makes the Declarer do some thinking. This situation would never come about if West, on the preceding deal, made his normal opening lead of a club. Without this unusual lead, South is almost certain to lead out the Ace and King of spades and play for the drop. The false lead, in other words, creates an element of doubt in the Declarer's mind which may or may not work out to West's advantage. Incidentally, it makes no difference whether East regards the lead of the Jack of trumps as honest or not.

It is also apparent why false-carding should be used only now and then. If West should open the Jack of trumps every time he happens to hold the Queen-Jack doubleton, the Declarer would soon catch on to this tendency and not be fooled. If, however, West has never made such an opening lead before to the Declarer's knowledge, the chances are pretty good that the Declarer will take the lead at its face value and be fatally misled. Sometimes the false-carding may have the tactics of double-crossing. If the Declarer has been led to believe that West is in the habit of leading the Jack of trumps from Queen-Jack doubleton, the sudden shift to the lead of the Queen from the same combination may fool the Declarer.

The effectiveness of the ruse depends entirely on the unexpectedness of it, and that depends, in turn, on the imagination and cleverness of the player making use of the trick.

The following deal contains an example of a play which was once actually made by Mr. Ely Culbertson, undoubtedly the most famous of the world's great Bridge players and authorities.

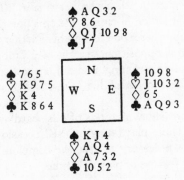

♠ A Q 3 2
♡ 8 6
♢ Q J 10 9 8
♣ J 7

♠ 7 6 5
♡ K 9 7 5
♢ K 4
♣ K 8 6 4

N
W E
S

♠ 10 9 8
♡ J 10 3 2
♢ 6 5
♣ A Q 9 3

♠ K J 4
♡ A Q 4
♢ A 7 3 2
♣ 10 5 2

With neither side vulnerable, the bidding happened to go:

SOUTH	WEST	NORTH	EAST
One No-trump	Pass	Two Diamonds	Pass
Two No-trump	Pass	Three Spades	Pass
Three No-trump	Pass	Pass	Pass

West's opening lead was the five of hearts, and East played the Ten, Mr. Culbertson winning the trick with the Ace! It seems pretty silly to go up with the Ace when the Queen would take the trick just as well, but Mr. Culbertson had a sound reason for his apparently foolish action. At the second trick he led a low spade over to the Dummy's Queen, and took the diamond finesse. This lost to West's King, and West immediately returned a low heart, a play for which he cannot possibly be criticized. Declarer's going up with the heart Ace on the first trick almost certainly indicated that the Queen and Jack lay with East, and that the heart suit was established. Of course, Mr. Culbertson simply won the trick with the Queen and proceeded to run off all his diamond and spade tricks.

What good did the play of the Ace do? Just look at the hand for a moment, if you do not see the point.

Consider what would have happened if the Declarer had made the normal play of the Queen of hearts on the first trick. West would still have regained the lead with the King of diamonds, but he would then have known that the Declarer held the Ace of hearts. (Had East held it, he would have played it.) Since West could see that the diamonds and spades were established for the Declarer, he would consider it futile to continue with the heart suit. There might be a chance in the one other suit—clubs. At this point, West would certainly shift to a club, whereupon he and his Partner would have taken 4 club tricks without opposition, setting Mr. Culbertson's contract. The Declarer saw all this coming, and did his best to keep West from shifting suits. The success of his false-carding strategy was well deserved.

The next diagrams show methods of false-carding available to the Defending Side. These plays may be used occasionally, but not all the time. It is not necessary to give the complete deals, since each illustrates only one feature of play at a time.

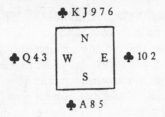

♣ K J 9 7 6

♣ Q 4 3   W   E   ♣ 10 2

♣ A 8 5

Here the Declarer is trying to establish his suit, which—for the sake of illustration—is clubs. He leads the Ace from his own hand, on which West plays low, and a low card is played from the Dummy. East should now play the Ten, not the deuce. The Ten is bound to start a train of thought in the Declarer's mind. Having previously made up his mind to take the second round finesse, he may change and decide that East's other club is the Queen. He may then play for the drop, thereby setting up West's Queen for a third-round winner. If it should turn out that Declarer had held the Queen (from East's point of view, that is), East need not worry, for no harm has been done by his play of the Ten. Of course, if this play is made every time the opportunity presents itself, the adversaries will eventually "catch on" and fail to take the play of the Ten at all seriously.

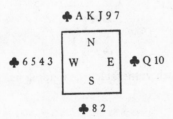

♣ A K J 9 7

♣ 6 5 4 3   W   E   ♣ Q 10

♣ 8 2

The example above is very similar to the one before it, although in other ways it is almost the reverse of it. Assuming that this club suit is the one the Declarer is trying to establish (at no-trump), South leads out the Ace before deciding whether or not to take the finesse. On the Ace lead, East should drop his Queen. This almost certainly places the Ten in the West hand—so far as the Declarer is concerned. South will then probably return to his own hand in order to finesse the nine-spot on the second round. You see, he cannot postpone this play, as the lead of another round of clubs leaves him with no card of the suit in his own hand.

Of course, it is true that, in the example just given, the Declarer might have taken the finesse even if the Ten had been played, but the Queen makes it almost a certainty that he will do so. It is also true that the play should not be made <u>unless East is certain of the distribution of the suit</u>, as it might turn out to be disastrous if the Declarer happens to hold three clubs instead of two. All of these features should be carefully weighed before the play is made.

REFUSING TO PLAY THIRD HAND HIGH

The type of play in the following deal is of rather frequent occurrence, and yet it is not commonly used. It refutes the well-known principle of playing Third Hand high.

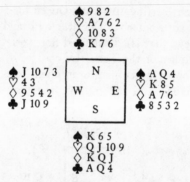

♠ 9 8 2
♡ A 7 6 2
♢ 10 8 3
♣ K 7 6

♠ J 10 7 3
♡ 4 3
♢ 9 5 4 2
♣ J 10 9

N
W E
S

♠ A Q 4
♡ K 8 5
♢ A 7 6
♣ 8 5 3 2

♠ K 6 5
♡ Q J 10 9
♢ K Q J
♣ A Q 4

With North and South vulnerable, the bidding has gone:

SOUTH	WEST	NORTH	EAST
One Heart	Pass	Two Hearts	Pass
Two No-trump	Pass	Three Hearts	Pass
Three No-trump	Pass	Pass	Pass

West makes his natural opening lead of the three of spades (fourth best). When the Dummy plays low, East should play the Queen! The Declarer will then be forced to play the King, because he will think that the Ace is with West, and that a lead through his King will annihilate it. Therefore he must take the trick while he is sure of it. Trying then the heart finesse, the Declarer will lose to East's King, whereupon East will continue spades, and East and West will take a total of 5 tricks, including 3 spade tricks. If East plays the Ace of spades on the first trick, the Declarer must make three no-trump. To be sure, East returns the Queen of spades on the second trick, but the Declarer holds up his King, and West's fourth spade is shut out of this hand forever. A moment's consideration should be needed to show you that East's play of the Queen cannot lose, and that it may gain.

An Unusual Play

The feature of the following deal is not a deceptive play, but an unusual play made to preserve entries in Partner's hand.

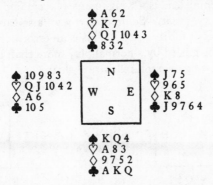

```
                    ♠ A 6 2
                    ♡ K 7
                    ◇ Q J 10 4 3
                    ♣ 8 3 2
      ♠ 10 9 8 3         N          ♠ J 7 5
      ♡ Q J 10 4 2                  ♡ 9 6 5
      ◇ A 6         W       E       ◇ K 8
      ♣ 10 5                        ♣ J 9 7 6 4
                        S
                    ♠ K Q 4
                    ♡ A 8 3
                    ◇ 9 7 5 2
                    ♣ A K Q
```

With North and South vulnerable, the bidding has gone:

South	West	North	East
One No-trump	Pass	Two No-trump	Pass
Three No-trump	Pass	Pass	Pass

The play proceeds as follows:

Trick 1. West leads ♡Q, North plays ♡7, East plays ♡5, and South plays ♡3. Declarer's hold-up on this trick is correct. If East has only two hearts, the play may prevent him from knocking out the second stopper if he should regain the lead in diamonds.

Trick 2. West leads ♡4, North plays ♡K, East plays ♡6, and South plays ♡8.

Trick 3. North leads ◇3, East plays ◇K, South plays ◇2, and West plays ◇6. East's play seems rather spectacular, but actually it is absolutely necessary. Furthermore, it is very unlikely to lose a trick.* If South happens to hold the Ace of diamonds, East knows

---

* Only if West has the lone Ace, giving South five diamonds.—S. F. Jr.

that his King is of no use anyway. If West should have the Ace, it will serve as a natural entry after the hearts are established.

Trick 4. East leads ♡9, South plays ♡A, West plays ♡2, and North plays ◇4.

Trick 5. South leads ◇5, West plays ◇A, North plays ◇10, and East plays ◇8. West can now run off 2 heart tricks and set the contract. Note that if East had played low on the first diamond lead, West would have been forced to win the trick with his Ace, and the entry which enabled him to cash his good hearts would have been lost.

MISLEADING THE OPPONENTS BY PLAYING NORMALLY

When the opening lead is a King, many players find the temptation to false-card very great. Sometimes they false-card whether the situation really calls for it or not. This is an error, for sometimes the Opponents can be misled by a normal play more than by an abnormal play. The following examples illustrate this:

```
                ♡ 9 6 4                              ◇ Q 10 5
             ┌─────────┐                          ┌─────────┐
             │    N    │                          │    N    │
1. ♡ A K 7 5 │ W     E │ ♡ J 10 3     2. ◇ A K 8 7 6 │ W     E │ ◇ 4 3
             │    S    │                          │    S    │
             └─────────┘                          └─────────┘
                ♡ Q 8 2                              ◇ J 9 2
```

In No. 1, West opens the King against a suit contract (some other suit is trump); East plays the three, as he does not want his Partner to continue the suit in the event that the lead is from an Ace-King holding; and South should play the eight. South knows that East's three-spot is meant to be a discouraging card, for he holds the deuce himself. Consequently there is no danger of the third round being ruffed—which is exactly what East is trying to signal his Partner. South therefore plays the eight, rather than the deuce, to conceal the lower card, hoping thereby to induce West to read the three-spot as the beginning of an echo. If West thinks that the trey is encouraging, he will continue with the Ace, thereby establishing South's Queen.

In No. 2, however, the situation has changed. (Some other suit is trumps.) West opens the King and East plays the four, thereby beginning an echo. South cannot be absolutely sure that East holds a doubleton, but he should certainly not ignore the possibility. This time he should play the deuce, thereby creating a doubt in West's mind as to the position of the three-spot, and hoping, therefore, that the suit will be abandoned. If South plays the nine or the Jack, West will probably not be misled, as this leaves both the deuce and the trey missing, and increases the chances of East's holding a doubleton.

Of much the same sort is the variation of the false-card of the Ace when holding Ace-King or Ace-King-Queen. Suppose that you have been bidding no-trump furiously, and hold, among other assets, the Ace-King-Queen of clubs. Suppose further that a low club is opened, on which you play low from Dummy, and the Opponent on your right plays the Jack. If you now go up with the Ace, to false-card West into continuing clubs, you will probably discourage West instead, for he is not likely to believe that his Partner holds both the King and the Queen—you have bid your no-trump too confidently. The best play here is the King (middle card), which gives West the suggestion that you hold the Ace but lack the Queen. This play stands the best chance of persuading West to continue the suit. If you hold only the Ace and King, however, and wish to *discourage* continuation, the best card to play is probably the Ace.

DESPERATION TACTICS BY THE DECLARER

Frequently a Declarer finds that after the opening lead a contract is well-nigh impossible if the Opponents realize the full strength of their combined values. In such cases it is sometimes possible to play in such a fashion that the Opponents may not appreciate each other's strength quickly enough and may allow the necessary extra trick or tricks to be sneaked through in time. For example:

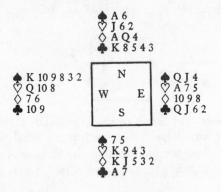

With neither side vulnerable, North and South reach a contract of three no-trump, with South the Declarer. West opens the Ten of spades and South sees at once that the hand cannot be made by normal means, as he holds only 8 top tricks. So many spades are outstanding against him that any attempt to establish clubs must result in losing at least 5 tricks immediately. On the other hand, if the diamonds are started at once, the Opponents (chiefly East, who is the player who must be fooled) will soon know the exact situation.

Declarer therefore goes up with the Ace of spades in the Dummy at the first trick and leads out the Jack of hearts. East is on the spot. He cannot be sure that his Partner holds the King of spades and it looks as though the Declarer is going to let the Jack of hearts ride. He therefore plays low, South goes right up with the King, and proceeds to run off 5 diamond tricks and 2 club tricks for his contract. Of course, East probably should go up with the Ace and lead spades, but—would everyone?

It is true that the Declarer might go down 5 tricks if West held the Ace of hearts. However, not vulnerable and not doubled, the play is worth while, as long as the loss risked is not too great. The play is not recommended if a set of 1000 points, or even 500 points, is threatened.

A DESPERATION SURPRISE LEAD

Although it is usually not good defense to lead a King out of nowhere, the situation may sometimes be so desperate that unusual tactics are urgently needed. The abnormal lead of a bare King is occasionally effective in such emergencies.

Suppose, for example, that you hold the following hand in the West position:

```
♠ 7 6 3        ┌─────────────┐
♡ K 5          │      N      │
♢ Q 10 6 3     │  W       E  │
♣ 10 7 4 2     │      S      │
               └─────────────┘
```

Let us also suppose that South opened the bidding with *one spade*, North responded with *three spades*, and South rebid to game, *four spades*. It seems from the bidding that the chances of defeating the contract are very slight. Therefore some lead which savors of the unusual is likely to be your best bet. Your hand does not offer much choice. About your only hope, therefore, is to lead the King of hearts. If your Partner happens to have the Ace, you may be able to ruff the third round and thereby obtain a trick you could not get any other way. Even if Partner holds only the Queen, you may still have a chance to inflict a telling blow on the Declarer, for Partner may be able to obtain the lead on the first or the second round of trumps. Of course, you may sacrifice a trick by this mad lead of the King of hearts, but what if you do? The chances are that the loss of the heart trick will merely mean giving the Declarer an extra trick —a negligible loss to your side, as against the possibility of occasionally defeating a game contract by such bold tactics as these.

A Deceptive and Unusual Lead

The following deal illustrates a lead which combines the deceptive with the unusual:

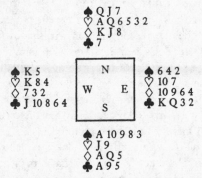

```
                    ♠ Q J 7
                    ♡ A Q 6 5 3 2
                    ◇ K J 8
                    ♣ 7
  ♠ K 5              ┌─────────┐              ♠ 6 4 2
  ♡ K 8 4           │    N    │              ♡ 10 7
  ◇ 7 3 2           │ W     E │              ◇ 10 9 6 4
  ♣ J 10 8 6 4      │    S    │              ♣ K Q 3 2
                    └─────────┘
                    ♠ A 10 9 8 3
                    ♡ J 9
                    ◇ A Q 5
                    ♣ A 9 5
```

With North and South vulnerable, the bidding has gone:

South	West	North	East
One Spade	Pass	Two Hearts	Pass
Two No-trump	Pass	Four Spades	Pass
Five Spades	Pass	Six Spades	Pass
Pass	Pass		

The bidding tells West that North and South almost certainly have some sort of fit in hearts. In fact, they are probably relying somewhat on those hearts for the success of their Small Slam contract. West sees that he can probably count on making 1 trick with his King of spades, but there seems little chance of obtaining another and setting trick by any normal attack. But if the Declarer can be made to guess at the start, before he has quite got his bearings, he may be defeated by a ruse. Such a ruse is available to West in hearts. By leading the eight of hearts, he makes the Declarer wonder about the whereabouts of the King. West's lead may be a singleton!

Of course, this play may not work. That is quite true. But it will certainly make the Declarer catch his breath in momentary alarm. He may decide that the eight of hearts is a singleton, and may then go up with Dummy's Ace immediately, deciding to rely entirely on the trump finesse. Of course, he may not be particularly frightened at all, but may simply play low, finessing without thinking. But West can lose nothing by making the lead, and it has a good chance of robbing the Declarer of his Slam.

LEADING AGAINST SLAMS

Many, many pages could be written on the subject of leading against Slams. Much depends on a most careful analysis of the bidding by the opening leader in conjunction with his own holding. Fortunately for the Defender's cause, Slams are usually reached after quite a few bidding rounds of cautious probing; rarely do we encounter the slam-bang "one spade, six spades" style. Because of this fact, a lengthy discussion of leads against Slams might better be included in a book on bidding. In any event, for that reason and for space considerations, we will merely touch the highlights.

1. Review the bidding carefully and look for a clue.

2. At most *suit* Slam contracts, you have to strike quickly, as Dummy usually has a long suit which can be set up for discards. It is your aim to set up immediately one side suit trick as the setting trick in case, as you hope, you or your Partner can get a first trick in either trumps or Dummy's or Declarer's side suit.

Thus a lead from a King or Queen of an unbid suit or a suit bid secondarily by Dummy is often desirable. The shorter the suit the better. Attacking from two or three or four to the King or Queen is more likely to be productive than from five or more. We're looking for a *second* round winner since Declarer is most likely to be able to handle the third round of any side suit by ruffing or otherwise.

3. Review the bidding carefully again and look for a clue!

4. Obviously, use to the hilt your honor combinations—but they are seldom available to you against Slams.

5. If no side suits are shown (and against no-trump Slams in particular) tend to make the safest lead possible. This is doubly true if you have a considerable smattering of high cards. In such cases lay back and hope Declarer must come to you or possibly misguess the hand.

6. Review the bidding carefully once more and look for a clue!

7. Be on the special alert for Partner's doubles, or for *failures to double* any later round bids made by the eventual Dummy. Cue bids, and in particular artificial responses to Blackwood, Gerber and the like, can be pure gold to alert defenders and thus boomerang against their users. The negative inference of Partner's failure to double a Blackwood response can be equally useful. Which leads us back again to:

8. Review the bidding *carefully* and look for a clue!

9. Against Grand Slams, against sound opposition, look for the safest, don't-give-up-a-trick lead.

LEADING AGAINST DOUBLED SLAMS

The double of a Slam bid, like any other double, is never made on sheer speculation. But since the occasion rarely arises against good opposition that a Defender has the "stuff" in his own hand to soundly browbeat a voluntarily reached Slam contract, the double of a Slam has come to have a special meaning.

When the Partner of the opening leader doubles a Slam contract he is asking the leader to make an unusual lead. (When the opening leader himself doubles, that's his business.) If the doubler has bid a suit, the one fairly clear-cut message conveyed is that the leader should not lead that suit. One Slam doubling convention known as the Four Aces Slam Double insisted that the double calls specifically for Dummy's *first* bid suit. (Since this almost invariably is an honest, good suit, such a lead is obviously unusual.)

The more prevalent convention, originally called the Lightner Slam Double does not definitely specify Dummy's first suit. The Lightner Double can be that, but very frequently can be showing a void suit and asking for that lead. And occasionally it may be smoking out a "phony" second suit shown by Declarer. How is the opening leader to tell? Again, one must "review the bidding carefully and look for a clue" in conjunction with a careful study of one's hand.

We will give one example, without the entire deal, of such a double and the leader's hand. The more general Lightner Double is being used. Here is how the bidding went:

South	West	North	East
One Spade	Pass	Three Diamonds	Pass
Three Spades	Pass	Four Diamonds	Pass
Four Spades	Pass	Five Spades	Pass
Six Spades	Pass	Pass	Double
Pass	Pass	Pass	

As West, on lead against six spades, you hold ♠ 8 4, ♡ J 10 9, ◇ K 3, ♣ Q 8 6 4 3 2. With this hand, after Partner doubles you may think fleetingly of Dummy's first bid suit, diamonds. But because of Dummy's diamond rebid, and your own King and your own shortness in the suit, Partner is not very likely to have the holding to wish a lead there. Partner must be doubling on a void suit elsewhere (plus the certainty or at least good hope of a trick somewhere else). Based on your length that void should be in clubs. So you forego your natural lead, the Jack from that nice heart sequence, and lead some low club.

Most of the time though, the desired lead, even under the Lightner convention, turns out to be Dummy's first suit. So in the long run there is little difference in effect between the two conventions. But the more rigid Four Aces convention would lose out in situations like the example given.

Leading Away From an Ace

At a suit contract, an opening lead away from an Ace is usually frowned upon as very undesirable. Yet, as already stated, in Bridge there is no such word as Never. The lead away from an Ace, against an adverse trump contract, may occasionally have its advantages.

Such a lead was actually made by Josephine Culbertson, wife of Ely Culbertson, who had a place in her own right among the master players of the world, in the following deal:

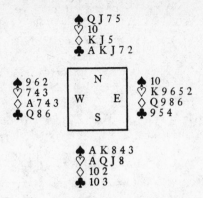

With North and South vulnerable, the bidding has gone:

SOUTH	WEST	NORTH	EAST
One Spade	Pass	Three Clubs	Pass
Three Hearts	Pass	Three Spades	Pass
Four Spades	Pass	Four No-trump	Pass
Six Spades	Pass	Pass	Pass

Mrs. Culbertson, sitting West, struggled with the problem of what to open against South's Slam contract in spades. The situation seemed fairly hopeless. Obviously the Queen of clubs is of no use, and, if Partner should turn up with any strength in hearts, this strength is also unfavorably placed. The only chance, as Mrs. Culbertson saw, seemed to lie in the diamond suit. Yet the Ace meant only 1 trick, and North's forcing take-out and subsequent no-trump bidding[*] almost certainly placed the King of diamonds in his hand. The one chance left, which Mrs. Culbertson took, was to lead the *trey* of diamonds!

The Declarer (South) went into long self-communion, studying his own hand and the Dummy. The opening lead appeared to bother him. He cannot be blamed much for finally deciding to play low from the Dummy, hoping that West's lead was away from the Queen. This low play made East hesitate slightly, but he quickly realized that there was little point in finessing the eight-spot. East therefore won the trick with the Queen and returned the suit to Partner's Ace, setting the contract. Clearly the first lead of the Ace of diamonds would have done no good.

---

[*] The four no-trump bid was a natural, unconventional call at the time.—S. F. Jr.

Lest the reader regard this unconventional lead with an excess of enthusiasm, a humorous incident may be related to show the other side of the picture. The experience befell Mr. Oswald Jacoby and Mr. David Burnstine, both ranking well up in the first ten of Contract Bridge players in the world, in an important match. Their Opponents were Mr. Howard Schenken and Mr. Sherman Stearns, two top-notch players also, who had reached a contract of six spades on remarkably strong bidding. The Dummy went down with the Queen and two small clubs, as Mr. Jacoby (holding only the Ace of clubs as a likely winner) opened a small club. A small card was played from the Dummy, whereupon Mr. Burnstine, holding King-Ten, decided (after profound and placid reflection) to finesse the Ten. The Declarer had abandoned all hope of avoiding 2 club losers. Seeing the Ten fall from East, Declarer perked up brightly and won the trick with the Jack, eventually discarding his other loser, thereby taking all 13 tricks. Thus you see that the underlead of an Ace against a Slam, or even against a game, may not always work out as hoped.

ANOTHER UNCONVENTIONAL OPENING LEAD

In the following hand another situation develops in which an unusual lead is the only way the contract can be defeated. Mr. Samuel Fry, Jr., who in 1933 was the author's Partner in winning the All-American Contract Team-of-Four Championship and the All-American Contract Pair Championship of the American Whist League, was sitting West and was the opening leader.

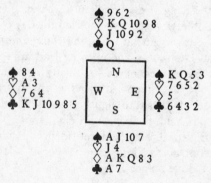

With East and West vulnerable, the bidding has gone:

SOUTH	WEST	NORTH	EAST
One Diamond	Two Clubs	Two Hearts	Pass
Two Spades	Pass	Three Diamonds	Pass
Three No-trump	Pass	Pass	Pass

After some consideration, Mr. Fry opened the King of clubs. His logic in making this choice was really quite simple. There could be no doubt that the Declarer held the Ace of clubs, so that the only card he had to worry about was the Queen. If the Queen was in the Declarer's hand, the lead was immaterial; even if Mr. Fry's Partner held the Queen, the lead was immaterial. But if the Dummy held the Queen, and held it alone, the normal lead of the Jack would give the Declarer 2 club tricks instead of 1. As it turned out, Mr. Fry had made a good guess, and he was eventually able to set the contract 2 tricks when he got in with the Ace of hearts.

Notice that any other lead by West will enable the Declarer to make his contract. Mr. Fry saw a possibility of defeating the contract, or of having a better chance to defeat it, if the Dummy should turn up with the singleton Queen of clubs. He made his opening lead, therefore, on the assumption that the Dummy did contain the singleton Queen. Of course, it would not happen to turn out this way very often, but it is the one time that it works—assuming that it does not lose anything—that a play of this kind justifies itself.

Mr. Fry's magnificent opening lead is the sort of play one has come to expect from this brilliant young player, whose rapid rise to the heights in the last few years has been phenomenal. *

A PAIR OF UNUSUAL DECEPTIVE PLAYS

The situation below gave Mr. Albert H. Morehead a chance to make a deceptive play which the author has always greatly admired:

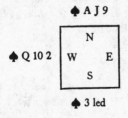

♠ A J 9

♠ Q 10 2   N / W   E / S

♠ 3 led

---

* It was my inclination to delete this paragraph, but since it proves I once was young, I left it in. So there, John Crawford!—S. F. Jr.

The writer must admit that the play was made against him (sitting South). Having to make 2 spade tricks, South (the author) led the trey to finesse Dummy's nine-spot on the first round. Mr. Morehead, sitting West, played the Queen, inducing the play of the Ace from Dummy on the logical assumption that West also had the King. When South regained the lead, another small spade was led, upon which Mr. Morehead played the deuce. This made the finesse of the Jack seem exactly right, but of course East won it with the King, and eventually West's Ten also made a trick. Had Mr. Morehead played normally, by putting the deuce on the first round, the nine would have been finessed, and on the second round the Jack would have been finessed, making 2 spade tricks for South. Even if the author had been aware of what was happening, he still could not have been sure of guessing aright, for West might still be playing normally.

The following diagram shows another interesting deceptive play:

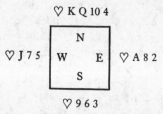

♡ K Q 10 4

♡ J 7 5   N W E S   ♡ A 8 2

♡ 9 6 3

South leads the trey, and plays the Queen from Dummy. East should refuse to win with the Ace, as by so doing he practically compels the Declarer (South) to take the finesse against the Jack the second time. When South returns to his own hand after the holdoff, and leads another low heart, he is forced to guess as to the location of the Ace and the Jack, respectively. He may very easily go wrong and place the Ace with West and the Jack with East. If he does, he will play the King from Dummy, which will permit East and West to make 2 heart tricks.

Two Deceptive Ace Leads

Mr. Howard Schenken, one of the greatest master players of the world, made the following interesting deceptive lead in an important tournament.

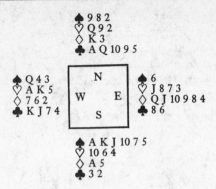

With both sides vulnerable, the bidding has gone:

SOUTH	WEST	NORTH	EAST
One Spade	Pass	Two Clubs	Pass
Two Spades	Pass	Two No-trump	Pass
Four Spades	Pass	Pass	Pass

Mr. Schenken, sitting West, had to make the opening lead. His first thought, as is natural, was to open the King of hearts. But he saw that this lead would probably not defeat the contract. He was pretty sure that North held an honor in hearts because of the no-trump bid. His own shortness in hearts made it unlikely for his Partner to be short enough for a third-round ruff. Furthermore, he held all the missing honor strength in clubs, which could be of no use.

His decision was that East must hold a hand practically blank, and that, if this was true, he could take only 3 tricks himself. A fourth trick had to be found if South was to be deprived of h s game. So Mr. Schenken laid down the Ace of hearts instead of the King. Dummy played low, and East, feeling that he did not want a shift, played the seven of hearts—an encouraging card. This gave Mr. Schenken his chance. He led a low heart next, and the Declarer, already led astray, played the nine from Dummy. East won with his Jack and returned the suit, making Mr. Schenken's sure spade winner the setting trick.

It might be argued that Declarer should have gone up with Dummy's Queen, but he really cannot be blamed for not doing so. As a general rule, the lead of an Ace denies the King, and Declarer thought that the nine-spot might possibly force the King from East's hand, in the event that West held the Jack.   Mr. Schenken's brilliant reasoning was highly deserving of success.

In the following hand another type of lead completely misinforms the Declarer about a suit distribution.   The lead was made in this deal by Mr. Albert H. Morehead and ranks as one of the most brilliant defensive plays on record:

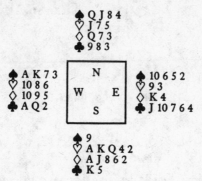

With East and West vulnerable, the bidding has gone:

South	West	North	East
One Heart	Pass	One No-trump	Pass
Two Diamonds	Pass	Two Hearts	Pass
Four Hearts	Pass	Pass	Pass

The bidding was very illuminating to Mr. Morehead, who was sitting West.   South's insistence on playing the hand at a game contract, in the face of North's repeated sign-offs, certainly marked South with a very strong hand, including probably two five-card red suits.   However, both of the long suits could not be solid, as then South would have bid *three diamonds* over *one no-trump*.   The chances were in favor of his holding some side honor as well, such as the King of clubs.

Mr. Morehead therefore opened the Ace of spades, deliberately concealing the King.   A glance at the Dummy's hand confirmed most of his suspicions.   He felt that South must hold five hearts headed by at least the Ace-King, and, if so, his Partner's Queen (if he held it) would be useless.   With the Queen of diamonds in the Dummy, it also seemed as though the only missing diamond could be the King.   Therefore, if there was any hope at all of beating the contract, it must depend on Declarer's play of the diamond suit.   With the Ten and nine both missing, Declarer could only lead low from Dummy once to finesse the Jack.   Then he would have to lay down the Ace in the hope of catching the King.   This, of course, would be entirely a gamble, but Mr. Morehead knew that the play would succeed!   He therefore decided to try and deceive the Declarer. With this object in view, he led the nine of diamonds at the second trick.

At this point the picture looks very dark for the Declarer.   It certainly seems as though both the King and the Ten of diamonds are in the East hand.   He therefore goes up with the Queen in Dummy, and tops East's King with the Ace.   Three rounds of hearts put him in the Dummy with the Jack, and he now leads the seven of diamonds, finessing against East's hypothetical Ten.   When Mr. Morehead won the trick with the Ten, the Declarer was fit to be tied.   But when he got over his momentary fury at being outwitted, he congratulated Mr. Morehead on his superb bit of deception.

Summary

The art of deception in Contract Bridge play is simply to lead or play a card which tells your adversary a story quite different from your actual holding. You must always bear in mind that, when playing defensively, you are likely to mislead your Partner as well as the Declarer, and almost never make a deceptive play when it may plunge your Partner into trouble.

Let it be said here, lest some reader misunderstand, that this form of deception is entirely ethical—for the simple reason that it *does* mislead Partner as well as the Declarer.   Any player may play any card he wishes, just so long as he follows suit when able.   If he sees fit to depart from the usual or expected play, and makes an unusual or "false" play, that is his privilege.   If his Opponent falls for the ruse, he cannot always be blamed, but the player who practiced the deception may well receive proper credit for his perspicacity in seeing the chance and his initiative in taking it.

CHAPTER XI

PLANNING THE PLAY

A PLAN is necessary in all enterprises, and the play of a hand at Contract Bridge, whether in attack or in defense, is no exception. To form a plan, it is not necessary for you to keep in mind every bit of strategy you have learned in this book. That would be manifestly impossible. However, you should try to learn to recognize the different *types* of hands so that you can apply the proper principles at the proper times.

PLAN OF THE DECLARER

The following are some of the general thoughts which should pass through your mind when you are Declarer, before you have even played to the first trick:

At a No-trump Contract:

Is the card led an honor lead, a length lead, or a short-suit lead?

What is the relation of the card led to that particular suit in the Dummy?

Does the lead help me to establish tricks, or does it threaten to establish tricks for the Opponents?

If the lead is a length lead, what does the application of the Rule of Eleven tell me?

If the lead is an honor lead, or a short-suit lead, where are the missing honors most likely to be?

How many sure winners have I?

How many possible winners have I?

What does the bidding tell me about the location of the missing honors?

What does the bidding tell me about the adverse distribution?

What long suits have I in my own hand and in the Dummy which can be established?

Which suits should I try to establish first?

Which suits, if any, are already established and can be left alone for awhile?

Which suits are dangerous?

460

What are my controlling cards which I must try not to relinquish?

Which finesses *must* I take, and which ones *might* I take?

What is the entry situation to both hands?

Which of the Opponents' hands should I try to keep out of the lead?

In which hand do I want to take the first trick, supposing I can take the first trick?

All these thoughts should go on in your mind before the first card is played from Dummy. With practice the process will not take as long as you think. After the first trick, you will already have some plan in mind and you can proceed along definite lines until developments prove to you the necessity for changing your tactics. You may frequently find that you will be forced to abandon your original plan, but this should not be any cause for worry. Meanwhile, you might see opportunities for making use of all the fundamental and advanced plays you have learned in this book, such as hold-ups, unblocking plays, ducking plays, finesses, safety plays, end plays, squeeze plays, etc. Furthermore, be sure to start counting.

At a Suit Contract:

What is the trump situation in my own hand and in the Dummy?

How many trumps are outstanding?

How many high trumps are outstanding which might win tricks?

How many sure losing tricks do I hold in side-suits?

How many losing tricks might I be able to eliminate by ruffing or discarding?

Is the opening lead an honor lead, a length lead, or a short-suit lead?

What is the relation of the card led to the particular suit in the Dummy?

Does the Rule of Eleven help me?

What information can I gain by reviewing the bidding?

Should I draw the trumps at once?

Should I postpone drawing trumps in order to get in a finessing situation?

Should I postpone drawing trumps in order to retain ruffing power in the Dummy?

Should I postpone drawing trumps in order to take discards of losing tricks?

Should I postpone drawing trumps in order to develop a side-suit first?

Should I consider developing a cross-ruff situation?

Is there any danger of ruffing by the Opponents?

Where do I want to take the first trick?

You are now ready to play to the first trick. Your plan must also include many of the principles which you have learned from a study of no-trump tactics. Also, as in no-trump hands, your plan may change as necessity demands. By all means, remember to count.

PLAN OF THE DEFENDING SIDE

An explanation of the thought processes of the defense is very difficult to chart. The chief thing that the Defending Side must bear in mind is that it is important to try to find out what plan the Declarer is making. After this is discovered, some means should be found, if possible, to circumvent it. In the beginning this is fairly impossible. The thoughts of the Defending Side might be divided up something like this:

The Opening Leader Against a No-trump Contract:

What have I learned from the bidding?

If Partner has bid, should I open his suit or my own?

If Partner has not bid, have I any good honor-sequence lead?

If I lead from my long suit, what are my chances of establishing it?

Is the situation so desperate that I must depend on my Partner and open some other suit?

The Opening Leader Against a Suit Contract:

What have I learned from the bidding?

Can I make an honor lead in Partner's suit?

Can I develop ruffing power in Partner's suit?

Have I a good honor lead available?

Have I a good length lead available?

Have I potential ruffing power in some side suit?

Should I lead through strength immediately?

What about the time element?

Third Hand:

What does Partner's opening lead convey to me?
Can I apply the Rule of Eleven to any advantage?
What has the bidding taught me?
What is the Dummy's holding in the suit led?
What does the Dummy hold in the trump suit?
What does the Dummy hold in side suits?
What card should I play on Partner's lead to encourage, discourage, or temporize?
If I win the first trick, am I going to return the suit or shift?

Beyond this it is impossible to go. As each trick is played, new influences come into play and each influence should start a new train of thought. Remember that it is just as important for the defense to count as it is for the Declarer.

SUMMARY

One sentence summarizes this chapter effectively: *Look before you leap!*

CHAPTER XII

SOME MODERN INNOVATIONS

Very little has happened that is startlingly new in the play of the hand since Louis Watson wrote this book in 1933 and 1934. True, play in general has improved because of the increased experience of hundreds of thousands of individual players as the popularity of Contract Bridge pyramided. Players have become better able to tie in the bidding with the play. We can, however, offer one widely used and valuable playing convention which cropped up a few years after Watson; and also one currently-up-in-the-air change in thinking on an old playing convention.

Suit-Preference Signals When Ruffing

During the late Thirties a good many players in a good many different localities began, more or less simultaneously, to experiment with a new form of defensive signal. (*All* new conventions which are worth their salt, crop up that way. No one genius invents them, although frequently one expert does a lot of legwork and deservedly gets most of the credit. Excuse us, Messrs. Blackwood, Stayman, Gerber, Fishbein, et al.) This new playing convention first got publicity through an article by a Mr. Hy Lavinthal; then B. Jay Becker gave it his worthy attention and efforts. It has become known variously as the Lavinthal convention, Becker convention and simply as Suit-Preference. Extensions of this convention beyond ruffing situations (explanation of which follows) should be looked upon solely as "exceptions proving the rule."

In brief: When leading to give your Partner a ruff, or in following suit to Partner's ruffing trick, you can assist your Partner to choose a suit for his return lead, by the size of the card you play. The signal is simply described by the catch phrase "high-high,

low-low." To explain: There are only two suits left after we eliminate the suit which is being ruffed and the trump suit. A high
card played by you in leading or following suit on the trick Partner
ruffs, tells your Partner you are prepared for him to continue with
the *higher* ranking of the two remaining suits. A *low* card by you
in the same situation tells Partner you prefer him to continue with
the *lower* ranking of the two remaining suits.

Let's take a typical example:

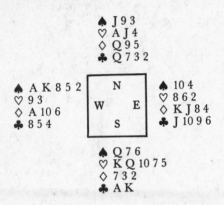

```
                    ♠ J 9 3
                    ♡ A J 4
                    ◇ Q 9 5
                    ♣ Q 7 3 2
♠ A K 8 5 2      ┌─────────┐      ♠ 10 4
♡ 9 3            │    N    │      ♡ 8 6 2
◇ A 10 6         │  W   E  │      ◇ K J 8 4
♣ 8 5 4          │    S    │      ♣ J 10 9 6
                 └─────────┘
                    ♠ Q 7 6
                    ♡ K Q 10 7 5
                    ◇ 7 3 2
                    ♣ A K
```

With both sides vulnerable, the bidding has gone:

SOUTH	WEST	NORTH	EAST
One Heart	One Spade	Two Hearts	Pass
Pass	Pass		

West sets about his task of trying to defeat the two heart contract
by leading his spade King. East starts his normal echo with the Ten
and West continues with the Ace. East follows with his four this
time and South drops his Queen. This of course does not fool West
after his Partner's echo and he leads a third round of spades,
carefully selecting the eight. East, trumping the trick, equally carefully notes the eight. From the fall of the cards to the first 2 tricks,
he knows the eight to be an unnecessarily high card. Following the
high-high principle, he now knows his Partner is calling for a lead
of the higher ranking of the two remaining suits other than trumps,
in this case diamonds.

So East returns his fourth best diamond. West after winning the Ace continues the suit, and the Defense garners 3 diamond tricks to defeat the contract. Note that without this bit of helpful assistance from his partner, East would have been sorely tried at trick 4. It's not too likely that a diamond lead away from the King-Jack up to Dummy's Queen would have looked more inviting to him than the safe-appearing club lead. At any rate, the Suit-Preference signal gives East a sure thing. Obviously, without the immediate diamond lead Declarer will make his two heart contract, what with Dummy's club Queen affording one diamond discard.

Here's another example of how Suit-Preference signals admirably serve to assist the defense in ruffing situations. Here a high card is read as actually being a low card.

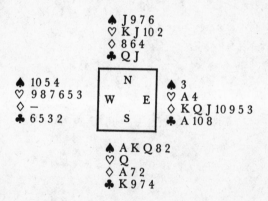

```
                    ♠ J 9 7 6
                    ♡ K J 10 2
                    ◇ 8 6 4
                    ♣ Q J
   ♠ 10 5 4          ┌─────────┐      ♠ 3
   ♡ 9 8 7 6 5 3     │    N    │      ♡ A 4
   ◇ —               │ W     E │      ◇ K Q J 10 9 5 3
   ♣ 6 5 3 2         │    S    │      ♣ A 10 8
                     └─────────┘
                    ♠ A K Q 8 2
                    ♡ Q
                    ◇ A 7 2
                    ♣ K 9 7 4
```

With both sides vulnerable, the bidding has gone:

South	West	North	East
One Spade	Pass	Two Spades	Four Diamonds
Four Spades	Pass	Pass	Pass

West, despite his horrible looking array of cards is a most active participant in this defense, proving one of Louis' admonitions mentioned in a very early chapter. Having none of his Partner's diamonds to lead, West guesses a low heart. East wins with the Ace and returns the diamond *nine*. Declarer plays the Ace and West ruffs. At this point, before the days of Suit-Preference, West would be on the spot. Who has the missing low heart? If Declarer has it, West should lead that suit again for his Partner to ruff. Or, does East have the club Ace and Declarer only the King or vice versa, either being plausible on the bidding?

But, playing Suit-Preference, West reads his Partner's diamond nine as a low one, undoubtedly the lowest of some sequence. It can't be East's highest diamond or anything like it, on East's vulnerable four diamond bid. So, since East is obviously leading as *low* a diamond as he can afford (he must lead a high enough card to force a high card from Declarer) East must want clubs, the *lower* ranking "other" suit. (Hearts in this case is the higher ranking "other" suit.)

Reasoning this way, West shifts to his fourth best club. East wins the Ace, cashes two good diamonds and Declarer is down 2 tricks. A second heart lead by West at trick 3, hoping his Partner will ruff, gives Declarer his contract, South's two losing diamonds going on Dummy's good hearts.

EXTENSION OF SUIT-PREFERENCE SIGNALS

We enter this subject with great fear and trepidation, because we have seen many players essay to scrap the entire normal sound structure of defensive play and replace it with Suit-Preference signals. Needless to say, these efforts have not been crowned with success, even with expert highly experienced partnerships.

Suit-Preference was designed basically for ruffing situations, as in the previous examples. In other normal situations a high card still means "Partner, please continue the suit," and a low card still means "shift" or at least "continue at your own risk." Even when Dummy has a singleton, at a suit contract, the signaller may want Dummy's trump holding shortened. Or perhaps the signaller's holding in both of the other side suits is so bad that he wants at least to warn Partner against a dangerous shift. So Suit-Preference, like fire, is valuable when properly used and controlled, but highly dangerous if played with indiscriminately.

The following example of a non-ruffing Suit-Preference signal is so clearcut that we feel safe in giving it. Don't go much further than this!

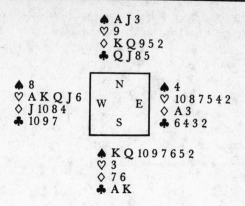

♠ A J 3
♡ 9
♢ K Q 9 5 2
♣ Q J 8 5

♠ 8   N   ♠ 4
♡ A K Q J 6   W   E   ♡ 10 8 7 5 4 2
♢ J 10 8 4   ♢ A 3
♣ 10 9 7   S   ♣ 6 4 3 2

♠ K Q 10 9 7 6 5 2
♡ 3
♢ 7 6
♣ A K

With neither side vulnerable and West dealer, the bidding has gone:

WEST	NORTH	EAST	SOUTH
One Heart	Double	Four Hearts	Six Spades
Pass	Pass	Pass	

West's opening bid, not vulnerable, as a potential lead director certainly is not to be criticized. And one can't blame South, with his huge hand, for taking the flyer he did in leaping to six. The opponents have badly crowded the bidding for him, pretty well closing the door on more scientific probes.

West opens the heart King and East plays the *Ten!* On this particular deal, with this particular Dummy and, most important, on this particular bidding, there should be no confusion. This *must be* a Suit-Preference signal. East can't want hearts continued as East must know and, furthermore, must know that West too must know, that the danger of a ruff-and-discard on a second heart lead is too great. In fact on East's triple raise it should appear to West as just about a certainty.

So West reads the heart Ten as calling for a diamond shift rather than a club shift. This obviously is the only way to beat the hand. But, in view of Dummy's holding in the two minors, which shift would normally look more inviting without help from Partner? It's certainly no better than a toss-up.

This final example of a Suit-Preference variation can be used without any danger to the rest of normal defensive signalling structure. This type of situation arises frequently.

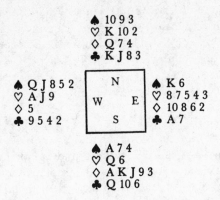

```
                        ♠ 10 9 3
                        ♡ K 10 2
                        ◇ Q 7 4
                        ♣ K J 8 3
        ♠ Q J 8 5 2        N         ♠ K 6
        ♡ A J 9                      ♡ 8 7 5 4 3
        ◇ 5            W       E     ◇ 10 8 6 2
        ♣ 9 5 4 2          S         ♣ A 7
                        ♠ A 7 4
                        ♡ Q 6
                        ◇ A K J 9 3
                        ♣ Q 10 6
```

With neither side vulnerable, the bidding has gone:

SOUTH	WEST	NORTH	EAST
One No-trump	Pass	Two No-trump	Pass
Three No-trump	Pass	Pass	Pass

South's very nice opening bid of one no-trump, concealing the five card diamond suit, might have had a better fate were it not for the very fine use of Suit-Preference employed by the Defense. Against South's three no-trump contract West opens the spade five and East's King is permitted to hold the trick. Declarer, not knowing that East has only one more spade, properly holds up his Ace again on the spade continuation, West's Jack winning.

West now continues with the spade *Queen*. East is able, from the fall of the cards to the first two rounds of spades, to tell that his Partner has the spade eight and almost certainly, for that matter, the spade deuce also. Otherwise there is just no accounting for Declarer's hold-ups. Why therefore did West carefully choose the Queen when the eight (or deuce) would have cleared the suit equally well.

The answer is that West is trying to say that his entry card is in a high *or* higher ranking suit. Declarer in his quest for 9 tricks naturally goes after clubs first and East wins with the Ace. Now it is doubly clear to East that of the two remaining suits (hearts and diamonds) hearts are what West was signalling for. So East returns a heart to West's Ace and the contract is defeated 2 tricks. Without the signal a diamond lead up to relative weakness will seem much more logical than a heart lead up to Dummy's King. But that will give the Declarer 9 tricks and his contract: one spade, five diamonds and three clubs.

What Do You Lead From Three Card Suits?

The passing of time has brought one unanimous minor change from Louis' writings on this subject and another more drastic change which has received only partial acceptance in expert circles. For the latter reason — because nothing is truly definitive — we will be brief in our discussion of this subject and tend to generalize.

Keep two things in mind. That "never say never" adage applies doubly to the subject of which card to lead from a three card suit. If you and your Partner happen to agree to lead the lowest from 9 7 2, the bidding of the very next hand may give you good and sufficient reasons to prefer the nine that time. So never say *never* lead the nine or the seven or the deuce. The other thing to keep in mind, whatever method of leading you choose, is to be sure you and your Partner know what each other tends to do.

When Partner has bid a suit:

Lead Ace from A x x against a suit bid and low against no-trump.
Lead low from K x x, Q x x and J x x against either a suit bid or no-trump. (That J x x combination is the one definite swing away from Louis. He preferred the Jack but only slightly.)

With 10 x x and x x x we have differences of opinion. The low card rather than the top card from both of these holdings in Partner's bid suit is now preferred by most top players. (The middle card is preferred by no one.) If you and Partner agree to lead low from these worthless tripletons you have this corollary going for you: If you have raised the suit during the auction you will then lead the top card. Partner, because of your raise, still knows you have three.

In leading an unbid suit:

If you hold x x x against either a suit or no-trump contract, a sizeable block of experts votes for the low lead. We won't give the arguments pro and con — they are too lengthy and get one almost into metaphysics. We personally have come around to preferring the low lead as a general thing, reserving the right to make many exceptions depending on exact hands and exact bidding. We believe Louis Watson would also belong to that school today. But either method is playable so long as it is not played woodenly and so long as Partner is let in on your secrets.

CHAPTER XIII

SOME LOOSE ENDS

Delaying for a Squeeze

WATSON's earlier discussion of the squeeze in this book is famous for being far and away the most lucid explanation of that family of plays. Portions of his text have been paid the compliment of being copied just about verbatim by some of his fellow bridge writers in their tomes. So we feel a bit diffident about wanting to add anything to Watson on squeezes.

But there's one phase of the squeeze that Watson hinted at in a single line in his end-of-chapter summary but pretty much skipped over in the text. So we're going to fill in that — to our mind — fairly large gap with two sample hands on the subject.

"A squeeze is effective only when Declarer has sure tricks within one trick of the contract [he is squeezing to make]," Louis said. Thus, if you want to squeeze for twelve tricks you have to have 11 winners (barring the very rare progressive squeeze). But also you have to *have lost 1 trick.* If you want to squeeze for 10 tricks you have to have nine winners and have to have *lost 3 tricks.* And so on. Note the past tense of the word "lost." Your squeezes won't work if you're ahead of yourself any more than if you're behind schedule in winners.

Here's a typical delaying tactic to prepare for the squeeze.

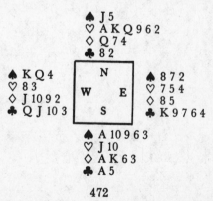

South has become the Declarer at six no-trump — the bidding is irrelevant — and West opens the club Queen. Declarer sees that he has 11 sure tricks and 12 if the diamonds are 3-3. Since the club opening has taken away Declarer's timing to try to work on the spade suit, his only possibility for 12 tricks other than the 3-3 diamond break is a possible squeeze. If the diamonds break adversely, but the long diamond hand also has the King and Queen of spades — a not too remote possibility — that player can be squeezed out of one or the other.

But neither Defender can be squeezed out of the 12th trick unless that point can be reached on schedule. The Defense must be given *1* trick earlier or else there will be room in the Defender's hand for both his spade and diamond guards. The only way on this deal for Declarer to lose that 1 trick and prepare for his squeeze position is to let the club Queen *hold the opening lead.* Declarer, by winning the opening club and trying to lose that loser at any later point, will obviously expose himself to several losers. So by ducking the first club Declarer prepares his squeeze position and still keeps control with his club Ace.

We suggest you play out the hand carefully by yourselves and see the squeeze operate on West through the running of Dummy's heart suit. South throws spades and keeps all four diamonds, with Dummy's spade Jack operating as the other squeeze card. Then try it without ducking the first club and watch West get off the hook.

Here's another example of how Declarer can take delaying action to prepare a squeeze:

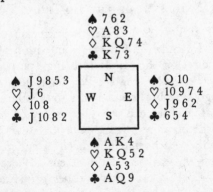

```
                    ♠ 7 6 2
                    ♡ A 8 3
                    ◊ K Q 7 4
                    ♣ K 7 3
                         N
   ♠ J 9 8 5 3                    ♠ Q 10
   ♡ J 6                          ♡ 10 9 7 4
   ◊ 10 8      W         E        ◊ J 9 6 2
   ♣ J 10 8 2                     ♣ 6 5 4
                         S
                    ♠ A K 4
                    ♡ K Q 5 2
                    ◊ A 5 3
                    ♣ A Q 9
```

South's opening two no-trump bid is carried directly to six by North. West opens the club Jack. South counts 11 certain top tricks and 12 if either hearts or diamonds break 3-3. (He has 13 if both suits break, but that is of no consequence.) But if neither suit breaks, there is one extra chance for a 12th trick, and no good player will fail to try for it. If one opponent has four (or more) cards in both red suits, the old squeeze play can be put to work.

But again, to squeeze for 12 one must not only have 11 winners but must have lost 1 trick. To inspect this particular hand more closely, Declarer can only run 5 fast tricks, outside of the red suits in which he hopes to squeeze an Opponent. After cashing three clubs and two spades the Opponent — East in this case — will still have eight cards left, four in each red suit and thus not be squeezed. But if 6 tricks can be played first, bringing East down to only seven cards he'll have to unguard one of the suits.

So South hits on the one way he can delay and lose a trick to get his squeeze on the road. He can't impair the squeeze suits themselves by giving up a heart or a diamond trick. So he simply leads out his low spade from his hand at trick 2. That losing four spot is thrown to the winds with nothing in Dummy to back it up.

The enemy garners that trick but is now through. Play out the rest of the cards with Declarer cashing his black suit tricks first and watch East suffer. Then try it without giving up that spade trick and watch Declarer suffer.

An Extension of the No-Trump Echo

Chapter VII of Part II included a discussion of the no-trump echo in which a Defender, in following suit with his low cards, gives his Partner a count on the suit by echoing (playing high-low) to show only two. This often enables Partner to know just how long to hold up a high card in the suit to destroy Declarer's communications. The negative inference was also explained. Failure to echo would show three or more low cards in the suit.

This very valuable echo has now been extended. (At just what point during the 24 year period the extension became widespread we cannot say — perhaps the early Forties.) The defending player following suit with his low cards echoes with either *two or four* cards in the suit. This enables the Partner to get valuable information much more rapidly in many cases. Let's look at this situation:

1. ♦ A 5 3
KQJ10

N
W   E
S

84

9 7 6 2

2. ♦ A 5 3
KQJ10

N
W   E
S

8 7 4 2

9 6

In both cases Declarer (South) leads a low card and West ducks. In both instances East plays the eight on the first trick, completing his echo by playing a lower card on the continuation of the suit from Dummy. West then knows for certain that East doesn't have exactly three cards in the suit. He doesn't know for certain, either time, whether East is showing two or four. But in this case he doesn't really care and this holds good in many other similar situations.

Either way his action is clear cut: he can win his Ace on the second round with impunity. If Partner has a doubleton (Case 1) that gives Declarer four cards in the suit and Dummy the same number, so holding up the Ace till the third round will do no good. And, if, as in Case 2, Partner's echo is from a four card holding that leaves Declarer with only two. So again the Ace should be taken on the second round and this time it may prevent Declarer from even winning a second trick in the suit (if Dummy is entryless).

In any event, it is most valuable in these situations to know that when Partner "goes up," that is, plays low and then high, that he has exactly three cards in the suit (or, rarely, five). Sometimes a Defender can get the entire picture on the *first* round of the suit when the low card Partner plays is clearly the lowest one that he can have. He thus can't be showing two or four and therefore must have either three or a singleton. The singleton possibility can usually be eliminated by simple deduction.

Incidentally, the title "no-trump echo" is somewhat of a misnomer. This type of signal is very frequently used to advantage in suit play as well, in the same type of situation. However, in suit play, the player with four small usually doesn't echo as Partner may erroneously play him for two and try to give him a ruff.